Cities, Space, and Behavior

Cities, Space, and Behavior: *The Elements of Urban Geography*

Leslie J. King
McMaster University

Reginald G. Golledge
University of California, Santa Barbara

Prentice-Hall, Inc., Englewood Cliffs, New Jersey 07632

Library of Congress Cataloging in Publication Data

KING, LESLIE J. (date)
Cities, space, and behavior.

Includes bibliographical references and index.
1. Cities and towns. 2. Anthropo-geography.
I. Golledge, Reginald G., (date) joint author.
II. Title.
GF125.K48   301.36   77-20243
ISBN 0-13-134601-6

Printed in the United States of America

10   9   8   7   6   5   4   3   2   1

PRENTICE-HALL INTERNATIONAL, INC., *London*
PRENTICE-HALL OF AUSTRALIA PTY. LIMITED, *Sydney*
PRENTICE-HALL OF CANADA, LTD., *Toronto*
PRENTICE-HALL OF INDIA PRIVATE LIMITED, *New Delhi*
PRENTICE-HALL OF JAPAN, INC., *Tokyo*
PRENTICE-HALL OF SOUTHEAST ASIA PTE. LTD., *Singapore*
WHITEHALL BOOKS LIMITED, *Wellington, New Zealand*

To Stephanie, Loren, Linda, and Andrew

Contents

PART II. SPATIAL ORGANIZATION OF URBAN SOCIETY

A. World-Wide Patterns, 14

B. National and Regional Patterns, 55

PART III. CHANGING THE SPATIAL ORGANIZATION OF URBAN SOCIETY: SOME POSSIBILITIES

Preface

The cooperation that produced this book began in the Department of Geography at the University of Canterbury, New Zealand, in 1961. As faculty members in the department, we shared the responsibility for urban and economic geography courses at the undergraduate and graduate levels. With other members of the University faculty, we also cooperated in a major planning study of transportation and land use in Christchurch, at that time a city of approximately 250,000 persons.

Some five years later we were associated again as colleagues in the Department of Geography at The Ohio State University. Our research interests by that time had taken us along somewhat different paths in urban and economic geography. King's interest in spatial analysis and urban economic growth characteristics tended to focus on inter-city contrasts and fairly aggregative statements about the spatial structure of urban society. Golledge's interests, in contrast, had focused on questions of individual behavior, especially in regard to consumer shopping trips and, more recently, the cognitive images that people have of the city and its features. This approach concentrates more on the specific parts of individual cities.

We have sought to merge our specific interests in the organization and writing of this book. There is an overriding interest in the spatial organization of urban society and we use an analytical method to uncover and shape spatial dimensions. The text begins with international considerations (Chapter 2), proceeds through national and regional topics (Chapters 3–5) and patterns within the city (Chapters 6–8), and then focuses on migration and interaction between and within cities (Chapters 9–11). But throughout the major part of the book, Part II, we discuss not only aggregative statements about spatial structure and trends but also micro-level statements about individual perceptions and behavior. In the final part of the book, Part III (Chapters 12 and 13), we discuss some of the primary contemporary questions concerning the planning and reshaping of urban society.

It is our experience that most, if not all, of the subject matter in this book can be handled by undergraduate urban geography classes over a two-semester period. Chapters 5 and 7 and sections 10.3 and 10.5 however, deal with more advanced topics in theoretical analysis and may be omitted without destroying the sequence of the presentation. These sections would provide a particularly useful review for beginning graduate students.

We acknowledge with thanks all of the indirect contributions made to this book by the numerous scholars in Geography and related disciplines from whose work we have liberally drawn results and examples. Having made such demands upon their published works, it seemed unreasonable to impose further upon any of these persons by asking them to read the text! As a consequence, we unfortunately have no one to whom we might attribute some of the blame for the errors that remain in the text. They are our responsibility.

Although the manuscript has taken much longer to complete than was planned, we doubt very much that our spouses, children, and the other sundry relatives who are usually accorded liberal thanks in such prefaces, had to make any of the "sacrifices" that appear to be demanded in the preparation of so many books! But, lest we offend the gods of marketing, we thank them profusely.

Early drafts of the manuscript were typed by Allison Cahill-Golledge and Betty Glasgow, and the final drafts by Diane Lane. We offer them our sincerest thanks for their patience and splended assistance.

Hamilton, Ontario, Canada   Leslie J. King
Santa Barbara, California   Reginald G. Golledge

Cities, Space, and Behavior

part 1

Introduction

chapter 1

Viewpoint of Urban Geography

1.1   An Emphasis on Spatial Dimensions

Almost all societies today are urban societies; that is to say, their social, political, and economic life is organized around and is increasingly dominated by the roles and characters of their cities, especially the big cities. The old saying that "when Paris sneezes, the whole of France catches cold" could also be applied to a variety of other countries and regions, admittedly with different emphases and shades of meaning, but with essentially the same point in mind, that the cities are the major elements of these contemporary societies.

Not surprisingly, many of the pressing social, political, and economic problems of today are also associated with the cities and their growth. These *urban problems* span the range of human knowledge and experience; they involve purely *physical* and *technical* problems, for example, water and air pollution and transportation; they involve *social* problems, for example, the integration of different ethnic groups, immigration policies, and the occurrence of poverty, crime, and despair; they involve *economic* considerations, for example, unemployment and meeting the costs of providing urban services; they involve *political* problems in the overlapping and competition of numerous jurisdictions and in the implementation of plans and policies; they encompass *humanistic* considerations as regards the quality of urban life and concern for aesthetic issues; and they involve *spatial* considerations.

We dwell on this last point because it is the major theme throughout this book, namely, that the character of urban society involves a number of important spatial dimensions. What is meant by the term *spatial dimensions*? In this book it means at least two things:

1. There are some simple concepts of *distance, direction, relative location, areas, groups, and regions* that we can use to describe the character of a city or a number of cities and that we can use to make generalizations about cities. Thus, for example, we can describe average distances separating cities of particular sizes. Or we can describe how particular land uses in a city are grouped together into areas that have particular shapes and also characteristic locations relative to other land uses. Or, as another example, we can describe the volume of traffic or the number of telephone calls between cities or between places within a city as being related in some way to the distance separating the cities or places. Many other examples of this approach will be given later in the book.
2. Cities involve people. The relationships between the behavior of these people and the environmental features of the city are complex. Human behavior is influenced by the spatial form of the city (for example, in choosing a route to work a person is constrained in his choice by the form of the transportation network), and, in turn, the spatial form of the city is shaped by human behavior (for example, by way of the locational decisions of manufacturers or the choices made by city officials). By studying patterns of human behavior in the city, by seeking to comprehend the different mental pictures that people have of the city and its parts, and by probing into how these pictures or images develop and change, we can begin to appreciate the complex interaction between the spatial form of the city and patterns of human behavior.

Both of these meanings of the term spatial dimension are developed side by side in this book. In the discussion of national and regional systems of cities in Chapter 3, for example, attention is given not only to the quantitative description of the numbers and sizes of cities in countries but also to the mental images that people have about the distance relations between particular cities. Later, when analyzing the patterns of human movement within cities (Chapter 11), we shall describe not only the volume and direction of these flows but also the mental images that people form of the city based on what they see along the routes that they travel frequently.

Issue of Scale

One other issue in regard to studying the spatial dimensions of urban society must be mentioned. This is the matter of *scale*. The chapters in this book deal with questions about urban society as it exists on the international, national, and local levels. World patterns of urbanization, for example, are analyzed in Chapter 2; this is followed by a discussion of the urban systems in two countries in particular, the United States and the U.S.S.R. Then, in Chapter 6 the emphasis is placed on the examination of urban land-use patterns within any single large metropolitan area. The distinction between these different chapters does not simply lie in the nature of the topics that are being discussed. The spatial scale of the investigation also varies from the one discussion to the other.

The importance that is to be attached to scale is an issue that geographers have sought to come to grips with for some time now. Is it possible, for example, to make any statements about the spatial dimensions of urban society that are independent of scale, statements that seem to hold true regardless of the scale at which they are applied? If not, in what ways do the statements have to be qualified to take account of scale differences? It has been suggested that "our descriptions of spatial form are entirely dependent on scale. And the relevant scale of analysis can be determined only in terms of the spatial variability and significance of a given process. There are therefore strong interdependencies between pattern and process and the only way we can avoid purely circular argument is to recognise very clearly the nature of these interdependencies."[1]

1.2 Relating Spatial Form to Patterns of Human Behavior

In a sense, the city is what people think it is. The city that its residents know personally—the city of their minds—largely determines the world in which they have their life's experiences and through which they strive to gain their many daily satisfactions. This city of the mind is built on acquired information and experience. Beginning with the world of early childhood, knowledge of the city grows eventually to influence the form of the many interactions between adult man and his environment.

Although cities exist as physical objects, as collections of buildings, highways, and open spaces, we suggest that there is no real evidence that they are perceived by the individuals living in them in the same way that they are objectively structured. The suggestion is made that it may be legitimate to think of a city as having both an objective physical structure and a psychological or cognitive structure. The psychological structure has been termed the *mental map*, or the perceived city. Although as yet there is little information about the nature of mental maps of cities, there is an increasing amount of research being undertaken in order to discover what types of regularities exist in the minds of groups of individuals living in urban areas. These studies range from broad ones of the mental images of national urban systems, through studies attempting to reconstruct the perceptual images of large cities such as Boston and Los Angeles, to studies of the accuracy with which people locate individual places within urban areas. Individual subparts of the city such as neighborhoods or areas in the vicinity of freeways also have been extensively examined by researchers. In this book, we shall discuss some of these different mental images or *cognitive structures* of cities and parts of cities.

An issue that has often been debated in geography concerns the relationship between studies of spatial form and studies of human behavior. In some contexts, for example in studying the location of manufacturing plants among a number of cities, it would be reasonable to argue that one could not understand the spatial form (the location pattern of the manufacturing plants) without understanding the decision processes that led up to the different locations being chosen. Why did the businessmen make the particular choices that they did? In this case, we would be interested in studying their behavior as a means toward understanding the observed spatial form, namely, the location pattern of the manufacturing plants.

But suppose one were interested in studying peoples' attitudes toward their neighborhoods and in determining the bases of their sense of belonging to such a neighborhood. Then one would be more interested in questions like those suggested earlier: What mental images do people have of certain areas or territories? How do these mental images relate to their sense of belonging to a neighborhood? In this context, the objective spatial form (the streets, the public buildings, and so on) probably would be taken as given. The concern would be with the perceived or mental form of the city and the sharp distinction between spatial form and human behavior would disappear. Throughout this book, both of these conceptions of the form-process relationship will be illustrated.

1.3 How Explanations Are Provided

In this book we shall describe different patterns of urban phenomena as they occur over the surface of the earth, and whenever possible we shall seek to make generalizations about these patterns that seem to hold true regardless of which country or region is being discussed. For example, we shall note how a relationship between the number and size of cities, known as the *rank-size rule,* seems to be characteristic of many different urban systems in different parts of the world and also at different times throughout history. Similarly, we shall suggest that certain economic relationships exist between the activities carried on in cities and the demands existing in the surrounding rural regions (the so-called *central place relationships*) and that these economic relationships are characteristic of many different regions. In emphasizing the search for generalizations in the discussion of urban society we are making a conscious choice, but there are many other very different approaches that might have been adopted. There are, for example, books on urban geography that concentrate on descriptions and analyses of particular cities. The emphasis in those studies is on acquiring an understanding and appreciation of the very particular characteristics of the cities in question with little concern for drawing generalizations about all the cities. There are other books that focus more on the constituent parts of the city, the central business district, the suburbs and the rural–urban fringe, and commercial, manufacturing, and residential activities; again these studies may not search for generalizations that seem to apply to many different cities.

Scientific Method

The approach adopted in this book largely dictates the choice of existing studies that are drawn upon for material. Almost all of these studies generally rely, or at least insist that they rely, upon what is known as a *scientific approach* to the study of urban phenomena. Since there are any number of books and writings on the scientific approach in geography that may be consulted, we do not intend to dwell long on this subject.[2] We shall simply characterize the scientific approach as a method of study that involves the following steps:

1. Observations are made about something that is of interest to the observer, for example, about the location of cities or the frequency of travel patterns. Some regularities or orders are either discerned or suspected in these observations. An explanation of why these regularities exist is desired.
2. The explanation is sought by constructing or developing a set

of logically connected statements (a theory) that by virtue of its logic yields a number of predictions about the phenomena under study. If, for example, we were studying shopping travel patterns, a theory might be constructed so that it would tell us something about how long the average trip length is or what the frequencies of trips are at different times of the day.

3. These theoretical predictions are then matched against other observations. The degree of correspondence will suggest whether or not the theory is a good one.

4. If the theory appears to be a weak one that provides very poor estimates of existing patterns, then either a new theory has to be developed or some modification has to be made of the existing theory.

The subject of theory building and testing is an extremely complicated one. The grossly oversimplified outline above pays no reference whatsoever to the vast literature that exists on various aspects of the subject. Consider, for example, some of the following related questions. How does one derive the "set of logically connected statements" to begin with? In this context, we often speak of formulating *hypotheses*. These hypotheses are unconfirmed hunches about the phenomenon in question and they can be woven into a logically connected set. In some cases, the hypotheses may be based on or suggested by past observations; in other cases, they may be the result of intuition and insight. These possibilities alone are the subject of much philosophical discussion. Then there is the question of how does one test the adequacy of a theory and its predictions? In the physical sciences it is usually possible to perform laboratory experiments designed to test the theory, but in the social sciences this form of testing is for the most part inapplicable. Often the development of the theory is prompted by one set of observations and the testing of its predictions has to be carried out with another set of observations.

Theory and Values

Another very important line of questioning in regard to the use of the scientific method in geography or any other social science focuses on the role of *values* in the whole approach. Traditionally, in the physical sciences the scientific approach is considered to be value-free in the sense that it does not address questions that have to do with human values and that it does not concede that human values enter into the conduct of scientific inquiry. But in the social sciences, many people argue, such value-free approaches are neither possible nor desirable. The argument is made that human values not only color or shape the investigator's questions, but they may also strongly influence the conclusions that are drawn from any study. This is a critical consideration if the study in question is of interest to those involved in making public policies and plans. An increasing number of geographers, in particular those who are students of Marxism, are insisting that geographers must acknowledge the biases that may be inherent in their studies as a consequence of their values and ideological convictions.

Classification of Social Science Theories

It has been suggested that social science theories, including those of human geography, can be classed into three categories depending on what they prescribe in regard to society and social change.[3] *Status-quo* theories are firmly based in the reality that they deal with and accurately represent this reality at any particular point in time, but by their very nature they can only perpetuate the status quo, that is, the existing situation. *Counterrevolutionary* theories are ones that may only appear to be grounded in the reality that they purport to represent and that typically obscure the comprehension of that reality. They may be, nevertheless, attractive by virtue of their logical elegance or fashionability, but they do not yield statements that are productive for social change. Finally, *revolutionary* theories are firmly grounded in reality, but their statements or propositions may become either true or false depending on the courses and outcomes of social change. These last theories identify the choices that are available in directing this change.

In this book we shall attempt to outline a few theories about aspects of urban society, more specifically theories of the spatial organization of urban society, that are perhaps best described as status-quo theories. We do not deny the possibility that in the eyes of those concerned with social change the examples may even appear to be better categorized as counterrevolutionary theories, but since this is not a book on social change, the *correct* classification of the examples chosen need not concern us.

Mathematics and Theory

One further point needs stressing. A theory may or may not be capable of mathematical expression. In the physical sciences, mathematics has proven essential in the higher development of theories, for by virtue of its logical character mathematics allows for the predictions to be drawn from these very complex theories. In other words, mathematics is the language in which the theorizing is carried on. Without mathematics many of the predictions of the theories would never have been realized. These predictions, of course, have proven to be remarkably good ones and have contributed to our fairly sophisticated level of understanding of how the physical universe works, at least compared to what was known a hundred or even fifty years ago. But not all theories can be expressed in mathematical form, and this is certainly the case with many theories of society. Marx's theory of social change is a notable example, and although many aspects of this general theory have been developed later in mathematical form, the main theory is still best expressed in verbal form. Whether or not it will ever be possible to structure mathematical theories of social change remains an open question. Many people argue that the appropriate mathematics does not yet exist for the task.

One other point on mathematical representation has to do with the use of the terms *theory* and *model*. A distinction between these two terms is not always required, but it seems as though in the social sciences it is often useful to draw one. A model may be thought of as a symbolic representation of a theory or parts of a theory. Usually, the representation is in the form of mathematics, but other forms are possible—for example, a physical model at a different scale (such as a model of an engineering project or an architect's model of a building) or an analog model (such as an electrical circuit used to represent a transportation network). In many cases, we may use a mathematical model for which the underlying theory is extremely simple and very restricted when expressed in verbal terms. Indeed, we often speak of a model based on a few simple hypotheses that can be thought of only as a very crude theory. Nevertheless, underlying any model is some such theoretical framework concerning the behavior and nature of the phenomenon being studied. Questions concerning the adequacy of this framework should not be obscured by discussions of the form of the particular symbolic representation used in the model.

In summary then, this book illustrates some very particular forms of explanation, but it makes no claim that these are the only or the best forms of explanations. Some may prefer lines of analysis that do not conform to the scientific approach; others may be happy to ignore mathematical formulations while still emphasizing scientific approaches to the analysis of social change. The different approaches have their relative strengths and weaknesses and, depending on the questions that the investigator wishes to study, they will prove more or less valuable to him.

1.4   Relevance of Findings to Planning

A comment was made at the beginning of this chapter on the range of the so-called urban problems that exist today. Along with those specialists who are trained as urban planners, almost all social scientists, including geographers, are involved to varying degrees in seeking solutions for these problems of society. Their contributions vary in scope and emphasis from those of the scholar in the ivory tower who may propose new ways of viewing the urban problem and may discuss in purely academic terms some particular solutions to it; through those of the social activist who seeks and advocates by word and deed solutions through revolutionary change and a consequent restructuring of the social and political order; to those of the scholar-consultant who advises government on the development of particular policies and plans and may also be involved in their evaluation. These are roles, and there are undoubtedly others that could be mentioned, that the social scientist may choose to play in society. For him, more than for the physical scientist, there is an intellectual obligation, perhaps even a moral one also, to say something useful about the patterns of change in society, about how these might indeed be shaped or directed, and about the possible consequences of such actions.

Urban geographers, for the most part, have not been very active participants in the area of policy making and urban planning. Almost all of the studies referred to in the main body of this book have focused on existing or past patterns of urban spatial structure. They have sought to develop explanations of these patterns by using in a sense ex post facto arguments, that is to say, arguments in respect to things that have already happened. The question of how these explanations might then be used as the basis for saying something about the future, in the form of statements about either how it should be shaped (planning) or how it is likely to evolve (forecasting), is difficult to answer. Almost all applications of social science knowledge, including that of urban geography, to social issues usually assume that causal explanations that seem to have held in the past will continue to do so in the future and that the planner by manipulating the causes should be able to achieve the ends that he desires. For example, in Chapter 2 the relationship between the level of economic development of a country and the number and relative sizes of the cities found in that country is discussed. This evidence has prompted the suggestion that if subregional disparities in economic well-being within any country are to be removed, then steps must be taken to create a well-ordered hierarchy of urban centers in the country.[4] In a similar vein, geographers have completed a wide range of studies dealing with the patterns of travel to different sized urban places by people living in rural areas. In some countries, notably Sweden, these studies have provided the foundation for many planning proposals ranging from the location of hospitals and schools to the reorganization of administrative districts.[5]

The difficulty with this bridging of what has been observed to exist and what ought to exist is that it is very difficult (indeed some say impossible) to place a great deal of confidence in the assumption that the same cause and effect relationships will hold in the future as held in the past. Might it not be possible, for example, assuming changed economic and political arrangements in the future, that the role of cities as centers of power will be altered and that regional development might not be so closely tied to urban development as it has been in the past? Similarly, is it unreasonable to expect that with changing patterns of transportation technology and preferences, and with shifts in peoples' living styles and tastes, future travel patterns might be very different in character from those in the past and not at all in harmony with the location patterns of facilities that are planned by using existing knowledge?

These considerations prompt many people to suggest that the proper role of the social scientist is that of the critic of existing policies and plans and not that of the fashioner or designer of policy. Such evaluations should take notice not only of the means employed, the location of new factories or the building of new towns, for example, but also the goals that are aimed for and the value system that these in turn imply.

Part 4 of this book reviews some of the approaches that have been suggested for solving different urban problems. Whenever possible we shall mention the particular contributions that geography and geographers have made and we shall attempt to highlight the difficulties and issues that seem to remain unresolved.

Notes

1. D. HARVEY, *Explanation in Geography* (London: Edward Arnold, 1969), p. 386.

2. HARVEY, *ibid;* W. BUNGE, *Theoretical Geography* (Lund: Gleerup, 1962); D. AMEDEO and R. G. GOLLEDGE, *An Introduction to Scientific Reasoning in Geography* (New York: J. Wiley & Sons, Inc., 1975).

3. D. HARVEY, *Social Justice and the City* (London: Edward Arnold, 1973), pp. 150–52.

4. J. W. SIMMONS, "Canada: Choices in a national urban strategy," *Research Paper 70,* Center for Urban and Community Studies, University of Toronto, 1975.

5. A. R. PRED, "Urbanization, domestic planning problems and Swedish geographic research," *Progress in Geography,* **5,** 1973, pp. 1–76.

part 2

Spatial Organization
of Urban Society

A. WORLD-WIDE PATTERNS

chapter 2

Extent and Growth of Urbanization
at the International Scale

No matter how one chooses to define urbanization, it is a fact that the phenomenon is becoming more and more pronounced throughout the world. In the developed countries, high levels of urbanization are already characteristic, while in the developing countries the levels are increasing rapidly, often at a faster rate than was the case in the past in the now developed areas.

In this chapter, following discussions of urbanization as a process and the history of urbanization throughout the world, several different measures of urbanization are considered, along with the locational patterns and the spatial contrasts in today's world that these measures reveal.

2.1   Interpretations of the Urbanization Process

The story of the development of urban life has not been an easy one for scholars to unravel and there are still many parts of it unknown

14

and incomplete. Moreover, there are still disagreements over the definitions of *urbanism* and *urban society,* over the interpretations that are to be placed upon archaeological findings in different parts of the world, and over the factors and forces that should be stressed in any theory of the urbanization process.

We shall now briefly review some of the themes that have emerged in the debate over the nature of urbanism and the process of urbanization.

Indices of Urbanism

A number of scholars have proposed that specific indices or criteria be used in defining urbanism. One such index is the invention of writing. This is considered by certain experts to be the best single criterion for distinguishing *urban* from other types of settlements.[1] Their argument runs as follows: A writing system suggests that there existed first, a highly specialized non-agricultural class of people who had the time to develop such skills; second, an educational system of some kind that could spread and teach the skills; third, a stable political power that would permit its continued use and acceptance; and finally, classes of merchants and servants who could supply the required goods and services. Other investigators have proposed that only those spatially compact communities with reasonably high population densities, and perhaps bounded by a city wall, deserve to be regarded as true cities in the early course of human history.

But there have been just as many critics as there have been advocates of these rather simple definitions. These criticisms are reflected in the following comment: "The truth of the matter is that the relationship between political, social, and economic institutions on the one hand and their material expression in the landscape on the other is nothing like so direct as these indices of urban development would seem to imply, and the search for a single indispensable criterion of city life, as for a suite of physical features diagnostic through all cultural contexts, betrays a misunderstanding of what the city is and does."[2] In a similar vein, the use of the writing index as a definition of urbanism has been criticized on the grounds that "the literate group which is likely to invent it represents only one class of specialists whose emergence in an urbanized society may or may not be delayed."[3]

But if no single simple index will suffice, how is urbanism to be defined? Sociologists have sought to define urbanism in terms of the patterns of social organization and have emphasized the existence of social differentiation as the distinguishing characteristic of the urban community. Geographers have preferred to focus on the functional role and "to look upon the city as an instrument for the organization of dependent territory. In other words, they define the city as a principle of regional integration, as a generator of effective space."[4]

Geographical Interpretations

This view of urbanism, which sees the city as an integral and yet dominant element in a wider spatial system and which stresses the political, social, and economic interdependencies that exist between the city and the surrounding region, is the common starting point for almost all interpretations of the urbanization process found in the geography literature.

One such interpretation identifies four major spatial processes of urbanization, which are as follows:[5]

1. *Spatial concentration of power, decision making, and control.* The role of the city in the organization of the surrounding countryside demands that groups or classes within it have power and the means of exercising it.

2. *Flows of capital and investment and the location of economic activities.* Cities function primarily as the centers of accumulation of wealth drawn from the surrounding areas and also as centers for the redistribution of this wealth. Capital and investment may also flow from the cities to the rural areas but at a much lower level. For economic reasons almost all manufacturing activities are attracted to the city and hence reinforce the concentration of economic power there.

3. *Diffusion of innovations and change.* Cities are the focal points for the introduction of new ideas and for economic, social, and political innovations (for example, new forms of communication, social clubs, and public services), which then spread down to smaller centers and perhaps into the rural areas.

4. *Migration and settlement.* As urbanization continues and as the patterns of economic and political power represented by the cities continue to force changes on the rural areas and their economies, migration to the cities is encouraged even further. Surplus rural labor migrates to the city to join there the ever-increasing pool of urban unemployed.

A different interpretation of urbanism and the urbanization process from the historical viewpoint has been given by Paul Wheatley.[6] He contends that at some stage in the historical evolution of ancient cities in different parts of the world these "cities" existed as "ceremonial centers." These centers were overwhelmingly religious in their function, but they also served as centers for the political, economic, and social organization of the areas in which they were located. Wheatley describes them as follows:

> Beginning as little more than tribal shrines, in what may be regarded as their classic phases these centers were elaborated into complexes of public ceremonial structures, usually massive and often extensive, and including assemblages of such architectural items as pyramids, platform mounds, temples, places, terraces, staircases, courts, and stelae.[7]

The economic importance of such a center was associated primarily with its role as "an instrument of redistribution." This involved

> in some instances ... a physical ingathering and storage of produce, with perhaps a subsequent partial reapportionment to the countryside, but in other cases it seems to have been merely appropriational, involving only rights of disposal over certain goods.[8]

Explanatory Factors

The three major factors that are usually mentioned in discussions about the origins of urban society are environment and ecology, demography, and technological change. We shall comment briefly on each of these.

Environment and ecology. An often repeated argument is that the emergence and development of urban society must have demanded as a prerequisite a combination of favorable climatic and soil conditions such that an agricultural surplus would then be available to support the emergence of an urban class.

The definition of what this surplus was is an issue on which there is fundamental disagreement among present-day scholars, as we shall note shortly. Wheatley thought of a surplus in relative terms, as something that a particular society could designate and that would be collected and redistributed by the leaders of that society. Wheatley is sceptical of the environmental arguments, for his studies suggested that

> it is abundantly evident that no fixed constellation of environmental conditions and resources could have constituted a precondition for the generation of ceremonial centers.[9]

In the work of other scholars there is certainly confirmation of the viewpoint that increased agricultural specialization, higher yields, and greater dependability all accompanied the emergence of urban settlement.[10] But there is no insistence that these same factors either caused, or were required for, the development of urban society.

On a different level, the relative importance of the physical environment in shaping the later patterns of city development has been a controversial subject in urban geography. It is indeed possible to note certain relationships between city location and natural environmental features, for example:

1. Cities are frequently located at points where some break in transportation occurred, for instance, at the head of lakes, on good harbors, or at river crossings.
2. Cities that were originally fortress towns often are located on hilltops or peninsulas; important trade centers often developed at river junctions or at the entrances to mountain passes.
3. Cities frequently developed at the sites of particular natural resources—the location of cities on coal fields is one such obvious occurrence. Water spring lines, precious metals, ore deposits, and climatic amenities provide other examples of resources that often attracted city development. Many of these cities continued in existence long after the attraction of the particular resource may have disappeared.

In addition, it is clear that natural environmental features are important in shaping certain aspects of urban development. The need for huge quantities of water, for example, is an important consideration. Today, the growing concern for environmental protection influences many decisions within the city. But even allowing for all these different considerations, the importance of natural environmental factors in shaping the pattern of city development should not be overstressed, and certainly not to the extent that some earlier geographers attempted to do.[11] The physical environment did impose certain limitations, often very rigid ones, on the process of urban development and restricted what was indeed possible in many areas. But the forces driving the urbanization process were more basic social and economic ones and were not shaped in any fundamental way by the physical environment.

Demography. The suggestion that urban development occurred in response to a rapid increase in population levels and densities is difficult to support. Admittedly, with the development of sedentary agriculture and the gradual emergence of urban settlement there was a sharp increase in population, but again this seems to have been more a related feature of the process rather than a simple determinant of it.

Technological change. The overall relative importance of such developments as improved agricultural methods (including irrigation, trade, and transportation) and the Industrial Revolution on the growth of urban society generally is not disputed. But the interpretations of these developments do differ. Some scholars prefer to consider technological change in a very limited sense, for example, by changes in the techniques of field cultivation and the forms of metal crafts. These developments could not be considered critical in the emergence of urban centers. By contrast, trade and marketing, irrigation, and warfare, along with religion, are usually emphasized by these scholars as the more important factors in the basic process whereby society was transformed from one having an extremely simple and undifferentiated structure in the hunting and collecting era of early human history into the more complex, differentiated form associated with urban life.

An alternative view is that these technological developments are agents of the process whereby the *surplus* is generated and distributed. To appreciate this point, we must pause and consider this notion of a surplus because it is central to an understanding of different interpretations of urbanization and it often seems to be the main bone of contention among proponents of the different interpretations.

The Concept of Surplus Product

One approach regards the concept of a surplus product in terms of the needs of the society in question. This relativistic viewpoint suggests that the agricultural surplus that allowed for the emergence of the urban class was not of a fixed quantity determined by absolute environmental features but was determined rather by the needs and particular institutional forms of the society involved.[12] This concept of a surplus product emphasized not only that the surplus was relative but also that it was particular to the institutional context and presumably that it would differ from one society to another.

Others accept the definition of the surplus product in the relative sense but reject the notion that it must be defined in terms of the particular needs of any single society or set of institutions. Instead, they prefer to consider it from the viewpoint of Marxist theory, that is, as a social surplus associated with a particular mode of production. Then it is defined as "the quantity of labor power used in the creation of product for certain specified social purposes over and above that which is biologically, socially, and culturally necessary to guarantee the maintenance and reproduction of labor power"[13] in that mode of production. In this sense, the notion of a surplus is a universal one related to human needs, although it is not fixed and it may change as the conditions of production, consumption, and distribution vary, and for a number of reasons it also may be easier to extract and distribute such a surplus under some conditions than under others. The reasons for cities, then, lie in the organization, the extraction, and the geographic concentration and redistribution of the surplus. Urbanization at all scales—the international, national, and regional—is seen as the process whereby the capitalist system promotes the creation, the circulation, and the concentration of the surplus.

We shall now turn to an overview of the history of urban development throughout the world.

2.2   Sketch of the History of Urban Development

It is possible to identify certain regions in the world where cities appear to have developed at an early time quite independent of any developments in other regions. There appear to have been at least seven such regions of *primary urban generation,* namely, Mesopotamia, Egypt, the Indus Valley, the North China Plain, Mesoamerica, the central Andes, and southwestern Nigeria. These areas are located on the map in Figure 2.1.

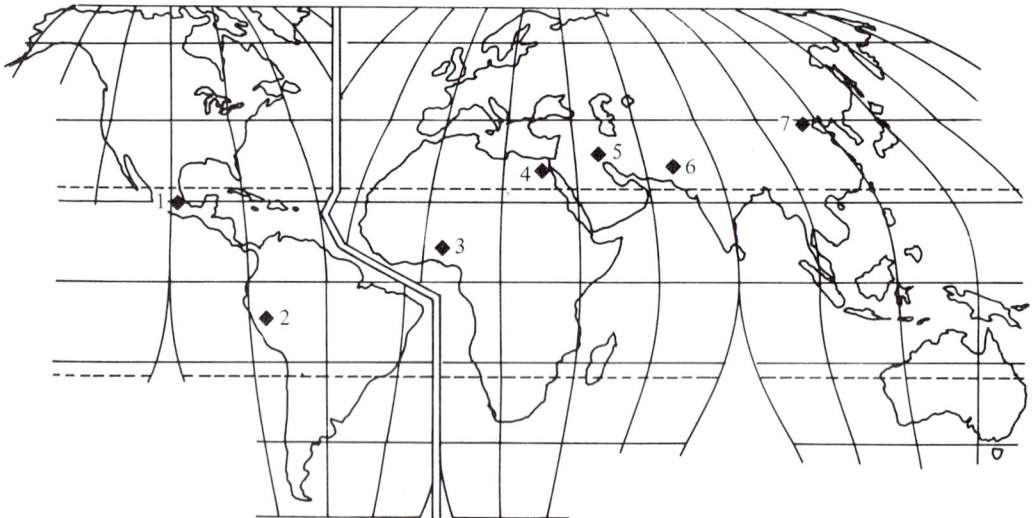

Figure 2.1   Areas of primary urban generation. Key: (1) Mesoamerica, (2) Central Andes, (3) Southwestern Nigeria, (4) Egypt, (5) Mesopotamia, (6) Indus Valley, (7) North China Plain.

Diffusion Hypothesis

In many past accounts of the history of urbanization it was popular to suppose that city life spread out from such primary regions into other areas. But this so-called *diffusion hypothesis* has to be regarded with a great deal of caution, for, there is still no universal acceptance of the designation of the seven areas mentioned as being the only possible areas of primary urban generation. In this regard, for example, there seems to be no clear agreement on whether or not Palestine, which includes the ancient city of Jericho, was an area of independent urban development.

More importantly, there are at least three different forms of diffusion process that may apply in the development of cities.[14] *Primary diffusion* involves the direct introduction of new city forms into a region by some outside authority, as in the case of the old colonial empires. The introduction of the Spanish style city into South America or the European form into North America would be examples of this. There are 11 cities in the United States that had walls during the early stages of their development. This feature may be related to the European origins of the early settlers in those places. *Secondary diffusion* involves the direct borrowing of cultural traits. This undoubtedly was a factor in the emergence of city forms in parts of Asia and Europe. Finally, *stimulus diffusion* involves the acceptance of ideas relating to different technical processes. Developments in urban transportation and their acceptance in different cities around the world might be thought of as an example of this form of diffusion.

It has been pointed out that given the lower levels of technology, especially in communication that prevailed in ancient times, it is difficult to imagine how any form of city or urban living could have spread by any of these diffusion mechanisms.

Primary Urban Areas in the Middle East-India

The rise of urban civilization in Mesopotamia seems to date from 3500 to 3000 B.C., although some ceremonial centers may have existed even earlier. The cities were located on or near the Tigris and Euphrates Rivers, especially in the southern part of the Mesopotamia plain (Figure 2.2). Uruk, which was one of the larger centers, has been described as a city containing much open space and even gardens within its 1,100-acre area and having a population between 24,000 and 50,000 inhabitants. The cities began as religious centers, but they gradually developed other functions such as handicrafts, especially pottery-making and metal-working. These cities appear to have had trading connections with regions as far away as the Indus Valley, but within the cities themselves the marketplace does not seem to have been an important feature.

Over the period 3200–1760 B.C. the cities of southern Mesopotamia or Sumeria were the principal centers of urban life. Then they gave way in importance to more northern cities, of which Babylon and Nineveh are perhaps the most famous (Figure 2.2). These were the capitals at different times of the powerful Babylonian and Assyrian empires that were finally overthrown by the Persians around 500 B.C.

Figure 2.2   The ancient cities of the Tigris-Euphrates Valleys. Key: (1) Ergani, (2) Cayönü Tepesi, (3) Edessa, (4) Tell Halaf, (5) Dura-Europas, (6) Mari, (7) Mosul, (8) Guagamela, (9) Tepe Gawra, (10) Nineveh, (11) Nimrud, (12) Tell Hassuna, (13) Ashur, (14) Kirkuk, (15) Jarmo, (16) Behistun, (17) Samarra, (18) Choga Mami, (19) Mandali, (20) Eshnunna, (21) Baghdad, (22) Akkad, (23) Sippar, (24) Agade, (25) Seleucia, (26) Clesiphan, (27) Kish, (28) Babylon, (29) Jemdet Nasr, (30) Nippur, (31) Isin, (32) Shuruppak, (33) Umma, (34) Uruk, (35) Larsa, (36) Tell al'Ubaid, (37) Eridu, (38) Ur, (39) Lagash (Telloh), (40) Susa, (41). Tepe Sialk. [Based on M. Hammond, *The City in the Ancient World* (Cambridge: Harvard University Press, 1972), pp. 32, 48.]

In this succession of empires and continuing with the Persians, the Greeks, and the Romans, the role of the city as the base for the territorial expansion of the empire and as the center of political, social, and religious organization became firmly established.

The Indus Valley cities developed in the period 2500–1500 B.C. The two largest known centers are Mohenjo-Daro and Harappá (Figure 2.3). The former has commanded the attention of scholars because it provides evidence of a city both well-planned and laid out in a regular rectangular grid pattern with elaborate drainage systems.   It is

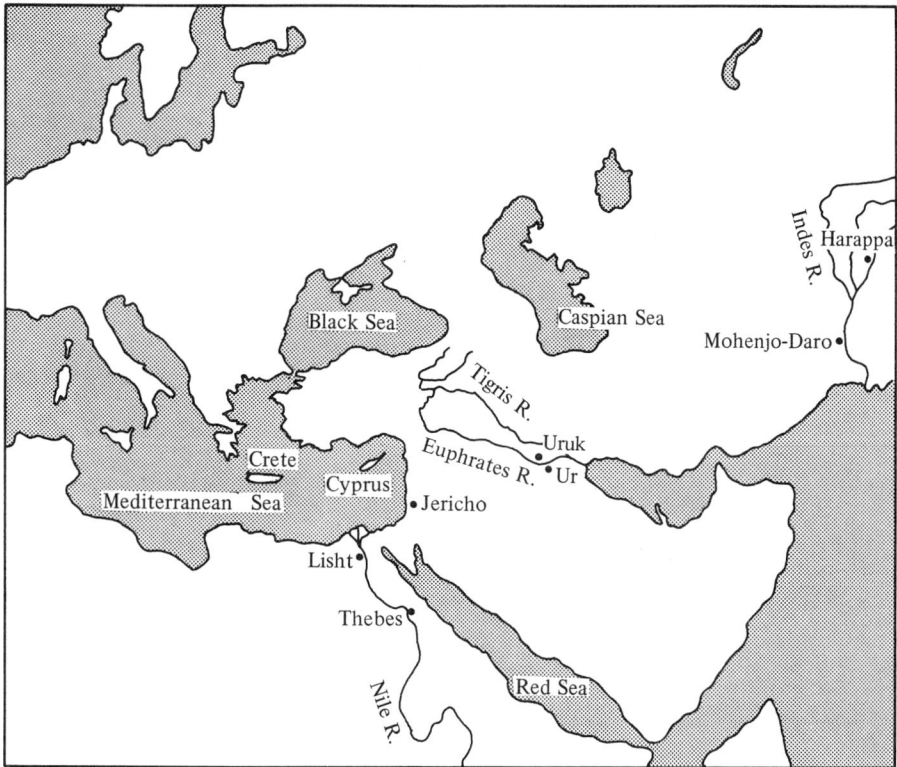

Figure 2.3   Early cities in the Middle East.

estimated that it must have been a city of some 40,000 persons.[15] There is strong evidence that these cities were engaged in trade with cities in Mesopotamia. The extent to which urban development in this Indus Valley region was truly independent of influences from Mesopotamia is still unresolved. The idea of city life may have been introduced from outside, but it apparently developed there in its own fashion. The development was not a lasting one, for as a result of either invasion or natural calamities or a combination of both, this urban civilization faded out after 1500 B.C.

The early Nile Valley urban civilization is not as well known to present-day scholars as is that of Mesopotamia simply because many of the ancient cities are now buried deep beneath the alluvium of the Nile delta. The main period of urban development seems to date from around 3100 B.C. at which time the ancient territories of Upper and Lower Egypt were united. The dynasties of the pharaohs that followed were centered in part on cities such as Memphis and Thebes and also on the so-called *mortuary cities* that were associated with the pyramids and temples that the pharoahs built as their burial places. Civili-

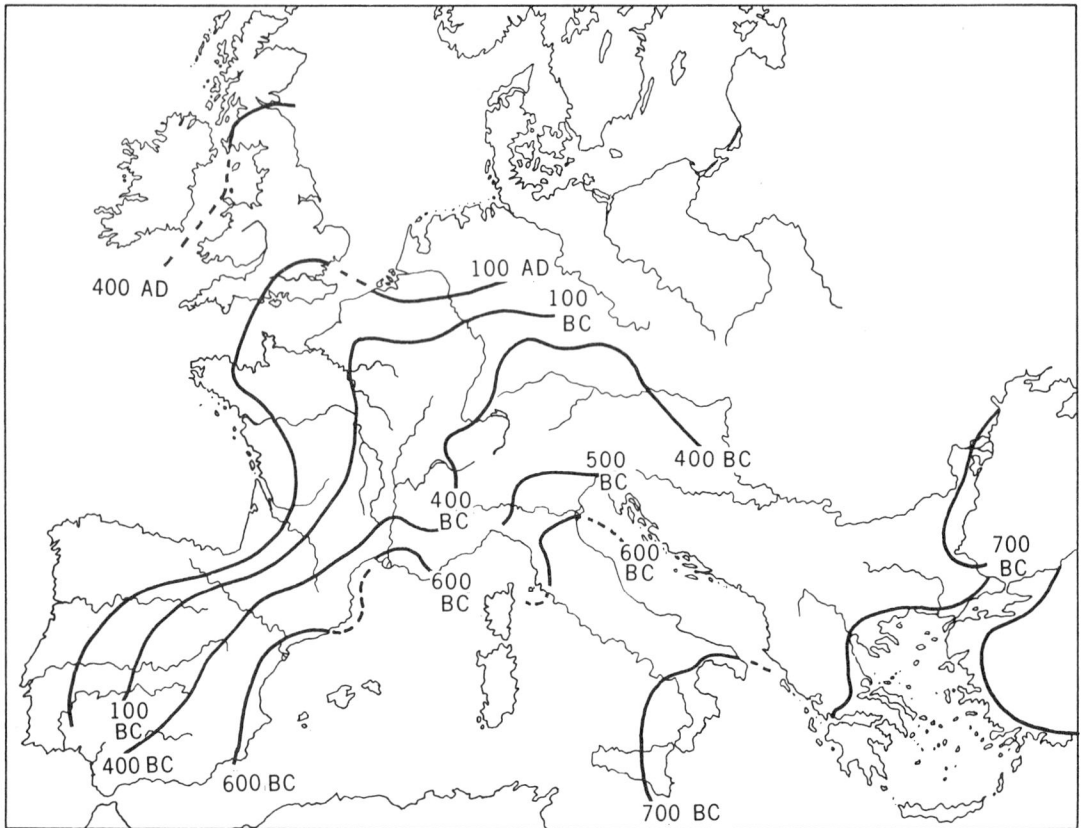

Figure 2.4 Diffusion of the polis. [N. J. G. Pounds, "The Urbanization of the "Classical World"; reproduced by permission from *Annals* of the Association of American Geographers, vol. **59**, 1969, p. 148.]

zation in Egypt was not a consequence of city development, but rather the reverse was true. Evidence suggests that cities such as Memphis and Thebes probably were neither as large nor as functionally important as the cities in Mesopotamia.

Later Developments in Europe and the Middle East

The subsequent history of urbanization in the Middle East and Europe was complex and it involved elements of independent development and diffusion. Along the eastern Mediterranean coast in the countries now known as Israel and Lebanon there were cities developed in connection with commerce, especially under the Phoenicians between the eighth and tenth centuries B.C. In Crete and mainland Greece in the second millenium B.C. the great palace-citadels such as

Knossos and Athens appear to have had many of the characteristics of city life.

But it was with the development of the great empires of the Greeks and the Romans, and to a lesser extent the Muslims, that city life spread widely throughout the Middle East and Europe.

The Greek city-state, or *polis,* in which government was vested in some form of popular assembly, is revered as one of the ancestors of the modern democratic state. Along with this new form of government the Greek city-state brought a new emphasis on city planning and civic design serving the needs of its inhabitants. The subsequent diffusion of the Greek polis throughout Europe is shown in Figure 2.4. The map probably overemphasizes the strength and extent of this diffusion, but there is little doubt that the Greeks did much to encourage the development of cities around the Mediterranean and in Southern Europe. These cities, in turn, were the agents whereby the splendid achievements of Greek civilization spread throughout the ancient world.

The primary diffusion of the city form that occurred under the Greeks was intensified under the Roman Empire in the first three centuries A.D. In Italy itself, a major phase of city building had been associated with the Etruscan culture that reached its peak in the sixth century B.C. These cities, in the region lying west of a line drawn north of Rome, apparently had trading relations with the Egyptians and Phoenicians. Rome's emergence as a city appears to date from the latter half of the sixth century B.C.

Under the Roman Empire extensive networks of cities and highways were built in the occupied areas. Around the Mediterranean, and in Italy particularly, the Romans further developed numerous existing cities, many of which were originally poleis. Hence, the density of cities in these areas was very high (Figure 2.5). But since in the newer conquered areas of Gaul (now France) and Britain the Romans were more methodical in their location of towns, a more even spacing resulted. The modern-day cities of London, Brussels, Cologne, Paris, Vienna, and Belgrade are but a few of those whose developments date from Roman times. The new Roman cities typically were of three types:

1. Colonies established in virgin areas and inhabited by exlegionaires. These colonies were more typical in Italy than elsewhere.
2. Towns tied to a specific location because the location was important for defense, trade, or resource development.
3. Former "capitals" of the Celtic tribes conquered by the Romans.

Following the final collapse of the Roman Empire in the face of the German invasions in the fifth and sixth centuries A.D., city life in

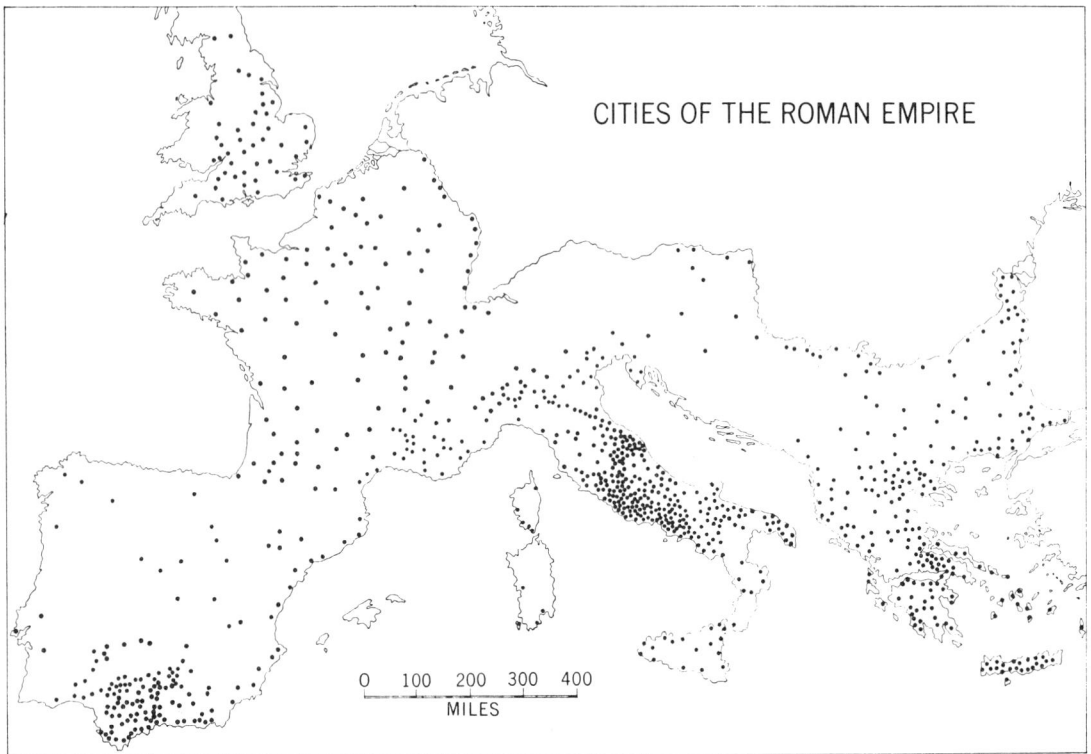

Figure 2.5 A tentative map of the cities of the Roman Empire during the second and third centuries A.D. [N. J. G. Pounds, "The Urbanization of the Classical World"; reproduced by permission from *Annals* of the Association of American Geographers, vol. **59**, 1969, p. 155.]

Europe declined, and it was not until the tenth and eleventh centuries that city development once again became pronounced. Then emerged the Italian city states of Venice, Milan, Florence, and Genoa and the important trading cities in the Low Countries and along the Rhine. In the twelfth century urban development began to spread across Northern Germany and around the Baltic, prompted in large part by the trading activities of the Hanseatic League. In central Russia city development became pronounced between the seventh and thirteenth centuries A.D. The map in Figure 2.6 shows the major European cities in the thirteenth century. The map bears out the following point: "The overwhelming majority of the settlements of today, throughout the whole of western, central, and southern Europe, were in existence at the end of the Middle Ages."[16] In the next chapter we shall look at the development pattern of cities in the Soviet Union in greater detail.

Figure 2.6 European cities in the thirteenth century. [J. C. Russell, "The Metropolitan Region of the Middle Ages," *Journal of Regional Science*, **2**, No. 2 1960, p. 57.]

India-Africa

The diffusion of the city was equally spectacular elsewhere in the world. In India, the Indus Valley Civilization (referred to earlier) disappeared around 1500 B.C. under the invasion of the Aryans from the northwest, and urban life probably did not revive there until about the sixth century B.C. Diffusion of cities over the southern parts of India dates from the Mauryan empire that emerged toward the end of the fourth century B.C. The city emerged in Southeast Asia after about the first century A.D. and seems to have been strongly influenced in its development by the spread of the Hindu temple-city form out of India. This phase of city development apparently reached maturity in Java in the second half of the eighth century A.D.

In the Mediterranean regions, the Middle East, India, and Southeast Asia the Muslim empire had an important impact on the history of urbanization, although in general it was not a strongly positive one. Like the Germanic invaders in the West, the Muslims were essentially non-urban in their traditions and they viewed the city mainly as a

religious center. Nevertheless, throughout the period of their domina-
tion, beginning in the seventh century A.D. and extending up to the
present day in the Middle East, there was a continuity in urban development and many present-day cities such as Teheran, Basra, Cairo,
Tangiers, Kano, Mombasa, Hyderabad, Agra, and Lahore were creations of this empire.

Mention of Kano serves to focus attention for the moment on urban developments in tropical Africa. Kano and other cities of West
Africa such as Timbuktu and Katsina were associated with the trading
routes that connected this region with Egypt in the east and the Mediterranean in the north. The associated trade in slaves, metals, manufactured goods, and agricultural products was a flourishing one up
until the sixteenth century. To the south, in what is now southwestern
Nigeria, there was one of the regions of primary urban generation,
the so-called *Yoruba territories*. Ceremonial centers may have appeared
in this region as early as the end of the first millenium A.D. This suggestion is in accord with the descriptions given of the Yoruba as an immigrant group that probably moved into the region from the northeast
sometime between the seventh and tenth centuries A.D.[17] Their first
palace complex, or *afin*, appears to have been established in the city
now known as Ife. Then other cities were founded around this one as
centers of dominance or control over the territory.

Apart from Egypt, the Mediterranean coastlands, and the Nigerian regions, urbanization on the continent of Africa had to await the
development of the European trading empires of the eighteenth and
nineteenth centuries. Then urbanization was most evident in South
Africa where the Dutch and English were responsible for the creation
of the European-style cities that exist there today.

China and Japan

One of the areas of primary urban generation was located in
China in the north of the alluvial plain created by the Huang River.
There, the earliest city forms based on the ceremonial center appear
to date from sometime early in the second millenium B.C. These centers were primarily religious and administrative complexes, but they
also served as the centers for the collection, storage, and redistribution
of the surplus product (agricultural and craft goods) from the surrounding regions. This economic function, of course, was later to
dominate urban development everywhere.

From the northern plain of China, city life diffused to the east and
south to the Yangtze River in the early centuries of the first millenium
B.C. But the really spectacular urban development involved the spread
of the small walled *hsien* or capital in the period of the third century

B.C. to the third century A.D. The diffusion was strongest on the northern plains area, but it also spread westward along the silk-trading route to the "western" world and into the river basins and valleys to the south (Figure 2.7). The vast majority of cities in China today were originally *hsien* capitals. Apart from the later development of centers such as Shanghai and Hong Kong by the Europeans, the urban pattern of China seems to have been fairly well determined by the end of the third century A.D.

A Chinese influence seems to have been important in the development of Japanese cities in the early centuries A.D. Under the Yamato state from the fifth to the seventh centuries there was "an imperial system based on Chinese techniques of land distribution and administration. Increased control of resources by members of the imperial court

Figure 2.7 Distribution of walled cities from 206 B.C. to 221 A.D. [Sen-dou Chang, "The historical trend of Chinese urbanization;" reproduced by permission from *Annals* of the Association of American Geographers, vol. **53**, 1963, p. 117.]

and officials associated with it was reflected in the development of capital cities."[18]

Many of these capitals were short-lived; some others, notably Heian (Kyoto), grew to very large size in the ninth and tenth centuries. Heian probably attained a population of around 500,000. But from the tenth to the twelfth centuries the imperial system weakened and with this came a decline in urban development that was not checked until around the fourteenth century. Thereafter, urban development in Japan became most pronounced.

Central and South America

In the new world of the Americas urban development dates from the early cities located in Mesoamerica and the central Andes. These were both areas of primary urban generation. The ceremonial complexes in Mesoamerica seem to date from around 1000 B.C., and many of the great architectural achievements associated with these centers are still to be admired today. The complex at Teotihuacan in the Valley of Mexico apparently covered an area of more than 11 square miles. The cities that evolved in this region were much more involved in trading activities than was the case with the early cities in Mesopotamia and this found expression in well-developed *marketplaces* within the cities.

In the central Andes, in Peru, major ceremonial centers appear to date from approximately 500 B.C. The development of cities around such centers continued up until the sixteenth century A.D. when the Spaniards arrived. In the central Andean region, Cuzco became the ceremonial center of the Incan empire that flourished in the fourteenth and fifteenth centuries. Along the coastal lowlands there also emerged cities in the valleys leading down from the mountains.

All of these early urban civilizations in the Americas crumbled under the invasions of the Spaniards in the sixteenth century. These conquests saw the introduction of Spanish-style cities as the bases for colonization and political control. A majority of these cities still survive today.

North America

The primary diffusion of the European-style city into South and Central America associated with the Spanish Empire from the sixteenth century onward was more than matched by the developments in North America beginning a century later. There the city was introduced following the conquests of territory at different times by the Spanish, Dutch, French, and English invaders. The consolidation of British rule and the eventual founding of the two nations of Canada and the United States set the stage for the spectacular growth of cities that was to characterize the nineteenth and twentieth centuries. With the emergence of the manufacturing economy, the building of the vast railway networks, and the development of the complex patterns of trade and commerce, urban growth diffused quickly westward across the whole continent. The elaboration of the development pattern for the United States will be taken up in the next chapter.

Australasia

The extensive and powerful European trading empires and colonial regimes of the nineteenth and twentieth centuries also had their impact on urban development in other parts of the world. Notably in Australia and New Zealand English-style cities were the focal points of the colonization efforts. In Asia the growth of the great port-cities of Rangoon, Singapore, Hong Kong, Bombay, and Calcutta all bear witness to these historical forces. It is when one views the impact of these trading empires on urban development at the local, national, and international levels that one can appreciate the force of such arguments as the following:

> Urbanism, as a general phenomenon, should not be viewed as the history of particular cities, but as the history of the system of cities within, between, and around which the surplus circulates. When Florence declined, Nuremburg and Augsburg took over; when Antwerp fell, Amsterdam rose and when Amsterdam fell, London emerged as the main arbiter in the circulation of the surplus. The history of particular cities can therefore be understood only in terms of the circulation of surplus value at a moment of history within a system of cities.[19]

2.3 Contrasts Today Between the Developed and Developing Societies

If we define *urbanization* in terms of the percentage of a country's or region's population living in cities, then some interesting comparisons can be made between countries and regions. This comparison would be made easier if there was universal agreement on what is meant by a city or urban area, but as far as individual countries are concerned no such agreement has been reached. A quotation from a United Nations publication emphasizes this point:

> Countries vary considerably with respect to the minimum

size of locality defined as urban. In Denmark, Finland and
Sweden, localities containing as few as 200 residents may
qualify as urban. In Australia and Canada the minimum
size is 1,000 inhabitants; in Mexico and the United States
it is 2,500 inhabitants. Even higher minimum criteria are
observed elsewhere. In Iran, Austria, Belgium, and Pakistan localities must contain at least 5,000 inhabitants to
qualify as urban, while in Switzerland, Turkey and Nepal,
the minimum population is 10,000. The minimum popula-
of Japanese urban municipalities has long been 20,000.[20]

In the discussion that follows we shall assume that the urban population of any country is as defined by that country. No attempt is made
to establish a single statistical criterion of urbanization.

Twentieth-Century Urban Growth

The first important point to be emphasized is that up until the
mid-nineteenth century the cities throughout the world, with one or
two exceptions, were not particularly large in terms of size of population, and urban populations generally were not very large in comparison to rural populations. But with the rapid growth of manufacturing,
the expansion of trade, the lowering of death rates, and accelerated
population growth in the second half of the nineteenth century and
thereafter, urban populations began to grow at an increasingly fast
rate.

The trends in urban growth after 1925 are illustrated in Tables
2.1 and 2.2. Table 2.1 shows the proportions of the population that
were classed as urban in the world and eight major areas. We see that,
expressed in these terms, the level of urbanization in the world was
only 21% in 1925 but that by 1975 this proportion almost doubled.
By the end of the century it is estimated that one-half of the world's
population will be urban.

Urbanization trends in the eight major areas generally are more
pronounced than the world as a whole. In Northern America (U.S.A.
and Canada) more than one-half of the population was urban in 1925
and 50 years later the proportion increased to more than three-quarters. An even more dramatic increase in urbanization has been experienced in the U.S.S.R. where the proportion classed as urban has
risen from 18% in 1925 to 61% in 1975. The trend in all areas is upward and over the next 50 years it is estimated that the urban proportion in all major areas will increase to over 50%, and in the cases of
Northern America, Europe, U.S.S.R., Latin America, and Oceania the
proportions will all be over 80%. Naturally, the characteristic nature
and quality of urban life of these areas will differ markedly, but un-

Table 2.1 Percentage of Total Population in Urban Localities in the World and Eight Major Areas, 1925–2025. [United Nations, *Concise Report on the World Population Situation in 1970–75 and its Long-Range Implications* (New York: United Nations, 1974), p. 63.]

Major Area	*1925*	*1950*	*1975*	*2000*	*2025*
World total	21	28	39	50	63
Northern America	54	64	77	86	93
Europe	48	55	67	79	88
U.S.S.R.	18	39	61	76	87
East Asia	10	15	30	46	63
Latin America	25	41	60	74	85
Africa	8	13	24	37	54
South Asia	9	15	23	35	51
Oceania	54	65	71	77	87

doubtedly there will be many common problems of congestion, unemployment, housing shortages, rising costs of providing services, and health.

The total size of each urban population is shown in Table 2.2. Two facts stand out. First, the rate of growth of each population is very high. The world urban population, it can be noted, grew by three-quarters from 1925 to 1950 but then doubled over the next 25 years. In the different regions, except for Europe, the growth was even more spectacular. In Northern America and Oceania the urban population

Table 2.2 Urban Population in the World and Eight Major Areas, 1925–2025 (millions). [United Nations, *Concise Report on the World Population Situation in 1970–75 and its Long-Range Implications* (New York: United Nations, 1974), p. 64.]

Major Area	*1925*	*1950*	*1975*	*2000*	*2025*
World total	405	701	1,548	3,191	5,713
Northern America	68	106	181	256	308
Europe	162	215	318	425	510
U.S.S.R.	30	71	154	245	318
East Asia	58	99	299	638	1,044
Latin America	25	67	196	464	819
Africa	12	28	96	312	803
South Asia	45	108	288	825	1,873
Oceania	5	8	15	26	38

trebled over the half century from 1925 to 1975, in the U.S.S.R. and East Asia it grew fivefold, in South Asia sixfold, and in Latin America and Africa nearly eightfold. The United Nations' estimates for the next 50 years call for almost all of these trends to continue.

The second point to be noted from Table 2.2 is that the distribution of the world's urban population is changing. Whereas in 1925 two-fifths of the world's urban population was in Europe, by 1975 this proportion had fallen to one-fifth. Meanwhile, East and South Asia, which together had about one-quarter of the world's urban population in 1925, had increased their joint share to around 38% by 1975. If present trends continue, it seems as though these two areas together will have about one-half of the world's urban population by 2025. By the same date the urban populations of both Africa and Latin America will also exceed those of Europe.

The prospects faced by the rapidly urbanizing nations of East and South Asia are viewed differently by Western scholars and depend on their own ideological biases. A fairly typical North American attitude is reflected in the following statement:

> The likely way the massive urbanization projected for Asia can take place is by a totalitarian government, highly competent and rigorously committed, ruling a docile mass of semi-educated but thoroughly indoctrinated urbanites existing at a low level of consumption, working very hard, and accepting passively what is provided for them.[21]

By contrast, scholars who have studied and viewed the achievements of modern China often present a much more optimistic viewpoint. Consider, for example:

> China has overcome almost all the tragic problems of Asia's cities. It has eliminated its worst slum housing, and renovated or built housing for all those tenants as well as for the tremendous population growth within its cities. It has provided water, public latrines, electricity and transportation, covered sewage systems, and is continuing to build. The problems that are left, and there are many, are not tragic by Asian or American standards.[22]

Urban-Rural Growth Comparisons

Urbanization as a process implies something more than just the growth of cities. For example, the cities of a nation might continue to grow, but the level of urbanization would remain fairly constant if the rural population continued to increase. What is indeed disturbing

Table 2.3 Rural Population in the World and Eight Major Areas, 1925–2025 (millions). [United Nations, *Concise Report on the World Population Situation in 1970–75 and its Long-Range Implications* (New York: United Nations, 1974), p. 64.]

Major Area	1925	1950	1975	2000	2025
World total	1,555	1,784	2,439	3,215	3,352
Northern America	57	60	56	40	24
Europe	177	177	156	115	70
U.S.S.R.	138	109	101	76	50
East Asia	513	558	706	735	606
Latin America	73	95	130	161	142
Africa	144	189	305	522	676
South Asia	452	591	980	1,559	1,778
Oceania	4	4	6	8	6

Table 2.4 Estimated and Projected Annual Percentage Rates of Growth in Total Urban and Rural Population, 1960–1970 and 1970–1975. [United Nations, *Concise Report on the World Population Situation in 1970–75 and its Long-Range Implications* (New York: United Nations, 1974), p. 34.]

Area	Total Population		Urban Population		Rural Population	
	1960–1970	1970–1975	1960–1970	1970–1975	1960–1970	1970–1975
World total	1.9	1.9	3.0	3.0	1.4	1.3
More developed regions	1.0	0.9	2.1	2.0	−0.6	−0.9
Less developed regions	2.3	2.4	4.1	4.2	1.8	1.7
Europe	0.8	0.6	1.6	1.4	−0.6	−0.8
U.S.S.R.	1.3	1.0	2.7	2.3	−0.4	−0.9
Northern America	1.3	0.9	1.9	1.5	−0.4	−1.0
Oceania	2.1	2.0	2.7	2.4	1.0	1.1
South Asia	2.5	2.6	4.1	4.3	2.1	2.2
East Asia	1.6	1.6	3.3	4.0	1.2	0.7
Africa	2.6	2.7	4.8	4.9	2.1	2.0
Latin America	2.7	2.7	4.3	3.9	1.3	1.1

these days is the fact that, especially in the areas of South Asia, Latin America, and Africa, the very spectacular increases in the level of urbanization are accompanied by large increases in the rural population. Table 2.3 illustrates this point. In the half century from 1925 to 1975 the world's rural population increased by about 57% (1,555 million to 2,439 million), whereas the corresponding increases were 78% in Latin America, 112% in Africa, and 117% in South Asia. For the last two areas, this trend seems certain to continue over the next 50 years.

Table 2.4 shows the estimated annual growth rates for both the urban and rural populations. It can be seen that in the developed areas (Northern America, Europe, U.S.S.R., Oceania) where the growth in total population is moderate, continued urbanization is at the expense of a declining rural population. In these areas, urbanization levels already are high. By contrast, in the less developed regions where total population growth is rapid, both the urban and the rural populations are increasing, the former by about 4% per year and the latter by about 1.7% annually.

2.4   Growing Dominance of the Larger Cities

One feature of the recent history of urbanization that deserves special mention is the increasing importance in many countries of a few very large metropolitan centers. A general overview of this trend is provided by Table 2.5. Allowing for many possible difficulties associated with the delimitation of such large metropolitan areas in different countries of the world, the figures in the table bear out the general point about the increasing relative importance of these large cities with population of over 1 million in the population distribution of each major region. A number of points deserve mention. First, the number of million-cities in the world almost doubled over the period 1960–1975, and almost all of these new million-cities were in the less developed regions of the world. By 1975, in fact, more than one-half of the million-cities were in the less developed regions. Second, the total population living in these large cities increased more than two and one-half times in the less developed regions from 1960 to 1975, and it almost doubled in the more developed regions. Third, the proportion of total population living in the million-cities increased in all areas over the period 1960–1975, with the more spectacular increases occurring in Northern America (a gain of almost 7 percentage points), East Asia (a gain of 5 percentage points), and Latin America (a gain of over 7 percentage points).

The figures for Northern America in Table 2.5 show that the proportion of the total population living in these larger cities has risen

Table 2.5   Number and Population of Million-Cities, and Percentage of Total Population in Million-Cities, 1960 and 1975, in the World and Major Areas. [United Nations, *Concise Report on the World Population Situations in 1970–75 and its Long-Range Implications* (New York: United Nations, 1974), p. 36.]

Area	Number of Million-Cities		Population of Million-Cities (Millions)		Percentage of Total Population in Million-Cities	
	1960	*1975*	*1960*	*1975*	*1960*	*1975*
World total	109	191	272	516	9.1	12.8
More developed regions	64	90	173	251	17.7	21.9
Less developed regions	45	101	99	265	4.9	9.2
Europe	31	37	73	93	17.3	19.3
U.S.S.R.	5	12	13	25	6.1	9.7
Northern America	18	30	52	80	26.2	32.9
Oceania	2	2	4	6	24.7	26.9
South Asia	16	34	32	88	3.7	6.8
East Asia	23	45	60	131	7.7	12.9
Africa	3	10	6	22	2.4	5.5
Latin America	11	21	31	71	14.5	21.9

NOTE: These estimates still correspond to earlier population estimates and projections of the United Nations.

to almost one-third and that this trend seems to be continuing. We shall examine this development in more detail in Chapter 3.

Urban Primacy

The trend toward a concentration of population in very large urban agglomerations is consistent with what has been described as increasing *primacy* in a country's urban structure. In Table 2.6 the ratio of the population of the largest city to that of the second largest city is given for a number of selected countries. The table shows that the levels of primacy vary widely throughout the world. At the one extreme are the values of 9 and 10 for countries such as Peru and Argentina, while at the other extreme value close to 1 characterize Canada, India, and Australia.

There is no strong or consistent relationship between the level of economic development and primacy.[23] Primacy occurs in developed economies such as Denmark, Sweden, and the Netherlands and in underdeveloped economies such as Peru, Mexico, Thailand, and Sri

Table 2.6 Primacy Levels For Selected Countries. [United Nations. *Demographic Yearbook 1973* (New York: United Nations, 1974)].

Country and Cities	Year	Population (Millions)	Ratio of Largest to Second Largest
Kenya			
Nairobi*	1969	0.509	2.06
Mombassa*	1969	0.247	
Nigeria			
Lagos†	1971e‡	0.901	1.19
Ibadan†	1971 e	0.758	
Egypt			
Cairo†	1970 e	4.96	2.44
Alexandria†	1970 e	2.03	
Morocco			
Casablanca*	1971	1.561	2.92
Rabat–Sale*	1971	0.534	
South Africa			
Johannesburg*	1970	1.432	1.31
Cape Town*	1970	1.096	
Argentina			
Buenos Aires*	1970	8.352	10.31
Rosario*	1970	0.810	
Brazil			
São Paulo†	1970	5.186	1.22
Rio de Janeiro†	1970	4.252	
Colombia			
Bogota†	1972 e	2.680	2.46
Medellín†	1972 e	1.091	
Peru			
Lima†	1972	2.862	9.41
Arequipa†	1972	0.304	
Dominican Republic			
Santo Domingo†	1970	0.671	4.33
Santiago de los Caballeros†	1970	0.155	
Mexico			
Mexico City†	1970	6.874	5.76
Guadalajara†	1970	1.193	
China			
Shanghai†	1970 e	10.820	1.43
Peking†	1970 e	7.570	
India			
Calcutta*	1971	7.031	1.18
Bombay*	1971	5.970	
Japan			
Tokyo†	1970	8.840	2.97
Osaka†	1970	2.980	

Table 2.6   (cont.)

Country and Cities	Year	Population (Millions)	Ratio of Largest to Second Largest
Thailand			
Bangkok†	1970	1.867	2.97
Thonburi†	1970	0.628	
Sri Lanka (Ceylon)			
Colombo†	1971	0.562	3.63
Dehiwela-Mount			
Lavinia†	1971	0.155	
Turkey			
Istanbul†	1970	2.247	1.86
Ankara†	1970	1.208	
U.S.S.R.			
Moscow†	1970	7.061	1.79
Leningrad†	1970	3.949	
Austria			
Vienna†	1971	1.614	6.51
Graz†	1971	0.248	
Denmark			
Copenhagen*	1970	1.380	7.38
Arhus*	1970	0.187	
France			
Paris†	1968	2.590	2.91
Marseille†	1968	0.889	
Netherlands			
Amsterdam†	1972 e	0.799	1.21
Rotterdam†	1972 e	0.662	
Sweden			
Stockholm†	1970	0.746	1.65
Göteborg†	1970	0.451	
United Kingdom			
London†	1971	7.452	3.12
Manchester†	1971	2.386	
United States			
New York†	1970	11.571	1.65
Los Angeles†	1970	7.032	
Canada			
Montreal†	1971	2.74	1.05
Toronto†	1971	2.62	
Australia			
Sydney*	1971	2.725	1.14
Melbourne*	1971	2.394	
Brisbane*	1971	0.818	

*Population figure is for the city proper.
†Population figure is for the urban agglomeration.
‡e identifies years for which only U.N. population estimates are available; otherwise the years are national census years.

Lanka (Ceylon). Again, primacy as defined in Table 2.6 may be characteristic of small countries that have low income (for example, Peru), export-oriented and agricultural economies (for example, Denmark), a colonial history and fast population growth (for example, Mexico); on the other hand, it is also characteristic of many highly developed economies for which no straightforward relationships can be identified (for example, Austria). What does seem to be important is the tradition of urbanization, that is, the more recent the history of urbanization in a country and the less complex its associated socio-political system, the more probable it is that the country will be dominated by a primate city. A related argument is that in highly centralized and closed political and economic systems primacy will be higher than in countries in which power is more decentralized and dispersed as evidenced by the existence of several large regional capitals.[24] The contrast between Mexico and the United States seems to support this argument.

One other argument on this question of primacy is worth noting. It has been suggested that in underdeveloped economies, primate cities tend to obstruct economic growth because they are tied in more with overseas trading empires and hence funnel out the country's resources without contributing either to the development of their own hinterlands or to a network of cities in the country. But the evidence is not convincing in support of this point. We have noted already that there is little or no indication that primacy is associated with the level of urbanization, and even underdeveloped countries with strong ties to a major country are not *unduly* likely to have a primate-city urban structure. But it does seem to be the case that lesser developed economies that have a heavy dependency on exports of raw materials *are* likely to have a primate city structure.

Clearly, we do not know as much as we would like to know about the nature of primacy in urban structure. For one thing, we do not have a really good measure of primacy for comparative study. The use of the ratio of the largest to the second largest city populations is not satisfactory for comparing large countries with small ones. Also, primacy might be more appropriately defined in some countries with respect to one or two of the larger cities and not just the largest. This is the case in Australia, for example, where primacy is low (1.14 in Table 2.6) when measured by the ratio of Sydney's population to that of Melbourne, but it is much higher when measured by the ratio (2.93) of Melbourne's population to that of the third city, Brisbane.

We also do not know what the true effects are of primacy in a country, either in economic or socio-political terms. In a small country such as New Zealand, for example, it can be argued very effectively that there are too many urban centers and that increased primacy of the five or six larger centers could allow for greater efficiencies to be achieved in transportation and marketing services.

2.5   Rank-Size Relationship: A Statistical Generalization or an Ultimate Form?

Another approach to studying the relationship between the number and size of cities in any country or large area is to rank the cities by

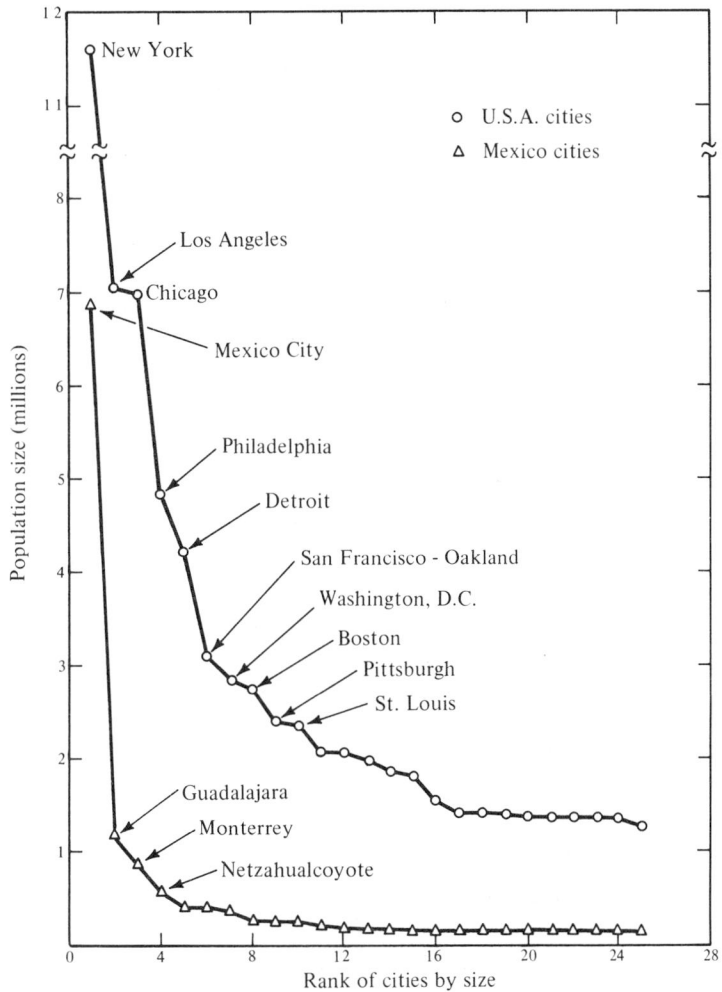

Figure 2.8 Rank-size distributions for Mexico and the United States, 1970. [United Nations, *Demographic Yearbook 1973* (New York: United Nations, 1974).]

their populations and then to graph the ranks against the population sizes. This technique is illustrated in Figure 2.8 in which symbols for the 25 largest cities in both the United States and Mexico are plotted. The curve joining the points in each case shows the general shape of this rank-size relationship.

Primacy would be reflected in such a graph by a large gap between the point representing the largest city, ranked number one, and that for the second largest city. This gap is present in both cases shown in Figure 2.8, but it is more pronounced in the case of Mexico. It will be noted also that in the case of the United States there are many more *intermediate*-sized cities than is the case in Mexico. If a similar graph were to be plotted for Canada, which had a much lower level of primacy in Table 2.6, the curve would appear closer to a straight line.

Rank-Size Rule

This relationship between city size and rank can be expressed in a number of ways. Figure 2.8 shows one way using a simple plot of rank against size. It may also be expressed by a simple formula relating population size P, to rank r, and k, the population of the largest city. Thus, for any city i,

$$P_i = \frac{k}{r_i}$$

In other words, given the population of the largest city (k), we can predict the population size of any other city (P_i) by dividing k by the rank (r_i). For example, if the largest city is 10 million, then the tenth ranked city has a population of 10 million ÷ 10, or 1 million. This formula is referred to as the *rank-size rule*. Some simple calculations using the population figures given in Table 2.7 suggest, however, that the relationship is not as precise as the use of such a formula would suggest.

Cumulative Frequency Distribution

The relationship may also be studied by plotting the cumulative frequency distribution curve of the towns against the actual population sizes. This is a development of the technique used in Table 2.7. It is possible to compute the cumulative frequencies of the towns and to express these as percentages (columns 3 and 4 of Table 2.8). These values can be plotted. In such cases it is conventional to make the plots on special graph paper that is scaled so that the plots tend toward straight lines. In Figures 2.9 and 2.10 the population size is also compressed on a logarithmic scale. For mathematical reasons that need not

Table 2.7   Twenty-five Largest Urban Centers in Mexico and the United States, 1970. [United Nations, *Demographic Yearbook 1973* (New York: United Nations, 1974).]

Rank	U.S.A.	Population	Mexico	Population
1	New York	11.571	Mexico City	6.874
2	Los Angeles–Long Beach	7.032	Guadalajara	1.193
3	Chicago	6.978	Monterrey	0.858
4	Philadelphia	4.817	Netzahualcoyotl	0.580
5	Detroit	4.199	Ciudad Juárez	0.407
6	San Francisco–Oakland	3.109	Puebla de Zaragoza	0.401
7	Washington, D.C.	2.861	Leon	0.364
8	Boston	2.753	Mexicali	0.263
9	Pittsburgh	2.401	Chihuahua	0.257
10	St. Louis	2.363	San Luis Potosí	0.230
11	Baltimore	2.070	Mérida	0.212
12	Cleveland	2.064	Aquascalientes	0.181
13	Houston	1.985	Hermosillo	0.176
14	Newark	1.856	Acapulco	0.174
15	Minneapolis–St. Paul	1.813	Culiacán	0.167
16	Dallas–Fort Worth	1.555	Morelia	0.161
17	Seattle-Everett	1.421	Durango	0.150
18	Anaheim–Santa Ana–Garden Grove	1.420	Nuevo Laredo	0.148
19	Milwaukee	1.403	Matamoros	0.137
20	Atlanta	1.390	Reynosa	0.137
21	Cincinnati	1.384	Cuernavaca	0.134
22	Paterson-Clifton-Passaic	1.358	Colonia Agricola	0.124
23	San Diego	1.357	Jalapa	0.122
24	Buffalo	1.349	Poza Rica de Hidalgo	0.120
25	Miami	1.267	Mazatlán	0.119

NOTE: Data are for cities in Mexico and for Standard Metropolitan Statistical Areas (SMSA's) in the U.S.A.

be explored here, the use of this logarithmic probability graph paper will produce straight-line plots of the cumulative frequency data, such as are given in Table 2.8, in those cases in which there is a fairly regular progression in population size from the smallest to the largest city. However, the plots in Figures 2.9 and 2.10 that show only the 25 largest cities are far from being straight lines, although particular segments of each curve could be so represented.

If graphs or plots of the kind we have just described are made for different countries using information on all cities of over 20,000, one finds that straight-line relationships are characteristic of developed economies such as Italy, Belgium, U.S.A., West Germany, and Switzerland and lesser developed countries, notably India, China, Brazil, and El Salvador. At the other extreme, primate distributions for Peru,

Table 2.8   Cumulative Frequency Distribution of Cities by Size.

U.S.A. City	Size (Millions)	Cumulative Frequency of Cities	Percentage Cumulative Frequency of Cities	Size	Mexico City
New York	11.571	1	4	6.874	Mexico City
Los Angeles– Long Beach	7.032	2	8	1.193	Guadalajara
Chicago	6.978	3	12	.858	Monterrey
Philadelphia	4.817	4	16	.580	Netzahualcoyotl
Detroit	4.199	5	20	.407	Ciudad Juárez
San Francisco– Oakland	3.109	6	24	.401	Puebla de Zaragoza
Washington, D.C.	2.861	7	28	.364	Leon
Boston	2.753	8	32	.263	Mexicali
Pittsburgh	2.401	9	36	.257	Chichuahua
St. Louis	2.363	10	40	.230	San Luis Potosí
Baltimore	2.070	11	44	.212	Mérida
Cleveland	2.064	12	48	.181	Aquascalientes
Houston	1.985	13	52	.176	Hermosillo
Newark	1.856	14	56	.174	Acapulco
Minneapolis– St. Paul	1.813	15	60	.167	Culiacán
Dallas– Fort Worth	1.555	16	64	.161	Morelia
Seattle–Everett	1.421	17	68	.150	Durango
Anaheim– Santa Ana– Garden Grove	1.420	18	72	.148	Nuevo Laredo
Milwaukee	1.403	19	76	.137	Matamoros
Atlanta	1.390	20	80	.137	Reynosa
Cincinnati	1.384	21	84	.134	Cuernavaca
Paterson-Clifton– Passaic	1.358	22	88	.124	Colonia Agricola
San Diego	1.357	23	92	.122	Jalapa
Buffalo	1.349	24	96	.120	Poza Rica de Hidalgo
Miami	1.267	25	100	.119	Mazatlán

NOTE: Compiled from data in Table 2.7.

Mexico, Dominican Republic, and Sri Lanka (Ceylon) plot as curves with sharp angular breaks in them, often reflecting the absence of a particular size range in the urban distribution. These results suggest that "primacy is the simplest city size distribution, affected by but few simple strong forces.... At the other extreme, rank-size distributions are found when, because of complexity of economic and political life and/or age of the system of cities, many forces affect the urban pattern in many ways."[25]

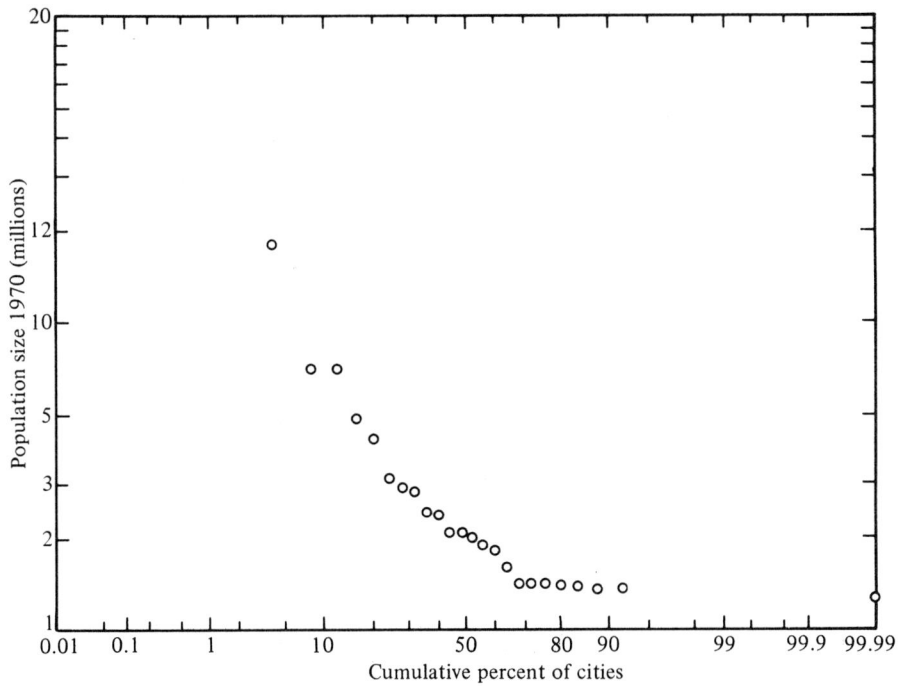

Figure 2.9 U.S.A. city-size distribution.

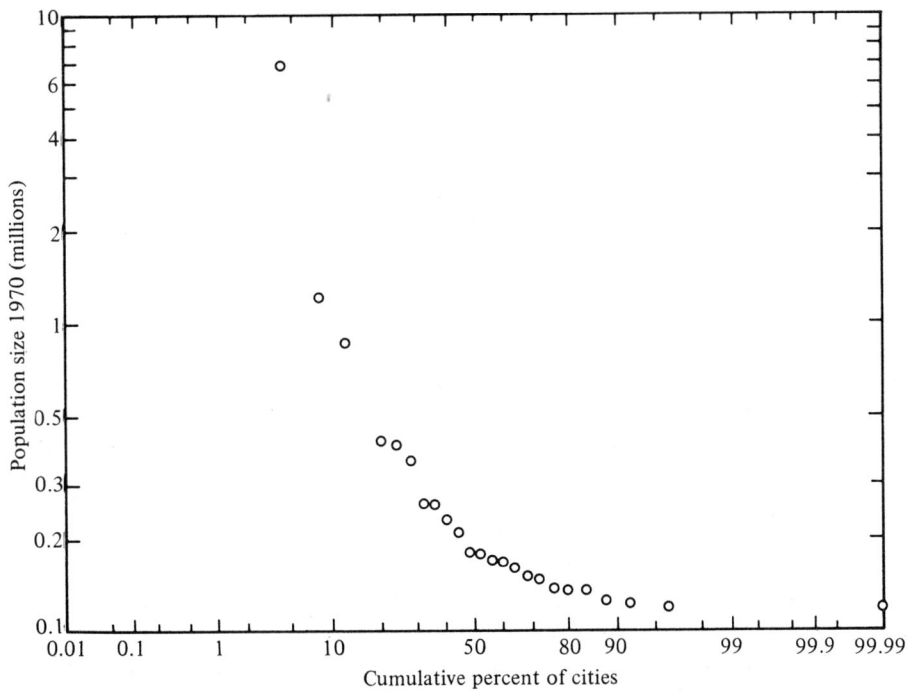

Figure 2.10 Mexico's city-size distribution.

Percent
of
cities

Population size

Early stage of urban development. A few large "primate" cities, but no intermediate sized or smaller cities. Urban system embryonic.

Gradual emergence of a few smaller urban centers. A few large cities still dominant.

Urban hierarchy beginning to emerge. Growth of intermediate sized cities seen in the "straightening" of the size distribution curve.

Mature urban system exists. A well-developed hierarchy of cities has emerged with all size classes represented. A straightline rank-size distribution now persists over time.

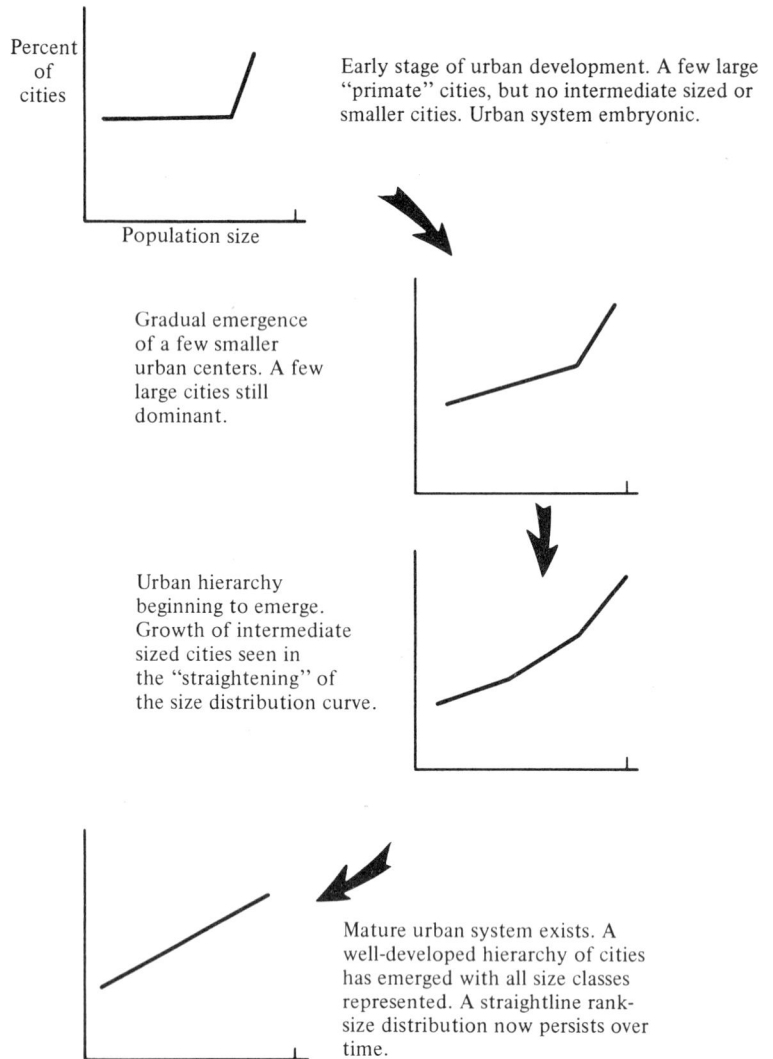

Figure 2.11 Berry's developmental model for the city-size distribution. [Based on B. J. L. Berry, "City size distribution and economic development," *Economic Development and Cultural Change,* **9**, 1961, p. 583. © 1961 by the University of Chicago. All rights reserved.]

Evolutionary Model

According to the above interpretation, the history of urbanization in a country may show a gradual development in the city-size distribution through the stages shown in Figure 2.11. In this model the straight-line rank-size distribution appears as the ultimate or limiting form.

Unfortunately, there are too few studies available to allow for any strong confirmation or denial of this evolutionary hypothesis. In support of the model one can point to the case of New Zealand where there has been some filling in of the intermediate part of the size distribution over time. Studies of the United States' urban system, however, have suggested that something approaching a straight-line relationship has always described this system; indeed, the stability of the relationship portrayed in Figure 2.12 is very remarkable. In the following chapter the United States picture will be examined more closely. All that can be concluded now is that the evolutionary model suggested in Figure 2.11 seems at least to be plausible and is confirmed by some limited examples. But much more careful historical analysis of how

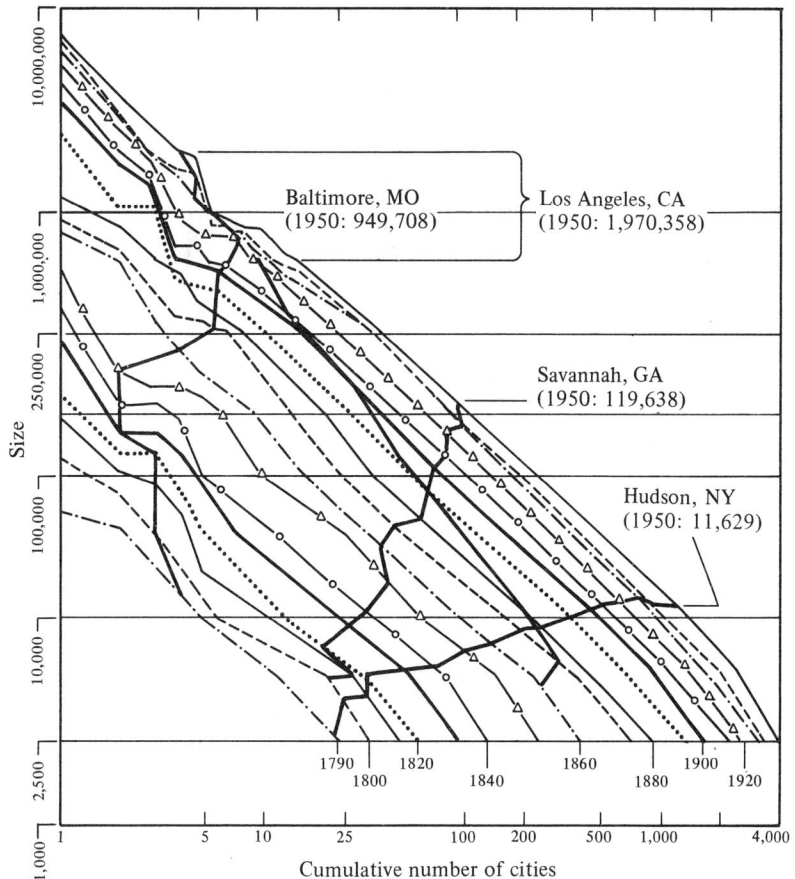

Figure 2.12 The rank-size distributions of the U.S., 1790–1950. The changing positions of four cities in these distributions are traced out on the graph. [C. H. Madden, "On Some Indications of Stability in the Growth of Cities in the United States," *Economic Development and Cultural Change*, **4**, 1956, pp. 236–52. © 1956 by The University of Chicago. All rights reserved.]

rank-size distributions develop over time is needed before any final judgment can be made on its correctness.

In concluding these sections on primacy and rank-size relationships it is well to keep one or two points in mind. One is that we have been dealing with national figures and patterns and these often represent simply an averaging of different regional effects that are present within a country. This is illustrated in the case of Australia. For that country as a whole, urban primacy is not strong, but within each of the states making up the Federation it is indeed very extreme.

> This situation, known locally as "centralization," has existed for a century and more; it forms a staple of political debate and inaction at both the state and federal levels, has been the fulcrum behind the maintenance of the third major political party, and has been the subject of endless public comment and criticism.[26]

A similar contrast between the national picture and the regional situations also shows up in Canada (Figure 2.13).

Finally, we should not overlook the fact that these general questions about the nature of the city-size distributions are obviously important in discussions of regional planning and economic development. On the one hand, a country might encourage primacy in its urban structure by investing heavily in the growth of only one or two major cities in the hope that growth might spill over from these centers into surrounding regions. On the other hand, a strategy that encouraged growth in a range of intermediate-sized and smaller cities could foster the emergence of a straight-line rank-size relationship. Later in this book we shall discuss in more detail these different approaches and some contrasting strategies.

2.6   Other Urban-Related Contrasts

Our discussions of the rapid growth of metropolitan centers and the different changes in the city-size distributions do not exhaust the ways of discussing the different consequences of the urbanization process. After all, these particular developments, in a sense, are only statistical creations and the statistics may conceal very important changes occurring in the nature and quality of urban life.

There is not a great amount of information on these more detailed considerations, but some facts are known. For one thing, it seems clear that from the economic point of view, urbanization is occurring prematurely in many of the developing countries. The rapidly increasing

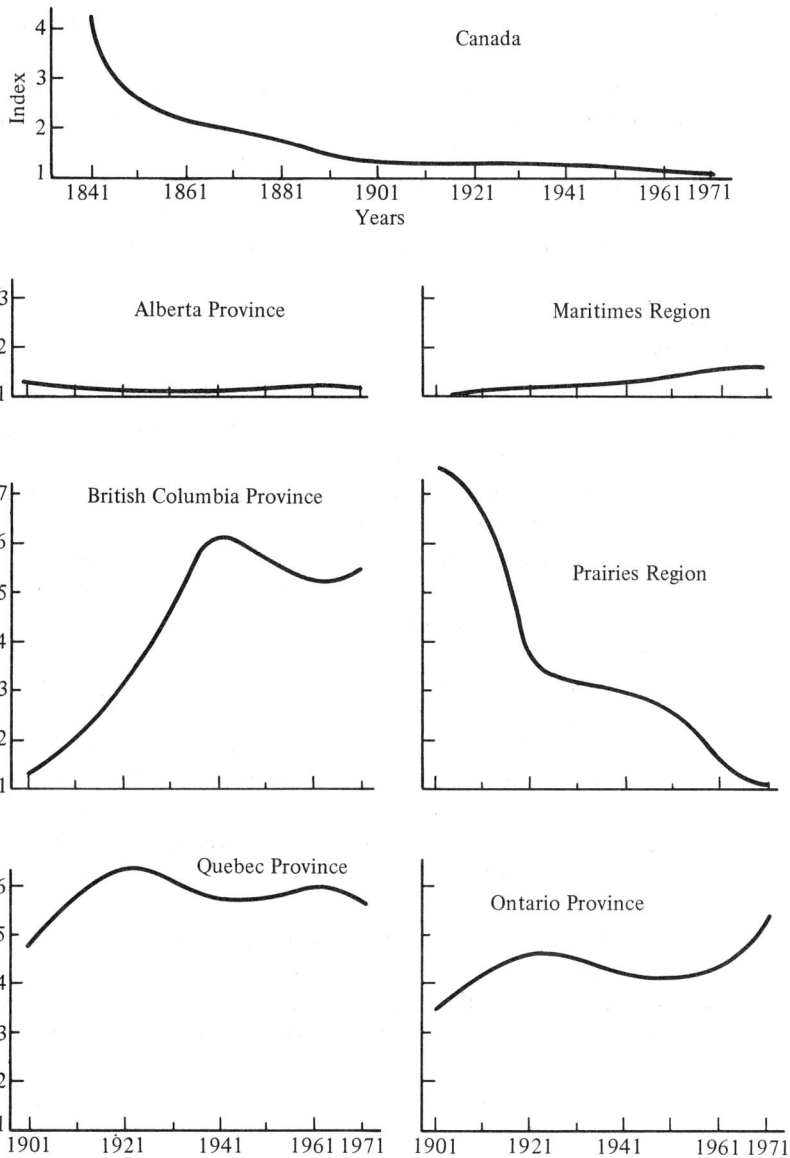

Figure 2.13 Primacy indices for Canada (1841–1971), provinces, and regions (1901–1971). The index is the ratio of the population of the largest city to that of the second largest. The "Prairies" region includes Alberta. [Based on D. Kerr, "Metropolitan dominance in Canada," in J. Warkentin, ed. *Canada: A Geographical Interpretation* (Toronto: Methuen, 1968), p. 539.]

flow of migrants into the cities of these countries far exceeds the growth of employment opportunities for the new inhabitants in these cities. One consequence of this has been that in many of the cities in the developing areas these recent migrants have been forced into very marginal service activities with extremely low productivity. The numerous sidewalk vendors and pedicab operators in the cities of Asia are expressions of this problem.

Housing

Another consequence of rapid urbanization is that the supply of housing lags far behind the increase in population. It is questionable whether or not the housing supply in the cities of the developing world could even keep pace with the natural increase in urban population, let alone cope with the influx of new immigrants. The results are very high land prices, high cost of housing, overcrowding, and large colonies of squatters. A 1968 United Nations report highlighted the problem in the following way:

> Over one-third of the population of Mexico City, 1.5 million people, live in the *colonias proletarias*—known originally as *barrios paracaidistas* or "parachutists' neighborhoods"; nearly half of Ankara's population of 1.5 million in *gecekondu* districts—the squatter settlements whose name describes a house built overnight; the area of the *villes extra-coutumiers* of Leopoldville is greater than that of the city itself.[27]

The problem of an urban housing shortage is not confined to cities of the developing countries. Similar problems exist in all too many cities of the so-called developed countries, and housing policies in the countries of North America and Western Europe are very live political questions.

Associated with the problems in housing are very great deficiencies in services and utilities. Again, even in the cities of the developed countries, for example, the United States, the spiraling upward costs of fire and police protection, of public transportation, and of water, power, sanitation, and other services are subjects of considerable concern and frequent political sensitivity. But in the cities of the developing world the levels of these services are greatly inferior, indeed often absent, and their real cost cannot even be approximated.

Health

The health picture is a rather conflicting one. It is possible to argue that measures of health have improved very rapidly along with increasing urbanization. This is certainly the case with such indicators as the rate of infant mortality and life expectancy. Improvements in these areas have kept pace with the increase in urbanization, and the associated gaps in standards between the developed and developing countries have been narrowed (Figure 2.14). But when we look at the pattern of health services within particular countries the picture is not so bright. In the developing countries particularly, and in the developed ones to a lesser extent, there is a marked disparity between the town and the countryside in the provision of medical services. In Latin America, for example, there are five times as many physicians in the capitals and large cities as in the countrysides, and the situation is no better in Africa and Asian countries.[28] But overcrowding and poor housing frequently result in higher mortality rates and disease levels in the cities than in the countrysides.

The urban-rural contrasts that exist in health services also show up in education. Urban schools appear to be better equipped and have

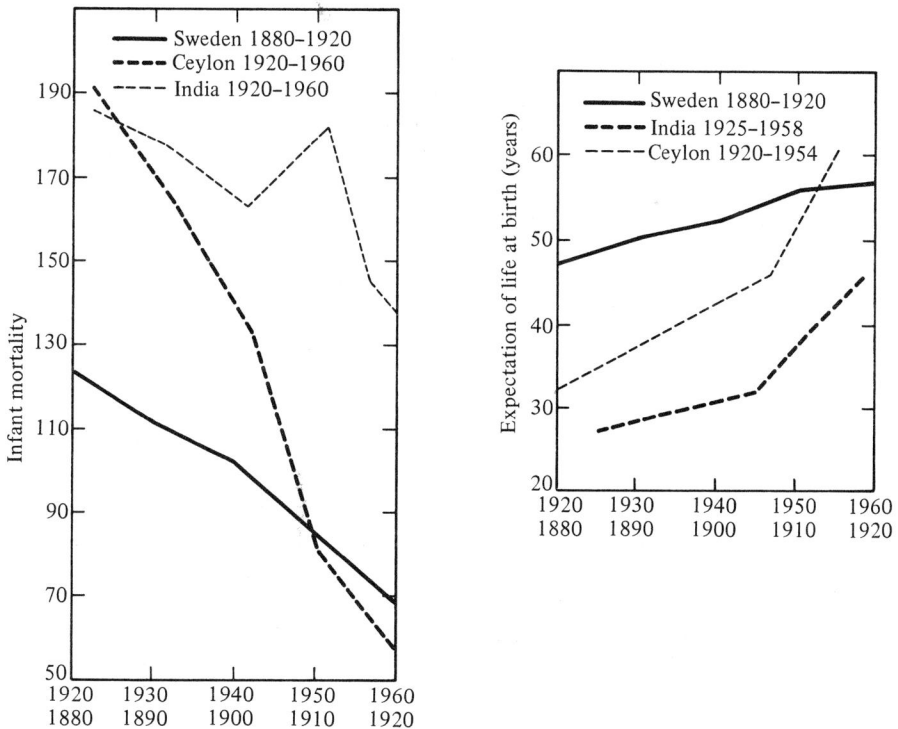

Figure 2.14 Demographic indicators for Sweden, India, and Sri Lanka (Ceylon). [United Nations, "Urbanization: Development policies and planning," *International Social Development Review*, 1, 1968, p. 107.]

smaller classes than those in the rural areas, especially in the developing countries.

One other social corollary of urbanization is noted here. The higher urban densities that characterize many cities in both the developed and developing countries possibly take their toll of the psychological well-being of the inhabitants. It is easy to point to higher crime rates and increased levels of deviant social behavior in the urban centers of today, but the possible causal relationships between these features and the changed conditions of urban living have yet to be clearly established. We shall have more to say on this question later in the book.

2.7 Summary

In this chapter we have discussed a number of issues having to do with the world-wide patterns of urbanization. We began with a discussion of the process of urbanization itself and noted some of the different interpretations that can be given to this process. We stressed a functional interpretation that emphasizes the role of a city in its regional setting, as the focal point for the organization, integration, and even control of the region. We critically reviewed the factors of environment and ecology, demography, and technological change that are often offered in explanation of the emergence of urban societies. Taken individually, they do not suffice to explain most developments. We noted, in particular, the different views on the concept of surplus product and how they related to theories of urban development. Some scholars prefer a relativistic definition, that is, the surplus product that allowed for the emergence of an urban class is seen as being determined by the particular institutional forms and needs of the society in question. The Marxists, by contrast, stress the notion of universality in speaking of surplus product, and cities are seen as the means whereby this surplus is organized, extracted, and distributed.

We sketched a brief history of the world's urban development noting that seven areas of independent, primary urban generation have been identified. We stressed, however, that this history is far from being completely written and that other independent centers of urban development may yet be recognized. The relative significance of different types of diffusion in the emergence of urban forms and patterns was given attention.

The modern picture of urban development was described in terms of the sharp contrasts between the developed and developing societies (with emphasis on the rapidly accelerating urban growth in the latter), the growing dominance of the larger cities in almost all countries throughout the world and the related variation in the levels of urban primacy, and the tendency in older and/or more mature societies for straight-line urban rank-size distributions to emerge. These generalizations about the world-wide patterns of urbanization provide a backdrop against which we shall view the more detailed characteristics of urban societies in particular countries.

It is unfortunate, but understandable, that a great deal more is known about the nature of urban societies in the developed countries than in the developing ones and this bias will become apparent in later chapters. The danger that we must guard against is assuming that what holds true for the developed societies is true also of developing ones. There is growing evidence that this is certainly not the case and whenever possible we shall acknowledge this important point.

Notes

1. See, for example, V. G. CHILDE, "The urban revolution," *Town Planning Review*, **21**, 1959, pp. 3–17.

2. P. WHEATLEY, *The Pivot of the Four Quarters* (Edinburgh: Edinburgh University Press, 1971), pp. 386–87.

3. A. L. MABOGUNJE, *Urbanization in Nigeria* (New York: Africana Publishing Co., 1968), p. 41.

4. WHEATLEY, *op. cit.*, p. 388.

5. J. FRIEDMANN and R. WULFF, "The urban transition: comparative studies of newly industrializing societies," *Progress in Geography*, **8**, 1976, pp. 1–93.

6. WHEATLEY, *op. cit.*

7. *Ibid.*, p. 225.

8. *Ibid.*, p. 264.

9. *Ibid.*, p. 269.

10. For example, R. McC. ADAMS, *The Evolution of Urban Society* (Chicago: Aldine Publishing Co., 1966).

11. Notably, G. TAYLOR, *Urban Geography* (London: Methuen & Co. Ltd., 1949).

12. See WHEATLEY, *op. cit.*, p. 268.

13. D. HARVEY, *Social Justice and the City* (London: Edward Arnold, 1973), p. 238.

14. See WHEATLEY, *op. cit.*, pp. 6–7.

15. M. HAMMOND, *The City in the Ancient World* (Cambridge: Harvard University Press, 1972), p. 59.

16. R. E. DICKINSON, *The West European City. A Geographical Interpretation* (London: Routledge & Kegan Paul Ltd., 1951), p. 279.

17. See MABOGUNJE, *op. cit.*

18. G. Rozman, *Urban Networks in Ching China and Tokugawa Japan* (Princeton: Princeton University Press, 1973), p. 20.

19. Harvey, *op. cit.,* p. 250.

20. United Nations, "Growth of the world's urban and rural population, 1920–2000," *Population Studies,* No. 44, 1969, p. 10.

21. K. Davis, "Asia's cities: problems and options," *Population and Development Review,* 1, 1975, p. 83.

22. Committee of Concerned Asian Scholars, *China! Inside the People's Republic* (New York: Bantam Books, Inc., 1972), p. 122.

23. See, for example, S. K. Mehta, "Some demographic and economic correlates of primate cities: a case for re-evaluation," *Demography,* 1, 1964, pp. 136–47.

24. Friedmann and Wulff, *op. cit.*

25. B. J. L. Berry, "City-size distribution and economic development," *Economic Development and Cultural Change,* 9, 1961, p. 582.

26. A. J. Rose, "Dissent from downunder: metropolitan primacy as the normal state," *Pacific Viewpoint,* 7, 1966, pp. 2–3.

27. United Nations, "Urbanization: development policies and planning," *International Social Development Review,* 1, 1968, p. 107.

28. *Ibid.,* pp. 92–93.

B. NATIONAL
AND REGIONAL PATTERNS

chapter 3

Number, Size, and Location
of Cities in a Region

Chapter 2 discussed certain aspects of urbanization at the international level. That discussion was very general, especially as far as the statements about large countries such as Canada, China, India, the Soviet Union, and the United States were concerned. The urban societies in those countries are very complex ones, resulting from a complicated mix of economic, historical, social, environmental, and political factors. There was some indication of this point in the discussion of the urban rank-size relationship, for there it appeared that the picture at the national level could conceal significant regional differences in a country.

This chapter explores some of the more detailed features of urban societies as they exist at national and regional scales. The emphasis is still placed on questions of spatial structure and form, but the change in scale allows us to focus on some of the interrelationships among cities and between cities and the regions in which they are located. In the first section we shall examine some of the historical processes that gave rise to the city-size distributions of the United States and the Soviet Union, the two leading urban countries in the world in terms of the number of large cities within them and the total sizes of their urban populations.

3.1 Evolution of City-Size Distributions

The United States

Recall that we noted how the city-size distribution of the United States has been remarkably stable in its form for more than 150 years. This does not mean that particular cities have stayed at the same position in the rankings of the cities by size over the whole period of time. Instead, it has been the case that the cities holding different size rankings, for example, the fifth or tenth or one-hundredth position, have changed in identity and yet the regular progression in size rank has continued to approximate a straight-line relationship. This was illustrated earlier in Figure 2.12.

Four major stages have been identified in the urban history of the United States.[1] A brief description of each stage follows.

"Sail-Wagon Epoch, 1770–1830." There was no dominant city in 1790 since New York, Boston, and Philadelphia were then all about the same size. These cities were Atlantic coast ports as were most of the cities at that time. Over the period, the more spectacular rises in size importance were experienced by cities on the western frontier, especially those along the Erie Canal, on Lakes Erie and Ontario, and on the Mississippi. Nevertheless, by 1830, with the exception of Pittsburgh, all of the cities in the top three size categories were still located east of the Appalachian mountains or in western New York State.

"Iron-Horse Epoch, 1830–1870." This period saw the early development of the rail networks and the rapid growth of the inland port cities on which these networks were focused. Cities such as Cleveland, Detroit, Chicago, and St. Louis all moved rapidly up the hierarchy. In the south, New Orleans overshadowed Charleston as the major regional city, while on the east coast New York grew rapidly ahead of Philadelphia and became the first-order center of the country. Table 3.1 shows that this period also witnessed the greatest increase in the number of second- and third-order centers.

"Steel-Rail Epoch, 1870–1920." With the completion of the extensive rail networks and the associated development of agricultural, forestry, and mineral resources, there occurred the emergence of the new metropolitan centers in the west, northwest, and Florida. Cities such as Seattle, Los Angeles, and Dallas moved quickly up the size

Table 3.1   Number of Centers and Total Population in Each of
the Size Orders Defined by Borchert. (Reprinted,
with permission, from J. R. Borchert, "American
Metropolitan Evolution," *Geographical Review*, vol.
57, 1967, p. 315.)

Size Order	1790	1830	1870	1920	1960
	Number of Centers				
First	0	0	1	1	1
Second	3	3	6	4	6
Third	8	8	14	16	19
Fourth	20	29	33	51	70
Fifth	8	12	37	75	82
Total	39	52	91	147	178
	Total Population (thousands)				
First	—	—	2,171	8,490	14,760
Second	514	1,120	3,301	10,364	28,826
Third	499	784	3,627	13,918	26,493
Fourth	530	1,812	2,533	12,829	30,473
Fifth	95	300	1,826	6,972	12,647
"SMSA" total	1,638	4,016	13,458	52,573	113,199
U.S. total	3,929	12,866	39,818	105,711	179,323

hierarchy. In the east, the development of the steel industry prompted
the rapid growth of the industrial centers in the states of Michigan,
Ohio, and Pennsylvania. This period also saw the decline in size–
order of first, the Ohio-Mississippi-Missouri river towns such as St.
Louis, Louisville, and Wheeling, and second, certain industrial centers
located at waterpower sites in the northeast.

Again, Table 3.1 summarizes many of the important changes.
What is especially noteworthy is the tremendous growth in the share of
total population accounted for by the five highest-order centers. Remember that in Chapter 2 we noted the increasing size and importance
of the larger metropolitan centers in the countries of the world and it is
now clear that in the United States, at least, this trend has been apparent for some considerable time.

"*Auto-Air-Amenity Epoch, 1920–.*" The most spectacular increases
in size-order in this period were among the cities of the southwest and
Florida that have particular attractions in regard to the way and style
of living. This growth is illustrated in Table 3.2 which shows that for
metropolitan areas such as Los Angeles, Miami and Fort Lauderdale,
Phoenix and Las Vegas over 80% of their 1960 populations were

Table 3.2 Percentages of Populations of Selected 1960 SMSA's Attained in Major Historical Epochs. (Reprinted, with permission, from J. R. Borchert, "American Metropolitan Evolution," *Geographical Review*, vol. **57**, 1967, p. 329.)

Size Order	SMSA*	Wagon-Sail Pre-1830	Iron Horse 1830–1870	Steel Rail 1870–1920	Auto-Air-Amenity 1920–1960
First	New York†	3	11	44	42
Second	Philadelphia	9	15	38	38
	Boston‡	9	18	48	25
	Chicago†	0	8	47	45
	Detroit	0	6	29	65
	San Francisco-Oakland and San Jose	0	7	27	66
	Los Angeles	0	0+	15	85
Third	Washington	5	5	19	71
	Pittsburgh	7	10	56	27
	St. Louis	2	21	34	43
	New Orleans	7	18	23	52
	Seattle-Tacoma	0	0+	42	58
	Denver	0	1	35	64
	Dallas and Forth Worth	0	3	30	67
	Miami and Fort Lauderdale	0	0	4	96
Fourth	Albany-Schenectady-Troy	23	25	23	29
	New Bedford and Fall River	13	12	65	10
	Scranton and Wilkes-Barre-Hazelton	4	20	63	13
	Birmingham	1	1	47	51
	Omaha	0	10	50	40
	Flint	0	7	27	66
	Jacksonville	0	3	22	75
	Phoenix	0	0	14	86
Fifth	Corpus Christi	0	2	8	90
	Altoona	0	21	72	7
	Charleston, S.C.	40	1	9	50
	Lubbock	0	0	7	93
	Las Vegas	0	0	4	96

*1960 SMSA except where noted to contrary.
†Standard Consolidated Area.
‡Norfolk, Suffolk, and Middlesex Counties.

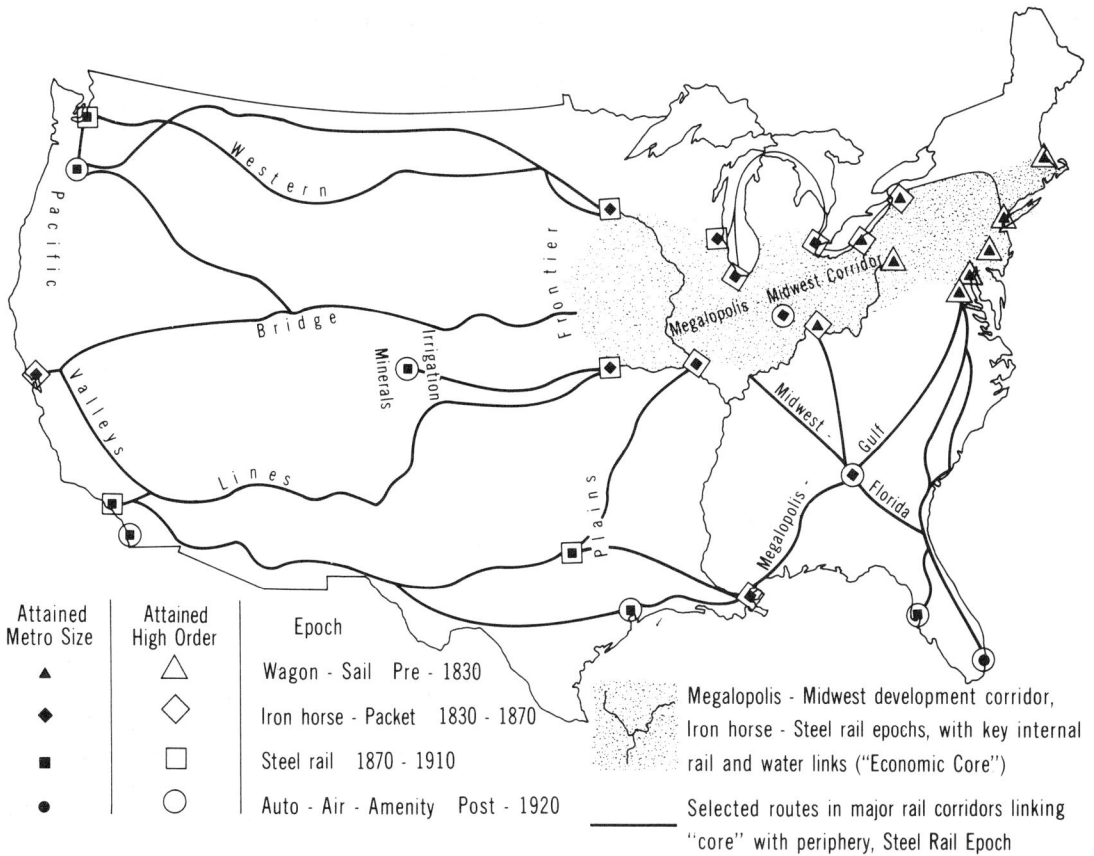

Western

Frontier

Pacific

Bridge

Minerals

Irrigation

Valleys

Lines

Plains

Megalopolis - Midwest Corridor

Midwest - Gulf

Megalopolis - Florida

Attained Metro Size	Attained High Order	Epoch
▲	△	Wagon - Sail Pre - 1830
◆	◇	Iron horse - Packet 1830 - 1870
■	□	Steel rail 1870 - 1910
●	○	Auto - Air - Amenity Post - 1920

Megalopolis - Midwest development corridor, Iron horse - Steel rail epochs, with key internal rail and water links ("Economic Core")

———— Selected routes in major rail corridors linking "core" with periphery, Steel Rail Epoch

Figure 3.1 The historical emergence of America's high-order metropolitan areas. [J. R. Borchert, "America's changing metropolitan regions"; reproduced by permission from the *Annals* of the Association of American Geographers, volume **62**, p. 355 (1972).]

achieved in the period 1920–1960. By contrast, the development of centers such as New York, Philadelphia, Boston, St. Louis, and Albany-Schenectady-Troy has been spread over a much longer time span. The industrial growth on the Gulf Coast and throughout the southeast and the dominance of Michigan in the automobile industry were reflected in accelerated growth of many metropolitan centers. Many former metropolitan areas in the Appalachian regions of New York and Pennsylvania failed to maintain population growth in their central cities and consequently lost their status as metropolitan areas.

By 1970 there were as many as 28 major metropolitan areas in the United States (see Figure 3.1), and these fell into three size groups. The area with the largest population was New York with more than

Table 3.3 Number of SMSA's and Emerging SMSA's Experiencing Shifts in Size Orders Defined by Borchert. (Reprinted, with permission, from J. R. Borchert, "American Metropolitan Evolution," *Geographical Review*, vol. **57**, 1967, p. 330).

Shift in Size Order	*1790–1830*	*1830–1870*	*1870–1920*	*1920–1960*
Up one rank	7	37	66	65
Up two ranks	11	16	15	6
Up three ranks	2	4	3	1
Up four ranks	0	1	0	0
Down one rank	10	14	25	20
Down two ranks	2	2	2	0
Steady	26	24	49	103
New entries	19	47	69	48
Dropouts	6	8	13	17
Net increase	13	39	56	31

15 million. Below it were 7 second-order centers that had populations in the range 3–10 million. Many of these, notably Boston, Philadelphia, Chicago, Los Angeles, and San Francisco, have played major roles at different times in the westward expansion of settlement in the country. The third-order centers included 20 different metropolitan areas, most of which were located in the northeast in the old centers of manufacturing. The newcomers to this group were located in the climatically attractive areas of the southwest, the Gulf Coast, and Florida.

One final note on the United States metropolitan system deserves mention. It is suggested by the information given in Table 3.3, which shows how over the different time periods there has been some stabilization in the total urban system in the sense that the number of centers moving more than one rank in an epoch has decreased. But it is also apparent that the same urban system has retained considerable flexibility, the "birth" and "death" of metropolitan areas continue, and the number of centers that shift either upward or downward by one rank remains fairly high from one time period to another.

The Soviet Union

In contrast to the straight-line rank-size relationship that we have noted to be characteristic of the United States, the situation in the Soviet Union is very different. This is illustrated by the graph of the rank-size distribution of the 1,576 cities of more than 10,000 popula-

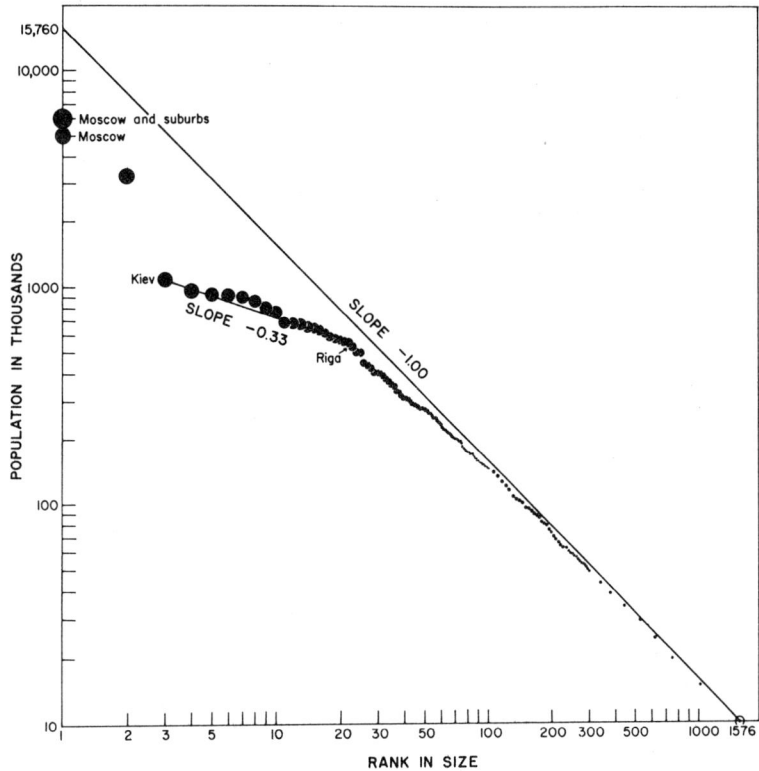

Figure 3.2 Rank-size distribution: 1,576 cities of more than 10,000 population in 1959, U.S.S.R. [C. D. Harris, *Cities of the Soviet Union* (Chicago: Rand Mc-Nally & Co., 1970), p. 137. Reproduced by permission of the Association of American Geographers.]

tion in 1959 (shown in Figure 3.2). Moscow and Leningrad are clearly separated from the remainder of the cities, although neither of the cities has as large a population as a straight-line rank-size relationship would suggest. From Kiev down to city number 22 (Riga) all the cities are plotted and both the height and slope of this section of the graph also are clearly less than might be expected. Beyond rank 22 every fifth city is plotted down to number 300. Thereafter, points are shown only at intervals of 5000 population. The overall shape of this graph, the fact that Moscow is not as large as expected, and the flattening of the slope between ranks 3 and 22 have been interpreted to mean that the urban system of the Soviet Union is not a highly integrated and unified system and that there are "several subgroups of city systems somewhat separated from one another and made semi-independent by the operation of space friction."[2] As many as 24 such subsystems are

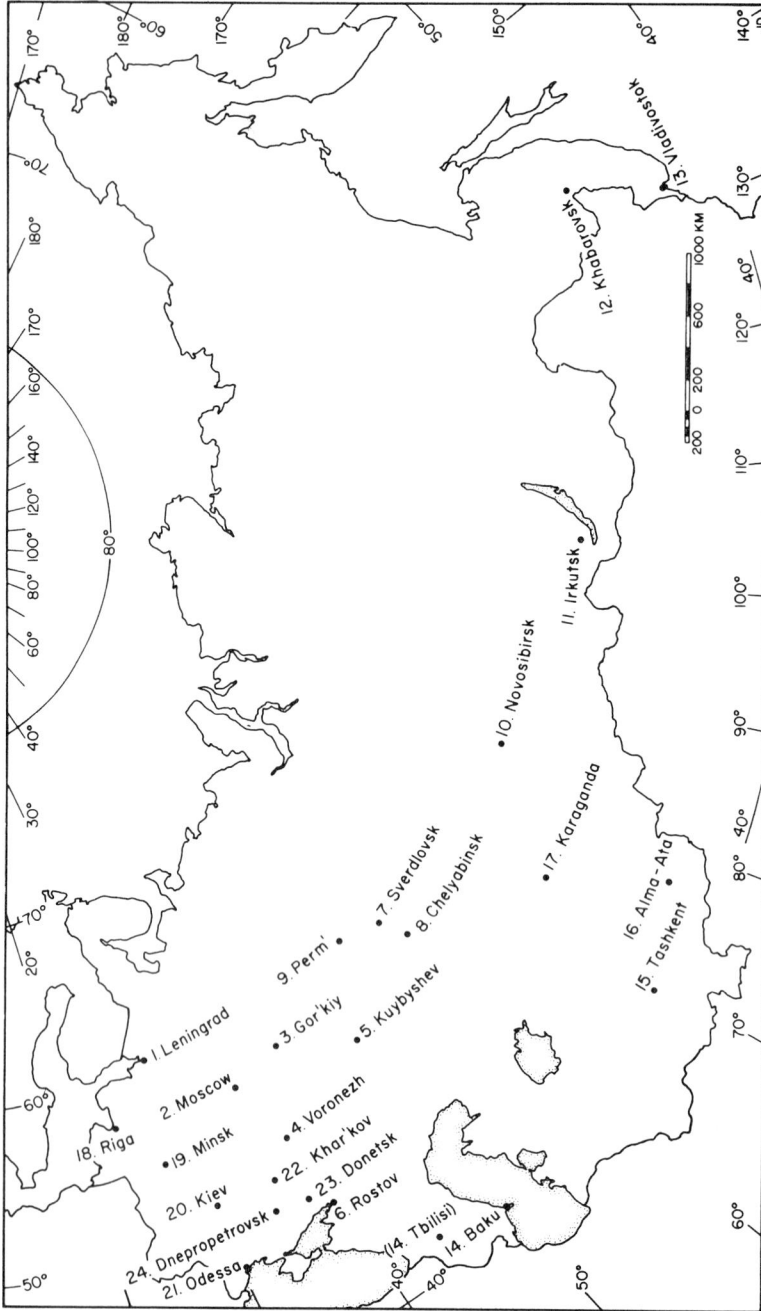

Figure 3.3 Centers of possible major urban regions based on size relations. [C. D. Harris, *Cities of the Soviet Union* (Chicago: Rand McNally & Co., 1970), p. 145. Reproduced by permission of the Association of American Geographers.]

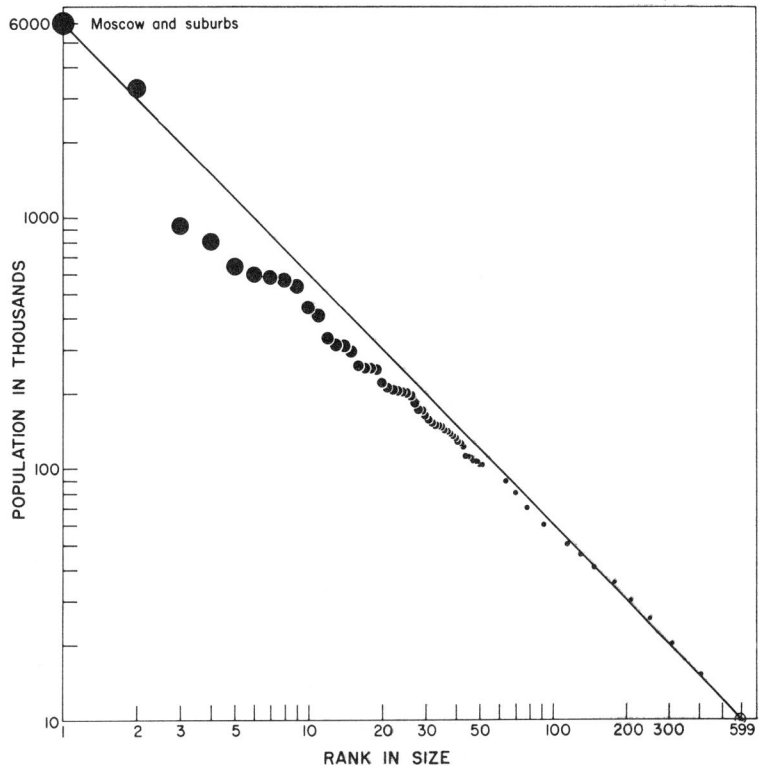

Figure 3.4 Rank-size distribution: Moscow and 599 cities of the European Subregion. [C. D. Harris, *Cities of the Soviet Union* (Rand McNally & Co., 1970), p. 140. Reproduced by permission of the Association of American Geographers.]

shown in Figure 3.3 and some examples of the regional rank-size distributions are shown in Figures 3.4 through 3.6. The major stages in the historical development of the urban pattern in the Soviet Union may be summarized as follows.

Pre-Soviet Period. City life in the area we know as the Soviet Union began in ancient settlements in Middle Asia and in the south around the Black Sea. Slavic towns first appeared along the rivers in the western regions in about the ninth century. Kiev was one of the earliest major centers. Moscow emerged in the twelfth century and its growth as a political and industrial center continued unchecked even though it lost its role as capital of the Russian Empire to St. Petersburg (now Leningrad) in 1713. In the second half of the nineteenth century urban growth became pronounced. As in the United States and elsewhere this surge was associated with the building of the railroads, the development of trade, the emergence of major iron and steel-producing centers (in this case around the city now known as Donetsk), the acceler-

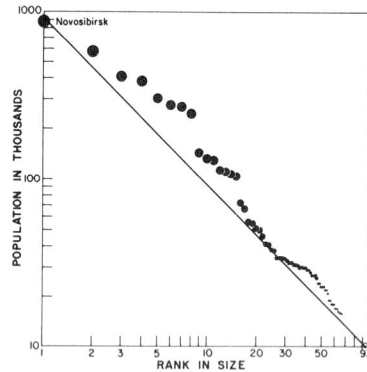

Figure 3.5 Rank-size distribution: Novosibirsk and 93 cities of western Siberia. [C. D. Harris, *Cities of the Soviet Union* (Chicago: Rand McNally & Co., 1970), p. 141. Reproduced by permission of the Association of American Geographers.]

ated growth of secondary industries such as textiles (especially in the area northeast of Moscow), and the exploitation of oil resources (in the southern Caucasian area).

The growth of the urban system over this period is partially reflected in Table 3.4 that gives the 20 largest cities for 4 different years. By 1915, on the eve of the Russian Revolution, Petrograd (St. Petersburg, then later Leningrad) and Moscow had pulled well ahead of the other cities. Some earlier centers of importance had already dropped out, notably Tobolsk in Western Siberia which, as a river junction town in the northern forested area, lost out in importance with the later development of the southern steppes for agriculture and the building of

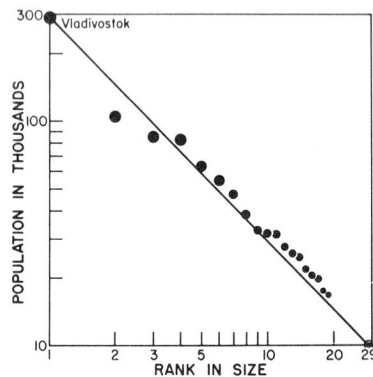

Figure 3.6 Rank-size distribution: Vladivostok and 29 cities of the Soviet Far East. [C. D. Harris, *Cities of the Soviet Union* (Chicago: Rand McNally & Co., 1970), p. 141. Reproduced by permission of the Association of American Geographers.]

Table 3.4 The Largest Cities of Russia and the Soviet Union. [C. D. Harris, *Cities of the Soviet Union* (Chicago: Rand McNally & Co., 1970), pp. 243, 244. Reproduced by permission of the Association of American Geographers.]

Rank		Name		Popu-lation	Rank		Name		Popu-lation
1811	1	St. Petersburg	(2)	336	1867	1	St. Petersburg		539
	2	Moscow	(1)	181		2	Moscow		399
	3	Vil'no	(59)	56		3	Odessa	(17)	121
	4	Kazan'	(14)	54		4	Kishinëv	(63)	104
	5	Tula	(45)	52		5	Riga		98
	6	Astrakhan'	(47)	38		6	Saratov		93
	7	Riga	(24)	32		7	Tashkent	(4)	80
	8	Saratov	(22)	27		8	Vil'no		79
	9	Orël	(93)	25		9	Kazan'		79
	10	Yaroslavl'	(33)	24		10	Kiev		71
	11	Kursk	(71)	23		11	Nikolayev	(64)	68
	12	Kiev	(3)	23		12	Tiflis	(11)	61
	13	Kaluga	(104)	23		13	Khar'kov	(6)	60
	14	Voronezh	(27)	22		14	Tula		58
	15	Revel'	(52)	18		15	Berdichev	(320)	53
	16	Tver'	(58)	18		16	Astrakhan'		48
	17	Tobol'sk	(x)	17		17	Kherson	(78)	46
	18	Vitebsk	(97)	17		18	Orël		44
	19	Tambov	(88)	17		19	Voronezh		42
	20	Penza	(53)	15		20	Nizhniy Novgorod	(7)	41
1915	1	Petrograd		2,165	1967	1	Moscow		6,507
	2	Moscow		1,806		2	Leningrad		3,706
	3	Kiev		610		3	Kiev		1,413
	4	Riga		569		4	Tashkent		1,239
	5	Odessa		500		5	Baku		1,196
	6	Tiflis		328		6	Khar'kov		1,125
	7	Tashkent		272		7	Gor'kiy		1,120
	8	Khar'kov		258		8	Novosibirsk		1,064
	9	Baku	(5)	237		9	Kuybyshev		992
	10	Saratov		236		10	Sverdlovsk		961
	11	Yekaterinoslav	(15)	220		11	Tbilisi		842
	12	Vil'na		204		12	Donetsk		840
	13	Kazan'		195		13	Chelyabinsk		836
	14	Rostov-na-Donu	(20)	172		14	Kazan'		821
	15	Astrakhan'		164		15	Dnepropetrovsk		816
	16	Ivanovo-Voznesensk	(38)	147		16	Perm'		796
	17	Orenburg	(56)	147		17	Odessa		776
	18	Samara	(9)	144		18	Omsk		774
	19	Tula		141		19	Minsk		772
	20	Omsk	(18)	136		20	Rostov-na-Donu		755

NOTE: Population in thousands; rank as of each date and also in parentheses for 1967; names as of the dates indicated.

the Trans-Siberian Railroad also in the south. By 1915 seven of the largest 20 cities were newcomers. These included three industrial cities (Yekaterinoslav, Ivanovo-Voznesensk, and Baku) and the others were all located in the new grain lands east of the Volga River.

Soviet Period, 1920–1939. Urban growth fell off during World War I and the Civil War, slowly revived in the early 1920's, and then accelerated rapidly in the period 1926–1939. During this latter period the urban population probably more than doubled, and eight cities, which already had populations of 100,000 or more in 1926, also individually doubled their populations. These eight cities were all industrial cities located in the three major industrial districts known as the Donbas, the Kuzbas, and the Urals. This was the period of very rapid planned industrialization, of collectivization and mechanization of agriculture, and of very high levels of rural to urban migration.

The Period 1939–1959. The early part of this period was marked by the devastating consequences of World War II with its heavy loss of life and destruction of cities. But over the whole period urban growth was very pronounced, especially to the east in the region between the Volga River and Lake Baykal (Figure 3.7). Again, much of this growth was associated with industrialization, but there was also rapid growth of some cities in new agricultural regions (see for example, Tselinograd in Figure 3.7).

Recent Growth, 1959–1966. The overall urban growth rate slowed down somewhat to around an average of 3.1% per year (compared to 6.5% for 1926–1939 and 4.1%, for 1950–1959). Nevertheless, there were still regions in which marked levels of above-average growth occurred, notably in the interior in Kazakhstan and Soviet Middle Asia where industrialization based on coal and minerals and expansion of the agricultural frontiers continued. Elsewhere throughout the major part of the country east to Lake Baykal urban growth was fairly widespread as a wider range of industrial development was encouraged, as small cities were boosted as alternatives to increasing the size of the larger centers (perhaps significantly, none of the largest 15 cities grew at a rate exceeding the national rate over this period), and as cities in the western parts of the country were revived after periods of considerable neglect.

For these two large countries, the United States and the Soviet Union, we have summarized the stories of how their urban city-size distributions evolved over time. In the case of the United States, certain general features of the urban system, especially the rank-size relationship, appear to remain fairly constant over time even though tremendous social, political, and economic developments are all the while unfolding. The example of the Soviet Union, by contrast, has shown how strong regional influences and the existence of urban sub-

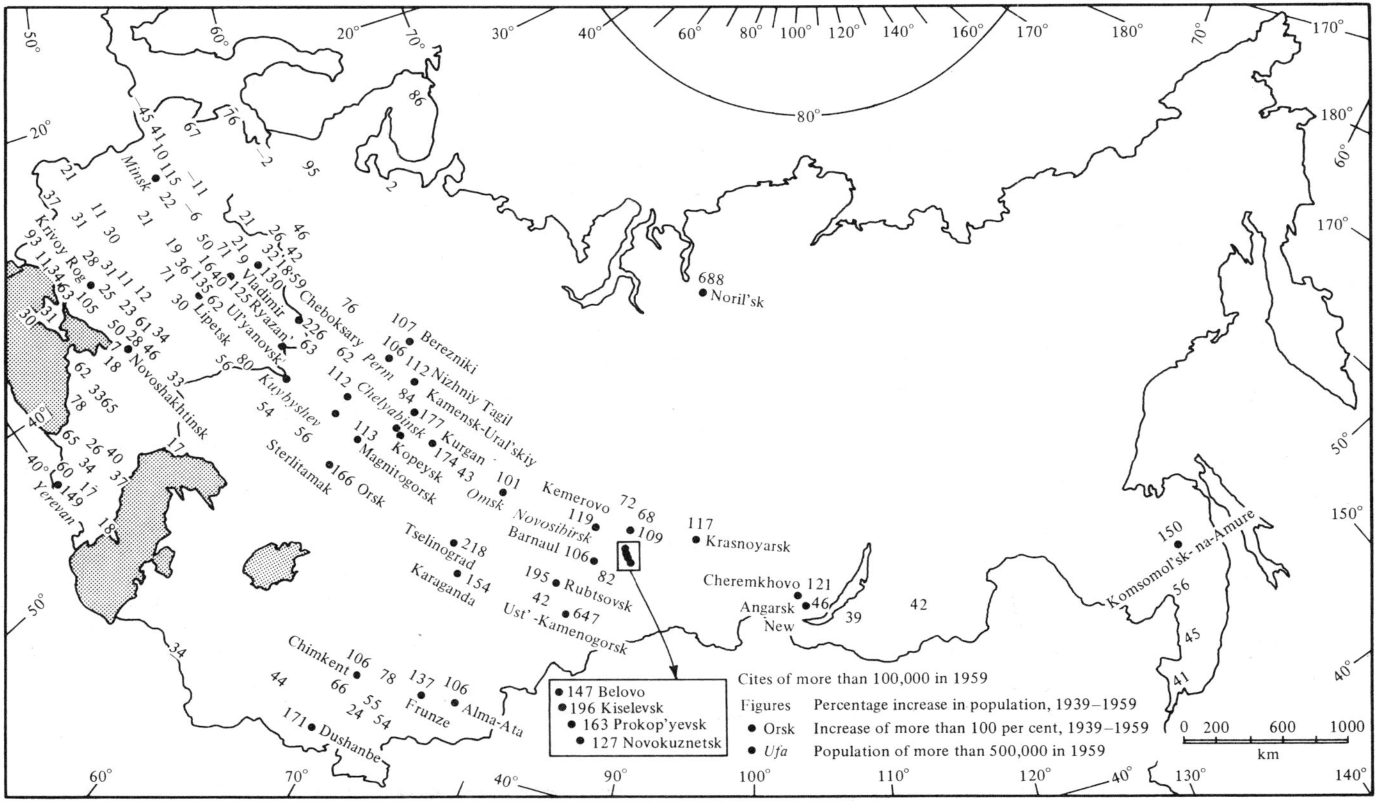

Figure 3.7 Percentage increase in population 1939–1959 of cities of more than 100,000 population in 1959. Cities with increases of more than 100% are named. [C. D. Harris, *Cities of the Soviet Union* (Chicago: Rand McNally & Co., 1970), p. 312. Reproduced by permission of the Association of American Geographers.]

systems can find expression in the city-size distribution for the nation as a whole. We might speculate on the one hand that greater integration of the different regions of the Soviet economy could result in a "straightening" of the national rank-size relationship; on the other hand, policies aimed explicitly at limiting the size of that nation's largest cities could reinforce the feature that the largest cities are not as large as the rank-size relationship would suggest they might be.

3.2 Locational Arrangement of Cities: Generalizations Based on Point Pattern Analysis

Statements about the size and number of cities in a country or region give no direct information about the locational pattern of the cities. But this is an important aspect of the spatial organization of any urban system, and we now consider this topic.

Nearest-Neighbor Distances

The term *locational pattern* can refer to the arrangement of cities, that is, the relative locations of the cities with respect to one another. One way of analyzing this feature of a locational pattern is to measure the distances between each city represented as a point on a map and the city (point) that is its nearest neighbor, and also possibly, the city that is its second nearest neighbor, the one that is its third nearest neighbor, and so on. The set of distances between cities and their different nearest neighbors can then be averaged over the set of cities to give for each map pattern an average first-order nearest-neighbor distance, an average second-order distance, and so on again.

This nearest-neighbor analysis has been applied in a number of studies of settlement patterns in the United States, Sweden, and the Soviet Union. In Figure 3.8, for example, there are a number of maps of the distribution of urban places in selected areas of the United States. For each of these map areas there is given the average distance between the urban places and their nearest neighbors. Note that in these maps all cities are treated alike simply as points; no attention is paid to such features as their population size or economic functions. The mean or average distances between towns and their nearest neighbors convey some information about these patterns, but on their own these measures do not allow us to discriminate sharply between the patterns.

A more detailed approach toward the analysis of the locational patterns of cities would be to distinguish between *different sized cities* before any distance measurements were made. An example of this is

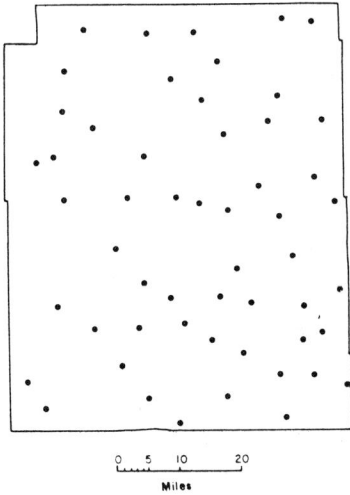

Minnesota: Otter Tail, Grant, and Douglas counties. Mean = 5.32 miles.

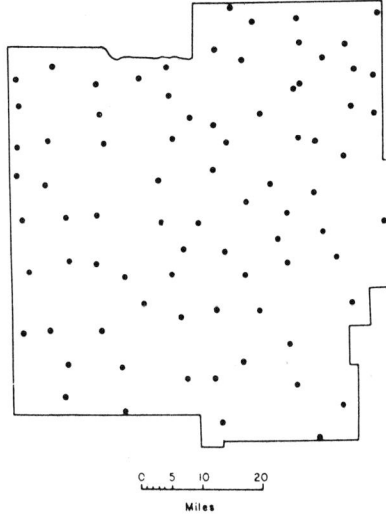

Missouri: Bates, Henry, Vernon, St. Clair, and Cedar counties. Mean = 4.67 miles.

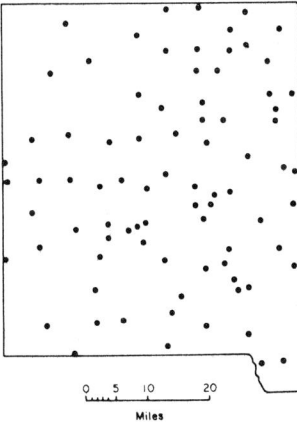

Iowa: Benton, Linn, Iowa, and Johnson counties. Mean = 3.86 miles.

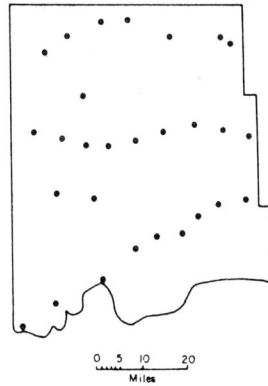

North Dakota: Divide and Williams counties. Mean = 6.13 miles.

Figure 3.8 Spacing of urban settlements in selected areas of the United States. The mean distance to the first nearest neighbors is given for each pattern. [After L. J. King, "A quantitative expression of the patterns of urban settlements in selected areas of the United States," *Tijdschrift voor Economische en Sociale Geografie,* **53**, 1962, pp. 4–6.]

Table 3.5   Nearest-Neighbor Distances for Different-Sized Urban Places in Iowa and North Dakota. (J. N. Rayner, R. G. Golledge, and S. S. Collins, Jr., "Spectral analysis of settlement patterns," *Final Report,* NSF Grant No. GS-2781, Ohio State University Research Foundation, Columbus, Ohio, 1971, pp. 60, 84.)

Population	N	Mean Distance to First Nearest Neighbor (miles)	Variance
Iowa:			
10–99	283	6.58	16.78
100–249	350	6.75	10.98
250–499	242	8.67	16.62
500–999	220	9.38	13.82
1,000–2,499	135	12.21	20.77
2,500–4,999	46	22.51	128.33
5,000–9,999	33	24.68	148.95
10,000–24,999	11	30.71	98.157
25,000+	14	42.77	218.09
North Dakota:			
10–99	153	11.322	32.241
100–249	151	11.719	32.075
250–499	84	14.584	63.879
500–999	45	18.317	105.80
1,000–2,499	50	21.165	90.762
2,500–4,000 5,000–9,999	7	56.531	245.48
10,000–24,999 25,000+	8	65.288	1266.0

provided by the information given in Table 3.5. This table presents information on the spacing of urban settlements in two states of the United States, namely, Iowa and North Dakota. In this case, an urban settlement is defined as any concentration of settlement involving 10 or more persons. The settlements in Table 3.5 have been grouped into various population-size classes. For the settlements in each population-size class there is then given the average distance to the first nearest neighboring settlement. (Distances are expressed in miles.) There is also given a measure of the variation in the distance measurements around the average value for the settlements in any one particular size class. Thus, for example, in Iowa the average distance among settlements of fewer than 100 persons was about 6½ miles, but the variation in these measurements was much greater, over 16 miles. In other words, there was substantial variation in the distances around the average value. This feature was characteristic apparently of all the different population-size classes not only for the Iowa data but also for the North Dakota data. In comparing the two sets of results it is worth noting that in both states the average distances between nearest neighboring settlements increase consistently with increases in population size. The fact that the number of settlements is smaller in North Dakota than in Iowa produces a range of average distances greater at both lower and upper population-size limits than in the case of Iowa. This point is reflected in the higher variances associated with the North Dakota data. It is also interesting to note that for each population-size group the distances for North Dakota are almost twice those of Iowa. This suggests a much more widely spaced settlement pattern with a definite scale difference.

If we were to expand on these studies of the spacing of settlements, we might consider the effects of other factors in addition to population size. For example, the variation in the distance measurements might be examined in relation to the importance of the towns as manufacturing centers (similar-sized manufacturing cities might be clustered together), the surrounding regional levels of population density and intensity of "farming" (higher densities should be associated with more closely spaced towns), and the role of the towns as service centers (spacing of service centers should increase along with size of centers). It is unlikely, however, that these different factors would provide anything more than a partial explanation of the variation observed in the nearest-neighbor distances. At these detailed scales, historical factors and aspects of the physical environmental setting would probably have to be taken into account in explaining the relative locations of urban centers.

All of the above approaches to studying the locational patterns of cities provide some measures of the relative locations of cities and of their spacing. These measures can also be related to other features of the cities and of the regions in which the cities are located. Experience alone would suggest to anyone who has done much traveling that there is some relationship between the size of a city and the distance at which it is located away from the next center of about the same size; usually, the larger the cities, the farther apart they are. This positive relationship was confirmed in some of the studies mentioned above. Indeed, it was on the basis of observing such regularities that Walter Christaller developed one of the better-known "theories" of geography, *central-place theory*, which will be discussed in Chapter 5.

Questions about the spacing of cities may not be simply abstract ones in studying the spatial organization of urban society. As we shall discuss later, they may indeed be very important issues in planning the location of new towns and devising new settlement patterns.

3.3 Further Generalizations About the Locational Arrangements Based on Network Concepts

Another approach to studying the locational arrangement of towns is to consider the towns as nodes in a network, the links of which may be the highways, the railways, or the airline routes that connect the cities. For example, Figure 3.9, which shows the cities and major highways of southern Ontario, may be represented by the diagram in Figure 3.10. In this diagram the direction and length of the connecting lines or *edges* are unimportant and the diagram may be drawn in a number of different ways; the presence or absence of edges between different pairs of cities is, of course, important. This representation of a locational pattern of cities allows for some particular questions about the spatial structure of the pattern to be answered.

Accessibility in a Network

One question that can be asked of the situation portrayed in Figure 3.10 is what is the level of *accessibility* of the different cities in the network? To assist in answering this question it is useful to represent the diagram by a table of numbers (a *matrix*), in which only zeros and ones appear. The zeros denote the absence of links between pairs of

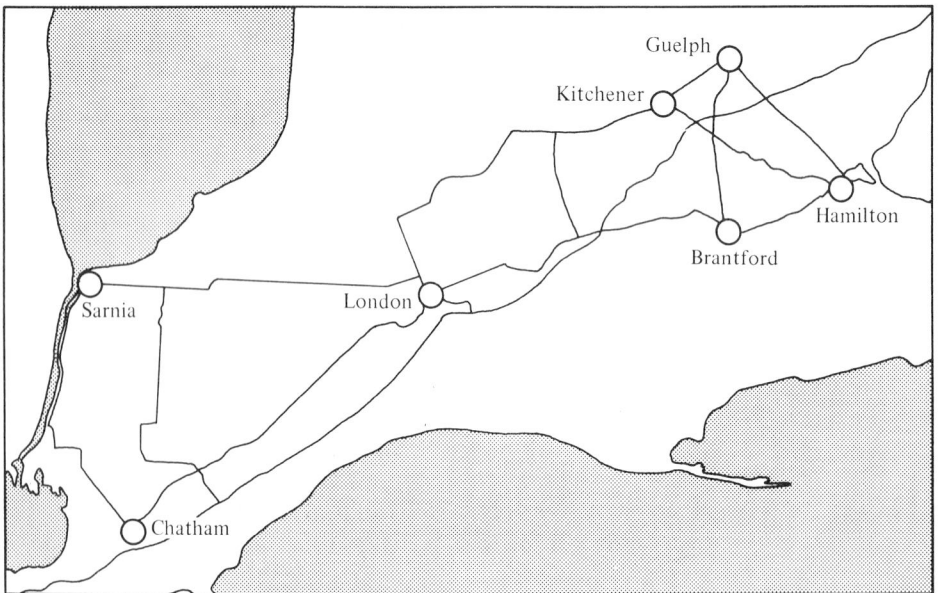

Figure 3.9 Main urban centers and main highways in area of southern Ontario.

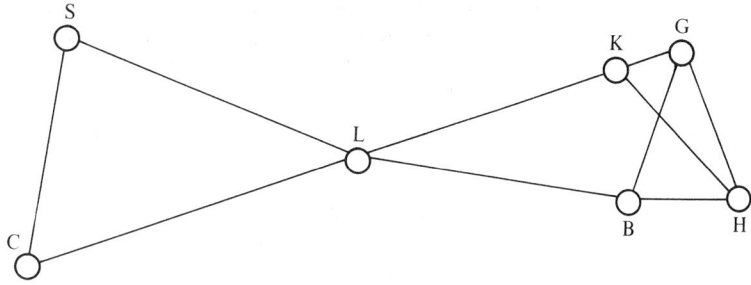

Figure 3.10 Graph-theoretic representation of urban network shown in Figure 3.9.

cities and the ones denote the presence of links. The matrix is known as the *connectivity matrix*. The one for Figure 3.10 is given in Table 3.6. The addition of the numbers along any one of the rows of the matrix provides a simple measure of the relative accessibility of the city on that row; in the example London shows up as being the most accessible node, having four links to other cities in the network.

A more technical approach to this same question involves raising the connectivity matrix to some power, such as either squaring or cubing it. Mathematically, this means that we treat the matrix in much the same way that we do an ordinary number when we square or cube it. There is no need to dwell on this matter of matrix algebra. It is enough to consider the results. For example, if the matrix in Table 3.6 is multiplied by itself, that is, the matrix is squared, then the resulting entries in the new matrix give the number of two-step connections between, say, cities K and B, which are K–L–B, K–H–B, and K–G–B

Table 3.6 Connectivity Matrix for the Graph in Figure 3.10.

	S	C	L	K	G	B	H	*Sum*
S	0	1	1	0	0	0	0	2
C	1	0	1	0	0	0	0	2
L	1	1	0	1	0	1	0	4
K	0	0	1	0	1	0	1	3
G	0	0	0	1	0	1	1	3
B	0	0	1	0	1	0	1	3
H	0	0	0	1	1	1	0	3

NOTE: In the matrix a town is not considered to be connected to itself; hence the zeros on the diagonal from upper left to lower right. Also, the matrix is symmetrical, that is, a connection from say S to C is the same as a connection from C to S.

Table 3.7   Multiplication of the Connectivity Matrix in Table 3.6 by Itself, That Is, Squaring of the Matrix.

	S	C	L	K	G	B	H
S	0	1	1	0	0	0	0
C	1	0	1	0	0	0	0
L	1	1	0	1	0	1	0
K	0	0	1	0	1	0	1
G	0	0	0	1	0	1	1
B	0	0	1	0	1	0	1
H	0	0	0	1	1	1	0

$\times$

	S	C	L	K	G	B	H
S	0	1	1	0	0	0	0
C	1	0	1	0	0	0	0
L	1	1	0	1	0	1	0
K	0	0	1	0	1	0	1
G	0	0	0	1	0	1	1
B	0	0	1	0	1	0	1
H	0	0	0	1	1	1	0

$=$

	S	C	L	K	G	B	H
S	_2_	1	1	1	0	1	0
C	1	_2_	1	1	0	1	0
L	1	1	_4_	0	2	0	2
K	1	1	0	_3_	1	3	1
G	0	0	2	1	_3_	1	2
B	1	1	0	3	1	_3_	1
H	0	0	2	1	2	1	_3_

NOTE: Readers who are unfamiliar with matrix algebra will have to accept this form of matrix manipulation.

(see Table 3.7). Note that the underlined numbers in the new matrix on the right give the number of two-step connections by which one can return to a city. Thus, there are four such connections for city L, namely, $L{\rightarrow}S{\rightarrow}L$, $L{\rightarrow}C{\rightarrow}L$, $L{\rightarrow}K{\rightarrow}L$, and $L{\rightarrow}B{\rightarrow}L$.

Groupings of Cities in a Network

A second general question that can be asked in regard to a network representation of cities and their connecting links is whether or not particular regional groupings of the cities can be identified. What is sought here is some breaking down of the network and its graph into subnetworks or subgraphs. This question may be answered by using statistical techniques that focus upon the patterns of connections that all the cities in the network have and that seek to identify certain basic or common patterns amongst them. The results of such an analysis are shown in Figure 3.11. In the network of some 59 cities in Venezuela and the airline routes connecting them there is identified a regional effect centered upon Caracas, the major city in the network, a western region focused upon Maracaibo and Santa Barbara, and an eastern one centered on Caracas and Maturin.

An alternative approach to this problem of identifying subsystems within an urban network is illustrated in the case of India. The network of airline connections for the 40 Indian cities that had populations of over 100,000 in 1960 along with three smaller cities, one a state capital and two relatively isolated centers at the end of air routes, is shown in Figure 3.12. Now assume that the connectivity matrix for this network is constructed and that this matrix is multiplied by itself repeatedly (that is, powered) until *all* the numbers in it are *positive* (that is, greater than zero). Some of the entries in the original connectivity matrix, of course, will already be positive (for those pairs of cities directly joined by an airline link) and we shall assume that this

Venezuela: Field effect

200 miles

Venezuela: Major regionalization effect

200 Miles

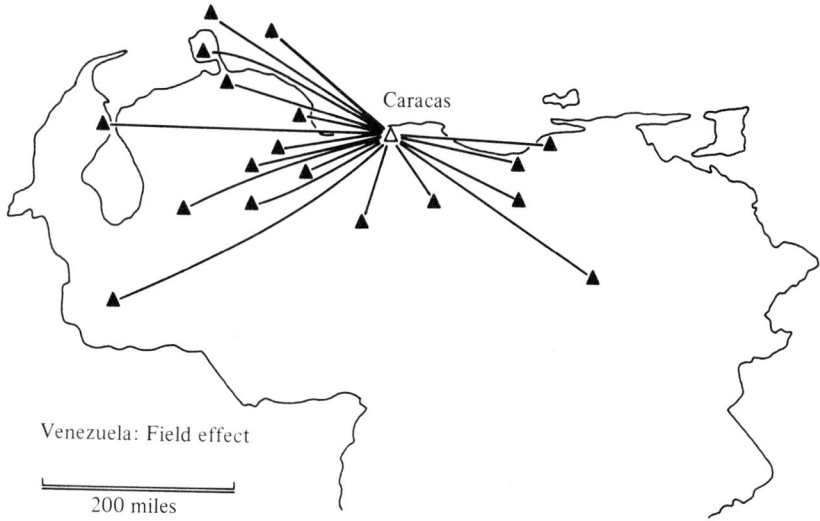

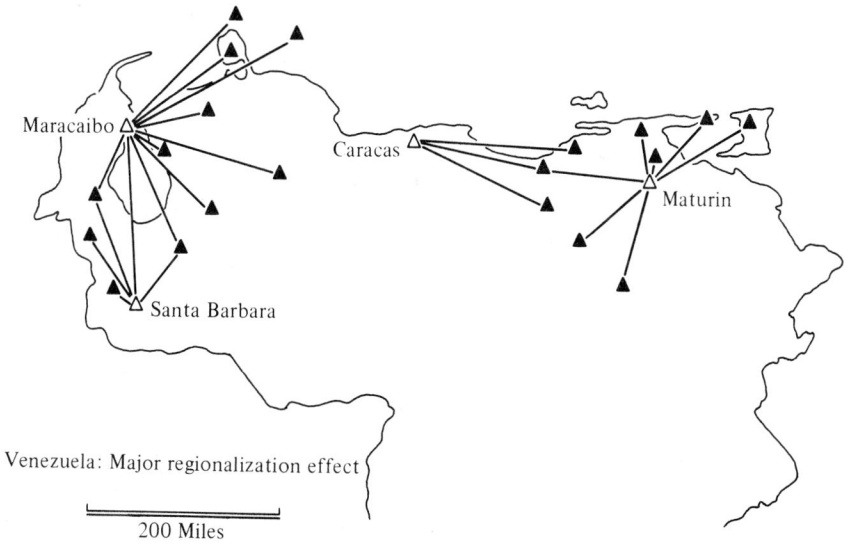

Figure 3.11 Basic elements in the Venezuelan airlines network. [W. L. Garrison and D. F. Marble, *The Structure of Transportation Networks* (Washington, D.C.: U.S. Depart. of Commerce, Office of Technical Services, 1961). p. 113.]

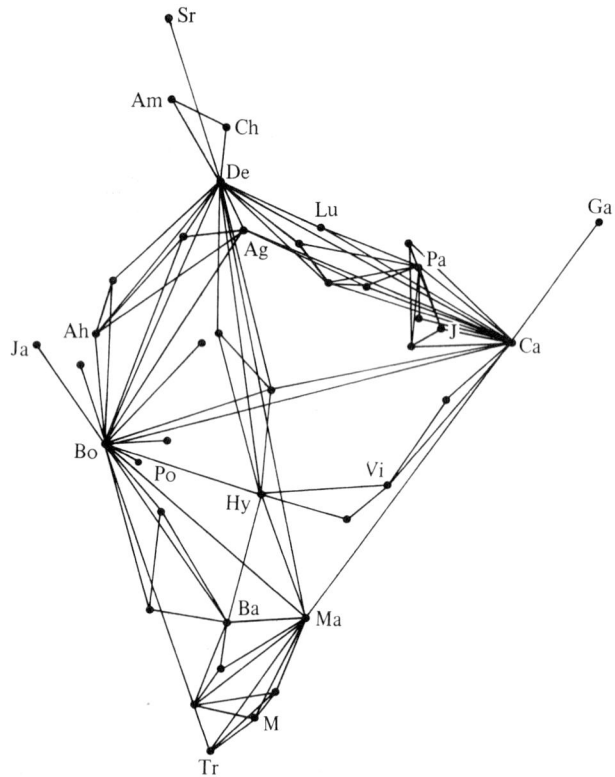

Figure 3.12 Network representation of India's airline routes. The relative locations of some of the nodes (cities) have been adjusted for clarity. Key: Ag, Agra; Ah, Ahmedabad; Am, Amritsar; Ba, Bangalore; Bo, Bombay; Ca, Calcutta; Ch, Chandigarh; De, Delhi; Ga, Gauhati; Hy, Hyderabad; Ja, Jamnagar; J, Jamshedpur; Lu, Lucknow; Ma, Madras; M, Madurai; Pa, Patna; Po, Poona; Sr, Srinagar; Tr, Trivandrum; Vi, Visakhapatnam. [Based on W. E. Reed, "Indirect connectivity and hierarchies of urban dominance"; reproduced by permission from the *Annals* of the Association of American Geographers, volume **60**, p. 775 (1970).]

information is recorded in another summary matrix by entering 1s in the appropriate places. When no direct links exist, the corresponding places in this table will be left blank. With the next step, the squaring of the connectivity matrix, some of the numbers will change from zero to a positive number; in other words, those pairs of cities connected by two step links will now show up. For these pairs in the summary matrix, the number 2 is now entered. The powering of the original connectivity matrix continues, as noted, until there are positive numbers for all pairs of cities. It may be, for example, that two cities are joined in the network only by a route involving four edges or links and a positive number for this pair will only appear in the connectivity matrix after it has been raised to the fourth power. For this pair, the number 4 would be entered in the summary matrix. Eventually, the summary matrix will be filled with numbers. The sums of these numbers along the different rows will show how many steps or edges are required to move from the individual cities to all the other cities in the network. This information is given in the columns headed "steps" in Table 3.8. A simple averaging (column 2 divided by column 3) gives an *average graph distance* for each city (column 4). Now, if particular cities are removed from the network, these statistics change for the remaining cities. This is illustrated in Table 3.8 when Delhi is removed.

Performing this sensitivity analysis with different individual cities and sets of cities removed in turn from the network allows for the following four major levels of connectivity to be identified in the Indian airline system:

First: Bombay, Calcutta, Delhi, Madras, Hyderabad
Second: Agra, Bangalore, Cochin, Patna, Varanasi, Visakhapatnam
Third: Jamshedpur
Fourth: (a) Mutually linked in triples: Ahmedabad, Jaipur, Udaipur, Madurai, Tiruchirapalli, Tirandrum
          (b) Mutually linked as pairs: Amritsar, Chandigarh, Kanpur, Allahabad, Muzaffarput, Rourkela, Bhopal, Nagpur, Belgaum, Mangalore
          (c) Singles: Srinagar, Jamnagar, Bhavnagar, Indore, Aurangabad, Poona, Gauhati, Coimbatore, Cuttack, Lucknow, Ranchi, Vijayawada

The use of this approach in identifying key centers in a network obviously could have wider applications and, indeed, this question is often important in transportation planning. When we come to consider flow patterns in a later chapter of this book, we shall see that the systems of rankings and hierarchical levels that are suggested by the network analysis can be nicely complemented and supplemented with studies of hierarchies based on behavioral patterns.

Evolution of Urban Networks

A final topic in regard to network structures has to do with their growth over time and the manner in which different cities are eventually connected into the network. Very few studies have addressed this question, perhaps because in the areas that today have highly developed urban networks the problem of untangling the historical sequences is extremely difficult and perhaps impossible to generalize

Table 3.8 Some Measures of the Connectivity of the Indian Airline Network. (Based on W. E. Reed, "Indirect connectivity and hierarchies of urban dominance"; reproduced by permission from *Annals of the Association of American Geographers*, volume **60**, p. 776, 1970.)

Selected Cities or Nodes	Total Network			With Delhi Links Out			Change in Average Graph Distance
	Number of Cities Reached	Steps Needed	Average Graph Distance	Number of Cities Reached	Steps Needed	Average Graph Distance	
Agra	39	77	1.97	35	71	2.03	.06
Ahmedabad	39	85	2.18	35	83	2.37	.19
Amritsar	39	97	2.49	1	1	1.00	1.49
Bangalore	39	85	2.18	35	74	2.11	.07
Bombay	39	60	1.54	35	53	1.51	.03
Calcutta	39	61	1.56	35	54	1.54	.02
Chandigarh	39	97	2.49	1	1	1.00	1.49
Delhi	39	60	1.54	—	—	—	—
Gauhati	39	99	2.54	35	88	2.51	.03
Hyderabad	39	75	1.92	35	73	2.09	.17
Jamnagar	39	98	2.51	35	87	2.49	.02
Jamshedpur	39	95	2.44	35	84	2.40	.04
Lucknow	39	88	2.26	35	86	2.46	.20
Madras	39	68	1.74	35	61	1.74	.00
Madurai	39	103	2.64	35	92	2.63	.01
Patna	39	82	2.10	35	80	2.29	.19
Poona	39	98	2.51	35	87	2.49	.02
Srinagar	39	98	2.51	0	0	0.00	2.51
Trivandrum	39	103	2.64	35	92	2.63	.01
Visakhapatnam	39	92	2.36	35	81	2.31	.05

about. Obviously, some cities attracted transportation routes (such as railways) to them; others clearly emerged as a result of the spread of the transportation routeways. By contrast, in the developing countries the historical sequence is often more easily recognized. In countries in which development begins along a coastline the network might evolve in four major stages (Figure 3.13). In the first stage there would be

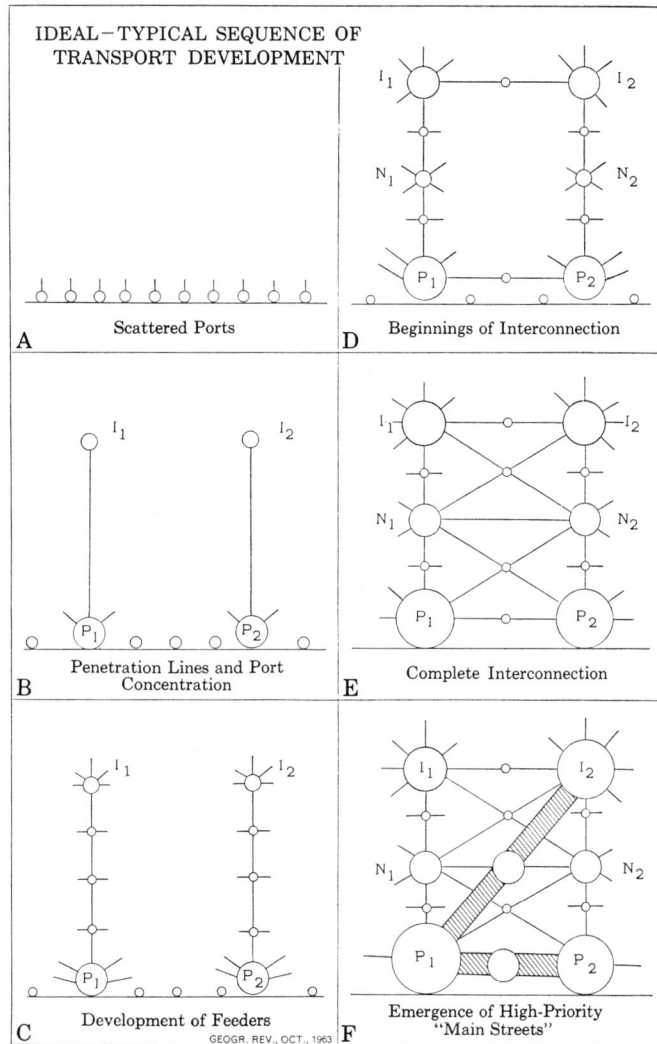

IDEAL—TYPICAL SEQUENCE OF TRANSPORT DEVELOPMENT

A — Scattered Ports

B — Penetration Lines and Port Concentration

C — Development of Feeders

D — Beginnings of Interconnection

E — Complete Interconnection

F — Emergence of High-Priority "Main Streets"

GEOGR. REV., OCT., 1963

Figure 3.13 Idealized schema of transport network development. [E. J. Taaffe, R. L. Morrill, and P. R. Gould, "Transport expansion in underdeveloped countries: a comparative analysis"; redrawn, with permission, from the *Geographical Review*, vol. 53, 1963, p. 504.]

small isolated urban centers which are ports or trading posts scattered along the coast. A second stage would see the accelerated growth of one or two of these centers as inland communication routes (to tap the country's resources or to expand the military/political spheres of influence) were focused on them, and there would also be the early growth of small inland trading centers. In the third stage these inland nodes would expand, others would be added, and small feeder routes and some lateral routes would develop. Finally, as the economic and political integration of the country advanced still further, major interconnecting routes would be built between the coastal and inland cities and smaller centers would also be interconnected.

3.4   Areal Extent of Cities: Sprawl and Coalescence

So far in this chapter, our emphasis has been on cities considered as *points* in a locational pattern or network. This idealization or abstraction was appropriate for the particular topics that were being considered. But the cities in which most of us live and work are far removed from this abstraction, they cover several square miles of area, and in many places they merge with one another in a way that makes their separate delimitation very difficult. It is important, therefore, that we give attention to this question of the areal extent of cities.

Standard Metropolitan Statistical Areas

The modern city is indeed more correctly described as a *metropolis,* and in such countries as the United States and Canada an attempt is made in the census definitions to reflect this fact. In the United States, a Standard Metropolitan Statistical Area (SMSA) is defined on the basis of detailed considerations regarding population size and economic and social relationships. There is always at least one central city of 50,000 or more population and the SMSA includes the county in which this central city is located and those adjoining counties that are essentially metropolitan in character. The determination of what is a metropolitan county is based on employment characteristics (at least 75% of the county labor force must be employed in non-agricultural activities), on population density characteristics, and on the extent of economic and social interaction of the county with the central city county (as measured, for example, by the percent of the county's workers working in the central county). The 1970 census recognized as many as 243 SMSA's, the locations of which are shown in the map in Figure 3.14.

Figure 3.14   Standard Metropolitan Statistical Areas: United States.

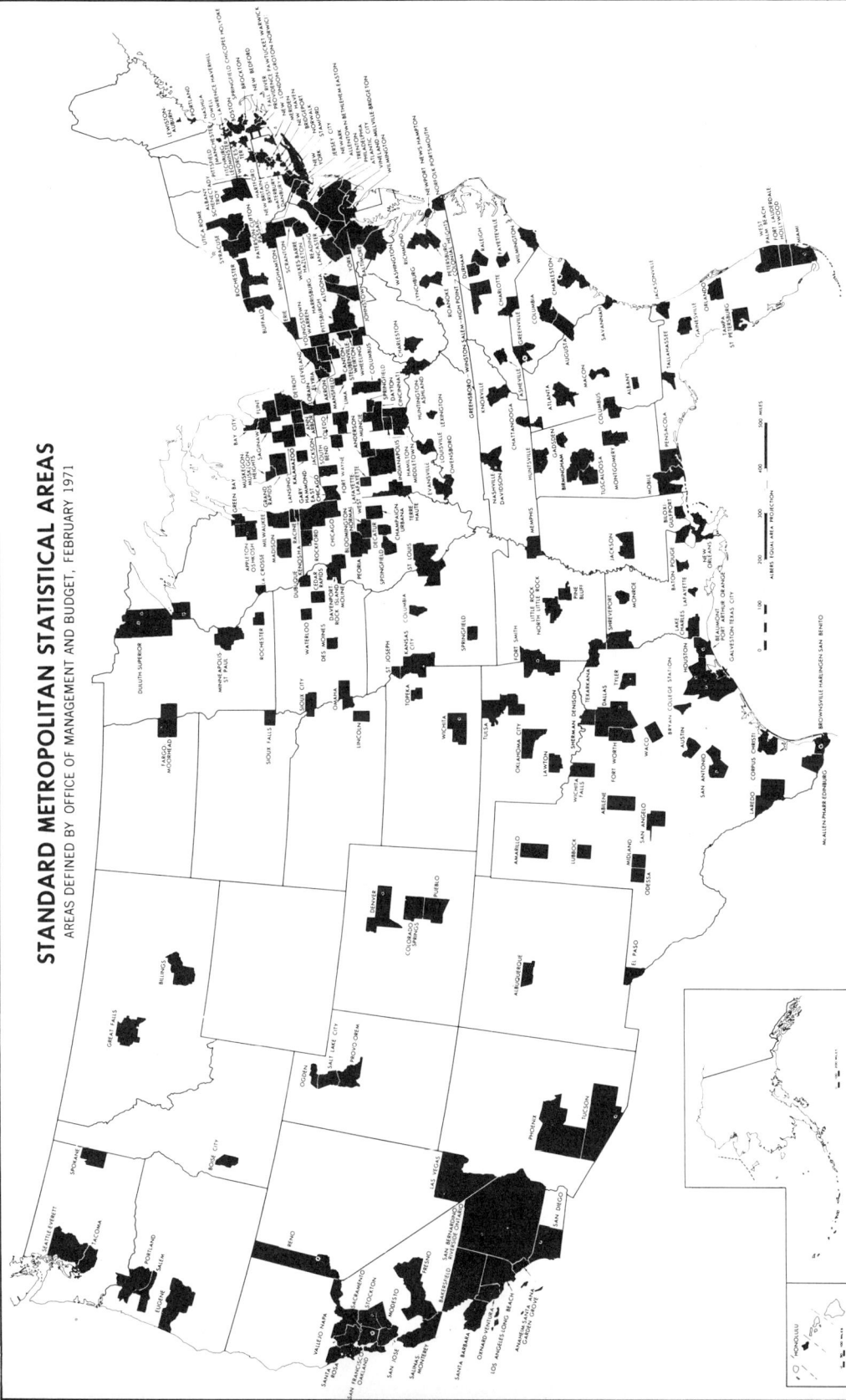

STANDARD METROPOLITAN STATISTICAL AREAS

AREAS DEFINED BY OFFICE OF MANAGEMENT AND BUDGET, FEBRUARY 1971

U.S. DEPARTMENT OF COMMERCE   SOCIAL AND ECONOMIC STATISTICS ADMINISTRATION   BUREAU OF THE CENSUS

Together these SMSA's covered an area of more than 387,000 square miles, approximately 11% of the land area of the United States. The population living within them in 1970 was over 139 million people, almost 69% of the total United States population. But an important point to remember is that this population was not evenly spread over the SMSA areas and was, in fact, heavily concentrated within the more restricted urbanized areas. These urbanized areas accounted for only 9% of the total SMSA land area but as much as 84% of the SMSA population. Hence, the impression created by the map in Figure 3.14 that all of the SMSA's are given over to urban uses tends to be an exaggerated one. A great deal of the land area within them remains devoted to rural uses.

Commuting Areas

Broad as the definition of a SMSA in the United States is, it still does not completely capture the very complex and spatially extensive patterns of influence that such a modern metropolis has over its surrounding areas. These zones of influence are suggested by other maps. For example, Figure 3.15 shows in black those areas from which some people at least travel each day to one of the metropolitan centers for work. Obviously, these areas are much more extensive than the SMSA's themselves. It has been estimated that in 1960 about 66% of the United States population lived in the SMSA's, another 21% lived in the commuting area of at least one central city of a SMSA, and 9% of the total U.S. population lived in the commuting areas of smaller urban centers located in between the metropolitan labor markets. In addition, as John Borchert has noted,[3] over the decade 1960–1970 four-fifths of the total increase that occurred in the United States population occurred within the SMSA's while most of the remaining increase occurred within the commuting fields of these metropolitan areas. Only around Buffalo and Pittsburgh did the expanding commuter fields not show high rates of population growth.

Additional information on the extent of the metropolitan fields of influence is given in Figures 3.16 and 3.17. These show the linkages between the different metropolitan areas in terms of the organization of banking. The point made by the author of those maps, John Borchert, is that "banks in a city of any given size order carry accounts in other 'correspondent' banks located in higher-order metropolitan centers,"[4] and that for any city these correspondent banking links are usually more numerous with metropolitan centers of a higher order. New York, of course, dominates the banking structure and is linked

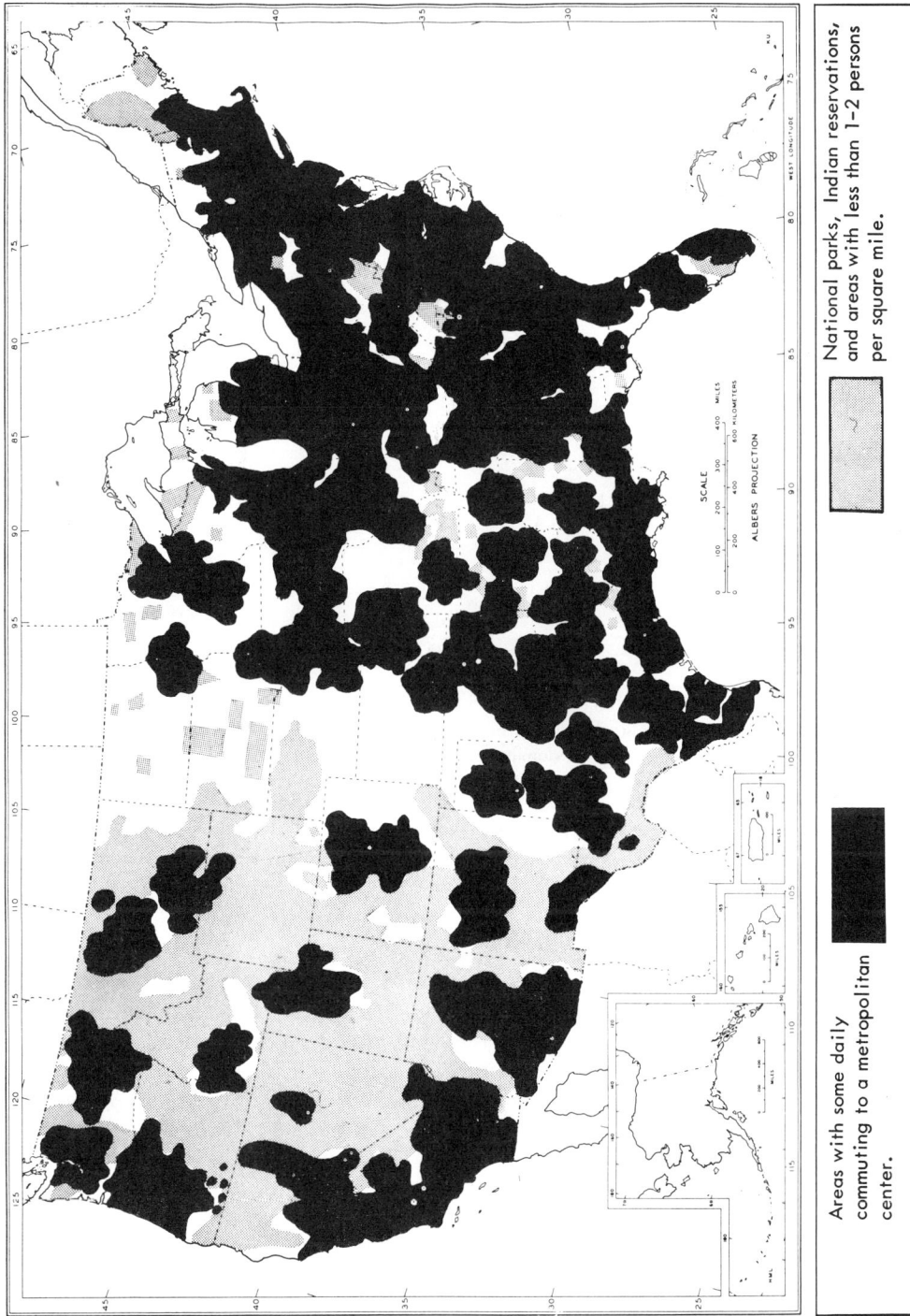

Figure 3.15 Areas with daily commuting to a metropolitan center in 1960. [B. J. L. Berry, *Metropolitan Area Definition: A Re-evaluation of Concept and Statistical Practice* (Washington D.C.: Bureau of the Census, Working Paper 28, 1968).]

Areas with some daily commuting to a metropolitan center.

National parks, Indian reservations, and areas with less than 1-2 persons per square mile.

SCALE

ALBERS PROJECTION

CORRESPONDENT BANKING LINKAGES TO SECOND ORDER METROPOLITAN CENTERS

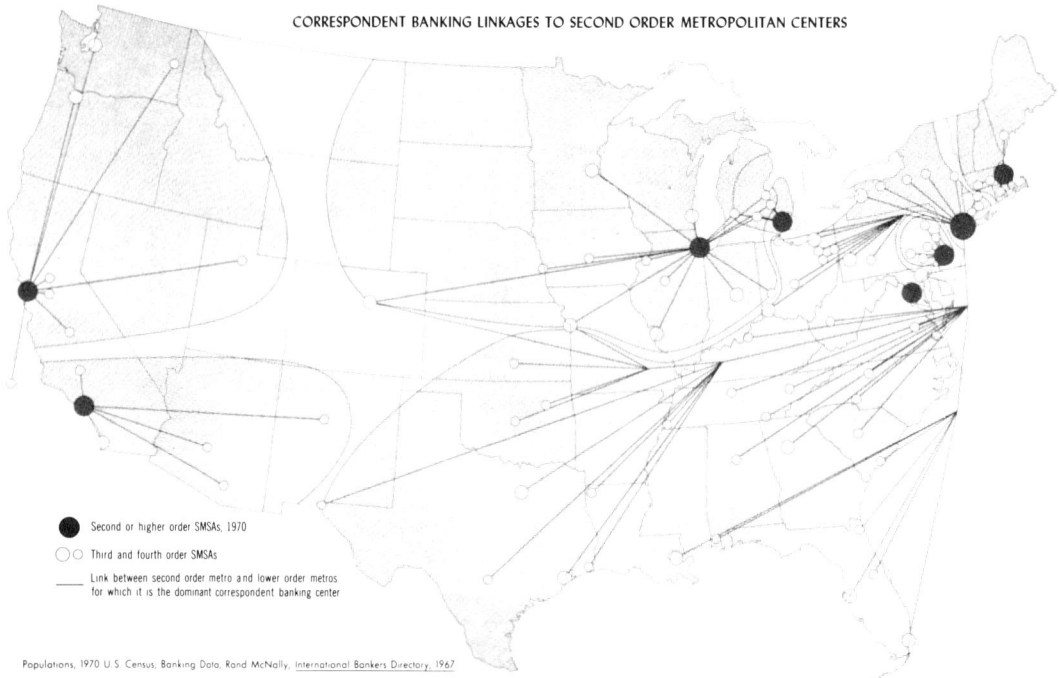

● Second or higher order SMSAs, 1970

○○ Third and fourth order SMSAs

―――― Link between second order metro and lower order metros
for which it is the dominant correspondent banking center

Populations, 1970 U.S. Census; Banking Data, Rand McNally, *International Bankers Directory*, 1967

Figure 3.16 Dominant correspondent banking linkages to second-order metropolitan centers from third- and fourth-order centers, 1967. New York is defined as the dominant second-order center for a given lower-order metropolitan area if it has more than twice as many correspondent banking links as any other second-order center. This assumes that half of that metropolitan area's links to New York result from New York's first-order function [J. R. Borchert, "America's changing metropolitan regions"; reproduced by permission from the *Annals* of the Association of American Geographers, volume **62**, p. 358 (1972).]

with virtually all cities of all sizes by way of these correspondent banks. The tributary areas of the 7 second-order metropolitan centers are shown in Figure 3.16, and those of the 20 third-order centers are mapped in Figure 3.17. The maps illustrate all too clearly that the metropolitan centers play a major role in the functioning and organization of the regional economies of the country.

Megalopolis

The coalescence of metropolitan areas and commuting zones in the United States is a significant current development. This dominates in the northeastern part of the United States where the area from Boston to Washington, D.C. is now almost one continuous metropoli-

CORRESPONDENT BANKING LINKAGES TO THIRD ORDER METROPOLITAN CENTERS

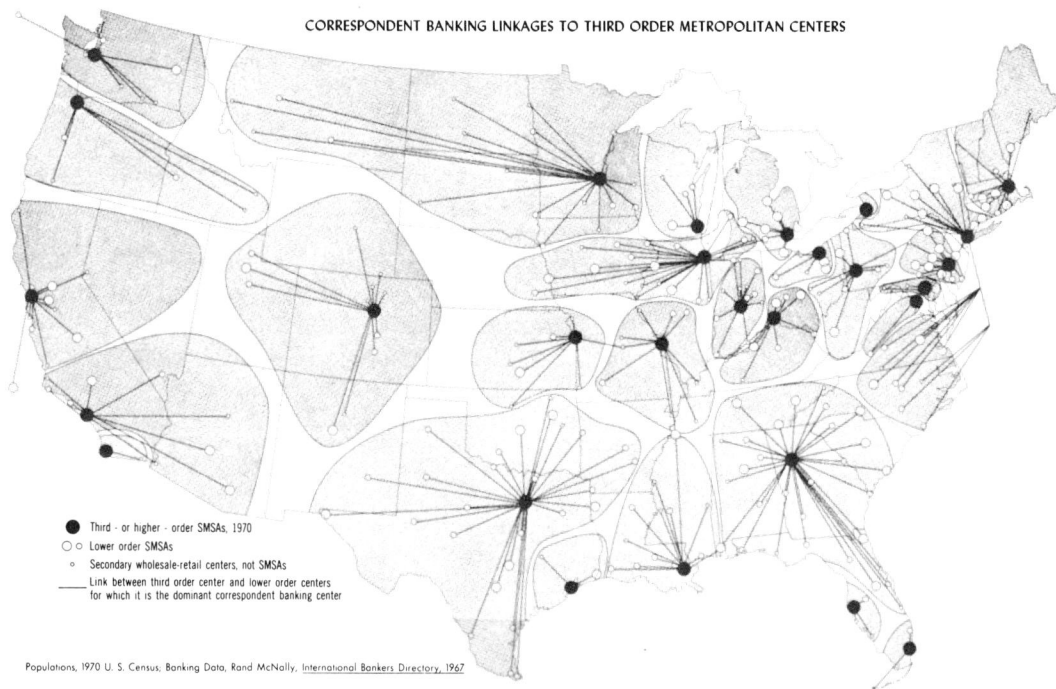

● Third - or higher - order SMSAs, 1970
○ ○ Lower order SMSAs
○ Secondary wholesale-retail centers, not SMSAs
──── Link between third order center and lower order centers
for which it is the dominant correspondent banking center

Populations, 1970 U. S. Census; Banking Data, Rand McNally, *International Bankers Directory, 1967*

Figure 3.17 Dominant correspondent banking linkages to third-order metropolitan centers from lower-order centers, 1967. New York is defined as the dominant third-order center for a given lower-order metropolitan area if it has at least four times as many correspondent banking links as any other third-order center. Second-order metropolitan areas are defined as dominant third-order centers if they have more than twice as many correspondent banking links as any other third-order metropolitan area. [J. R. Borchert, "America's changing metropolitan regions"; reproduced by permission from the *Annals* of the Association of American Geographers, volume **62**, p. 358 (1972).]

tan region. Jean Gottmann coined the term *megalopolis* for this particular region.[5] Although there are other extensive metropolitan regions throughout the world (for example, the Ruhr area in Germany, the Liverpool-Manchester region in England, and the Tokyo-Yokohama region in Japan) that merit the same name, we reserve it for the northeast section of the United States (Figure 3.18). *Connurbation* also has been used, especially in Europe, for these metropolitan regions. Gottmann described the Northeast as follows:

> . . . an almost continuous system of deeply interwoven urban and suburban areas, with a total population of about 37 million people in 1960, has been erected along the North-

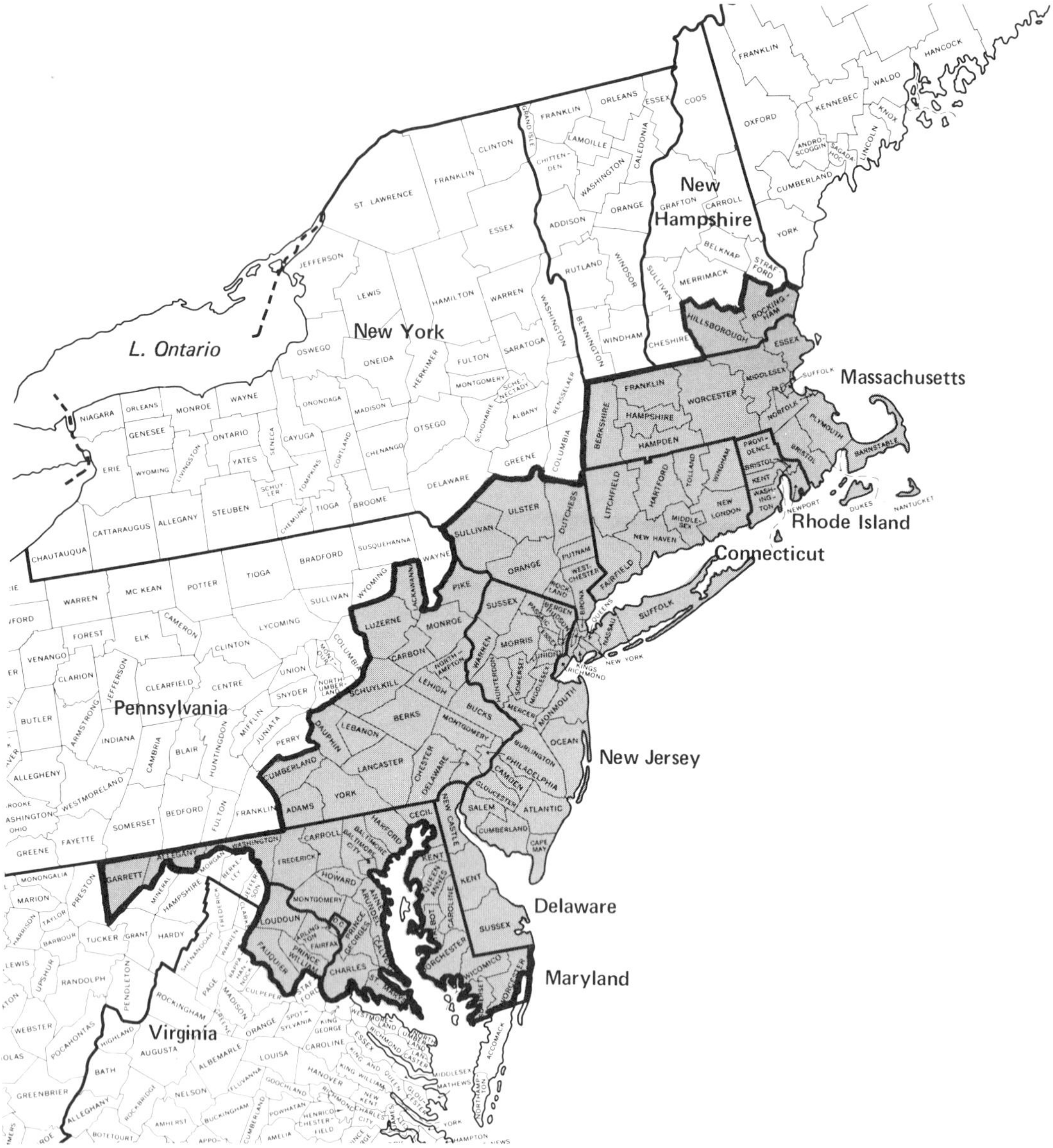

Figure 3.18 The extent of Megalopolis as defined by J. Gottmann, *Megalopolis: The Urbanized Northeastern Seaboard of the United States.* © 1961 by the Twentieth Century Fund, New York. Figure 9, p. 41.

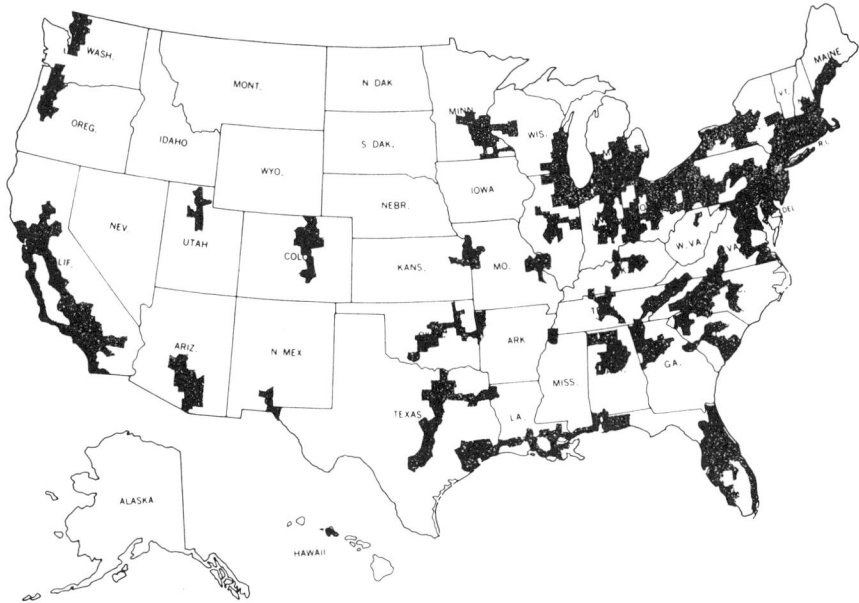

Figure 3.19 Urban regions, year 2000; based on a projection of two children per family. [L. J. Carter, "Land use law (I): Congress on verge of a modest beginning," *Science,* **182**, No. 4113, 1973, p. 694. Copyright 1973 by the American Association for the Advancement of Science.]

eastern Atlantic seaboard. It straddles state boundaries, stretches across wide estuaries and bays, and encompasses many regional differences. In fact, the landscapes of Megalopolis offer such variety that the average observer may well doubt the unity of the region. And it may seem to him that the main urban nuclei of the seaboard are little related to one another. Six of its great cities would be great individual metropolises in their own right if they were located elsewhere.[6]

Two other metropolitan zones like Megalopolis are emerging. One is the San Francisco–San Diego region (*Sansan*) and the other is the Chicago–Pittsburgh region (*Chipits*). Megalopolis is renamed *Boswash* in a forecast of the urban pattern of the year 2000. But these are only three of the massive urban concentrations that will exist in the United States in 2000. The map in Figure 3.19 is taken from a study of population growth for the United States and is supplemented by in-

Table 3.9 Population and Land Area of Urban Regions, 1920
to 2000. [L. J. Carter, "Land use law (I): Congress on
verge of a modest beginning," *Science*, **182**, No.
4113, 1973, p. 694. Copyright 1973 by the American Association for the Advancement of Science.]

	1920	*1940*	*1960*	*1980**	*2000**
Number of urban regions	10	10	16	24	25
Population					
Millions	35.6	53.9	100.6	164.6	219.7
Percent of total U.S.					
population	33.6	40.8	56.1	73.4	83.1
Land area†					
Square miles	60,972	94,999	196,958	395,138	486,902
Percent of total					
U.S. land area‡	2.1	3.2	6.6	13.3	16.4
Gross population density					
of people per square					
mile	584	568	511	417	451

*Based on Census Bureau series E population projection (based on a fertility assumption of 2.1
births per woman).
†Excludes urban region of Oahu Island, Hawaii.
‡Coterminous U.S. excluding Alaska and Hawaii.

formation given in Table 3.9. Both the map and the table show that by
the turn of the century there will be 25 major urban regions. Over 80%
of the total United States population will live in these regions and the
urban land area involved will be more than twice what it is today. No
shortage of land will be felt, however, because these estimated urban
land areas will still amount to only 16% of the total land area.

Today, unfortunately, certain lands are misused as urban areas
spread and often prime farm land is lost to urban development.
Southern California and Florida are two obvious examples of this
problem and in the Niagara Peninsula in Canada valuable land for
fruit growing increasingly is being developed for urban uses.

For the peoples of the United States and Canada the challenges
and issues that result are numerous. (1) Should metropolitan concentration continue unchecked? (2) Can suitable social, economic, and
political systems be devised to manage these supercities? (3) Can
growth and concentration be checked or halted and alternative spatial
forms of urban settlement be encouraged? These questions will come
up later when we discuss planning.

3.5 Generalization of the Metropolitan Area Growth Process

The United States Case

Can we describe generally the changing form of the United States' metropolitan areas over time? John Adams identified four important periods in the process as follows:[7]

1. The walking and horse-drawn car era: up to the 1880's.
2. The electric streetcar era: 1880–1918.
3. The recreational auto era: 1920–1941.
4. The freeway era: post-1945.

The first of these eras witnessed a building surge that peaked just prior to the 1893 depression (Figure 3.20). This period saw the construction of the *old cores* of almost all American cities. From 1900 to 1919 there was another important phase of building construction that often involved the erection of large frame houses on very narrow lots. This was the period of streetcar transportation.

With the coming of the recreational auto era, there was a tremendous increase in building construction, first in the 1920's, with the peak occurring in 1925, and second, in the decade 1935–1945, with a peak occurring in 1941. Separating these two booms were the depression years of the early 1930's, with the bottom of the trough occurring in 1933. The overall effect of these two building surges and of the greatly increased reliance on auto travel was a filling in of the areas of the cities between the main roads that were served by streetcars.

After the end of the war in 1945, building construction again boomed and reached an all-time high level just prior to 1950. Suburban construction was pronounced as the building of high-speed auto routes improved the accessibility of outlying areas to the cities. Much lower residential densities became characteristic of these newer developed areas.

Model of the Process

On the basis of these generalizations, John Adams described a *model* Midwestern city (Figure 3.21) in this way:

> Along traverse *A* one moves rapidly from the old walking–horse car core down a steep age gradient to newer neighborhoods of the 1920's and 1930's. Along traverse *B*, on the

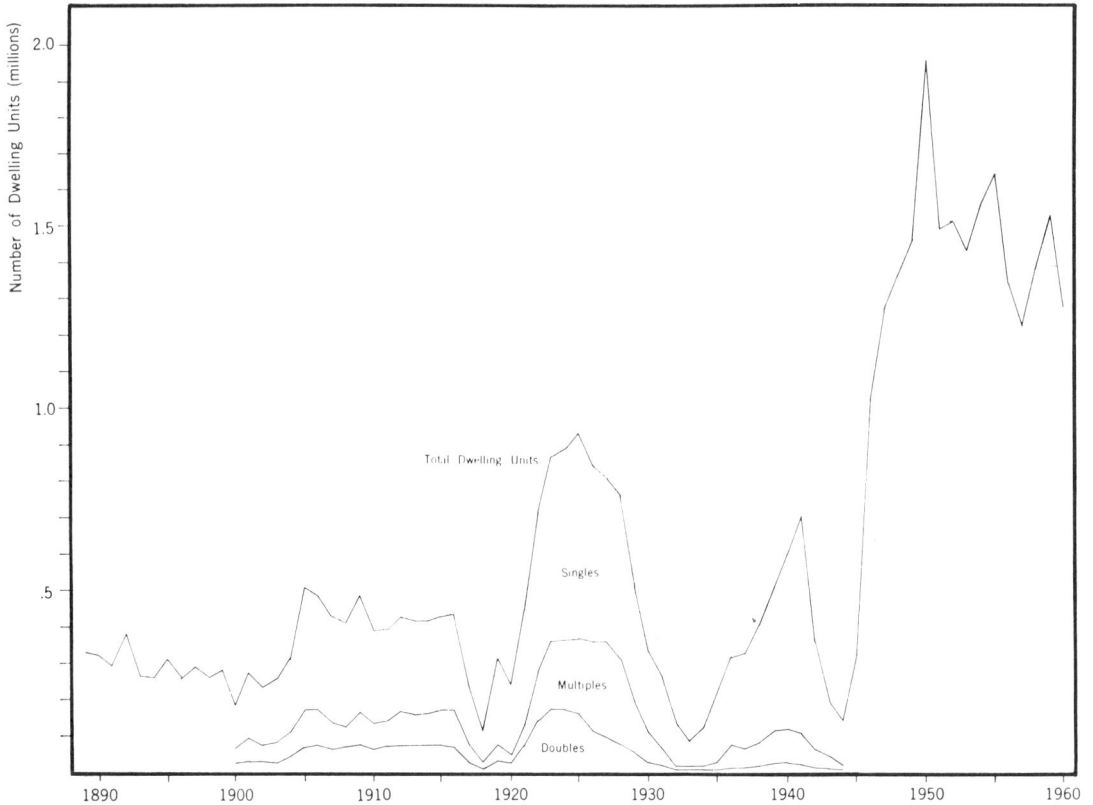

Figure 3.20 Estimated number of dwelling units started each year, 1889–1960. Dwelling units are built as single-family houses, in double houses, or in multiples. Estimated detail by type of structure is not available for units built before 1900 or after 1944. [J. S. Adams, "Residential structure of midwestern cities;" reproduced by permission from the *Annals* of the Association of American Geographers, volume **60**, p. 47 (1970).]

other hand, the age gradient per unit distance is more gradual. Traveling route *C* one moves up an age gradient approaching the old streetcar route, then down the gradient to newer housing on the other side of the route. Traverse *D* illustrates a similar pair of gradients that are more obvious from common experience. From rural land the traverse intersects residential areas of the recent construction era only, then passes into rural land once more.[8]

These descriptions, Adams found, fitted the city of Minneapolis very well.

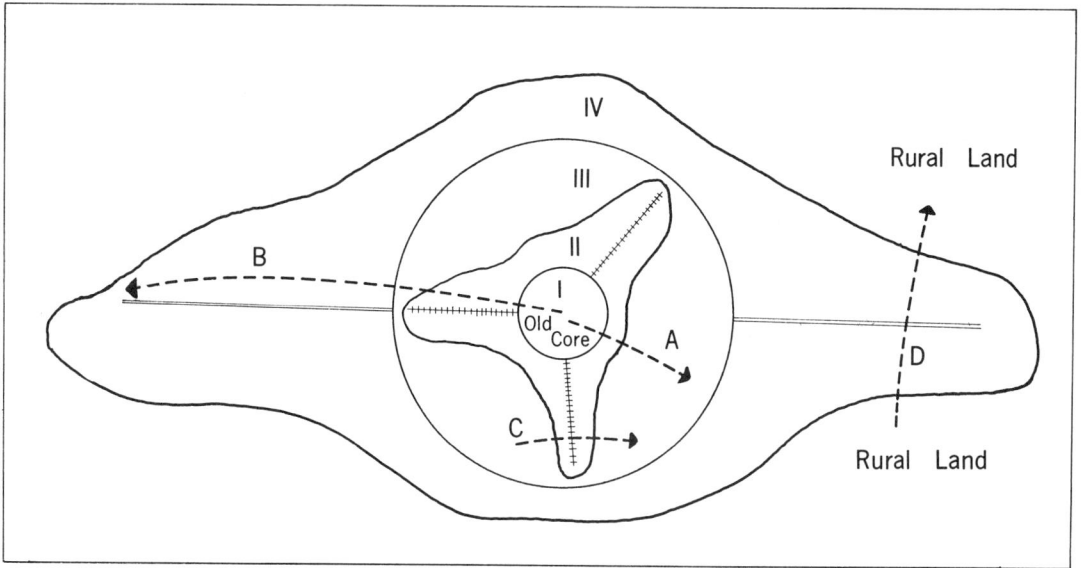

Figure 3.21   Expected distortions from concentric growth patterns. The highly articulated urban transport networks of transport eras two (streetcar lines) and four (freeways) promoted star-shaped deviations from concentricity. Transport eras one (foot travel) and three (recreational auto) promoted transport surfaces and compact, circular urban forms. Traverses *A* through *D* indicate the variety of contrasting age gradients. [J. S. Adams, "Residential structure of midwestern cities"; reproduced by permission from the *Annals* of the Association of American Geographers, volume **60**, p. 56 (1970).]

3.6   Simulations of Metropolitan Growth

This idea of describing a model city and comparing it with an actual city has been used in other studies that have attempted to *simulate* the growth patterns of cities over time. In this section we discuss two such attempts to simulate urban growth. The first of these was developed by planners in North Carolina and is strictly regional in nature. The second example uses cities from various states and was developed by a geographer.

Consider the spatial patterns of urban development that occurred in the Piedmont region of North and South Carolina around the cities of Greensboro, Winston-Salem, and Lexington (Figure 3.22). Can a model be made of this process to help us understand the process? One approach to this problem proceeds in this way. A regular grid network is overlaid on a map of the region. The map scale is such that the cells are 1,000 feet square. Each cell is divided into 9 equal parts. An *attractiveness index* for each cell is computed by using a formula that takes

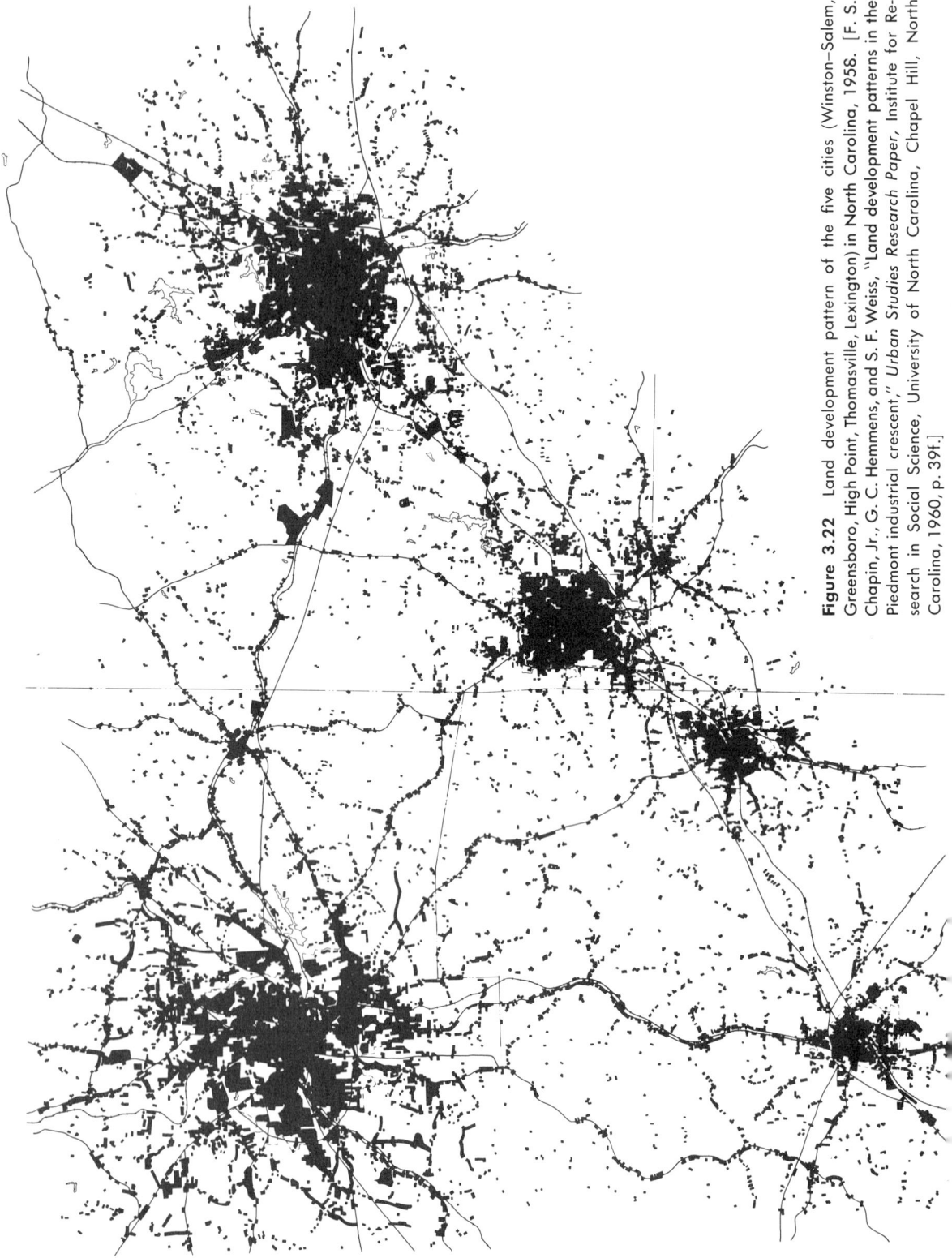

Figure 3.22 Land development pattern of the five cities (Winston–Salem, Greensboro, High Point, Thomasville, Lexington) in North Carolina, 1956. [F. S. Chapin, Jr., G. C. Hemmens, and S. F. Weiss, "Land development patterns in the Piedmont industrial crescent," *Urban Studies Research Paper*, Institute for Research in Social Science, University of North Carolina, Chapel Hill, North Carolina, 1960, p. 39f.]

into account the cell's accessibility to centers of employment, the travel distance from the cell to the nearest major street and to the nearest available elementary school, and whether or not the cell is served by a sewerage system. On the basis of the attractiveness indices for all cells, a value is then assigned to each cell that gives the probability of its being developed (or rather the probability that one of its 9 equal parts will be developed) as "urban" over the next time period. The higher the attractiveness index for a cell, the higher the probability that it will be developed.

The *simulation* of the pattern of urban development (Figure 3.23) requires that a scale of numbers consistent with these probabilities be devised, that some of these numbers be selected randomly (how many is determined by the number of units that have to be developed somewhere in the region over the time period), and that the cells to which these numbers refer be identified. The diagrammatic representation of the simulation in Figure 3.23 shows that at the "start" there are 8 cells with equal levels of attractiveness. This would mean that each cell has a probability of 0.125 of being developed. If we ignore the decimal points, a suitable number scale for the 8 cells would be as follows:

0 to 125	126 to 250	251 to 375
376 to 500		501 to 625
625 to 750	751 to 875	876 to 1,000

In Figure 3.23 there are 3 units of housing to be distributed in the first step; therefore, 3 numbers in the range 0 to 1,000 have to be chosen randomly. The diagram suggests that these could have been, for example, 117, 590, and 777. Once the units are located, then the attractiveness indices have to be recalculated for all cells and new number sets have to be devised. The simulation continues for as many steps or passes as are desired. The simulated patterns may then be compared with the actual map patterns of growth as is shown in Figure 3.24 (see pp. 96 and 97). The degree of similarity between the two patterns is an indication of how well the model has represented the processes going on in the real world.

A similar approach has been used by Robert Yuill in studying population growth in 11 medium-sized United States cities (the smallest was Lubbock, Texas, with a 1960 population of 129,000 and the

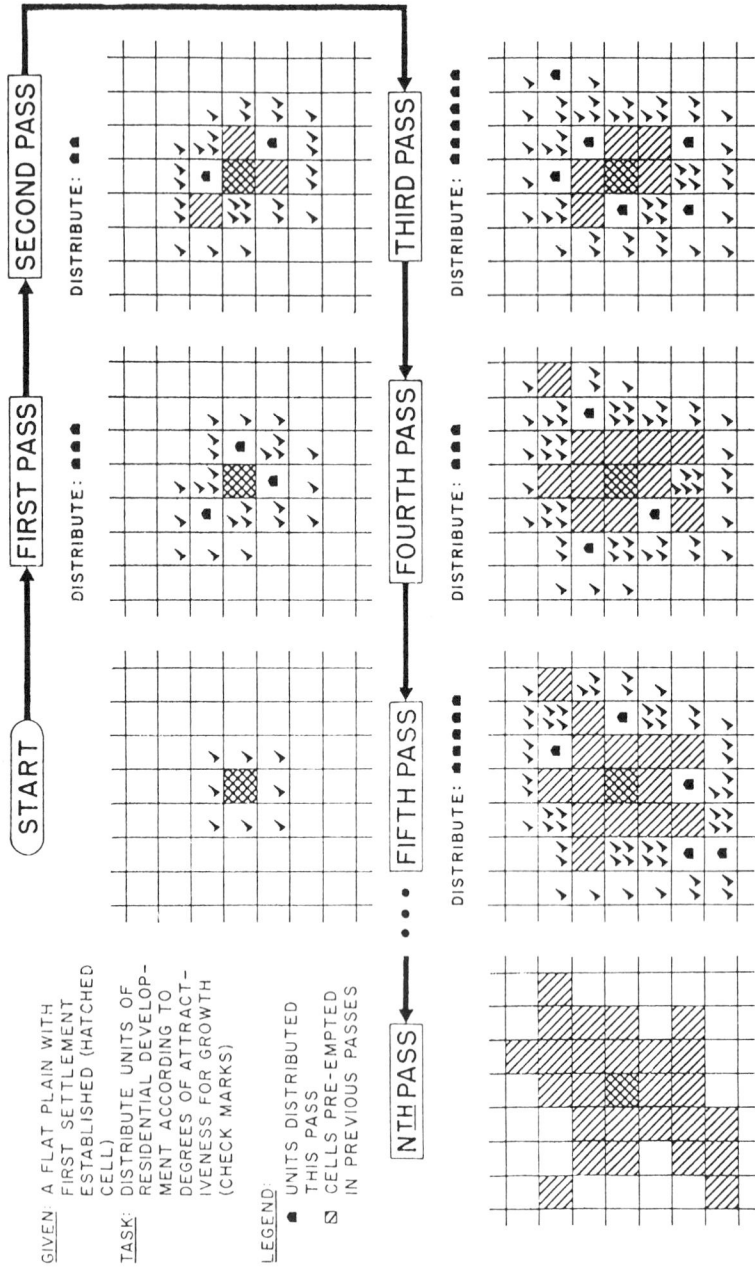

Figure 3.23 Diagrammatic representation of the simulation technique used by Chapin et al. At each step there are a certain number of residential units to be located in the region. Each small subregion or cell has a computed measure of attractiveness that may change from one step to another as the residential units are distributed. The number of checkmarks indicates the level of attractiveness. The actual allocation at each step is done by using random selection methods. [F. S. Chapin, Jr., and S. F. Weiss, "Factors influencing land development," *Urban Studies Research Monograph*, Institute for Research in Social Science, University of North Carolina, Chapel Hill, North Carolina, 1962, p. 37.]

largest was Baltimore with a population of around 938,000).[9]   His
model sought to take into account for each small area within the city
the *capacity* of the area in terms of the maximum amount of residential
population that it could accommodate, the features of its site that might
influence its rate of growth, and its accessibility. Figure 3.25 (pp. 98
and 99) shows two examples of the simulated city population density
profiles compared to the actual ones.

3.7   Cognitive Images of Intercity Differences

People form mental pictures or cognitive images of urban places as
they exist at different scales. At the macrolevel, our positive or negative attractions to different "world" cities are shaped by the information we have about the places, their locations, our emotional involvement with them, the images the cities project, and their specific
identifying characteristics. Few would deny that Chicago, Paris, and
Moscow project different "images," but preference rankings of these
places by different people may vary, depending on where these people
live.

The locational and nonlocational features of these cities shape the
mental frameworks that people use to organize and order information
about places in the environment. Information relevant to the framework either reinforces its form or leads to change. Information that
cannot be fitted to the scheme may be discarded. These mental
schemes seem to be based on features of the cities that can be designated precisely, for example, location, size, social composition, and
physical environment, and also on evaluations that people make on
such things as desirability, attractiveness, quality of life, and level of
economic opportunity.

Intercity Distances and Emotional Involvement: A Swedish Example

If we were to ask a sample of randomly chosen individuals to estimate the distance between pairs of cities, it might be expected that
the answers obtained would reflect the different features of the cities,
both the easily designated ones and the evaluative ones. This was
tested in a study that used Stockholm as a base.[10] A group of Swedish
residents were asked to estimate the distances to ten major cities of the
world. The major idea behind the study was that the estimated distances would be a function of the subjects' emotional involvements
with the cities. The *distance* data were gathered for this experiment
by asking the people to (a) compare the distance from Stockholm to
each of a pair of cities, (b) indicate which of the two distances was

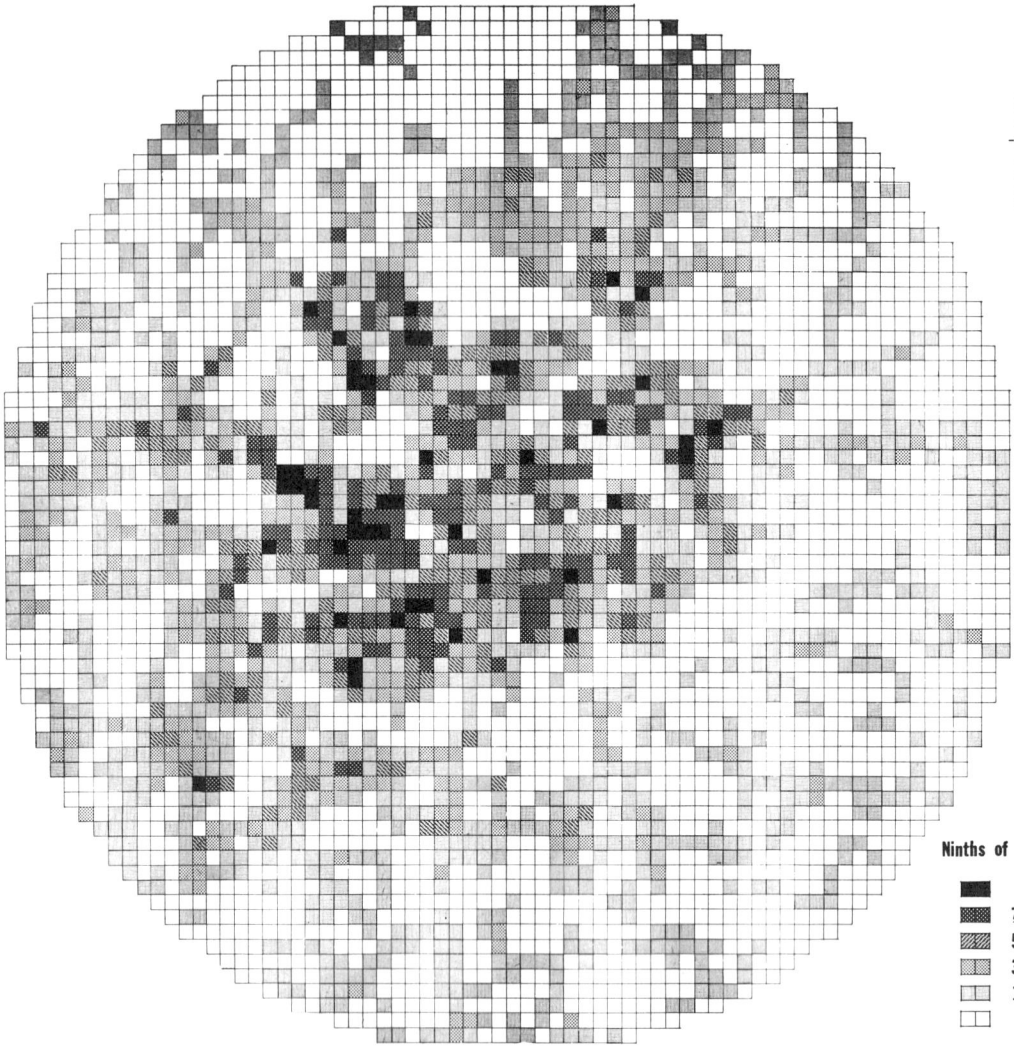

Ninths of Development

■	9
▨	7 - 8
▧	5 - 6
▦	3 - 4
□	1 - 2
□	0

LAND IN RESIDENTIAL USE, GREENSBORO, NORTH CAROLINA, 1960

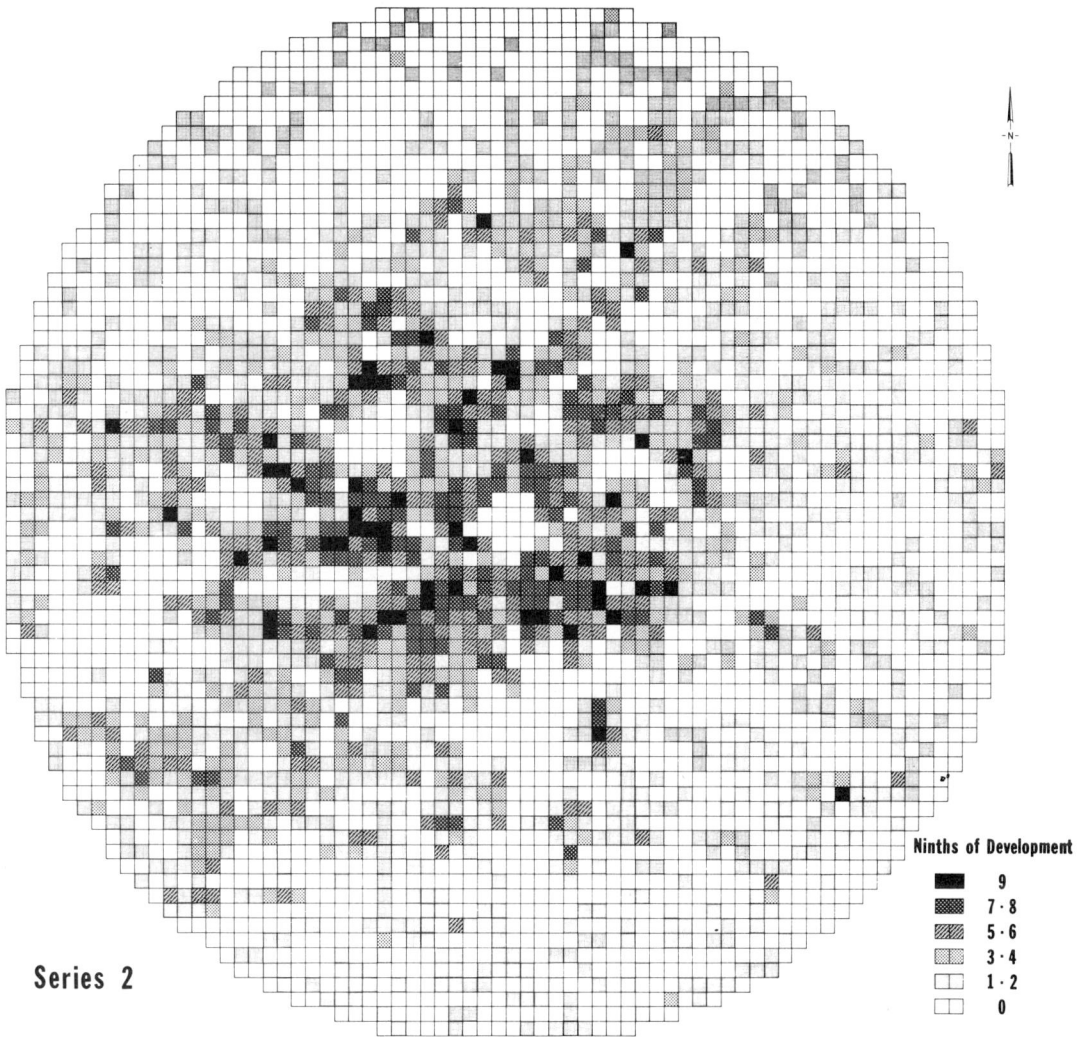

Ninths of Development

██	9
▓▓	7·8
▨▨	5·6
░░	3·4
☐	1·2
☐	0

Series 2

EXPECTED RESIDENTIAL LAND USE, GREENSBORO, NORTH CAROLINA, 1960 BASED ON USE OF PROBABILISTIC MODEL – MEDIAN OUTCOME OF 50 RUNS

Figure 3.24 Example of the comparison between actual residential-use pattern (see preceding page) and a simulated one. [F. S. Chapin, Jr., and S. F. Weiss, "Some input requirements for a residential model," *Urban Studies Research Monograph,* Institute for Research in Social Science, University of North Carolina, Chapel Hill, North Carolina, 1965, p. 28.]

CINCINNATI MODEL AND EMPIRICAL DENSITY SURFACES

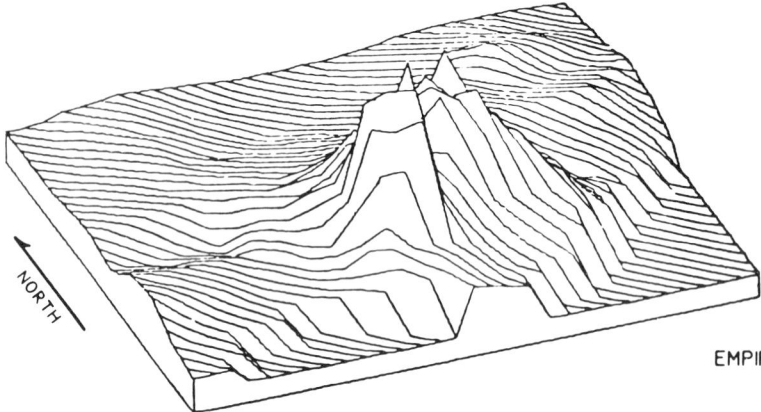

EMPIRICAL

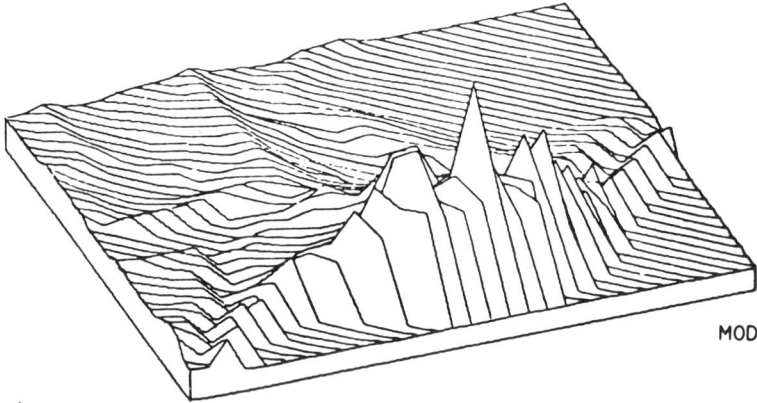

MODEL

0   1

MILES

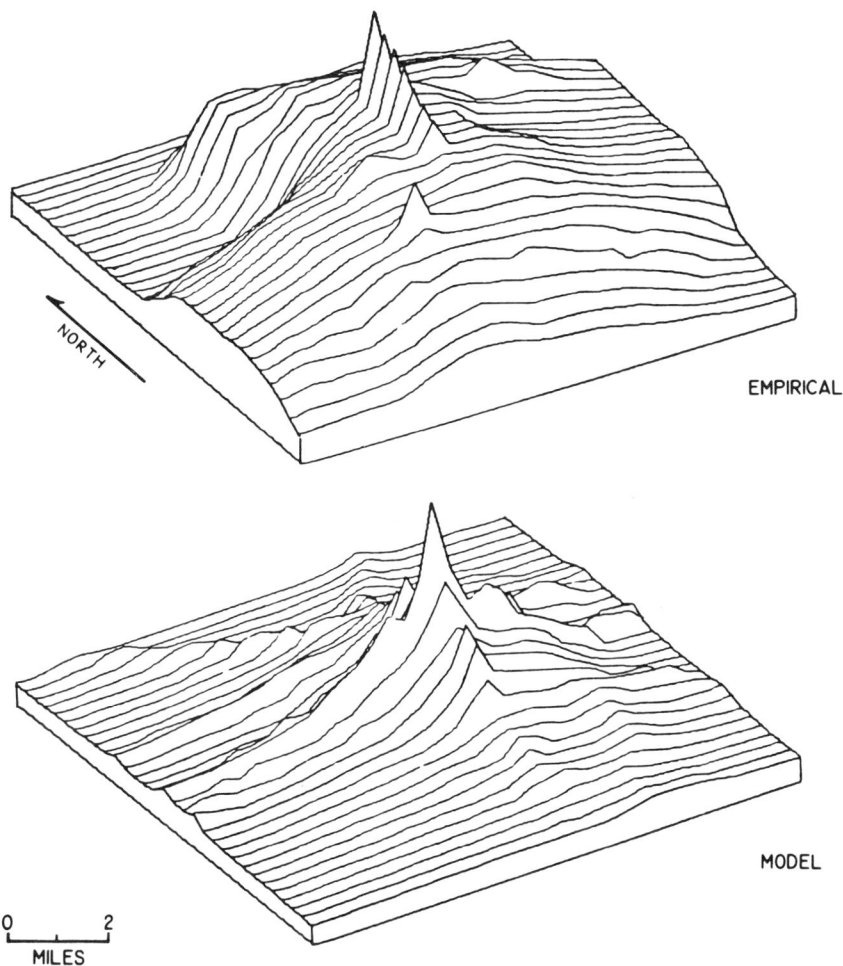

Figure 3.25 Comparison of actual city population density patterns with simulated ones for Cincinnati (see preceding page) and Lubbock models. [R. S. Yuill, "A general model for urban growth: A spatial simulation," *Michigan Geography Publication*, **2**, 1970, pp. 164–66.]

Table 3.10   Scales Constructed From Experimental Data.
(G. Ekman and O. Bratfisch, "Subjective Distance
and Emotional Involvement. A Psychological
Mechanism," *Acta Psychologica*, **24**, 1965, p. 448.)

City	Great-Circle Distance (kilometers)	Subjective Distance	Emotional Involvement	Estimated Importance
Budapest	1,328	2.43	1.71	23.9
Copenhagen	522	1.00	2.77	25.3
Hamburg	801	1.38	2.35	26.1
Kiruna	943	1.55	2.16	7.0
London	1,447	1.85	3.00	71.6
Montreal	5,886	6.35	1.00	23.8
Moscow	1,224	2.75	2.57	78.5
Peking	6,701	8.30	2.06	69.9
Reykjavik	2,127	2.28	1.51	21.2
Vienna	1,253	2.15	2.22	24.2

thought to be greater, and (c) estimate the smaller distance as a percent of the larger distance. Emotional involvement was determined by asking the people to imagine something important happening in the cities and to estimate their degree of emotional involvement in what might happen. Scale values were calculated from both estimates. As an additional variable, the people were asked to estimate the *importance* of the cities. The scale values obtained from these experiments are shown in Table 3.10.

The relationship between emotional involvement and subjective distance was found to be an inverse one, as is shown in Figure 3.26. That is, the higher the emotional involvement, the shorter the subjective distance; the lower the involvement, the greater the subjective distance. The three cities of London, Moscow, and Peking seemed to fall on a curve of approximately the same slope but at a higher level (diagram A). This suggested that these major centers "attract an emotional involvement additional to that related to subjective distance." When the values for these three cities were adjusted downward and when logarithmic values were taken, the straight-line relationship shown in diagram B resulted. This is known as an *inverse square root law*. It is also another expression of what is known as a *distance-decay effect*.

A number of subsequent studies have sought to confirm this relationship between emotional involvement and subjective distance. The results of similar experiments conducted on university students in Australia suggested that the exponent describing the inverse relationship between emotional involvement and subjective distance (the value of 0.50 in Figure 3.26) was not invariant as other studies had sug-

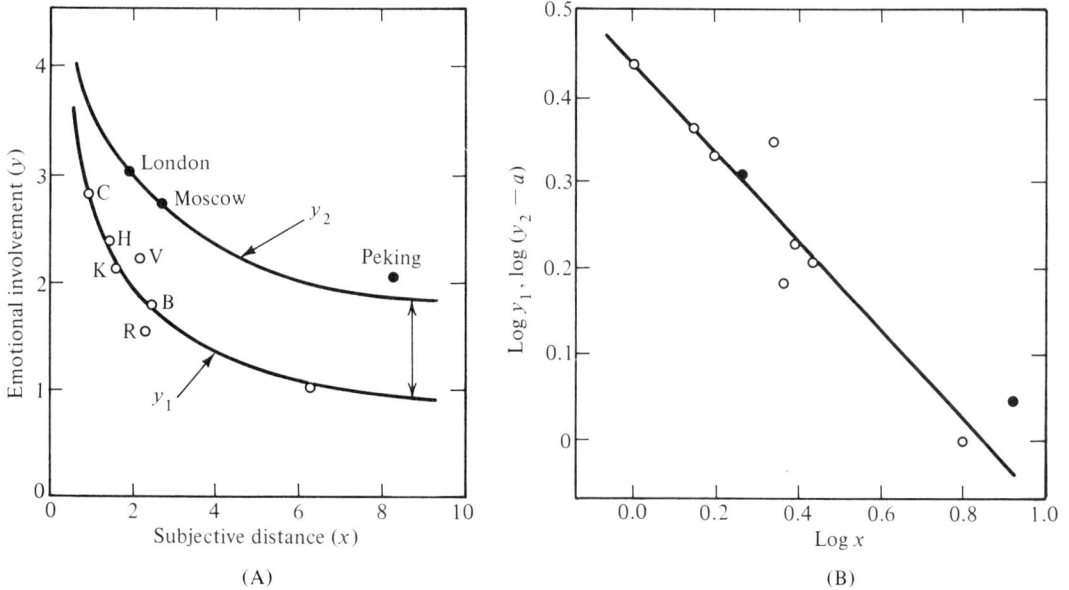

Figure 3.26 Emotional involvement as related to subjective distance. Two trends, y_1 and y_2, can be seen in diagram A, approximately parallel and separated by the constant $a = 0.95$. In diagram B, log y_1 and log (y_2—0.95) are plotted against log x. The trend is linear with the slope—.50. [G. Ekman and O. Bratfisch, "Subjective distance and emotional involvement: A psychological mechanism," *Acta Psychologica*, **24**, 1965, p. 450.]

gested and did in fact vary with "the physical range of the stimuli (in terms of distance)."[11] That is to say, the exponent was larger (1.89 to 2.40) when the cities being considered were located at relatively short distances from the base city or epicenter, and the exponent tended to be smaller the further the sample cities were located away from the epicenter (for the Australian students the exponent was 0.40 to 0.60 when cities in Southeast Asia were considered). These studies suggest that fundamental spatial properties (such as local neighborhood effects and distance-decay effects) exist not only in terms of their objective physical manifestations but also as factors that help shape peoples' cognitive images of systems of cities even at the world scale.

Subjective Appraisals of Cities in the United States

The cities of North America have been extensively studied and classified from the point of view of their economic functions, physical land use, social structure, and so on. But how do people regard them? Which places are perceived to be *similar* and what are the readily designated characteristics of these places?

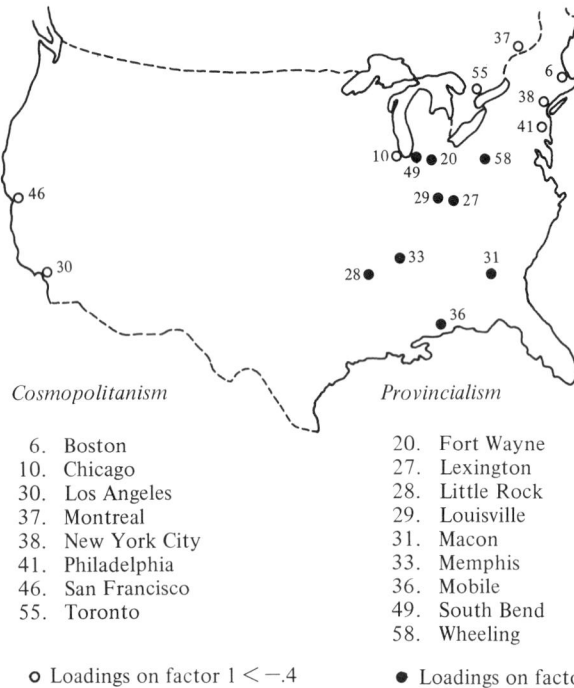

Cosmopolitanism   *Provincialism*

6.	Boston	20.	Fort Wayne
10.	Chicago	27.	Lexington
30.	Los Angeles	28.	Little Rock
37.	Montreal	29.	Louisville
38.	New York City	31.	Macon
41.	Philadelphia	33.	Memphis
46.	San Francisco	36.	Mobile
55.	Toronto	49.	South Bend
		58.	Wheeling

o Loadings on factor 1 < −.4   ● Loadings on factor 1 < +.4

Figure 3.27 Cosmopolitanism-provincialism: the first set of locational classes emerging from the factor analysis of city similarities. [K. R. Cox and G. Zannaras, "Designative perceptions of macro-spaces: Concepts, a methodology, and applications;" reprinted by permission from R. M. Downs and D. Stea, eds.: *Image and Environment* (Chicago: Aldine Publishing Company and London: Edward Arnold Ltd.); copyright © 1973 by Aldine Publishing Company and Edward Arnold Ltd.; p. 174.]

A study that attempted to answer these questions for a set of 60 United States cities of different sizes began by asking some university students to take each city in turn and then to select the three places *most similar* to it.[12] *Similarity* was evaluated in whatever manner the student chose, but it was expected that generalizations could be made over the choices of the whole group of students. The students appeared to use a variety of attributes to judge similarity. A statistical analysis had to be made of the results. This analysis summarized the different responses over a large number of attributes in terms of a few *common* underlying patterns. The three more important patterns were identified as cosmopolitanism, provincialism, and location. Figure 3.27, for example, shows the cities that were designated as cosmopolitan and provincial. Figure 3.28 locates groups of cities whose distinguishing attributes (in the minds of the students) were their locations.

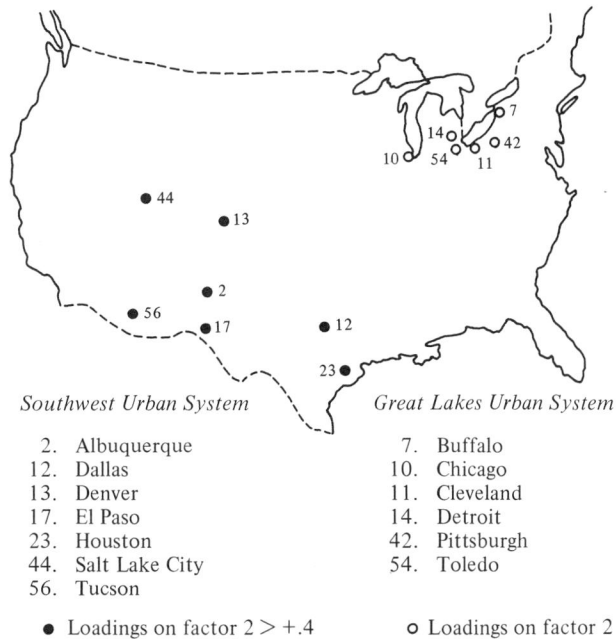

Southwest Urban System   Great Lakes Urban System

2.	Albuquerque	7.	Buffalo
12.	Dallas	10.	Chicago
13.	Denver	11.	Cleveland
17.	El Paso	14.	Detroit
23.	Houston	42.	Pittsburgh
44.	Salt Lake City	54.	Toledo
56.	Tucson		

● Loadings on factor 2 > +.4   o Loadings on factor 2 < −.4

Figure 3.28 The Great Lakes Urban System–Southwest System: the second set of locational classes emerging from the factor analysis of city similarities. [K. R. Cox and G. Zannaras, "Designative perceptions of macro-spaces: Concepts, a methodology, and applications"; reprinted by permission from R. M. Downs and D. Stea, eds.: *Image and Environment* (Chicago: Aldine Publishing Company and London: Edward Arnold Ltd.); copyright © 1973 by Aldine Publishing Company and Edward Arnold Ltd.; p. 175.]

3.8 Summary

In this chapter we have endeavored to present a variety of views about city systems. The scale of analysis was national and regional. At the national level, we discussed the evolution of two city systems, those of the United States and the Soviet Union. At the regional level, some fundamental spatial characteristics of size and spacing were presented. Since cities do not exist in isolation, connections among cities in various national and regional systems were examined. Levels of connectivity were defined by using ideas of networks and graphs. Expressing the intercity connections in this way allowed us to discuss the occurrence of regional clusters within larger national systems, to develop summary measures of network complexity for comparative purposes, and to outline an evolutionary view of city systems in terms of network development.

The view of a city system as a collection of points (nodes) and lines (edges) is but one way to discover characteristics of their spatial form. Another is to examine cities as distinct areal units with differing locational size, shape, and attractive powers. Some cities are large and complex enough to be considered as regions in their own right. Therefore, we discussed concepts of cities as statistical areas and the coalescence of these areas into supercities such as Megalopolis. This development of city-regions will be a major aspect of our urban future.

Our discussion of metropolitan growth in the United States was prompted by a desire to understand the metropolitan growth process itself. With this goal in mind, we showed how simulation techniques could be used to examine how cities grow and change.

Almost all of this chapter stressed the *objective* spatial form of city systems and their components. But people do not necessarily comprehend the complexity or structure of these systems, and in many cases they have very little knowledge of their specific elements. Consequently, we offered comments on the mental images that people have of city to city differences, stressing how locational information may be modified by emotional involvement, how subsets of cities may actually be seen as being "the same," and how particular groups of cities can be distinguished by relatively few characteristics.

Having introduced the idea of cities as being both real and perceived connected units in larger systems, we shall now turn to a discussion of a range of city-system characteristics, focusing at first on the economic activity in the cities.

Notes

1. J. R. Borchert, "American metropolitan evolution," *Geographical Review,* **57,** 1967, pp. 301–32.

2. C. D. Harris, *Cities of the Soviet Union* (Chicago: Rand McNally & Co., 1970), p. 139.

3. J. R. Borchert, "America's changing metropolitan regions," *Annals,* Association of American Geographers, **62,** 1972, pp. 352–73.

4. *Ibid.,* p. 356.

5. J. Gottmann, *Megalopolis: The Urbanized Northeastern Seaboard of the United States* (New York: The Twentieth-Century Fund, 1961).

6. *Ibid.,* p. 7.

7. J. S. Adams, "Residential structure of midwestern cities," *Annals,* Association of American Geographers, **60,** 1970, pp. 37–62.

8. *Ibid.,* p. 46.

9. R. S. Yuill, "A general model for urban growth: a spatial simulation," *Michigan Geography Publication,* **2,** 1970.

10. G. EKMAN and O. BRATFISCH, "Subjective distance and emotional involvement. A psychological mechanism," *Acta Psychologica,* **24,** 1965, pp. 446–53.

11. D. J. WALMSLEY, "Emotional involvement and subjective distance: a modification of the universe square root law," *The Journal of Psychology,* **87,** 1974, pp. 9–19.

12. K. R. COX and G. ZANNARAS, "Designative perceptions of macro-spaces: concepts, a methodology, and applications," in R. M. DOWNS and D. STEA, eds., *Image and Environment* (Chicago: Aldine Publishing Co., 1973), pp. 162–78.

chapter 4

Economic Characteristics and Functions of Cities

The modern city typically performs a wide range of economic, social, and political functions. In many cases, these modern-day functions may have been of no importance whatsoever in the original founding and location of the city; conversely, factors that were important in determining the initial role and location of the city may have been overshadowed for some time in its history and may even have disappeared. This is so, for example, with regard to many cities founded originally as fortress towns or religious capitals. In the case of cities such as Birmingham (U.K.) and Pittsburgh (U.S.A.), the depletion of local mineral resources and the locational shifts of the iron and steel industry have meant that these cities have had to diversify their functions and that they can no longer be identified simply as primary metals-producing centers. The substitution of functions in the development of city economies and a trend toward diversification are common features in the urbanization process.

4.1 Basic and Nonbasic Functions of a City:
A Simple Representation

A common approach to considering the employment structure of the city looks at the proportional distribution of the employed labor force over the different categories of economic activity. The larger the city, the more diversified its economy is likely to be, that is to say, no one or two economic functions are likely to have a disproportionately high percentage of the city's employment. Conversely, smaller cities are often more highly specialized and are harder hit by economic depressions in those industries on which they depend. The numerous small coal-mining towns in different parts of the world that declined as their resources were depleted and as the competition of other fuels increased are obvious examples.

Basic/Nonbasic Distinction

The distinction between *basic* or *export* activities and *nonbasic* or *local* activities is based on the idea that certain economic activities in a city generate the important flows of income into the city and hence are *basic* to the economic well-being of the city. These activities serve markets largely outside the city itself; in this sense, they are *export* activities. The automobile manufacturing plants in Detroit would be an obvious example. By contrast, many other activities carried on in a city exist primarily to serve the inhabitants of the city itself—bakeries, hairdressers, and taverns are examples—and these are considered nonbasic or local activities.

This distinction between basic and nonbasic urban activities has prompted many lines of discussion. First, there is the question of how one measures the levels of basic and nonbasic activities. They are exceedingly difficult to measure because some activities in a city (for example, newspaper publishing) serve both an internal and external market. How does one allocate employment or income in this activity between the basic and nonbasic sectors? Below we shall discuss a method of estimating the levels, the *minimum requirements approach*. It is a crude but practical method given the data that are available. But before we introduce this approach, we shall mention some other questions that have arisen from the basic/nonbasic distinction.

Multiplier Effect

One such issue emphasizes the measurement of a *multiplier effect*. If the basic employment is increased in a city, the argument goes, then

107

the nonbasic sector also increases as more service activities are required to support the new export activity. Overall, then, total employment and population in the city should increase. The discussion usually ignores the question of whether or not there are unemployed in the city who might thus be employed; in any case, if the argument is phrased in terms of income levels, this point is not important in elaborating on the idea of a multiplier effect.

There has been considerable debate over the usefulness of this multiplier concept and the distinction between basic and nonbasic employment in forecasting the growth prospects of any city. Some have challenged the view that growth requires expansion of the basic sector and they have argued that nonbasic activities may be as important in determining the future of the city. Over the short-run (5–10 years) the impact of basic employment growth may indeed be very important, but over the long-run (25–50 years) the performance of the service industries may be equally, if not more, important. The growth of urban centers in Florida and the southwestern part of the United States has certainly provided evidence in support of the last point, for in many of these communities the service activities are more important.

One implication of the multiplier concept is the assumption that

Table 4.1 Average Propensity to Spend Inside Area and Area Characteristics. (W. H. Oakland, F. T. Sparrow, and H. L. Stettler, "Ghetto multipliers: A case study of Hough," *Journal of Regional Science*, vol. 11, no. 3, 1971, p. 344.)

	Average Propensity to Spend Inside Area	*Population (1965)*	*Median Income (1965)*
Ghetto Areas			
Hough	0.38	59,000	4,050
South Central Los Angeles	0.38	168,000	3,884
East Los Angeles	0.48	178,000	5,106
Bedford-Stuyvesant	0.55	378,000*	4,648*
Nonghetto Areas			
Winnetka	0.30	15,000	
Redondo Beach	0.40	50,000	
Evanston	0.50	72,000	

*1960.

almost all the positive effects generated by new activity or income coming into the community are confined to the community itself and do not "leak" outside of that community. But these "leakages" may be very high and as a consequence multiplier effects may be relatively insignificant. In Table 4.1, for example, there are shown measures of the "average propensity to spend inside area" which are indicators of these leakages. In Hough, Cleveland, apparently only 38 cents out of every dollar are spent within that community and none of the other values is so high that one could have much faith in the notion of a multiplier effect being applicable in that community. Significantly, there is no sharp contrast between the value for ghetto and nonghetto areas even though the higher mobility of the populations in the non-ghetto areas might have prompted some anticipation that the values for these areas would be lower than for the ghettos.

Minimum Requirements

We made reference above to the minimum requirements approach to estimating levels of basic/nonbasic activity. The approach is not a sophisticated one, but it is easily applied by using data that are generally available. As the name suggests, the method calculates for a city the levels of employment in several different economic activities that are the minimum requirements *for a city of that particular population size.* The latter qualification is important because it is in its consideration of this size effect that the minimum requirements approach differs from other approaches that have been proposed.[1]

The minimum requirement level for each economic activity is calculated by a statistical *averaging* of the data for a set of cities of a given population size range. The argument is that if a city of a certain size can exist with only so many percent of its employed in a particular economic activity, then presumably this minimum level is all that is really required in any other city of about the same size. This level could be considered as the nonbasic part of that economic sector, and a summing of the corresponding employment percentage figures over all the sectors gives an estimate of total nonbasic employment (as a percent) for a city of that size class.

A minimum requirements study has been made of the 101 United States metropolitan areas that had populations greater than 250,000 in 1960.[2] The cities were grouped into the size classes shown in Table 4.2 although the 24 metropolitan areas of over 1 million populations were not included in the calculations of the minimum requirements levels. These levels for the 1940, 1950, and 1960 data are shown in

Table 4.2 Minimum Percentages Employed in Cities of Varying Size Classes, 14-Industry Classification, 1960. [E. L. Ullman, M. F. Dacey, and H. Brodsky, The Economic Base of American Cities (Seattle: University of Washington Press, 1969), p. 26.]

Sector	Metropolitan Areas Over 1,000,000*		300,000–800,000		Cities 100,000–150,000	25,000–40,000	10,000–12,500	2,500–3,000
Agriculture	0.4	New York	Bridgeport	0.6	0.9	0.3	0.1	0.0
Mining	0.1	13 cities	Several	0.0	0.0	0.0	0.0	0.0
Construction	4.0	Detroit	Flint	3.4	3.5	3.2	2.7	0.4
Durables manufacturing	2.8	Washington	San Antonio	3.8	1.5	1.3	0.5	0.9
Nondurables manufacturing	4.0	San Diego	Flint	3.5	3.4	3.0	1.0	1.0
Transportation	5.1	San Diego	Flint	4.0	3.3	3.2	2.5	1.8
Wholesale	2.2	Washington	Wilmington	2.3	1.7	1.4	0.6	—
Retail	12.9	Washington	Bridgeport	12.6	12.3	12.2	10.5	9.7
Finance	3.5	Buffalo	Allentown	2.6	2.2	2.1	1.4	0.4
Business service	1.9	Baltimore	Utica	1.6	1.6	1.0	0.6	0.5
Personal service	3.7	Milwaukee	Wilkes-Barre†	3.7	2.5	3.3	2.3	1.9
Entertainment	0.6	Philadelphia	Hartford	0.4	0.4	0.2	0.2	0.0
Professional	10.1	Chicago	Ft. Lauderdale	9.3	8.0	7.8	6.0	5.9
Public administration	2.9	Houston	Allentown	2.2	2.2	2.4	1.6	0.9
Total	54.2			50.0	43.5	41.4	30.0	23.4

*Based on 24 cities, and not used in any calculations; all other size classes contain 38 cities and form basis for minima. Only free-standing SMSA's used; suburbs such as Jersey City, Gary-Hammond, even if classified as SMSA's by the Census, are not used for minima; similarly, no suburbs are used for minima in smaller SMSA's or cities.
†Actually, the lowest is Providence, at 3.5.

Professional services 1940
Professional services 1940
Professional services 1950
Professional services 1960
Retail 1960

Personal services 1960
Personal services 1950

Personal services 1960
Personal services 1950

Retail 1940
Retail 1950

10,000,000

1,000,000

100,000

10,000

Population size

0   2   4   6   8   10   14   16

Minimum employment as percentage of
SMSA employment

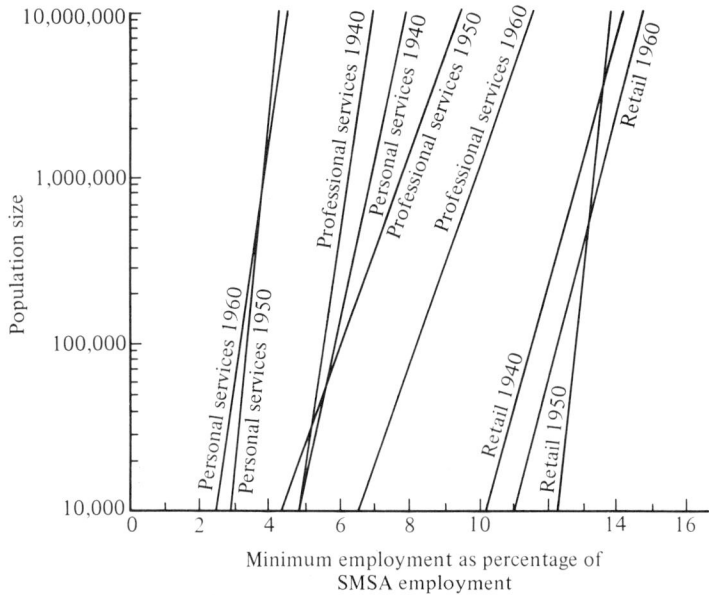

Figure 4.1 Minimum employment by industry and population size for U.S. SMSA's. [Based on E. L. Ullman, M. F. Dacey, and H. Brodsky, *The Economic Base of American Cities* (Seattle: University of Washington Press, 1969), p. 29.]

Figure 4.1. The graphs are read as follows: There are 14 different industries included, ranging from agriculture, through manufacturing, to professional services. Consider the example of retail trade. There are 3 lines or curves drawn under "Retail Trade," one each for 1940, 1950, and 1960. Looking at the 1960 line, we see that cities of around 10,000 population have at least 11% of their employment in retail trade. As the city size increases, this minimum level also increases until for cities of around 1 million population the percent is about $13\frac{1}{2}$.

There has been remarkable stability over time in the minima except in the cases of personal services and professional services. For the former, the 1950 and 1960 values are below that of 1940, which may reflect the decrease in the number of domestic servants. For professional services, the 1960 minima are higher than those of previous years, probably a function of the increases in the ranks of teachers and professional consultants.

Index of Diversity

Once the minima are computed, then the employment profile of each individual city can be compared with these values to determine the extent to which the city in question is specialized or diversified. An index of diversity, D, can be computed as follows:

$$D_k = \frac{\sum_i \left[(P_i - M_i)^2 / M_i \right]}{\left[\sum_i P_i - \sum_i M_i \right]^2 \Big/ \sum_i M_i}$$

where P_i is the percent of its labor force in industry i;

M_i is the minimum requirement in industry i for a city of the size of k;

$\sum$ is the sum of whatever term follows in the equation for all the values of i.

The calculation of this index by using the 1960 data gives the values shown in Table 4.3. At one extreme, high index values (but conversely low levels of diversity) are characteristic of mining and manufacturing cities such as Duluth-Superior (iron ore), Wilkes-

Table 4.3 Indices of Diversity for Selected U.S. Metropolitan Areas, 1960. [Based on E. L. Ullman, M. F. Dacey and H. Brodsky, *The Economic Base of American Cities* (Seattle: University of Washington Press, 1969), p. 62.]

SMSA	*Index*
Duluth-Superior, Minn.-Wis.	18.94
Washington, D.C.-Md.-Va.	11.80
Canton, Ohio	9.75
Wilkes-Barre–Hazelton, Pa.	7.79
Providence-Pawtucket, R.I.-Ma.	6.55
Tulsa, Okla.	6.10
Newark, N.J.	5.46
Utica-Rome, N.Y.	4.97
Springfield-Chicopee-Holyoke	4.73
St. Louis, Mo.–Ill.	4.32
Indianapolis, Ind.	3.94
Cincinnati, Ohio–Ky.	3.92
Seattle, Wash.	3.84
San Diego, Calif.	3.70
Phoenix, Ariz.	3.33
Houston, Texas	3.06
Tucson, Ariz.	2.92
Columbus, Ohio	2.67
Mobile, Ala.	2.62
Kansas City, Mo.–Kans.	2.26
Tacoma, Wash.	2.01
Omaha, Nebr.–Iowa	1.86
Jacksonville, Fla.	1.58
Spokane, Wash.	1.41

Barre–Hazelton (mining), while at the other extreme, low indices (that is, greater diversities) were characteristic of cities such as Omaha and Spokane.

What is the point of ranking cities using such an index? Obviously, it provides a basis upon which to classify cities, and we shall take up this topic in a following section. The measures themselves may also underline or emphasize the comparative roles that cities play in broader regional contexts. For example, the results in Table 4.3 suggest that in the state of Washington, Spokane (D = 1.41) is more diversified and serves more as a regional service center than does Seattle (D = 3.84). Again, Columbus, Ohio shows up as being more diversified in its role as a state capital than does Indianapolis, another state capital.

The computation of the index values also provides a measure of the probable sensitivities of different city economies to times of economic hardship. It might be expected that cities having highly specialized economies would be much more vulnerable to economic depressions, especially if the depressions occurred in the industries of specialization, than would cities having more diversified economies. This has proven to be the case for mining communities, as is illustrated in the regions of Appalachia. It has also been demonstrated in the case of specialized manufacturing cities, for example, Seattle with its overwhelming dependence on the aircraft industry. Serious problems of unemployment have occurred there since the early 1970's as a result of cutbacks in that industry's production.

We shall take up this question of urban sensitivity to economic change in a following section on city classification, but before we do this we must consider briefly one other approach to analyzing the external relations and interdependencies of a city's economic activities. This approach is called *input-output* analysis.

4.2 Urban Input-Output Analysis: A More Detailed Representation

As with the basic/nonbasic distinction, the emphasis here is on the fact that the economic functions of a city are tied in, to some degree or another, with activities that are located outside the city itself. But in input-output analysis there is even greater emphasis on the interdependencies that exist among the different activities making up the city economy, and it is only possible to consider the external relations of the city in a fairly aggregated manner. This difficulty reflects more the limitations of the available data rather than any weaknesses of the framework.

Input-output analysis is an accepted and very widely used tool of national economic planning. It involves partitioning the economy of a country into a number of sectors and analyzing the transactions that take place among these various sectors. The approach calls for very detailed information on the purchases and requirements of the various sectors of the economy and in those cases in which as many as 200 or 300 different sectors are identified the data requirements are tremendous. For the most part, input-output analysis has been mainly concerned with the interrelations among the sectors of particular national economies. An input-output table is a standard tool for national economic planning in almost all of the developed countries in the world. When the technique is applied in urban and regional analysis, there is an attempt to give greater emphasis to the relations that exist between the economy of the city or region and that of the rest of the country or nation.

The Stockholm Input-Output Model

This was an early attempt at fashioning an input-output model of an urban economy.[3] Sixty-two different production sectors in the city were identified along with 4 other groups of sectors, namely, industries in the rest of Sweden, foreign countries, government authorities, and households. The various transactions among these different sectors were then recorded in a table similar to Table 4.4. In this table each row of the production sectors shows how the total production from that sector was distributed among the various other sectors, and, in turn, any one of the columns from 1 to 62 showed where the purchases for that sector came from. The rows for "Foreign Countries" on the left represent imports that were used by the various production sectors in the city. The "Government Authorities" were the municipal government of the city of Stockholm, all other municipal authorities in Sweden, and the national government. The various rows under this sector represented forms of taxation. Finally, in the left-hand column the "Household Sector" involved households in Stockholm and households in the rest of Sweden. These rows presented data on wages and salaries and other forms of income.

The column headings across the top of the table show the same major groups of sectors. Any column among the 62 production sectors gives the information on the purchases made by that sector. The same holds true for the columns under the heading "Industries in Rest of Sweden" which are also purchasers of goods and services produced by the Stockholm economy. The "Foreign Countries" columns represent

Table 4.4 Stockholm Economy: A Diagrammatic Representation of the Intersectoral Flow Table. [After Roland Artle, *The Structure of the Stockholm Economy.* © 1965 by Cornell University. Used by permission of Cornell University Press.]

Outputs \ Inputs	Production Sectors 1 2 3 4 . . . 62	Industries in Rest of Sweden	Foreign Countries	Government Purchases and Transfers	Households	Grand Total
Production Sectors 1 2 3 . . 62	Transactions between productive sectors					
Industries in rest of Sweden						
Foreign countries						
Government						
Households						
Grand Total						

exports, and the "Government" columns represent the purchases made by the three different sectors of government. Similarly, under "Households" there is a column representing purchases made by households in Stockholm and another for purchases made by households in the rest of Sweden.

It should be noted, although it is not shown in the table, that certain other columns and rows have to be included in order to balance out the transaction table. This is particularly important in regard to the columns of the table that must include entries on investments, on increases in inventory, and on transfer payments. Similarly, in the set of headings on the left there must be balance items that represent depreciation, inventory decrease, and undistributed net profits.

Given these data on transactions and intersectoral flows, the next important step in an input-output analysis is to calculate the so-called *production* or *technical coefficients*. These are calculated only for the processing sector industries, in this case the 62, and they are calculated by dividing the entries in the 62 columns representing the production sectors by the corresponding columns totals. Any one of these technical coefficients is a measure of the amount of inputs required from each industry to produce one unit of output of a given industry. It is assumed that these technical coefficients are stable over time, or at least can be adjusted on the basis of new data, when the input-output table is used for forecasting the effects of changes in the output or demand of any sector on the whole economy.[4]

The method of input-output analysis has become a very useful tool in urban metropolitan planning in which agencies and decision makers are often interested in forecasting the effect of major decisions on the economy of their city. For example, the effects of cutbacks in military industries have been analyzed in this way.

The Philadelphia Input-Output Study

One of the most ambitious recent attempts to fashion an input-output analysis of an urban economy is the metropolitan Philadelphia study.[5] For this economy in 1960, information was gathered on approximately 1,000 manufacturing firms. Input-output coefficients were estimated for as many as 360 different manufacturing sectors (the vast majority of these were so-called *four-digit industries* in the SIC classification). This study has provided the basis for a number of different impact analyses of the Philadelphia economy and for certain studies that have thrown new light on the operation of a large urban economy.

Table 4.5 Distribution of Largest Input by Percent Locally Purchased for Four-Digit Philadelphia Manufacturing Industries. (G. Karaska, "Manufacturing Linkages in the Philadelphia Economy: Some Evidence of External Agglomeration Forces," *Geographical Analysis*, 4, 1969, p. 358. Reprinted by permission.)

Percent Locally Purchased	Number	Four-Digit Industries Percent	Cumulative Percent
0	78	27.7	27.7
01–10	46	16.3	44.0
11–20	24	8.5	52.5
21–30	17	6.0	58.5
31–40	14	5.0	63.5
41–50	16	5.7	69.2
51–60	9	3.2	74.2
61–70	9	3.2	75.6
71–80	14	5.0	80.6
81–90	13	4.6	85.2
91–99	13	4.6	89.8
100	29	10.3	100.0
Total	282	100.0	

Mean = 34.5%

An analysis of the various manufacturing linkages in the Philadelphia economy (Table 4.5) pointed up the fact that 44% of the Philadelphia industries purchased less than 10% of their largest input from local industries, and that the percentage of firms depending on local industries for more than half of their largest input was very small. In Table 4.6 the pattern of total purchases is analyzed in terms of the value of local versus imported purchases. The table shows that in terms of their dollar value, the imported inputs outweigh the local ones by about 4 to 1 in terms of the total figures. But it will be noted that for some industries the ratio is much higher, and only in the case of the newspaper industry (S.I.C. 27) does the value of local inputs exceed that of imported ones. A conclusion is that the effect of the Philadelphia economy on manufacturing location appears to be rather weak and the so-called *agglomeration effect,* which supposes that the existence of industries in a large urban area acts as an attraction to other industries, is not strongly borne out by these data. The industries examined seemed to rely much more heavily on suppliers from outside the city instead of on ones within.

Table 4.6   The Total Value of Four-Digit Inputs and the Value
of Locally Purchased vs. Imported Inputs, Sum-
marized by Two-Digit SIC in Thousand Dollars. (G.
Karaska, "Manufacturing Linkages in the Philadelphia Economy: Some Evidence of External Agglomeration Forces," *Geographical Analysis*, 4,
1969, p. 363. Reprinted by permission.)

Two-Digit S.I.C. (1)	Total Value of Purchased Inputs (2)	Value of Local Inputs (3)	Value of Imported Inputs (4)	Percent Local (3):(2)	Ratio (3):(4)
20	122,191	14,470	107,721	11.8	1:7.4
22	66,552	6,321	60,228	9.5	1:9.5
23	2,673	1,025	1,649	38.3	1:6.1
24	13,585	6,612	6,927	48.7	1:1.1
25	3,063	944	2,120	30.8	1:2.2
26	262,834	31,900	230,933	12.1	1:7.2
27	6,125	3,704	2,421	60.5	1:0.7
28	155,014	26,649	128,366	17.2	1:4.8
29	22,872	6,288	16,584	27.5	1:2.6
30	11,319	2,661	8,658	23.5	1:3.3
31	4,142	1,260	2,882	30.4	1:2.3
32	25,615	7,668	17,947	29.9	1:2.3
33	255,045	94,705	160,340	37.1	1:1.7
34	69,134	25,600	43,533	37.0	1:1.7
35	36,635	7,417	29,217	20.2	1:3.9
36	51,946	12,362	39,584	23.8	1:3.2
37	17,701	1,144	16,557	6.5	1:14.5
38	2,123	834	1,290	39.2	1:1.6
39	1,938	596	1,342	30.7	1:2.3
Other	284,838	543	284,842	0.0	1:524.6
Unclassified	74,994	37,535	37,463	50.1	1:1.0
Total	1,490,890	290,246	1,200,654	19.4	1:4.1

NOTE: Value is the dollar sum of the sample of Philadelphia manufacturing firms.

4.3   Central Place Functions: A Particular
Economic Role for Cities

In the above discussion we referred to a number of ways of studying the
total economic structure of cities. In many of their studies, however,
urban geographers have concentrated on only the service sector of the
urban economy and have given particular attention to the role of a city
as a service center for the surrounding rural region.

As was noted in the discussion of basic/nonbasic activities, cities
derive much of their economic support from their exporting goods to
regions outside the city itself. In an economic sense, *goods* may also
include services such as banking or hairdressing. Now the argument

in which we are interested goes as follows: In any farming region there will be a demand for goods and services originating with the farm population, and these people will be prepared to travel to nearby urban centers to obtain these goods and services. Certain patterns of farm-to-city travel result, and generalizations can be made about the sizes of areas that different cities serve. These questions are reviewed in Section 4.4. For the moment we are interested in the aspects of this discussion that have to do with the functions of the urban centers.

Central Place Functions

Economic activities whose continued economic well-being in the urban center is largely dependent on the location of the center somewhere central to a region of farm population demand are called *central place functions*. These are generally assumed to be service activities and do not include such activities as manufacturing that for the most part serve outside markets that may be more distant and very unevenly distributed. We do not mean to suggest that central locations are not sought after by manufacturing activities, for indeed they are; but their location in an urban center is not an expression of the *complementarity* in function that exists between that place as a central place and the surrounding rural region and its inhabitants.

In order to discuss some of the important central place considerations we need to establish one or two definitions. As noted above, a *central place function* is any activity carried on in the urban place that derives at least part of its support from people living in the rural areas around the place. For the most part, these are economic activities and in many studies the list of such functions has approached one hundred or so. The list typically includes such activities as "grocery and food provision," "laundering," "sale of hardware," "sale of clothes," "doctors," "dentists," and so on. Often the list is expanded to include social and cultural activities such as schools, churches, and clubs.

In most urban places any one central function will generally be offered by more than one business or unit. There may be, for example, five foodstores, several doctors and dentists, and two or three churches. Each operating unit offering a central function is counted as one *functional unit*. Obviously, the number of these must at least equal the number of central functions and it will usually be greater.

Finally, we note the possibility that any one building or *establishment* may involve more than one function and functional unit. For example, a general store that sold mainly food might also have a hardware section and serve as a post office. In this case, we have one establishment, three functions (sale of food, sale of hardware, post office) and three functional units. This distinction between establishment and functional unit may be important in certain cases, but on the

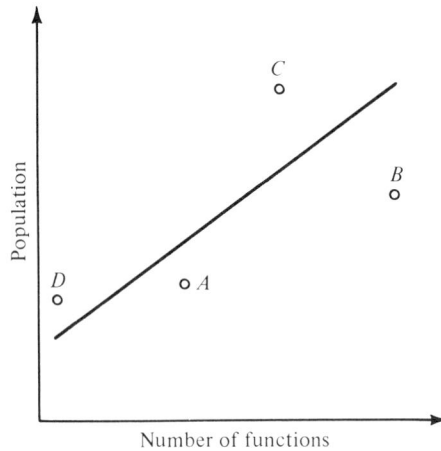

Figure 4.2   Hypothetical relationship between urban population size and number of urban functions in a central place.

whole it does not warrant much emphasis. In the following discussion we shall concentrate on number of functions and functional units.

Population Size and Central Place Functions

What relationships might we expect to exist between these features of an urban place and also between them and its population size?

First, we might anticipate that over a set of urban places the number of functions and population size should be positively related, that is to say, the larger-sized centers should offer more functions, the smaller ones fewer. The graph of this relationship should look something like Figure 4.2. This seems intuitively appealing since we can expect that more people will visit the larger centers and that this greater "pulling power" combined with the larger population in the town itself will enable certain more specialized functions to be offered there whereas these same ones could not be economically offered in the smaller places. By way of example, we can note that specialized medical clinics can be found in larger towns but they are absent in the very small urban places.

This positive relationship between size and number of functions has been confirmed in a number of studies for different areas all around the world. Table 4.7 presents a summary of some of these studies and we note the correlation coefficient that was obtained in each case for the number of functions-population size relationship. Clearly, the relationship is a strong positive one.

Assume that the data for a set of urban places is plotted on the

Table 4.7 Relationship Between Urban Population Size and Number of Urban Functions in Different Areas.

Study	Correlation Coefficient, r
Iowa[a]	0.890
Canterbury, N.Z.[b]	0.823
S. Illinois[c]	0.892
Barrie area, Ontario[d]	0.870
Wales[e]	0.87

[a]B. J. L. Berry, H. G. Barnum, and R. J. Tennant, "Retail location and consumer behavior," *Papers*, Regional Science Assoc., **9**, 1962, pp. 65–106.

[b]L. J. King, "The functional role of small towns in the Canterbury area," *Proceedings*, Third N.Z. Geography Conference, 1962, pp. 139–149.

[c]H. A. Stafford, Jr., "The functional bases of small towns," *Economic Geography*, **39**, 1963, pp. 165–75.

[d]J. U. Marshall, "The location of service towns. An approach to the analysis of central place systems," *Research Publications*, Dept. of Geography, University of Toronto, 1969.

[e]H. Carter, H. A. Stafford, and M. M. Gilbert, "Functions of Welsh towns: implications for central place notions," *Economic Geography*, **46**, 1970, pp. 25–38.

graph in Figure 4.2 and that one or two cases fall either well above (for example, points *A* and *B* in Figure 4.2) or well below (points *C* and *D*) the average relationship suggested by the straight line. How do we explain these deviations? The places represented by points *A* and *B* obviously have more functions than is suggested by the model. We might speculate that *A* is possibly a small center that enjoys a very advantageous location, for example, at the junction of two major highways, and can therefore support on the basis of a high volume of through traffic more functions than might otherwise have been the case. City *B* might also be similarly located or we might speculate that this is an important regional center comparatively isolated from other towns of a similar size and therefore able to offer a wider range of functions. By contrast, places *C* and *D* have fewer functions than are suggested by the model. Place *C* might be a suburban community located fairly close to a larger city and therefore cast in the role of a residential community. Since persons living there presumably rely upon the larger city in which many of them work for the provision of goods and services, place *C* does not need to offer them. Place *D*, however, could be a small place, a *hamlet*, as it is often called in North America, which has suffered from improved transportation systems that now enable people to bypass it on their way to larger centers.

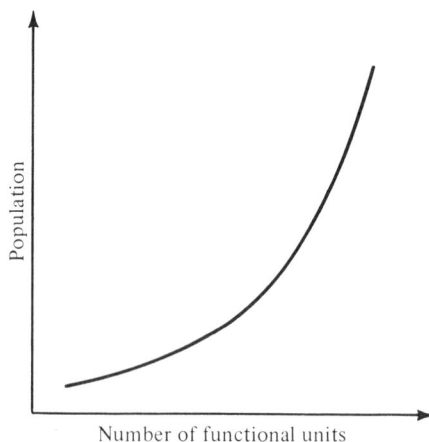

Figure 4.3 Hypothetical relationship between urban population size and number of functional units in a central place.

People, most probably older people, still live there but many of the center's economic functions have disappeared.

Population Size and Number of Functional Units

What of the relationship between the number of functional units and population size? In this case, we might reasonably anticipate some sort of nonlinear relationship such as is shown in Figure 4.3. This requires that as population size increases, the number of functional units increases, fairly rapidly up to a point and thereafter at a slower rate. This would be consistent with the notion that in larger centers certain economies of size become feasible and larger operating units begin to be substituted for several smaller ones. The point is illustrated in the case of foodstores; in large centers big supermarkets replace the separate foodstores that are more typical in the smaller urban places.

Again, deviations from this generalized relationship could be explained in terms of the town's particular location and/or the presence of functions other than central ones. Studies have confirmed that this relationship between size and the number of functional units is a strong positive one.

Threshold Sizes

This relationship has also provided a basis for estimating the *threshold* level for a function. The threshold level is defined as the minimum level of support, as measured by numbers of population, required to support a function in a particular community. For example, if there were 5 hairdressers serving a total population of 8,000 in both the town itself and its surrounding region, then a crude estimate of the threshold level for this function might simply be $8,000/5 = 1,600$ persons. But since this ratio is certain to vary from town to town, some form of statistical averaging is preferable.

One such statistical approach assumes that the relationship between population size (P) and number of stores (N) for each central place function is described by the following equation:[6]

$$P = A(B^N)$$

The coefficients A and B are calculated by using data on the number of stores for each central place function and the population sizes of a selected group of urban places. In the case of foodstores, for example, there would be for each town a measure of how many foodstores it has and its population size. These two numbers along with the corresponding ones for the other towns are used to determine the statistical estimates of A and B. The same procedure applies to every other central place function.

Once the values of A and B are determined for a given central place function, the corresponding population size can be calculated by substituting a value of $N = 1$ in the above equation. This is interpreted as the threshold population, the population that on the average is required to support one store of that function in the group of towns considered. There will be a different threshold population for each central place function.

The relationship of number of functional units to number of central functions should be of the same form as the one between population size and number of functional units; indeed, the same rationale should apply and a strong positive relationship between the two features should exist. This has been confirmed in a number of studies.[7]

Arising out of many of the analyses of population size/number of functions/number of functional units relationships have been attempts to identify *hierarchies* of functions and urban places. The approach usually has been as follows: In ranking the central functions, either with respect to the associated number of functional units or some computed threshold value, *breaks* are identified that separate levels of the hierarchy. This classification of either functions or places into hierarchies provides a means of organizing the information, but to date there is little evidence to suggest that the different hierarchies that have been identified have prompted any new or worthwhile generalizations about the functional role of the towns in question.

4.4   Elements of Economic Change in a Set of Cities

We have stressed in this book how cities differ in regard to their accessibility within the urban network and in the functions they perform. On the basis of these two comparisons alone, and ignoring for the moment the important contrasts that exist between cities in other significant factors such as the political structure, the progressiveness of the community leaders and local businessmen, income levels, quality of the labor force, and the nature of the amenities available, it might be anticipated that different cities in the system are going to experience very different rates and levels of economic change.

Sensitivity to Economic Fluctuations

One important element of economic change among cities is their differing sensitivities to cyclical fluctuations. How does the impact and the timing of economic fluctuations, either up or down, vary among the cities of a region or country?

Assume that an economic fluctuation has been introduced into the system from outside (for example, one stemming from a major decision at the national level on economic policy). It might be anticipated that in the transmission of this fluctuation some cities will be hit harder than others (witness Seattle's plight in comparison to say Chicago's as a consequence of cutbacks in the aerospace industry) and that the impact will be felt sooner in some cities than in others (for example, a strike by the national union of autoworkers in the United States is felt first in the cities of southern Michigan and then later in the cities that supply the steel, glass, rubber, and so on).

These issues have been studied in regard to unemployment levels in metropolitan areas in the United States over the period 1960–1965.[8] The aim was to try to explain variation in the levels of unemployment within each city over the time period in terms of the city's employment mix, the national trend in unemployment over the same period (allowing, however, for some possible time lag in this effect), and finally, seasonal effects. Figure 4.4 maps the values of one of the coefficients estimated for each city. This particular coefficient measures how sensitive the city's economy is to national changes. A value of 1 means that the city's unemployment pattern over the time period in question exactly mirrors the national effect, given that the city's industry mix is taken into account. Values greater than 1 (for example, Wheeling, West Virginia, 1.82) suggest that the cities in question are highly sensitive to the national effects, whereas cities that have values less than 1 (Denver, Colorado, 0.42) are much more stable and less responsive to the national trends.

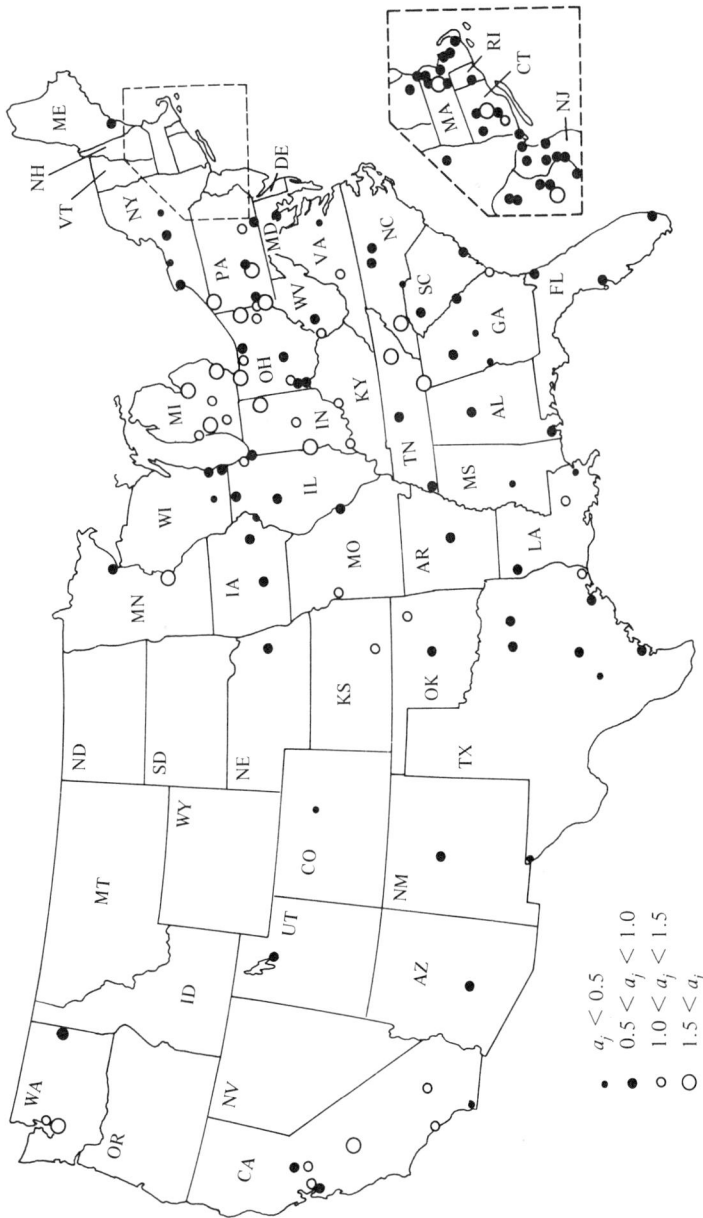

Figure 4.4 Measures of city sensitivity to national changes in unemployment. [L. J. King et al., "Cyclical fluctuations in unemployment levels in U.S. metropolitan areas," *Tijdschrift voor Economische en Sociale Geografie,* **63**, 1972, p. 351.]

Legend:
- $a_j < 0.5$
- $0.5 < a_j < 1.0$
- $1.0 < a_j < 1.5$
- $1.5 < a_j$

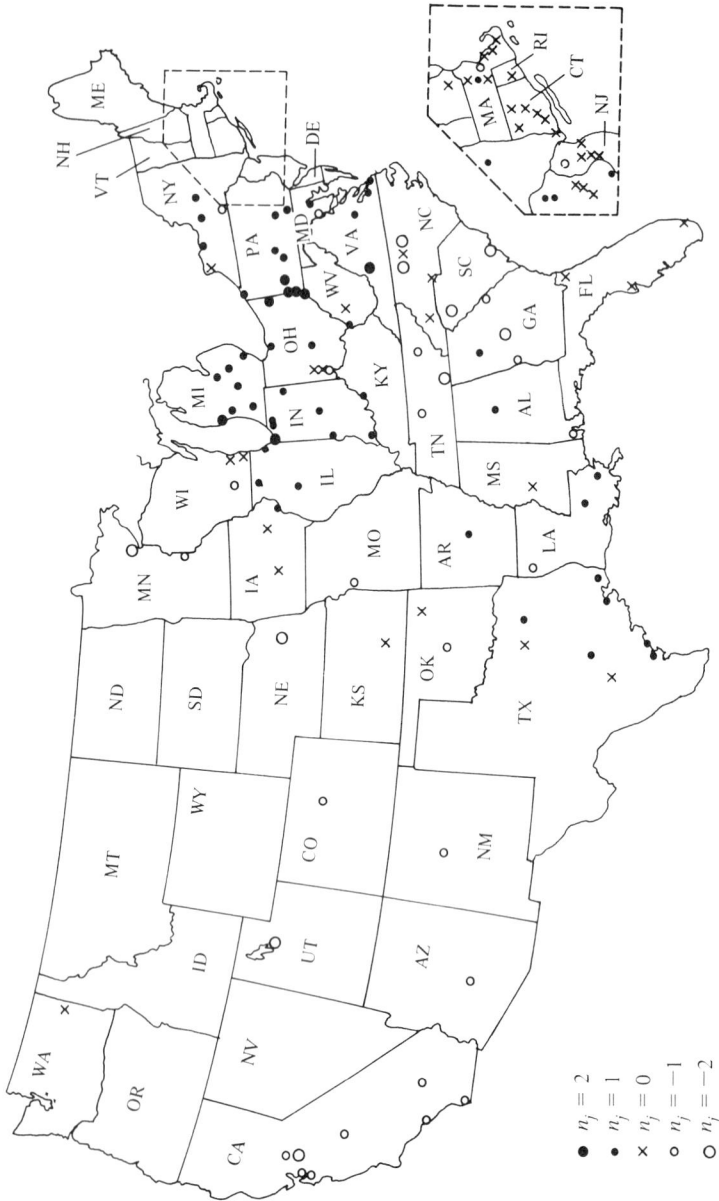

Figure 4.5 Time lags for the cities. [L. J. King et al., "Cyclical fluctuations in unemployment levels in U.S. metropolitan areas," *Tijdschrift voor Economische en Sociale Geografie*, **63**, 1972, p. 350.]

Legend:

- $n_j = 2$ ●
- $n_j = 1$ ●
- $n_j = 0$ ×
- $n_j = -1$ ○
- $n_j = -2$ ○

A second map, Figure 4.5, shows the pattern of values for the time lags associated with the varying responses of the cities to the national trend. The map reveals that Midwestern cities generally lead the nation by one month, and sometimes two, and that cities west of the Mississippi River typically lag behind. In New England and the northeast the city responses generally approximated the nation in their timing.

The above lines of analysis throw some light on the question of why certain cities outperform others in their growth. Obviously, the industry mix of the town in question is a major factor contributing to its growth characteristics. A town that is highly specialized in industries that experience marked fluctuations in the demands for their products as income levels rise or fall or as technological changes occur is likely to have a much more erratic growth record in employment and population than is a town that has a more diversified and balanced economy. Diversity is likely to mean greater economic stability, and, for the most part, diversity increases with city size.

Analysis of Urban Growth Rates

Table 4.8 shows the population growth levels for 1950–1960 for some 25 large metropolitan areas in the United States. There are two major lines of explanation usually offered for why some of the cities shown in Table 4.8 grow faster than others. The first is the *export-base hypothesis,* discussed in an earlier part of this chapter. This argument goes as follows. An increase in basic employment, which is determined by forces outside the region or city, is seen as the trigger in setting off an increase in the demand for labor in the production of nonbasic goods and services within the region (city). The effect of the increased demand for labor in the basic sector is thus multiplied, and the overall employment and presumably the population of the region or city is increased. An alternative hypothesis states that it is not so much the varying levels of demand for labor that account for the different growth performances of regions, but rather the differential shifts in the supply of labor available to the manufacturing activities in the regions. These shifts, it is argued, reflect migration and the relative importance of manufacturing in the region. The point is that whenever manufacturing is a smaller proportion of total employment, it is likely to be relatively more attractive in terms of earnings than other activities and it will attract employees from those activities.

A study of the growth rates in Table 4.8 by Richard Muth seemed to bear out the second hypothesis more than the first.[9] Although the results were not strongly convincing, Muth found that for the metropolitan areas employment change and migration levels strongly in-

Table 4.8 Population Growth Rates, 1950–1960, for Selected
U.S. Metropolitan Areas. [After R. F. Muth, "Differential growth characteristics among large U.S.
cities," in J. P. Quirk and A. M. Zarley, eds., *Papers
in Quantitative Economics* (Lawrence: University
Press of Kansas, 1968).]

City	*Percent Change 1950–1960*
Akron, Ohio	27.7
Allentown-Bethlehem-Easton, Pa.	12.4
Buffalo, N.Y.	20.0
Canton, Ohio	20.2
Cincinnati, Ohio	24.0
Columbus, Ohio	34.1
Detroit, Mich.	24.7
Erie, Pa.	14.3
Grand Rapids, Mich.	27.6
Houston, Texas	51.6
Indianapolis, Ind.	29.9
Kansas City, Mo.	28.7
Los Angeles, Calif.	45.5
New Orleans, La.	27.3
New York, N.Y.	11.9
Peoria, Ill.	15.3
Philadelphia, Pa.	18.3
Pittsburgh, Pa.	8.7
Portland, Oregon	16.6
Reading, Pa.	7.7
Rochester, N.Y.	19.1
San Diego, Calif.	85.5
San Francisco, Calif.	24.0
Toledo, Ohio	18.8
Utica-Rome, N.Y.	16.4

fluenced one another. The ratio of employment change to migration
change, called the *elasticity*, was very close to one.

A similar study has been made of the growth of cities in Ontario
and Quebec, Canada, from 1941 to 1961 in terms of the structural
characteristics of the urban system.[10] For some 70 cities having populations greater than 10,000 in 1961 (Table 4.9) it was possible to account for almost all the variation in the population growth levels by the
following factors:

1. Percent of the city's population aged 14 years or under in 1961.
   This measure of demographic structure distinguished between
   cities on the basis of their age structure. The cities having the
   more youthful populations were the faster growing cities.

Table 4.9 Growth Levels 1941–1961 for Ontario and Quebec Cities. (S. Golant and L. S. Bourne, "Growth characteristics of the Ontario–Quebec urban system," *Research Report No. 4*, Centre for Urban and Community Studies, University of Toronto, Toronto, 1968, pp. 26–27, Appendix A.)

Ontario		Quebec	
City	Percent Growth 1941–1961	City	Percent Growth 1941–1961
Barrie	117.7	Arvida	215.7
Belleville	95.1	Asbestos	94.1
Brockville	56.4	Cap-de-la Madeleine	125.1
Brampton	206.8	Chicoutimi	71.7
Brantford	72.8	Drummondville	164.4
Chatham	97.4	Grand Mère	83.6
Cobourg	78.2	Granby	121.6
Cornwall	209.1	Joliette	41.9
Fort William	47.8	Jonquière	107.6
Georgetown	302.0	Kénogami	79.6
Guelph	71.2	La Tuque	64.5
Hamilton	99.9	Magog	45.4
Kenora	40.8	Montréal	84.2
Kingston	77.7	Noranda	150.8
Kitchener	121.9	Québec	59.1
Lindsay	35.7	Rivière-du Loup	24.4
London	99.2	Rimouski	153.1
Niagara Falls	8.6	Rouyn	112.5
North Bay	52.5	Shawinigan	58.3
Orillia	56.6	Shawinigan-South	455.8
Oshawa	132.8	Sherbrooke	85.1
Ottawa	89.9	Sorel	40.0
Owen Sound	24.4	St. Hyacinthe	25.6
Pembroke	50.5	St. Jean	97.8
Peterborough	86.1	St. Jérome	116.7
Port Arthur	85.4	Thetford Mines	70.0
Port Colborne	112.9	Trois Rivières	27.3
Sarnia	172.1	Val D'Or	150.5
Sault Ste. Marie	67.0	Valleyfield	60.1
St. Catharines	179.0	Victoriaville	119.8
Stratford	20.1		
St. Thomas	31.2		
Sudbury	97.5		
Timmins	1.7		
Toronto	100.5		
Trenton	58.4		
Welland	188.6		
Whitby	148.7		
Windsor	56.0		
Woodstock	64.4		

2. Percent of rented dwelling units in the city in 1961. This, and the following two factors, were measures of the physical structure of the city. In this case, the relationship with population growth proved to be an inverse one. The cities having high levels of population growth were ones in which there was an emphasis not on rented units but on single-family housing construction.

3. Percent of dwelling units in the city in need of major repairs. Again, this measure was smaller in the case of the more rapidly growing cities in which the total number of housing units would also be growing and the proportion of substandard units would be falling.

4. Percent of dwelling units in the city occupied by the head of the household for more than 10 years. Perhaps not surprisingly, this measure of age was related in a negative manner to population growth. The faster growing cities had the lower values on this index.

5. Percent change in the value of industrial permits issued in the city, 1951–1961. This was an expression of the relationship between urban growth and the level of industrial development, specifically in new plant construction.

The fact that these different measures varied from city to city helped account for the fact that population growth also varied from city to city. When the same analysis was completed separately for the two provinces using the same mix of factors, the levels of explanation of city-to-city variations in population growth were even higher than for the combined system. This distinctiveness of the provincial groupings of cities in Canada shows up in almost all studies of urban growth in that country.

4.5 Classifying Cities:
A Statistical Exercise or an Aid in Predictions?

The literature on the classification of cities is extensive and yet often confusing in the sense that it is not always at all clear why classification is important. In any context, one usually seeks to classify objects as a way of organizing and summarizing a mass of information such that new insights will be gained or particular purposes will be served. Hence, in classifying cities on the basis of their economic characteristics, one might hope that new information would be yielded concerning, for example, the relative susceptibility of the different city types to economic downswings. Or, a classification of cities might be of use, for example, to a market researcher seeking to identify certain representative cities in which to test market some new products.

Classification may be based on a few selected features or on a very broad set of characteristics. We shall briefly illustrate this point by reviewing two examples of city classifications.

Cities of the Soviet Union

Table 4.10 shows a functional classification of the cities of the Soviet Union based on the proportions of the gainfully occupied persons in each city found in mining, manufacturing, construction, transportation, and communication; city size; and administrative functions.

Table 4.10 Functional Classification of the Major Cities of the USSR in 1959. [Based on C. D. Harris, *Cities of the Soviet Union* (Chicago: Rand McNally and Co., 1970), p. 68. Reproduced by permission of the Association of American Geographers.]

Functional Types	*Number of Cities*
Diversified Administrative Cities	
Capitals of Union Republics	
Population over 500,000	10
Population 250,000–499,999	6
Centers of oblasts or similar units	
Population over 500,000	21
Population 250,000–499,999	27
Population 100,000–249,999	57
Population 50,000–99,999	13
Total	134
Local Centers	15
Industrial Cities	
Manufacturing	
Population over 100,000	42
Population 50,000–99,999	40
Manufacturing and mining	
Population over 100,000	29
Population 50,000–99,999	15
Mining, primary processing, and energy	10
Total	136
Other Specialized Cities (transport, resorts, education and research, naval bases, suburbs)	19
Total Number of Cities	304

Table 4.11   Importance of Manufacturing and Mining in Occupational Structure of Soviet Cities of More Than
50,000 Population in 1959.   [Based on C. D.
Harris, *Cities of the Soviet Union* (Chicago: Rand
McNally and Co., 1970), p. 60. Reproduced by
permission of the Association of American Geographers.]

	Percentage of Gainfully Occupied in Manufacturing and Mining	*Number of Cities*
Soviet Average	Less than 30	39
	30–40	86
	41–50	76
	51–60	73
	Over 60	30
		304

The overwhelming majority of the cities are classed as either "diversified administrative centers" or "industrial cities," a reflection of the
centralized, planned society of the Soviet Union. The identification of
the specialized industrial centers is based in part on the information
given in Table 4.11.   This shows the distribution of the 304 cities
among employment percentage categories above and below the average value for the total of the two occupations of mining and manufacturing. It is worth noting that in almost one third of the cities (103 of
them), 50 percent or more of the gainfully occupied people are in
manufacturing and mining. This is in marked contrast to the situation
in the United States where more diversified economies are characteristic of the larger cities and the service sector usually looms larger in
relative importance. In addition to these 103 cities, Table 4.10 showed
that there were 33 other cities whose occupational structures were
dominated by manufacturing, mining, primary processing, or energy
production, or different combinations of these, such that they rated as
"industrial cities."

Employment Growth Patterns
Among United States Metropolitan Areas

As a second but different example of a city classification we consider a classification of United States metropolitan areas based upon
their patterns of employment growth over the period 1957 to 1969. A
statistical analysis of the employment growth measures for all cities revealed four underlying patterns or trends.[11] The first had to do with

the differences between the cities in the rate of employment growth after the effect of differing city size had been taken into account. Some cities, for example, those in the west and southwest of the United States, grew much faster than average while others, particularly those in the northeastern sections of the country, grew at a rate much slower than the average for all 128 areas.

The three remaining underlying trends or patterns all focused on differences between the cities in the timing of the employment growth. The first indexed the general timing of growth over the period with manufacturing cities in Indiana, Ohio, eastern Michigan, and north-western Pennsylvania experiencing almost all their growth in the latter part of the period 1957–1969, while almost all the remaining cities had growth more evenly distributed over the whole period. A second difference in the timing of growth involved the impact of short-term upswings and downswings on local employment growth. Some cities, especially those manufacturing centers in the northeast, appeared very sensitive to such short-run changes (for example, the 1958 and 1961 recessions), but cities in the south, southwest, and west had much more stable employment growth patterns. The third difference in timing reflected the importance of seasonal factors: the cities to the west of the Mississippi generally had greater than average seasonal fluctuations while those to the east were less sensitive to this element of change.

If the underlying patterns of the differences in the rates of growth, the general timing of growth, and the sensitivity to cyclical fluctuations are put together (that is, with only the seasonality factor ignored), then the classification of the cities as shown in Table 4.12 emerges. The

Table 4.12 Classification of U.S. SMSA's by Growth Characteristics. [Based on L. J. King *et al.,* "Classifying U.S. cities: Spatial-temporal patterns in employment growth," *Growth and Change,* **3,** 1972, p. 41.]

Group	Sign of Parameter for Reference Curve			Growth Characteristics	Number of Cities
	Rate	*Timing*	*Stability*		
1	+	−	−	Fast/Early/Stable	48
2	+	−	+	Fast/Early/Unstable	6
3	+	+	−	Fast/Late/Stable	0
4	+	+	+	Fast/Late/Unstable	1
5	−	−	−	Slow/Early/Stable	21
6	−	−	+	Slow/Early/Unstable	9
7	−	+	−	Slow/Late/Stable	11
8	−	+	+	Slow/Late/Unstable	32

major distinction revealed by the table is between groups 1 and 8 and this is essentially between the fast/early/cyclically stable growth of most southern, southwestern. and west coast cities such as Atlanta, Fort Worth-Dallas, Phoenix, Los Angeles, and Seattle (group 1) and the slow/late/cyclically unstable growth of the northeastern manufacturing cities such as Albany, Buffalo, Pittsburgh, Cleveland, and Detroit (group 8). In between these two groups are the cities of New England with slow but cyclically stable growth (group 5 cities such as Manchester, Boston, and Lowell), the cyclically sensitive southern Appalachian cities (for example, Chattanooga in group 6, Knoxville and Altoona in group 8, and Huntington-Ashland in group 4), the slow-growth but cyclically stable cities of Georgia and Alabama (Augusta, Savannah, and Birmingham in group 7), and the slow-growth midwestern cities such as Milwaukee, Peoria, Des Moines, and Omaha which had early and cyclically stable growth.

These are but two examples chosen from a very large number of classifications that have been made of cities in almost all countries of the world. These studies have in some cases been much simpler in design; in others they have been more complicated. One recent classification of United States cities, for example, considered as many as 97 different features for more than 1,700 communities.[12] But these statistical exercises often seem to serve little point other than to tax the ingenuity of the statistical analyst and the computer programmer! A classification should serve some purpose, either by providing new knowledge about the processes that are at work or as a means of predicting future developments. The classification of the Soviet Union cities on the basis of their economic characteristics gave results that seemed consistent with the planned character of that society. This was hardly new knowledge, but the classification did provide a summary of a large mass of information about the cities in question. In this sense, it contributed toward a simplification and, at the same time, a sharpening of the descriptions of that urban society.

The classification of United States metropolitan areas did something more. It grouped the cities on the basis of their past economic performances, specifically employment growth, and suggested that some cities were more susceptible than others to economic fluctuations. Here is information that might be used in predicting the future impact of various developments in the economy, be they planned or unplanned. If there is to be a recessionary development (associated with a national labor strike in some sector or a cutback in production stemming from trade imbalances), then it would be possible to identify in the classification of cities those communities that probably would be affected the most (and the earliest) by the trend. The more the classification was refined, the better would be these predictions.

4.6 Summary

In this chapter we have begun to look at the economic functions that cities perform. Although many other factors may have influenced the original founding and location of cities, it is the economic function that has come to be critical in their continued existence. With the development of trade and commerce both at the international and national levels, the cities have become the important economic centers in these trading networks.

We considered different ways of analyzing and describing the economic functions of cities. At first, we discussed the simple basic/ nonbasic distinction in regard to the activities of a city. Then with the input-output table we saw how the interrelations and interdependencies of the different activities could be analyzed. The recognition of the spatial interdependency of town and country, of the special roles that many cities play as service centers for the surrounding rural areas, led us then to a consideration of central places and their particular economic functions.

The economy of a city is a changing one over time. Therefore, we next examined some of the features of urban economic growth. We saw how in the United States certain cities were much more responsive than others to economic changes taking place at the national level. We also reviewed the factors that seem to best account for the varying levels of growth that occur among the different cities of both the United States and Canada. Finally, we noted how the economic characteristics of cities can be used as the basis for classifying those cities.

In all of this discussion we have been concerned with sets of cities, and our emphasis has been on the variation from city to city either in the economic functions performed or the level of economic change. In Chapter 6 we shall consider the economic activities of a city from the point of view of the internal patterns of land use within the city. But before we turn to this, in the next chapter we shall discuss some abstract statements or "theories" about systems of cities and their economic functions. The discussion builds upon the ideas we have introduced in this chapter, but it demands that we think much more precisely about the relations that are involved.

Notes

1. See earlier studies by G. ALEXANDERSSON, *The Industrial Structure of American Cities* (Lincoln: University of Nebraska Press, 1956); I. MORRISSETT, "The economic structure of American cities," *Papers,* Regional Science Association, **4**, 1958, pp. 239–56.

2. E. L. Ullman, M. E. Dacey and H. Brodsky, *The Economic Base of American Cities* (Seattle: University of Washington Press, 1969).

3. R. Artle, *The Structure of the Stockholm Economy* (Ithaca: Cornell University Press, 1965).

4. The use of input-output tables for forecasting requires mathematical analysis of the technical coefficients. Specifically, the inverse of the matrix of technical coefficients is required. See Artle, *op. cit.*, Chapter 2.

5. W. Isard et al., *The Philadelphia Region Input–Output Coefficient Table* (Philadelphia: Regional Science Research Institute, 1967).

6. See B. J. L. Berry and W. L. Garrison, "The functional bases of the central-place hierarchy," *Economic Geograpy*, **34**, 1958, pp. 145–54.

7. See J. U. Marshall, "The location of service towns. An approach to the analysis of central-place systems," *Research Publications*, Department of Geography, University of Toronto, 1969.

8. L. J. King et al., "Cyclical fluctuations in unemployment levels in U.S. Metropolitan areas," *Tijdschrift voor Economische en Sociale Geografie*, **63**, 1972, pp. 345–52.

9. R. F. Muth, "Differential growth among large U.S. cities," in J. P. Quirk and A. M. Zarley, eds., *Papers in Quantitative Economics* (Lawrence: University Press of Kansas, 1968).

10. S. Golant and L. S. Bourne, "Growth characteristics of the Ontario-Quebec urban system," *Research Report No. 4*, Centre for Urban and Community Studies, University of Toronto, Toronto, 1968.

11. L. J. King et al., "Classifying U.S. cities. Spatial-temporal patterns in employment growth," *Growth and Change*, **3**, 1972, pp. 37–42.

12. R. L. Forstall, "A new social and economic grouping of cities," *The Municipal Year Book 1970* (Washington D.C.: The International City Management Association, 1970), pp. 102–70.

chapter 5

Abstract Representations of City Systems

In Chapter 1 of this book we noted that one approach to urban geography considered as a social science has favored attempts to develop theories or models of the spatial organization of urban society. In this chapter we shall consider some of these attempts especially as they relate to the development of theories of urban settlement. In general, these theories seek to account for the size, number, and location of urban settlements in any large region.

5.1 Central Place Theory: Christaller's Intellectually Rich Abstraction

The theory first formalized by Walter Christaller in 1933[1] was essentially a verbal theory largely based on his observations of the Southern Germany of his time. It relied upon certain notions of rational economic behavior on the parts of the business firms and the farm populations. For the former this meant that in order to make maximum profits they had to capture as wide a market area in which to sell their goods and services as was possible. This meant trying to locate as far as possible from competitors. For the farm population who were the consumers, economic rationality was expressed in terms of a desire to minimize the costs of travel and, therefore, to purchase goods and services from the nearest firm selling them. Economic rationality also implied for both groups that they had perfect knowledge of the alternatives open to them.

Assumptions and Definitions

In the development of any theory of the real world it is always necessary to make certain limiting assumptions in order to be able to focus on those features that are of interest. Thus, for example, in attempting to develop a theory of an urban system that emphasizes the economic dependencies between towns and rural areas it would be inappropriate to attempt to consider such features as the importance of a defensible site or the existence of mineral springs thought to have healing powers as the reasons for the locations of particular towns. These factors may be important in other discussions, but they are irrelevant to the development of this theory and are excluded by the following assumptions:

1. There is an unbounded homogeneous plain with uniform soil fertility and resources; uniformly distributed over it is a population that is homogeneous in respect to income (purchasing power), the demands for goods, and patterns of consumption.
2. There is a uniform transport system that allows all urban places of the same size to be equally accessible; transport costs are directly proportional to distance, and movement is possible in all directions across the plain.
3. Producers and consumers are economically rational persons who have complete and perfect knowledge that allows them to behave in the optimizing fashion described above; that is, they maximize profits or minimize their transport costs.
4. Consumers patronize the nearest centers in which required goods and services are available and pay, therefore, the costs of the goods at the locations plus the transportation costs to their homes.
5. The demands of the rural areas are fully met by the minimum number of necessary central places; no areas are unserved and no restrictions other than economic ones limit the number of producers.

Given these simplifications the problem becomes one of defining an urban system that has the necessary minimum number of places and that satisfies the economic and behavioral constraints. Such a system of urban places will represent an *equilibrium solution* to the problem in the sense that if the above assumptions remain unchanged and if no changes occur in the other features such as population distribution and density, demands, and cost, then the urban system will remain unchanged.

At this point it is necessary to establish certain definitions. A *central place* is defined as a settlement at the center of a region. The dominant function of the place is to provide market and supply functions for the region. The *order* of a place depends on the size of the region that is served. Places serving large regions are higher-order places; those serving small market areas are lower-order places. Economic functions offered only by large places with their associated market areas are referred to as higher order functions than those offered by the smaller urban places. In order to define one of the other important concepts, that of the *range* of a good, it is necessary to consider some of the economic underpinnings of central place theory.[2]

Spatial Demand Curves

Consider a place on the plain that is producing a particular good demanded by the farm population (a brewery producing beer is the well-known example used in this discussion). What is the level of the demand for beer at different prices by any one farm household (remember our earlier assumption that the household has to pay the transport cost from the brewery)? Figure 5.1 shows that as the brewery price increases, the demand falls off. This is consistent with notions of consumer behavior. Assume that the household's income is fixed but the price of beer rises; there is less money to spend on other items and the associated trade-offs become more and more critical until at a certain beer price, P_0, the household decides to buy no beer at all and to spend its income on other items. The particular shape of the curve in Figure 5.1 will depend on the relative preference for beer as against the other items in the householder's budget and also on the degree to which other goods can be substituted for beer.

Now the information given in Figure 5.1 can be translated into another graph showing how the household's demand is related to the distance it is located away from the brewery. In Figures 5.1 and 5.2 we see that at the brewery the amounts demanded will be q_1, q_2, and q_3, depending on the brewery price. Adding transport costs to these prices means that the product becomes more expensive farther away from the brewery until at some distances the households cannot afford

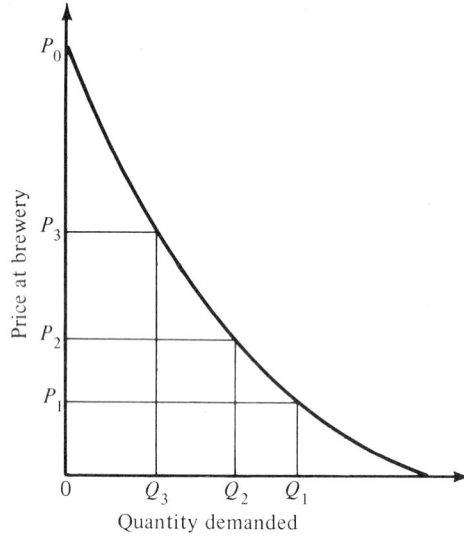

Figure 5.1   Quantity of beer demanded as a function of brewery price. [After J. B. Parr and K. G. Denike, "Theoretical problems in central place analysis," *Economic Geography*, **46**, 1970.]

to buy beer and, therefore, the demand is zero (the points s_3, s_2, and s_1 in Figure 5.2 that relate to the different fixed brewery prices of P_3, P_2, and P_1).

The above information can then be translated into a curve that shows the total market demand facing a single producer. This *free spatial demand curve* is shown as line D_1 in Figure 5.3. Also shown is a

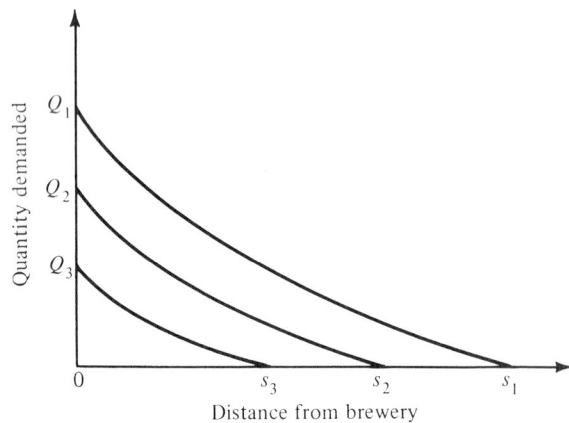

Figure 5.2   Demand curves for beer as a function of price and distance. [After J. B. Parr and K. G. Denike, "Theoretical problems in central place analysis," *Economic Geography*, **46**, 1970.]

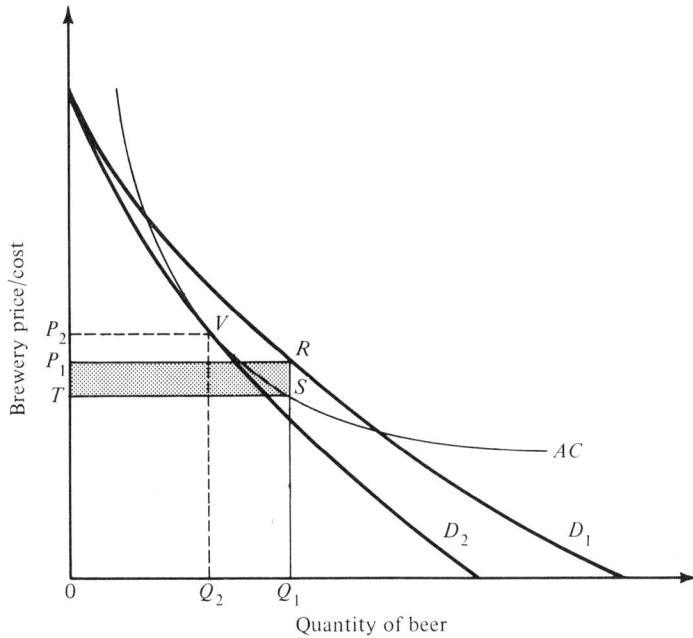

Figure 5.3 Cost and demand curves for a single brewery. [After J. B. Parr and K. G. Denike, "Theoretical problems in central place analysis," *Economic Geography*, **46**, 1970.]

line (AC) mapping the average cost of a unit of production (say a gallon of beer) for the producer, assuming that different levels of the quantity of beer are produced. At this point we have to draw on some introductory economic analysis. It is assumed that we are in a perfectly competitive situation in which the particular producer is powerless to set the market price for beer. Hence, this has to be taken as given for him. By the principles of introductory economics this price (or marginal revenue) is set equal to the firm's marginal cost (the cost of producing one additional unit of production) to determine the profit-maximizing price and level of output. These are shown in Figure 5.3 as OP_1 and OQ_1. In Figures 5.1 and 5.2 we saw that the price OP_1 generated an individual level of demand of q_1 at the brewery and that this fell off to zero at distance s_1. This distance was referred to by Christaller as the *ideal range* of the good in question.

Excess Profits

At this point there exists only one producer and we see from Figure 5.3 that he is realizing what are called *excess profits*. What does this mean? First, we note that in computing the average cost curve AC,

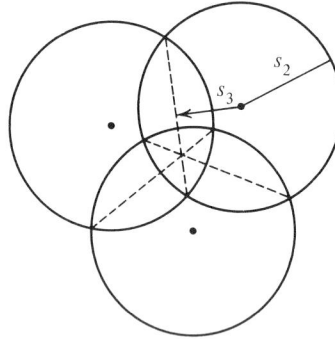

Figure 5.4   Ideal and real ranges of a central place good.

some allowance would be made for a normal profit needed to persuade
the producer to stay in business. But we see from Figure 5.3 that at
the profit-maximizing level of output OQ_1 the average-cost curve is
below the curve D_1, which may also be thought of as an average-
revenue curve for the producer. Hence, his excess profits are represented by the shaded rectangle P_1RST. Given our earlier assumption
about free-entry of producers, we then must assume that these excess
profits will continue to attract new breweries into the business until
such time as every firm is earning only normal profits and excess profits
are zero. This means that our initial producer's demand curve is
shifted to the left (to D_2) to the point of tangency with the average-
cost curve, that is, point V in Figure 5.3. The market price will now be
set at OP_2 and the output will be set at level OQ_2.

It is important to note that every brewery will now have the same
level of output because it is assumed that all firms in the same industry
have the same cost structure and production schedules. Now that the
price is OP_2 we note from earlier diagrams that the demand at this
price falls to zero at distance s_2 from each brewery. This is the new
ideal range. But with many producers now located on the plain this
ideal range will not be realized because at some distance away from
one brewery the consumers will find it advantageous to buy from a
different brewery. The boundary between the two market areas will
set the limit on the real range of the good. This point is illustrated in
Figure 5.4 in which s_2 defines the ideal range and s_3 is the real range.
If we recall our assumptions about the uniform distribution of farm
households and so on, we can appreciate how the plain will be covered
by a series of overlapping market areas for the breweries, and in
Figure 5.4 we see how a pattern of hexagonal market areas will serve
to divide up the total plain so that no area is unserved and no firm is
earning excess profits. The real range is conveniently defined as one-
half the distance between the locations of two competing firms and it

will, of course, not be equal in all directions within a hexagonal-shaped market area.

Threshold Range

Another concept requiring definition is that of the lower limit of the range, or as it has come to be called the *threshold range*. In the case of the single producer earning excess profits this threshold range would be defined as the distance to the perimeter of the area enclosing sufficient consumers to allow at least normal profits to be realized. When there are several producers each earning only normal profits, the threshold and real ranges are the same. In empirical studies of central place systems this notion of a threshold has been the subject of much statistical analysis, but in this case the concept is defined in terms of a level of population necessary to support an urban firm and not in terms of distance. In Chapter 4 we referred to this idea of a threshold population for an urban function.

Hierarchies of Urban Settlements

In developing his theory, Christaller assumed that a well-developed urban system with one large city, a small number of towns, and a large number of villages and hamlets already existed. In other words, his theory tells us nothing about how a system of cities is built up or why some centers are favored at the expense of others. The theory really assumes the existence of a central place system and concerns itself with prescribing the characteristics of that system.

The larger urban places will have larger tributary areas and they will be able to provide those goods and services that could not achieve the necessary threshold ranges in the smaller urban places. In addition, the larger places will be able to offer all of the goods and services provided in the smaller places.

Christaller emphasized the notion of a hierarchical structure in the types of urban places and in the sets of goods and services offered by the places. In his studies of Southern Germany he recognized seven such levels (Table 5.1).

Location Pattern and Its Geometry

Against the background of the above definitions and concepts we can now examine Christaller's theory of the location of central places. Two of the initial assumptions are of major importance here. First, all of the area's population must be served, and second, each center must be located centrally in its tributary region (that is, so that a condition of minimum aggregate travel is achieved for its uniformly dis-

Table 5.1 The Central Place System Discussed by Christaller.
[W. Christaller, Die Zentralen Orte in Süddeutschland (Jena: Gustav Fischer, 1933); trans. by C. W.
Baskin, *Central Places in Southern Germany* (Englewood Cliffs: Prentice-Hall, Inc., 1966), p. 67. © 1966;
reprinted by permission of Prentice-Hall, Inc.]

Type	Number of Places	Number of Complementary Regions	Range of Region (km)	Area of Region (sq km)	Number of Types of Goods Offered	Typical Population of Places	Typical Population of Region
M	486	729	4.0	44	40	1,000	3,500
A	162	243	6.9	133	90	2,000	11,000
K	54	81	12.0	400	180	4,000	35,000
B	18	27	20.7	1,200	330	10,000	100,000
G	6	9	36.0	3,600	600	30,000	350,000
P	2	3	62.1	10,800	1,000	100,000	1,000,000
L	1	1	108.0	32,400	2,000	500,000	3,500,000
Total	729						

tributed population). This implies further that centers of the same
order should be equidistant from each other. If we accept the idea that
a theoretical optimum market area system should be hexagonal, then
a regular hexagonal network of complementary regions would exist for
any given size level of urban places in the theoretical system. In other
words, each place of the same order has the same real range.

Consider an urban place offering goods of a high order. It is assumed that such a place would perform a variety of functions, each
with a different range. It follows that the tributary areas for all lower-
level goods will be contained within (or *nested* within) the larger tributary areas in the manner shown in Figure 5.5. It is also obvious that a
multiplicity of smaller places must be contained within the tributary
area of the highest-order function of any given place in order to satisfy
all potential demands for the lower-order functions. How are such
places located?[3]

Examine the 60°-plane lattice of points shown in Figure 5.6. Assume that each point on the lattice represents a potential city location.
The lattice allows us to focus on the smallest possible regular bounded
areas (triangles) and to consider the maximum packing density criterion (that is, obtain the smallest number of necessary places needed to
serve the given region). Note that each point in the lattice is a focal
point for six adjacent triangles—the sum of which form a regular hexagon. Further, if the centers of the triangles surrounding a lattice point
are joined, the region formed is also hexagonal. This represents the
fundamental region of the lattice and is called a *Dirichlet region*. In this

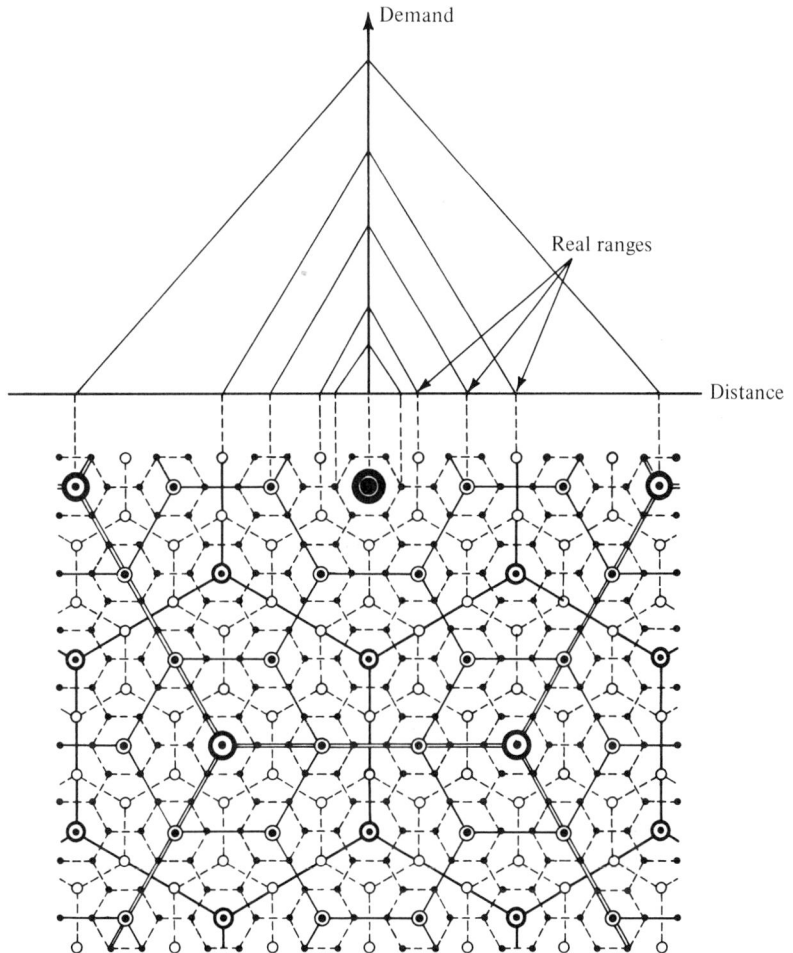

Figure 5.5 Diagrammatic representation of the nesting effect. The vertical axis in the top part of the diagram is not drawn to any scale.

region no other lattice points are found and it bounds the area that is closer to a given lattice point than to any other lattice point. This fundamental Dirichlet region containing only one lattice point, located at its center, is said to be of degree 1.

In general, the *degree* of a Dirichlet region is calculated as follows:

1. The number of lattice points in the region, plus
2. one-half the number of lattice points on the *edges* of a region, plus
3. one-third of the number of lattice points at the *vertices* of the region.

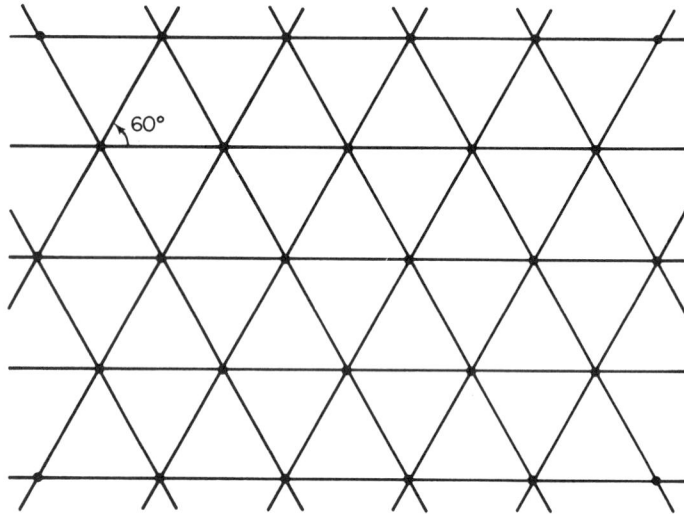

Figure 5.6   A 60°-lattice of points.

Different degrees are illustrated in Figure 5.7. In these diagrams the degree is designated by the constant, k.

Figure 5.7(a) illustrates a Dirichlet region with a degree of 3 (that is, one central lattice point plus one-third of all the six points located at the vertices of the region). Figures 5.7(b) and 5.7(c) represent the two other systems discussed in Christaller's work, as we shall note shortly.

Nesting of Tributary Areas

The degree of the system also supplies us with other relevant information on the nesting of tributary areas, the numbers of lower-order centers dominated by a larger one, and the distance between centers in the system. Referring again to Figure 5.7(a), we can visualize how, contained within the degree 3 region, there is one complete fundamental region of degree 1 and one-third of each of the surrounding six fundamental regions of degree 1 (that is, an equivalent of three complete fundamental regions). If we were to expand the lattice segment shown and impose on it consecutively larger tributary areas, we would find that each larger one contained an area equivalent to three of the immediately lower areas. This defines a hierarchical nested system of tributary areas with the following progression: 1, 3, 9, 27, 81, 243, ... That is, there is one largest region that contains the equivalent of three smaller ones (a total of three areas), each of which in turn contains the equivalent of three smaller ones (that is, a total of 3 × 3 or nine

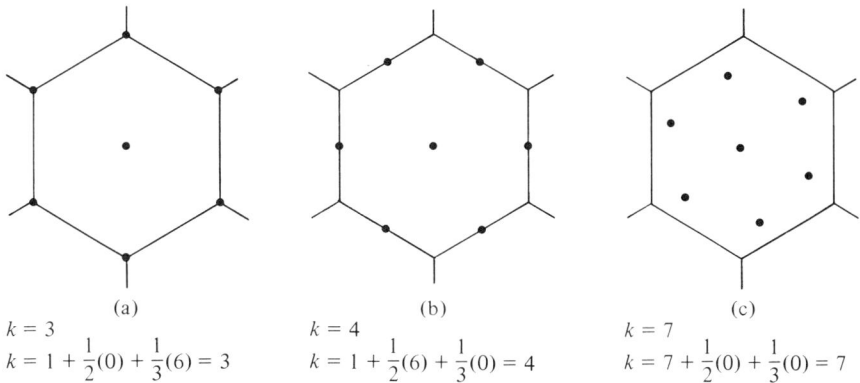

(a)

$k = 3$

$k = 1 + \frac{1}{2}(0) + \frac{1}{3}(6) = 3$

(b)

$k = 4$

$k = 1 + \frac{1}{2}(6) + \frac{1}{3}(0) = 4$

(c)

$k = 7$

$k = 7 + \frac{1}{2}(0) + \frac{1}{3}(0) = 7$

Figure 5.7   Dirichlet regions having different degrees.

areas), and so on. This progression is shown in the third column of Table 5.1.

Each central place is presumed to perform all the functions of lower-order places. The highest-order place, therefore, also acts as a second-order place, a third-order place, and so on. Consider now what is meant by saying that "the equivalent of three second-order tributary areas exist within the highest-order tributary area." It means that in addition to the first-order place (now also considered as a second-order place) there are two other centers. Similarly, the nine third-order tributary areas involve the first-order place, both second-order places all acting now as third-order places, and six other places. Hence, the progression describing the number of different-sized places in a system of degree 3 is: 1, 2, 6, 18, 54, 162 .... This is shown in column 2 of Table 5.1.

Spacing of Urban Centers

The degree of a system also defines the distance between places in the system (Figure 5.8). These distances are derived by applying simple rules of trigonometry. When a right-angled triangle is involved, for example, the triangle ABZ in Figure 5.8, then the distance AB between the two centers A and B can be determined by using the Pythagorean theorem. Thus,

$$AB^2 = AZ^2 + ZB^2$$

If the triangles are not right-angled, for example, ABD in Figure 5.8, then a different formula has to be used. The formula is the cosine rule and gives

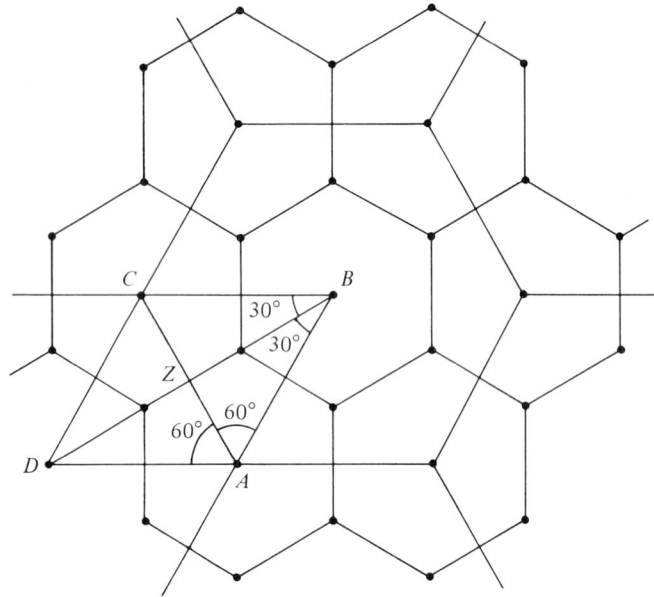

Figure 5.8   Distance relations in a Christaller *k* = 3 network.

$$BD^2 = AD^2 + AB^2 - 2AD \cdot AB \text{ cosine } \angle DAB$$

where $\angle DAB$ represents the interior angle of the triangle at vertex A.

The case of the right-angled triangle given above determines the distance between nearest neighboring centers of the same order in Figure 5.8. In other words, AB equals BC equals AC equals AD equals DC, and so on. The distance BD, however, is the distance between centers of the next higher order, they being the centers of the larger hexagonal market areas shown in Figure 5.8.

In order to illustrate these calculations, let us assume that the neighboring points in the lattice, A, B, C, D, and so on, are 1 distance unit apart. Then the distance BD is given as

$$BD^2 = AD^2 + AB^2 - 2AD \cdot AB \cos 120°$$
$$= 1^2 + 1^2 - 2(1)(1) \cos 120°$$
$$= 2 - 2 \cos 120°$$
$$= 2 - 2(-\tfrac{1}{2}) = 3$$

Therefore,

$$BD = \sqrt{3}$$

Now we generalize the argument by assuming the basic distance is not 1 unit but x units. Then, from triangle ABZ in Figure 5.8 we have,

$$AB^2 = AB^2 + BZ^2$$

and

$$BZ^2 = AB^2 - AZ^2 = x^2 - \left(\frac{x}{2}\right)^2 = x^2 - \frac{x^2}{4}$$

Therefore,

$$BZ = \sqrt{\frac{3x^2}{4}} = \frac{x}{2}\sqrt{3}$$

Now

$$BD = BZ + ZD = 2BZ = 2\left(\frac{x}{2}\sqrt{3}\right) = x\sqrt{3}$$

It can be shown that the distances between nearest centers of progressively higher orders in this hexagonal network will increase by the factor of $\sqrt{3}$.

In his study Christaller assumed that the basic distance AB was 7 kilometers. This meant that the distances between the successively higher-order places in the $k = 3$ system were $7\sqrt{3}$ kilometers, $7(\sqrt{3})^2 = 21$ kilometers, $7(\sqrt{3})^3 = 36.4$ kilometers, $7(\sqrt{3})^4 = 63$ kilometers, and so on.

In Christaller's discussion the system of order $k = 3$ was seen as developing in response to pure marketing forces (Figure 5.9). By

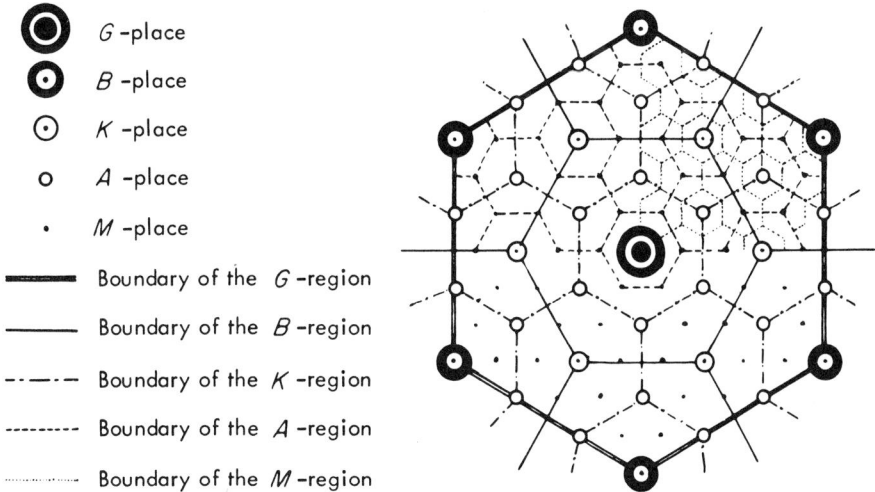

●   *G* -place

●   *B* -place

⊙   *K* -place

o   *A* -place

·   *M* -place

——   Boundary of the *G* -region

——   Boundary of the *B* -region

—·—·—   Boundary of the *K* -region

--------   Boundary of the *A* -region

·············   Boundary of the *M* -region

Figure 5.9 The marketing regions in a system of central places. [W. Christaller, *Die zentralen Orte in Süddeutschland* (Jena: Gustav Fischer, 1933); trans. by C. W. Baskin, *Central Places in Southern Germany* (Englewood Cliffs, N.J.: Prentice-Hall, Inc., 1966), p. 73. © 1966; reprinted by permission of Prentice-Hall, Inc.]

Only the *B*-place is traffic-oriented
B-distance = 31 km. = ½ *G*-distance
M-distance = 6 km.

Preference for one line
of traffic. *M*-regions

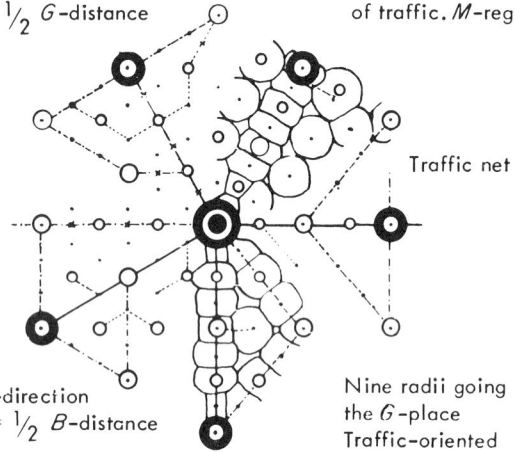

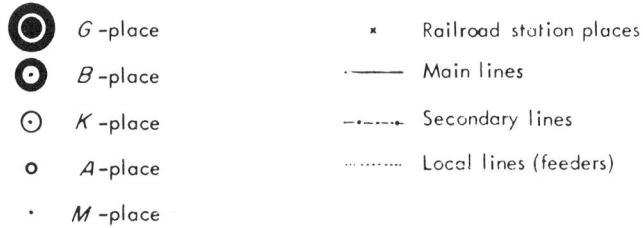

Traffic net

Nine radii going from
the *G*-place
Traffic-oriented

K-place lying on a *B*-direction
K-distance = 18 km. = ½ *B*-distance
M-distance = 6 km.

◎ *G* -place
◉ *B* -place
⊙ *K* -place
o *A* -place
· *M* -place

×   Railroad station places
——   Main lines
—·—·—   Secondary lines
············ Local lines (feeders)

Figure 5.10 A system of central places developed according to the traffic principle. [W. Christaller, *Die zentralen Orte in Süddeutschland* (Jena: Gustav Fischer, 1933); trans. by C. W. Baskin, *Central Places in Southern Germany* (Englewood Cliffs, N.J.: Prentice-Hall, Inc., 1966), p. 75. © 1966; reprinted by permission of Prentice-Hall, Inc.]

contrast, a system of degree 4 could arise in response to transportation forces that favored the locations of places on the routes between major centers (Figure 5.10). Finally, a system of degree 7 was seen by Christaller as evidence of political or administrative forces that make for separation of jurisdictions and clear-cut territorial rights (Figure 5.11).

5.2 Lösch's Theory of Settlement

Another German scholar, August Lösch, also formulated a theory of location of urban places.[4] We now discuss the nature of his theory and point to several critical differences between this work and that of Christaller.

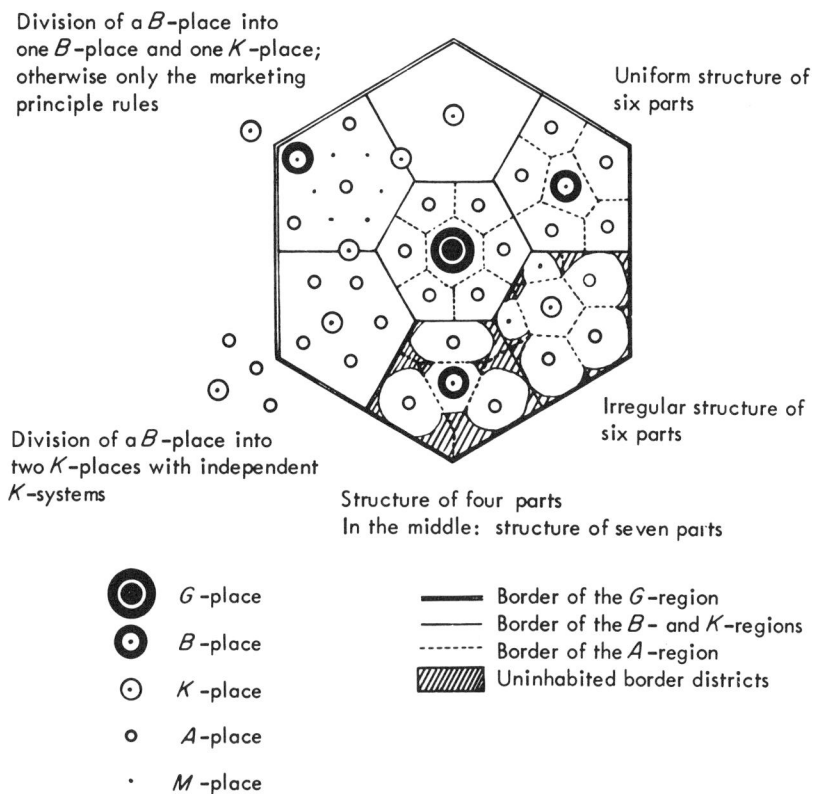

Division of a *B*-place into
one *B*-place and one *K*-place;
otherwise only the marketing
principle rules

Uniform structure of
six parts

Division of a *B*-place into
two *K*-places with independent
K-systems

Irregular structure of
six parts

Structure of four parts
In the middle: structure of seven parts

◉	*G*-place	━━━ Border of the *G*-region
◉	*B*-place	──── Border of the *B*- and *K*-regions
⊙	*K*-place	------- Border of the *A*-region
o	*A*-place	▨▨▨ Uninhabited border districts
·	*M*-place	

Figure 5.11   A system of central places according to the separation principle. [W. Christaller, *Die zentralen Orte in Süddeutschland* (Jena: Gustav Fischer, 1933); trans. by C. W. Baskin, *Central Places in Southern Germany* (Englewood Cliffs, N.J.: Prentice-Hall, Inc., 1966), p. 79. © 1966; reprinted by permission of Prentice-Hall, Inc.]

Basic Features

Unlike Christaller who constructed his system "downward" from the higher-order places, Lösch began at the fundamental level of a single producer and worked upward to a system of urban places.

Three basic steps in Lösch's analysis were as follows:

1. To find the optimal density of urban places (of all sizes) in a given area.
2. To show that this system of settlements, represented by points, forms a plane lattice.
3. To show that demand is maximized at each place if the surrounding market areas are hexagonal.

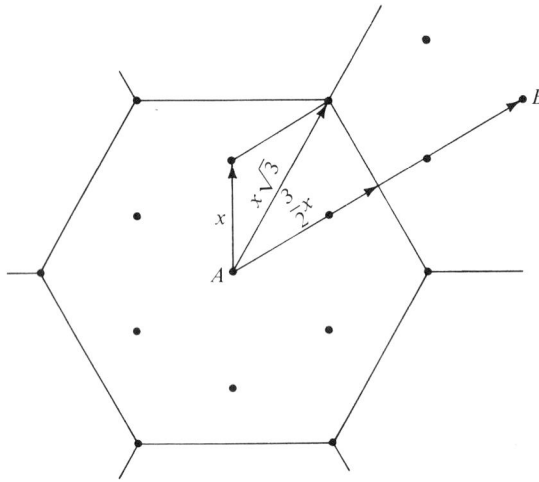

Figure 5.12   Distance relations in a Löschian system.

The selection of a hexagonal network of market areas based on a 60°-(sixfold) plane lattice is essentially a function of the space-filling requirement of central place theory. For example, when comparing the volumes of demand for a given good, Lösch argued that the demand in a cone with a hexagonal base is "2.4% greater than a square of equal size, about 10% greater than in a circle, if the empty corners are included, and at a maximum 12% greater than in an equilaterial tri-angle of the same area."[5] Since the superiority of the hexagon over the square is least, several researchers have suggested that urban sys-tems based on either squares *or* hexagons could theoretically be con-structed without undue loss of efficiency in location and service. In the strictest sense of obtaining the maximum packing density of places, however, the hexagonal distribution of places satisfies the criterion best.

The main economic features of Lösch's system were the same as those discussed earlier in regard to Christaller's work. In actual fact, it would be more correct to say that Lösch dealt explicitly with these features but that Christaller was not very concerned with the under-lying economic theory. If Christaller's work is thought of as proceed-ing from detailed observations to generalization, then Lösch's work proceeded more by way of logical reasoning.

Again, we assume that producers are trying to maximize their profits, the entire region in which population is uniformly distributed must be served by urban places, no producer can make excess profits, the market areas of each urban place must be as small as is economically possible, and the boundaries of market areas are lines of equal competition between places.

In contrast to Christaller who discussed mainly the network of degree 3, Lösch argued in more general terms. Consider, for example, the system in Figure 5.12 in which there is an urban place A serving the equivalent of nine customers, including itself. If we define the basic distance between the original settlements to be x again, then using the same relations as before we can show that the distance AB equals $3x$, which in general terms can be expressed as $x\sqrt{n}$, where n is the total number of *equivalent customers* served by a place (Table 5.2).

Table 5.2 Distance of Centers from Each Other. [After A. Lösch, *The Economics of Location* (Gustav Fischer Verlag), trans. by W. H. Woglom and W. F. Stolper (New Haven: Yale University Press, 1954), p. 131.]

Regional Level	$k = 3$	$k = 4$	$k = 7$
1	$x\sqrt{3^1}$	$x\sqrt{4^1}$	$x\sqrt{7^1}$
2	$x\sqrt{3^2}$	$x\sqrt{4^2}$	$x\sqrt{7^2}$
3	$x\sqrt{3^3}$	$x\sqrt{4^3}$	$x\sqrt{7^3}$
4	$x\sqrt{3^4}$	$x\sqrt{4^4}$	$x\sqrt{7^4}$
5	$x\sqrt{3^5}$	$x\sqrt{4^5}$	$x\sqrt{7^5}$
6	$x\sqrt{3^6}$	$x\sqrt{4^6}$	$x\sqrt{7^6}$
7	$x\sqrt{3^7}$	$x\sqrt{4^7}$	$x\sqrt{7^7}$

We can also note that the size of a market area in this system is $x^2 n\sqrt{3/2}$ and that the value of n increases according to the following formulae:

$$(5.1) \qquad\qquad n = (k\sqrt{3})^2 + j^2$$

$$(5.2) \qquad\qquad n = [(k + \tfrac{1}{2})\sqrt{3}]^2 + (j + \tfrac{1}{2})^2$$

These formulae are used as follows. First, k is set equal to 1 and then Equation 5.1 is applied with j taking on the values 0 and 1. Then k is increased to 2 and Equation 5.1 is again applied, but now with j equal to 0, then 1, and then 2. In other words, using Equation 5.1, we let k take on integer values from 1 to infinity and j takes on integer values from 0 up to k. This procedure gives the values of n in Table 5.3 for the first, second, fifth, sixth, seventh, eleventh, and so on, levels of

Table 5.3 Number of Settlements Supplied in Market Areas of Different Orders in Löschian System. [After A. Lösch, *The Economics of Location* (Gustav Fischer Verlag), trans. by W. H. Woglom and W. F. Stolper (New Haven: Yale University Press, 1954), p. 119.]

Level or Order of Market Area		Number of Places Served, n
1		$(1\sqrt{3})^2 + 0^2 = 3$
2		$(1\sqrt{3})^2 + 1^2 = 4$
	3	$(1\frac{1}{2}\sqrt{3})^2 + (\frac{1}{2})^2 = 7$
	4	$(1\frac{1}{2}\sqrt{3})^2 + (1\frac{1}{2})^2 = 9$
5		$(2\sqrt{3})^2 + 0^2 = 12$
6		$(2\sqrt{3})^2 + 1^2 = 13$
7		$(2\sqrt{3})^2 + 2^2 = 16$
	8	$(2\frac{1}{2}\sqrt{3})^2 + (\frac{1}{2})^2 = 19$
	9	$(2\frac{1}{2}\sqrt{3})^2 + (1\frac{1}{2})^2 = 21$
	10	$(2\frac{1}{2}\sqrt{3})^2 + (2\frac{1}{2})^2 = 25$
11		$(3\sqrt{3})^2 + 0^2 = 27$
⋮		⋮
	15	$(3\frac{1}{2}\sqrt{3})^2 + (\frac{1}{2})^2 = 37$
⋮		⋮
19		

market areas. The values of n for the third, fourth, eighth, ninth, tenth, fifteenth, and so on, levels are obtained by applying Equation 5.2 by using the same rules for the values of j and k.

Under this Löschian system, there is no real fixed-k situation as in the Christaller model; instead, there is a system of central places of which Christaller's $k = 3$, $k = 4$, and $k = 7$ are simply those systems having the three smallest sets of market areas (Figure 5.13).

Central Place Numbers

A general rule gives the set of all possible market sizes in Lösch's central place theory.[6] Stated simply, the rule is

$$Q = u^2 + uv + v^2$$

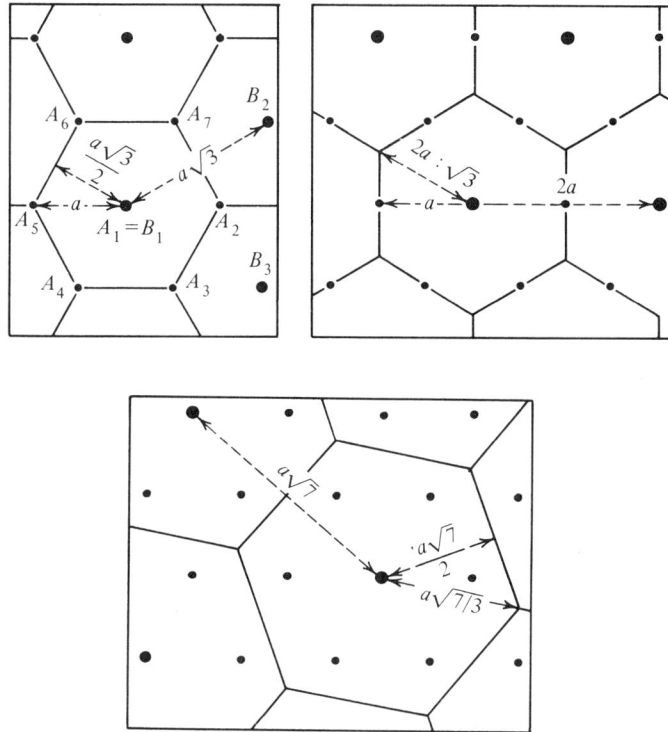

Figure 5.13 The three smallest market areas. [A. Lösch, *The Economics of Location* (Gustav Fischer Verlag), trans. by W. H. Woglom and W. F. Stolper (New Haven: Yale University Press, 1954), p. 117.]

where Q is the set of central-place numbers and u and v are non-negative integers, with $u \leq v$ and $v = 1, 2, 3 \ldots$. The set of numbers generated in this way is illustrated in Table 5.4. Of these numbers, only those that are powers of 3, 4, or 7 are possible in the Christaller system. The number 9 (equals 3^2), for example, is one such number and refers to the set of third-order markets in the $k = 3$ network. The numbers 13, 19, 37, 25, and 31 in Table 5.4 are illustrative of the Löschian market sizes for which there are no network counterparts in the Christaller system.

One of the significant differences between the formulations of Lösch and Christaller is associated with the fact that in the latter there is a *nested* hierarchy of places and market areas with the lower-order market areas completely contained within higher-order areas. This implies that if a center offers good m, it must also offer good $m - 1$, $m - 2, \ldots$, that is, all goods of a lower order than m. Lösch argued, however, that two centers of order m may have different functional mixes, that is, one may have a brewery and a bakery, while another

Table 5.4 Set of Central Place Numbers. (Based on M. F. Dacey, "An interesting number property in central place theory," *The Professional Geographer,* **17**, 1965, p. 33.)

	Integers															
v	1	1	2	2	2	3	3	3	3	4	4	4	4	4	5	5...
u	0	1	0	1	2	0	1	2	3	0	1	2	3	4	0	1...
$Q = u^2 + uv + v^2$	1	3	4	7	12	9	13	19	27	16	21	28	37	48	25	31...

may have a bakery and a laundry. Yet another center of similar size might conceivably contain all three functions. Places of the same size in Lösch's system would have the same number of functions, but they need not be the same functions. How could this situation arise?

Lösch's System of Market Areas

The explanation is found in the way that Lösch generalized from his economic analysis of the market area system for a single type of good or service to the case in which there are multiple goods and services offered by the urban places in the region.

The individual market area systems for different economic functions were put together by Lösch in such a way that when they were overlaid one on top of another there would be at least one central location (the metropolis) in common and as many other points as possible also would coincide. Then, if one imagines all the market area systems being fixed at the central location but free to move otherwise, Lösch was able to rotate them so as to generate a locational arrangement in which there were certain sectors with many urban places and certain sectors with few (Figure 5.14). These were referred to as the *city-rich* and *city-poor* sectors.

Several subsequent writers have pointed out that the method Lösch used in deriving his urban system contains inconsistencies. Consider, for example, Figure 5.15, a simple diagram that shows two market areas for two different goods centered on town *A*. In deriving the smaller set of hexagons consideration would be given to the necessary number of consumers. But now centered on that same urban place, *A*, is a larger market area for some other economic function. There must, therefore, be a certain population in *A* to supply this second good and this population presumably would now add to the demand for the first good. Excess profits may then arise. Another possibility arises if one allows for multiple-purpose shopping trips. Consider the consumers located in the larger market area centered on *A*. In journeying into *A* they may decide to take advantage of the oppor-

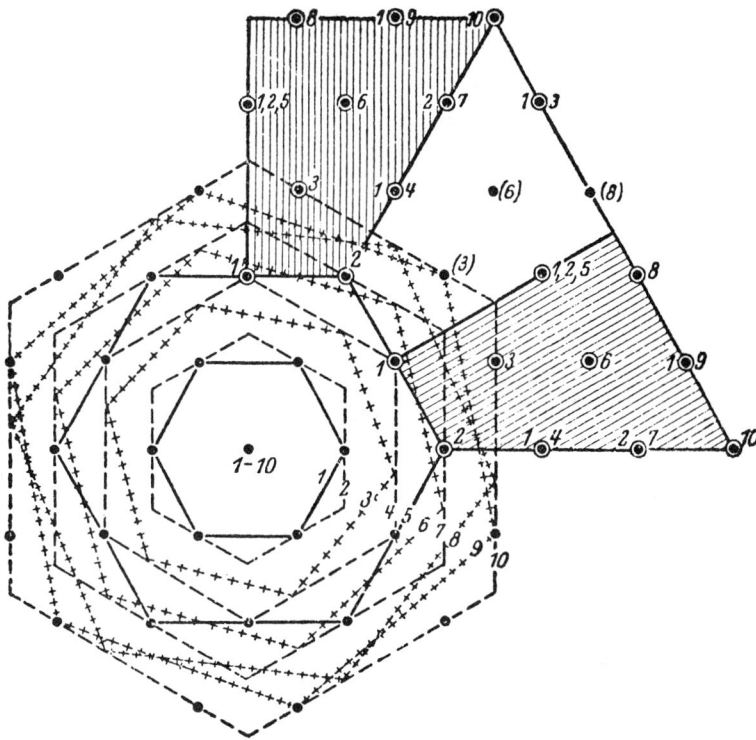

Figure 5.14 The ten smallest economic areas in Lösch's scheme. The sectors containing many towns are hatched. Alternative regional centers are in parentheses. Simple points represent original settlements. Those enclosed in circles are centers of market areas of sizes indicated by the figures. [A. Lösch, *The Economics of Location* (Gustav Fischer Verlag), trans. by W. H. Woglom and W. F. Stolper (New Haven: Yale University Press, 1954), p. 118.]

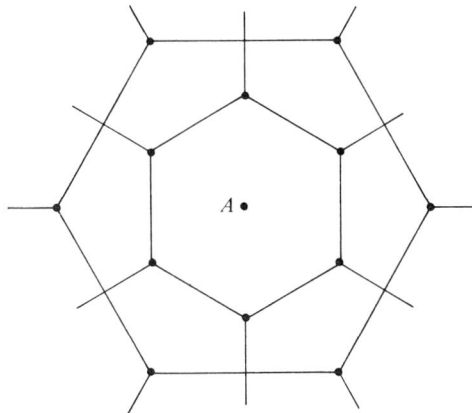

Figure 5.15 Two different-sized market areas centered on a town, A.

tunity to purchase the other good that is also available there. Again, the demand for the first good at A is increased (and presumably decreased at some other center). The failure to allow for such multiple-purpose shopping is a shortcoming of both Christaller's and Lösch's formulation.

The Legacy of Central Place Theory

It is perhaps an appropriate point in this discussion at which to stand back and attempt to assess the significance of the work of Christaller and Lösch.

There can be no denying the fact that these writers left a rich legacy in terms of intellectual stimulation and that many lines of scholarship have developed from central place theory. On the one hand, there has been a tremendous volume of work completed with the intention of testing the theory's predictions. Numerous studies of the spacing of cities, the size and number of cities, the relationships between the population sizes and functional complexity of urban places, and the patterns of consumer shopping behavior have usually been prefaced with restatements of parts of central place theory and have sought to test certain of its predictions. We have already reviewed some of the empirical findings that these studies have provided in earlier sections of this book.

It in no way detracts from the seriousness and scholarship of the studies of central place theory to suggest that on the whole they have not made significant contributions to the further refinement of the theory. Some scholars would argue that this matters little and they would contend that central place theory with its emphasis on the economic relationships between the urban place and the surrounding rural region is sadly outdated and provides little understanding of the complex modern urban societies that we live in today. A few other writers have pointed out that these disappointing results from the empirical studies were to be expected on logical grounds. They argue that in view of our inability to be able to set up control situations similar to those dictated by the assumptions in Christaller's and Lösch's formulations we can never really confirm or deny the predictions of these theories.

One other legacy of the work of Christaller and Lösch is that central place theory has been seen by many to provide a convenient framework for certain policies in regional planning. There are actual cases that one can point to in different parts of the world where settlement patterns have been planned in accordance with central place theory. We shall consider some of these applications and discuss the strengths and weaknesses of central place theory in this context in Chapter 13.

5.3 Related Issues in Settlement Theory

Another legacy of Christaller and Lösch is the interest in theorizing about settlement patterns that has been apparent in geography and other disciplines over the past decade or so. Three particular lines of work can be chosen to illustrate this point. These include research on city-size distributions in general, market area analysis, and studies of consumer behavior.

City-Size Distributions

How does one reconcile the apparent difference between the hierarchical step-like frequency distribution of city sizes predicted by central place theory and the more continuous and unbroken frequency curve suggested by the work on the rank-size rule? Recall that we discussed this rank-size relationship earlier.

One attempt to answer this question went as follows.[7] Represent the population size of a city at a given level of the central place hierarchy by P_m, where m denotes the hierarchy level. Then,

$$P_m = \frac{ks^{m-1}r_1}{(1-k)^m}$$

where

k is a proportionality factor that relates the city population to the total population served by that city (if the rural population component is r_m, then $k = P_m/(P_m + r_m)$ and this is assumed to be constant over the levels of the hierarchy);

s is the number of equivalent urban places of the $(m-1)$ level that are served by the mth level city; and

and

r_1 is population of the market area at the first or lowest level of the hierarchy.

Assume further that for each level m of the hierarchy there is a middle or average city with population P_m and the other cities at the same level have populations that show some variation above and below this middle value. In other words, all of the cities at a particular hierarchical level do not have the same population and there is a progression in size up and down from that of the midway city. Then, if the rank of this city in the overall hierarchy is multiplied by its population size P_m, the result will be approximately constant from one level to another which conforms to the rank-size rule.

Unfortunately, the formulation of the central place population-

159

size distribution in the above argument is inconsistent with the rank-size rule, when this rule is stated as[8]

$$R^q P_R = C = P_N$$

here, R is the rank of a city according to its size;
         P_R is the population of city of rank R;
         P_N is the population of the largest city;

and q and C are constants, with q either equal to or not equal to 1.

However, the city sizes in a central place system for which the constant proportionality factor k in the above argument is assumed to hold can be described by rank-size rule if the *endpoint* cities of each hierarchical level or size class are considered. This rank-size rule is

$$(K^{n-1})^q P_m = P_N$$

where K^{n-1} is overall rank of the endpoint city of the mth hierarchical level $(n = N - m + 1)$;
         N is total number of levels in the hierarchy;

and q, P_m, and P_N are defined as before.

In this formulation, q is greater than 1. Although the mathematical consistency between the two formulations can be shown in this case, there remains the problem of providing an appropriate rationale for the use of the endpoint cities in each class.

Spatial Competition and Market Area Analysis

Lösch's formulation in particular was very rich in questions concerning the spatial location of production and the nature of market areas. It is impossible to attempt to review here all of the work in location theory that references Lösch's contributions and there are excellent books on the subject. It is possible to discuss briefly two specific questions that will illustrate the type of analysis that is involved.

One issue has to do with the effect of there being free entry of new producers into an industry on the size and shape of the market area served by each producer.[9] Consider the diagram in Figure 5.16. There are three producers, P_1, P_2, and P_3 (in three central places), and they serve hexagonal market areas as shown. Now consider a particular consumer, a, located at the common apex of the three hexagons. Note that he is further away from any one of the producers than is, say, customer b who is closer to P_1. Hence, the price of the product at P_1 must be such that consumer a can still afford to buy it (remember, the consumer has to pay the transportation). If the price rises, consumer a may be priced

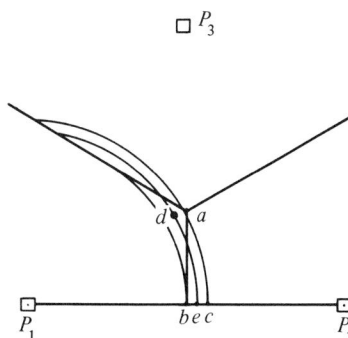

Figure 5.16 Affect of free entry of new producers on market area boundaries at equilibrium. [Based on K. G. Denike and J. B. Parr, "Production in space, spatial competition, and restricted entry," *Journal of Regional Science,* **10,** no. 1 1970, p. 54.]

out of the market and this would be true for him at P_1 or P_2 or P_3. The increase in price may not affect b or c or even e because they are all closer to producer P_2 (or P_1 in the case of b). If we assume that consumer d can still buy from P_1, even at the higher price, then all consumers at the same distance from P_1 as is d will be on the boundary of P_1's market area. In other words, the corners of the hexagons become rounded. If the price went even higher the market areas might become circular in shape and in the event that the producers were still not earning excess profits there might be customers who would remain unserved.

Consider a second question. In numerous empirical studies it has been pointed out that in any urban place there often will be several firms engaged in offering the same function. The central place theory would lead us to expect that only one producer would be present for each function. Why should there be more? An answer to this can be found in the theory of agglomeration economies which predicts that in competitive market situations two or more producers may find it advantageous to locate at a common point. There is a well-known illustrative problem involving two ice-cream vendors searching for locations for their ice-cream carts on a length of beach.[10] It can be proven that the two vendors maximize their sales if they locate together at the center of the beach strip. These same advantages of centrality can be assumed to hold for producers in many different situations.

Behavioral Postulates

The third and final example of theoretical analysis related to central place theory has to do with attempts to introduce more realistic assumptions about human behavior. A number of studies of the shopping trips made by the farm population in Iowa[11] have pointed up the fact that, contrary to the assertions of central place theory, people often do not go to the nearest urban place to purchase goods and services available there but prefer to travel further to alternative places. Some of these findings were discussed earlier in Chapter 4.

These results have generated an interest in the possible effects on a central place system of changes in the preference structure that is assumed to describe the consumers' choices among alternative locations for shopping.[12] It is found that the urban patterns are altered significantly and a number of places do not attain the status in the hierarchy predicted by Christaller's formulation.

Let us assume that each consumer in the urban system goes through a decision-making process during which *preference structures* for the different urban places are formed. These preference structures may be influenced by variables such as the number of functions offered in a center, the size of the place, and its distance from the consumer's home. The resulting patterns of shopping trips made to the places and their size development in turn would depend on their relative attractiveness as reflected in the preferences of the consumers. The effects of incorporating a preference structure assumption based on factors that influence consumer spatial behavior can be seen in the series of diagrams in Figure 5.17.

Figure 5.17(a) shows a cross section through a Christaller-type central place system in which the transport costs have the same gradient around each place and consumers travel to the nearest center offering the goods demanded. Center G is of a higher order than A. In Figure 5.17(b) the transport cost gradients around centers G and A are changed so that the one from G is less steep than the one from A. The rationale for expecting some difference in the cost gradient from each place lies in the simple fact that since a G-order center offers more goods and services than an A-order center, the probability of a consumer's satisfying more of his requirements in a single trip to a G-center is greater. Consequently, the perceived cost to the consumer of going to G would be less than that of going to A. This reduces the probability of his making a trip to A. It may even be possible for businesses located in the G-order center to lower their prices and subsidize the transport costs of people moving to the G-order center. The result of this lowering of prices is to automatically increase the size of G's trade area, as can be seen in Figure 5.17(c). The resulting tributary area of A_1 is restricted on the side of greatest competition. One can imagine the continuation of this process until A_1 is driven out of business altogether [Figure 5.17(d)]. The death of small hamlets and village commercial centers has been a common feature of the development of urban systems over time in North America. In this process,

(a) same transfer cost gradients from all centers

G   A   A   B

(b) transfer costs decrease with center size   G>B>A

G   A   A   B

(c) prices inversely related to center size   G>B>A

G A_1 A_2 B

(d) tributary area for A_1 now does not support threshold

G A_2 B

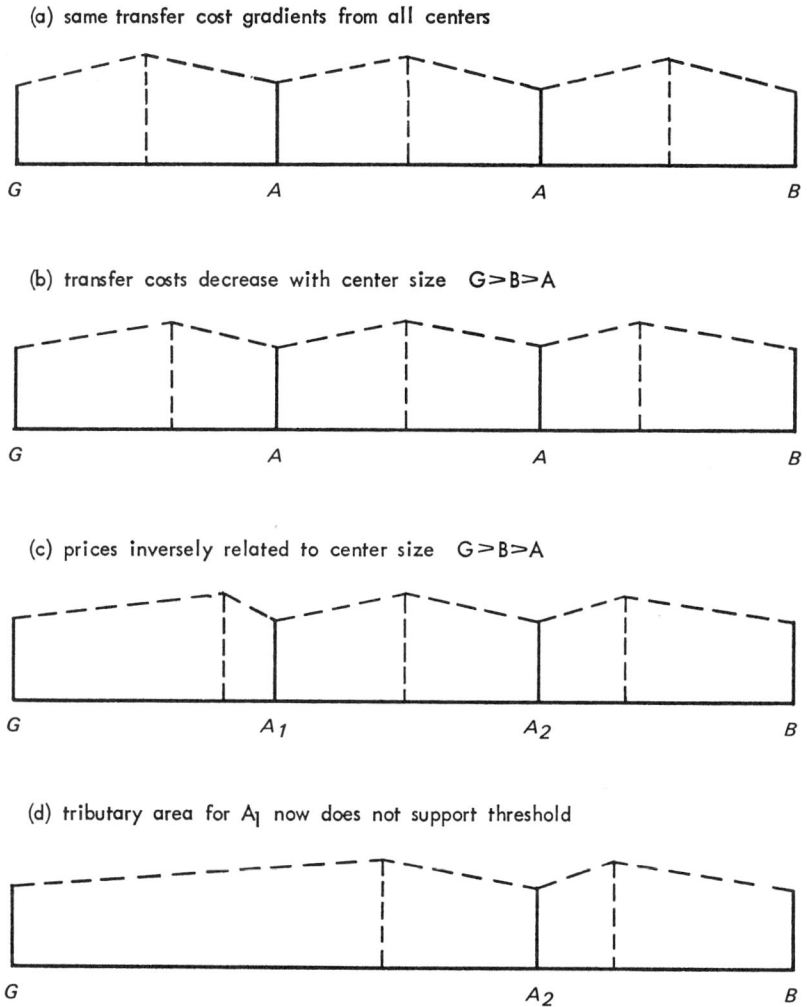

Figure 5.17 Cumulative effects of multi-purpose shopping trips and increasing internal economies of scale on the tributary area of firms. [G. Rushton, "Postulates of central place theory and properties of central place systems," *Geographical Analysis*, **3**, 1971, p. 143. Reprinted by permission.]

the B-order center (which is larger than A but, by assumption, smaller than G) would not be able to wage as successful a war against A_2. In addition, after the demise of A_1, there would be a gain of consumers to A_2 that would increase its viable tributary area and allow it to better withstand competitive pressures from B.

In addition to the above considerations, what might be the effects on the system of changing the assumption of uniform population densi-

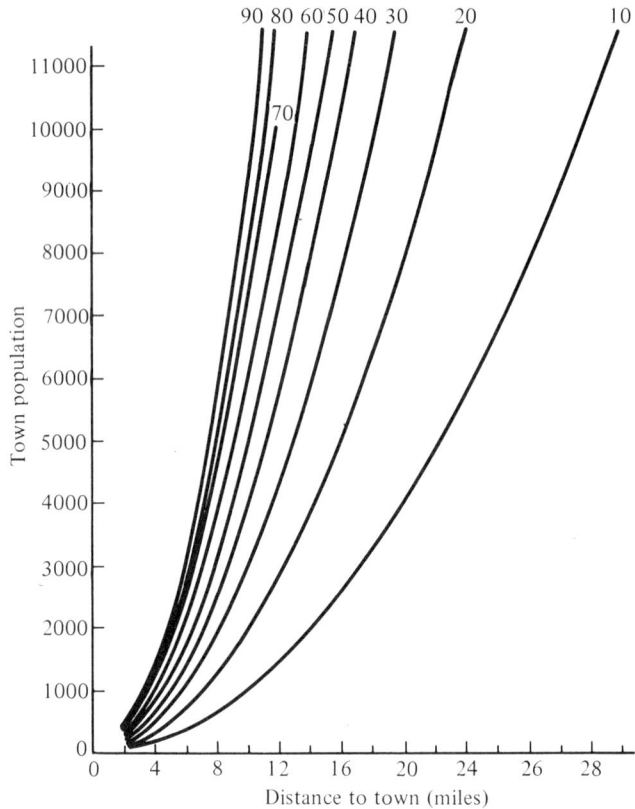

Figure 5.18 Indifference surface showing the spatial behavioral postulate used in a revised central place model. [G. Rushton, "Postulates of central place theory and properties of central place systems," *Geographical Analysis,* **3,** 1971, p. 149. Reprinted by permission.]

ties? It is then possible to produce a hierarchical system similar to that proposed by Christaller only if the fundamental behavioral postulate discussed above is also altered. This has been demonstrated by using the behavioral postulate suggested by the set of indifference curves shown in Figure 5.18.[13] These show a series of trade-offs between size of town and distance from potential consumers. For example, the rightmost curve indicates those sets of distance-town size combinations where 10% of the population would make particular trade-offs. That is to say, 10% of the population would show this indifference between the size of town visited and the distance that had to be traveled. They would be indifferent between traveling 33 miles to a town of around 11,000 population and traveling about 14 miles to a town of 2,000 population. By contrast, the left-hand curve shows the distance trade-off that would be acceptable to 90% of the population, and it suggests that the majority of persons are much less willing to travel longer distances to particular-sized towns.

By using a computer model, it is possible to examine the impact of these new assumptions on the size distribution of towns in a system. Not surprisingly, some centers fail to achieve the size suggested for them in a Christaller-type model while other places show up as being larger.

5.4   Introducing the Element of Chance into the Study of Urban Patterns

In the formulation of any theory there is always a choice involved in deciding which factors are to be emphasized and which factors are to be ignored. For example, in the theories discussed in the preceding section the emphasis was on economic factors and mechanisms and other factors, such as environmental factors, were ignored.

Some scholars in their theorizing choose to allow for the possibility that the phenomena being studied may be subject to the influence of chance factors in much the same way that certain physical phenomena are observed to be. We take for granted that the tossing of a coin and the outcome of whether it lands heads-up or tails-up are subject to chance and cannot be predicted precisely ahead of time before any one toss. We do know that if we tossed a coin for an extremely large number of times, the relative frequency with which either a head or a tail occurred would be very close to one-half. This belief is the basis for the often-made statement that the probability of either a head or a tail coming up on a single toss (before the toss is made) is one-half. Some geographers have argued that if we wish to talk about the locational distribution of towns over a fairly homogenous, large region, we are best to think of the problem as being analogous to a physical process subject to chance such as coin-tossing or the rolling of dice. We shall say more on this subject shortly.

Random Variables

In many physical processes it is often found that the description of particular features of the process cannot be made in an exact way but must allow for some variability. For example, the observed lifetime of a machine part may be so many machine-hours of operation, but there will be some occasions on which a part lasts a little longer and there will also be some occasions on which failure of the part occurs sooner than usual. Again, this outcome cannot be predicted ahead of time and it is assumed to be subject to chance.

In technical terms, the lifetime of the machine part is said to be a *random variable* for which it will be possible to compute an average or mean value and also a measure of the dispersion of the different values (made over time) around this mean. Naturally, in this case, the manufacturer is going to be most unhappy if there is considerable variability in the lifetime of the particular part in his machines.

In studying urban questions it soon becomes clear that many of the features of interest are best described as random variables that can be characterized by their mean and dispersion values. Urban population size, the densities of towns in particular-sized areas, urban income and employment levels, and so on, can all be thought of as random variables.

The use of the word *random* warrants comment. It is used here as an adjective to describe a phenomenon or a process that is subject to the influence of chance. This may be interpreted to mean that there are influences or forces at work that are simply not understood given our present state of knowledge. In this sense, the random or chance component is regarded as a composite effect of all the unknown forces acting upon the phenomenon under study and presumably, as knowledge is developed and refined, this random component would become smaller and smaller.

Alternately, the acknowledgment that there are random or chance factors present may be interpreted as meaning that some part of the behavior of the phenomenon under study will always defy explanation in terms of known laws and theories. In other words, this view implies that some effects or influences are purely chance ones and must be accepted as such.

The debate over which interpretation is the correct one occupied the attention of many distinguished physical scientists in the past, but now it is widely accepted that, depending on the area of study, the one or the other interpretation will be the more appropriate. The distinction then between the theories to be discussed now and those in the preceding section is largely one of how the problems are conceptualized.

Deterministic and Stochastic Models

A distinction is often made between *deterministic* and *probabilistic* or *stochastic* models in this context. Deterministic models allow for the exact determination of the state of the system under study and they make no allowance for chance factors. Probabilistic models, by contrast, incorporate these chance elements and make explicit allowance for them by using the language of probability theory, the mathematics of random variables and random processes. In the case of a random process operating over time (the occurrence of machine breakdowns) or over space (the location of disease victims in an area), the more specific term stochastic, rather than probabilistic, is used to describe the process.

The deterministic-probabilistic distinction is useful, but it should not be overemphasized. In the sense that it suggests the different conceptualizations referred to above, it is convenient, but it often leads to confusion if it is regarded too strictly as a commentary on the different mathematical forms used. Deterministic models usually are structured in equation form and are solved by using calculus; probabilistic models involve the mathematics of probability theory and expressions for the measures of variability (the variance and so on) that do not appear in deterministic models. But it must be appreciated that once a model has been structured as a probabilistic or random one, then its solution may be as precisely determined as that of any deterministic model! The distinction should be thought of as mainly a difference in the manner of thinking about the problem at hand and not primarily as a difference in the mathematical language used.

5.5   Random Spatial Economy: Patterns of Behavior in Both Time and Space

In the central place theories of Christaller and Lösch there was no allowance made for the operation of any factors of chance. The systems were strictly deterministic ones and the associated behavioral rules, for example, the requirement that all farm households obtained their goods and services of a particular order from the nearest urban center offering them, were assumed to apply exactly to all parts of the system.

In later work, as we saw, there have been attempts to change a part of this framework by allowing for some variation in the shopping habits of rural households. But this work has always stopped short of trying to develop a completely random central place model. It is another geographer, Leslie Curry, who has made an effort to develop this type of model.[14]

Curry's theory of central places in a random spatial economy is not easily understood, largely because the concepts and mathematics that he used, principally those of communications engineering, are not widely known by social scientists. We only sketch here the main features of Curry's theory.

Curry approached the problem of explaining the size, spacing, and economic functions of urban settlements from the viewpoints of the two main groups of actors involved in the urban systems, namely, the retailer (or firm) and the consumer. The behavior of each of these classes involves certain random elements both in its unfolding over time (for example, the maintaining of inventories of goods by the retailer over a time period) and over space (for example, the shopping at different centers by consumers).

No particular locational arrangement of either the consumers or the urban centers need be assumed at the start. Nor need there be very much said about the physical setting of the central place system except that the space is a bounded one. The emphasis is placed on the behavior of the actors in the system, the argument being that this is sufficient to generate predictions about many of the spatial properties.

Consumer and Retailer Behavior

The behavior of the consumers involves two components, their interaction over space with particular locations at differing distances from their residences and their demand over time for certain classes of goods and services. The first component involves a random element and may be described mathematically such that the probability of the consumer's visiting a point decreases as his distance away from that point increases. The demand for different goods over time is assumed to be both *aperiodic* (that is, there are no particular patterns that keep on recurring at a regular interval over and over again) and *stationary* (that is, over time there is no long-term trend apparent in either an increasing or decreasing direction). These same two assumptions of aperiodicity and stationarity also may be made about the retailers' behavior. For both groups of actors there also exists a limited time horizon. To the retailer this means the period over which he expects to sell his supply of goods; to the consumer it represents the time over which certain goods are needed.

The retailer has to establish himself and maintain his inventory of goods in the face of the uncertainty represented by the consumer's behavior. In the language of communications engineering, the consumer provides the *input* to the system and this consists mainly of a *signal* which is the demand for a set of goods. But for the retailer this signal is accompanied by a certain amount of *noise* representing the myriad consumer demands for all other goods and services and the uncertainties associated with the consumers' behavior. This noise level increases the overall uncertainty confronting the retailer.

In any communications problem involving a signal and associated noise it is the practice to use *filters* to separate out the signal from the noise. This is what is done in all forms of electronic communication. As an analogy to this, suppose that the signals in the central place system are acted upon by at least two filters. The first would be the existence of *household stocks*. These would be household inventories of goods that would do away with the necessity of the consumer making trips to replenish them immediately after they have been consumed. A trivial example would be the owning of a refrigerator by a consumer. This would eliminate his need to travel to a store to purchase ice every time he needed it. This filter may be ignored. The more important filter is the retailer or business firm that in some way *distorts* the signal. The distortion may be a temporal one whereby certain demands are not met until after some service time has elapsed, if even then, or it might be spatial in the sense that consumers at particular locations remain unserved.

Bandwidths and Sets of Goods

Curry sought to tie these different ideas together by using the concept of *bandwidth*. Assume that there are particular goods that are purchased by consumers at varying time intervals and that the pattern of these purchases over time can be broken down and summarized by diagrams as shown in Figure 5.19. In each diagram the *cycle* is shown and the *frequency* is defined in terms of the number of cycles per time unit. Figure 5.19(a) involves a higher frequency therefore than does

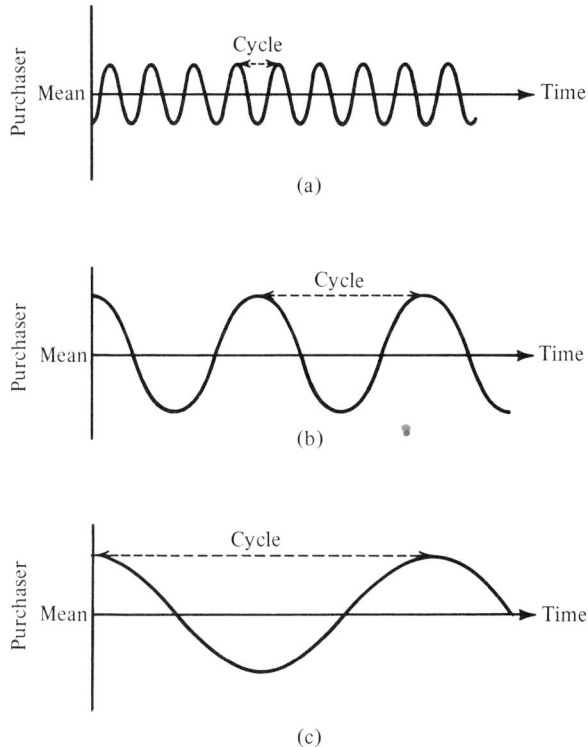

Figure 5.19   Variation in purchasing volume over time.

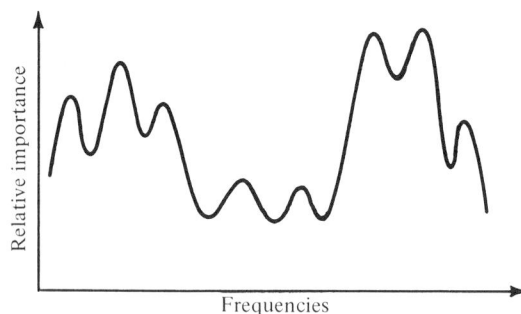

Figure 5.20   A hypothetical spectrum.

either Figure 5.19(b) or Figure 5.19(c). There are mathematical techniques for estimating the different frequencies in any set of observations recorded continuously over time or space. The result is a *spectrum*
that shows how the different frequencies contribute to the total variability in the observations. A plot of a hypothetical spectrum is shown
in Figure 5.20. A *bandwidth* is defined as the width of a band of frequencies measured in cycles per time unit. In Curry's theory *bandwidth* is used to define a range or variety of goods. That is to say, the
different goods and services have characteristic frequencies and a
bandwidth identifies a particular group of them. Now, associated with
the provision of any good there will be inventory costs for the retailer
and

> ... frequently demanded goods have relatively low suppliers'
> inventory costs per item but this cost goes up as frequency
> goes down. Thus a supplier will find that for a given order of
> magnitude of potential customers, there will be certain fre-
> quently demanded goods which it is obviously worth his
> while to stock, others of infrequent demand which are
> clearly not worthwhile, but in the intermediate frequencies
> there is a range of goods about which he must be uncertain
> depending on price margins and holding costs per item.[15]

Curry assumed that the bandwidth of frequencies (and hence
goods) in which the ratio of mean output (goods supplied) to mean input (stockpiling of goods) was not less than 0.7 would define an upper
limit to the bundle or set of goods stocked by the retailer. This limit
was arbitrary, but what is meant was that "the cost situation of the
least frequently demanded item stocked is such that on the average the
supplier will be out of stock three times in ten when the article is asked
for."[16]

Although the above discussion is only a very crude sketch of

Curry's theory, it does give the outline of a theory of the behavior of consumers and retailers in a central-place system in which elements of uncertainty and the frequency components of the behavioral patterns are all important. For those readers who are prepared to plunge into the technical aspects of communication theory and the related mathematics, there are many challenging implications of Curry's formulation that remain to be explored. In particular, the urban rank-size rule can be related to the spectrum interpreted as a set of bandwidths corresponding to different mixes of goods offered, if the assumption is made that urban populations are proportional to bandwidths. In the same vein, the theory has implications for the study of questions concerning the diffusion of purchasing power in a central place hierarchy, the economic base of an urban center, and the spacing of urban centers.

5.6   Locational Patterns of Cities Considered as Outcomes of Probability Processes

One set of predictions yielded by central place theory has to do with the spacing of cities. This subject also has been the focus of a great deal of empirical work, some of which was mentioned in an earlier section of this book. If we consider any particular locational pattern of urban centers in a region, then it soon becomes clear that a very large number of historical, economic, social, political, and physical factors have influenced the locations of the urban places and that it is virtually impossible to unravel all of these factors as they have operated over time. Furthermore, even if the historical records were available and could be studied closely, it might be anticipated that many of the locations would seem to have resulted from pure chance and would defy description in terms of any other factors. Perhaps it is not surprising to find that some scholars have attempted to formulate theories of the locational arrangements and distributions of towns that emphasize the randomness of the process involved.

Distribution and Arrangement of Towns

It is important to begin by drawing a distinction between the arrangement and distribution of towns. We do this by using a purely abstract situation involving a set of points on a map. Figure 5.21(a) is a map showing a set of points that we can think of as representing the locations of towns. If the map region is very large compared to the area of the largest town, this point representation of town locations poses no serious conceptual difficulty. How do we describe this point pattern?

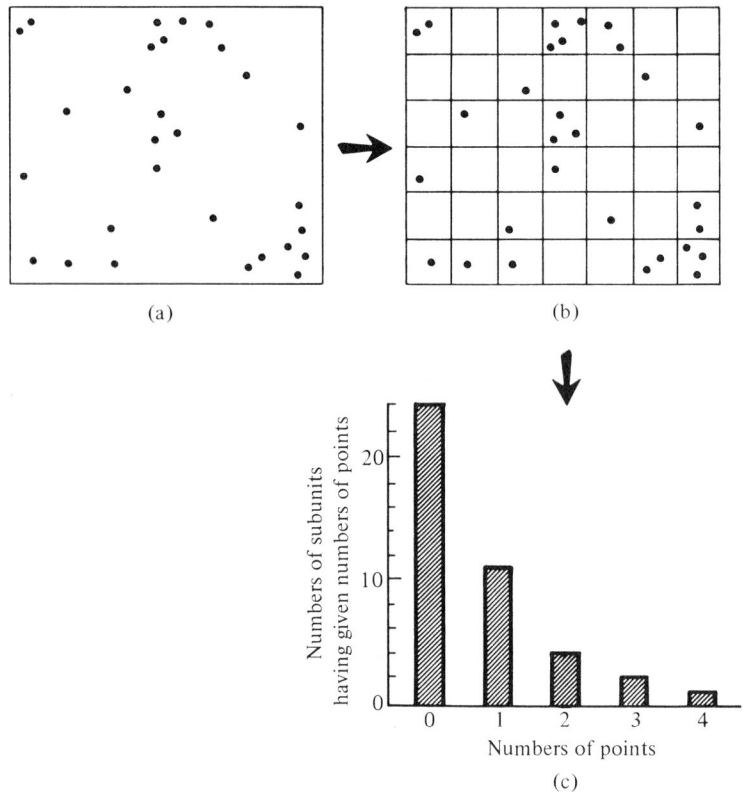

Figure 5.21   Analysis of a hypothetical point pattern.

One way involves dividing the map into a set of regular-sized sub-units [Figure 5.21(b)] and then recording the number of sub-units that contain 0, 1, 2, and so on points. The frequency distribution of these observations is shown in Figure 5.21(c). In this way we are measuring the *distribution* of the points over the map and it is really only the absolute locations of the points that are being considered.

The distinction between distribution and *arrangement* is illustrated graphically in Figure 5.22 in which the two maps obviously have the same distribution of points in the sense defined above, but they have drastically different arrangements of points. Recall from Chapter 3 that a different approach to describing these point patterns involves the measurement of nearest-neighbor distances.

We have now identified two features that are random variables. The first is the number of points per unit area and the second is the distance to a nearest neighbor, be it the first-, second-, third-, or even nth-nearest neighbor. It is possible to develop mathematical models to predict the values of these two different random variables.

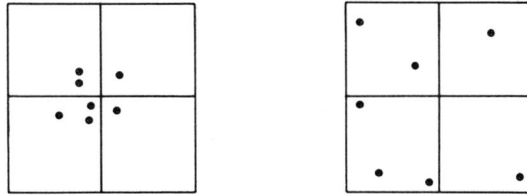

Figure 5.22 Illustration of the distinction between a distribution and an arrangement of points.

Poisson Function

We shall consider first the distribution of points per unit area and we shall assume that the points are town locations in a large region. If we make certain assumptions about the point pattern, it is possible to use a particular mathematical model, the *Poisson function,* to predict the frequency values shown in Figure 5.21(c). The necessary assumptions are that the distribution of points over the sub-units is random in the sense that every sub-unit has an equal chance of having a point within it and every point, in turn, has an equal chance of occurring in any sub-unit. Also, we shall assume that the location of any point is not affected by the locations of others, which is not a particularly appealing assumption when dealing with two locations, but it is a convenient one to make at this moment.

The Poisson function is

$$p(x) = \frac{e^{-\lambda}\lambda^x}{x!} \quad \text{for } x = 0, 1, 2, \ldots, \lambda > 0$$

$$= 0 \text{ otherwise}$$

The term λ is the mean density of points per sub-area; $p(x)$ is the probability of there being exactly x points in a sub-unit; e is a mathematical constant that is the base of the natural logarithm system ($e = 2.71828\ldots$); and $x!$ is read as x-factorial and equals $x(x - 1)(x - 2) \ldots (3)(2)(1)$. The Poisson function is used extensively in predicting the occurrence of fairly rare events either over space or time. It is defined only for integer values.

The County-Seat Model

In some early work on the spacing of towns the Poisson function was used, but the results were not very satisfactory. We consider here a more complex model, the so-called *county-seat model.*[17] Consider a large homogeneous region containing a total of N urban places and divided into c equal-sized counties. The situation is analogous to that shown in Figure 5.21(b), assuming that the counties are small in comparison to the total size of the region. Now assume that each county may have a county-seat town and that of the total N urban places, Z of them are county seats. The remaining $N - Z$ places are noncounty seats. The probability that a county has a designated county-seat town is stated as p and no county may have more than one such town, but it may have none. The process might be thought of as one in which *chance* distributes a set Z of towns over the region in such a way that only one town can land in any one county but some counties may receive none.

Now imagine that this same actor, chance, distributes the remaining $N - Z$ places over the region in a very random manner. That is to say, any county may get none, one, two, or more of this second assignment of towns. The probability that it receives one is assumed to be m and this is equal to $(N - Z)/c$.

Once the two assignments are completed, the following question is asked: What is the probability that a county received exactly x urban places in total? There are two possibilities that have to be considered in answering this question.

1. If the county received a county-seat town, in order for it to have a total of x places it must have $(x - 1)$ noncounty-seat towns. The probability of the first event we said was p; that of the second is given by the Poisson function as

$$\frac{e^{-m}m^{x-1}}{(x - 1)!}$$

    In this case, the density parameter equals m, which we noted above equals $(N - Z)/c$. Here we have two independent events and we can simply multiply their probabilities to get the probability of there being a total of x places in this first case. Thus,

$$p(x)_1 = \frac{pe^{-m}m^{x-1}}{(x - 1)!}$$

2. The other possibility, of course, is that the county did not get a county seat, for which the probability is $(1 - p)$; therefore, in order for it to have a total of x places, they must be all non county-seat towns. The latter possibility is also given by the Poisson function as

$$\frac{e^{-m}m^x}{x!}$$

and the probability is

$$p(x)_2 = \frac{(1 - p)e^{-m}m^x}{x!}$$

The above two possibilities are mutually exclusive, that is to say, if the one applies, the other cannot. Therefore, in answering the original question we must allow for both possibilities by adding the two probabilities. Thus,

$$p(x) = p(x)_1 + p(x)_2$$

$$= \frac{pe^{-m}m^{x-1}}{(x - 1)!} + \frac{(1 - p)e^{-m}m^x}{x!} \quad \text{for } x = 0, 1, 2, \ldots$$

$$= 0 \text{ otherwise}$$

In this model, the term p, which it will be recalled was the probability of a county having a county-seat town, may be interpreted as a measure of the tendency toward uniformity in an otherwise random pattern. If p were zero, the pattern of towns would be purely random, but if p were one, then every county would have at least one town.

This model has been used to predict the locational distribution of urban places of 2,500 population or larger among the counties in Iowa for different census years. The model gives fairly close predictions to the actual values as the figures in Table 5.5 suggest. These results are

Table 5.5   Analysis of Frequency Distributions of N Largest Urban Places by County, Iowa, 1950. [Based on M. F. Dacey, "A county-seat model for the areal pattern of an urban system"; redrawn, with permission, from the *Geographical Review*, vol. **56**, 1966, p. 538.]

Number of Urban Places Per County	$N = 20$		$N = 60$		$N = 100$		$N = 200$	
	Number of Counties							
	obs	*cal*	*obs*	*cal*	*obs*	*cal*	*obs*	*cal*
0	80	80	43	44	15	17	0	0
1	18	19	52	50	69	66	34	35
2	1	0	4	5	14	14	38	36
3				0	0	1	2	21	19
4							3	6
5							3	2
6							0	1

for 1950. In each column there are given the observed number (obs) of urban places per county (of which there were 99) and the number of places calculated from the above model (cal). The columns differ according to the value of N, the number of largest places.

There are a number of ways in which the above model has been modified, for example, by treating the terms p and m as random variables that vary over the counties. These modifications involve more complex mathematics and we do not consider them. Instead, we shall turn now to the problem of predicting the relative locations of towns in a region by using models that focus on the distances between neighboring towns.

Nearest-Neighbor Distances

Again we are concerned with a pattern of town locations considered as points. Assume that this point pattern is the result of some disturbance of an equilibrium central place pattern that is the regular lattice of points shown earlier in Figure 5.6. Is it possible to develop a model that would predict such a pattern of displaced points? Michael Dacey has formulated a probability model of this kind. Although it has very technical aspects, we shall try to sketch its framework here.[18]

Figure 5.23 shows a 60°-lattice. The solid points on this lattice are the equilibrium central place locations and the small open circles are the displaced locations. The distance r from a displaced point to its corresponding equilibrium location can be thought of as a random variable, and it is convenient to assume that all these distances are described by the one probability law. What form this law takes, that is to

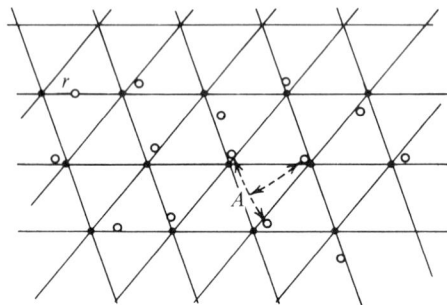

• Points represent central places in equilibrium pattern, H.
o Displaced points in pattern, M.

Figure 5.23 Displacement of points from equilibrium positions on lattice. [After M. F. Dacey, "A probability model for central place locations"; reproduced by permission from *Annals* of the Association of American Geographers, vol. **56**, 1966.]

say, which one of the many known mathematical probability laws is assumed, is a matter of choice to the theorist. Dacey used the *normal probability function* to describe this random variable, but other forms could be used.

Two questions can be answered in regard to the point pattern shown in Figure 5.23. First, for any point in the pattern *M*, what are the probable distances to its six nearest neighboring points? More precisely, what is the nature of the probability law that describes these nearest-neighbor distances for the first-, second-, third-, and so on up to the sixth-nearest neighbor? Second, if a sample point or locus is chosen anywhere within the lattice, for example, point *A* in Figure 5.23, what are the probable distances from this locus to the three points displaced from the lattice points that form the vertices of the triangle containing *A*? These three distances have been identified for this sample point *A* in Figure 5.23. Remember that point *A* could be anywhere in the lattice. The answer to the question involves a probability law that describes the distance from *A* to the *j*th nearest of the three points, for $j = 1, 2, 3$.

In testing the probability models that he derived, using again information on the pattern of towns in Iowa, Dacey found that the models yielded very good predictions. At the same time, he noted that this stochastic interpretation of central place patterns provided descriptions only and added nothing new by way of explanations about the underlying processes.

This last comment to the effect that the models provide good descriptions but no explanations of the underlying processes deserves some attention in concluding this section. Often the argument is made that probabilistic models are appropriate if one is dealing with the behavior of individuals in a system and that deterministic formulations are more appropriate for the aggregative and macro-level aspects. The distinction is apparent in the work of the two geographers that we have discussed in this section, Leslie Curry and Michael Dacey. Curry, we noted, used as the building blocks for his theory certain statements about individual behavior in the face of uncertainty, and his representation of the associated decision processes as ones involving random elements did not appear unreasonable. The formulations conveyed a sense of certain behavioral processes at work, and even though the assumptions that were used could be questioned, the emphases appeared consistent with our intuitive notions of how human behavior influences and shapes urban society. In Dacey's work, by contrast, there is no reference at all to the individual decision maker. The emphasis is solely on the location of points viewed as a stochastic process. The mathematics is much more rigorous, but the results seem far less satisfying in terms of contributing to our understanding of urban society. We are provided with very precise descriptions of point location patterns that may well prove useful in more ambitious formulations that seek to weld the behavioral processes with the point pattern analysis. But to date, no such synthesis has been successful.

5.7 Summary

In this chapter we have gone beyond the simple descriptions of spatial patterns and processes and have sought to develop theories and models of these same things. A great deal of the chapter was devoted to discussion of central place theory which seeks to provide an explanation of the number, size, and location of urban centers in any large region. The quest for explanation was founded on the belief that if we could discover patterns of order and regularities and formulate laws or generalizations about these, we would then have the means to predict other patterns and occurrences. This is, after all, what is done in other sciences.

But we should now realize that in order to develop the laws and theories such as Christaller and Lösch proposed, we have to make very restrictive assumptions about how people behave, both as consumers and businessmen, about the role of cities and the reasons for their existence, and about the constancy over time of different relationships and processes. We had to assume, for example, that people traveled only to the nearest urban center to shop and that businessmen always acted rationally in their choices of locations for their stores. We considered towns only as service centers and had to ignore their industries that might be exporting goods to far off places, perhaps overseas. We had to assume that people's preferences and tastes were not changing over time and that technological changes in transportation and so on could be ignored.

Given all these assumptions, little wonder then that the theories and models do not seem to fit the real world that we know and live in. But should this concern us? What are the real gains and advantages to be realized by theorizing about urban society as we have done in this chapter?

Three main advantages come to mind. First, the intellectual activity involved in developing a theory or model of some situation demands a high level of mental discipline. There are rules of logic to be observed and heeded and these are fundamental in the use of mathematics as the language for theorizing. We. are, of course, assuming that we are interested only in the scientific approach that we discussed in Chapter 1. There are other approaches and different sets of rules, but they are of no interest to us here. As an expression, then, of intellectual creativity and discipline of thought any social science theory should be of interest to us.

We always demand something more, however. The theory should be a sensible one. Its insights and predictions should seem plausible. This suggests the second main advantage of theoretical work. It forces us to think very carefully and critically about those aspects of urban society that are of interest to us. The assumptions of the theory must be reasonable ones and the analysis of the processes at work should be critical and unbiased. Whether the latter goal is attainable is questioned by many who argue that biases are always present in social science research and that they must be recognized explicitly.

Finally, it is worth stressing that theories and models provide at least a set of frameworks within which one can reflect on future developments and change. Theories of urban society will never allow for precise predictions to be made about the future, but they do permit speculations to be made against the background of certain stated assumptions. They allow for such statements as "if such and such hold true then this should (or, "may possibly") be true also" to be made and commented on. Without these frameworks provided by the social sciences, society is left to rely on the prophets and soothsayers.

Notes

1. W. Christaller, *Die zentralen Orte in Süddeutschland* (Jena: Gustav Fischer, 1933); trans. by C. W. Baskin, *Central Places in Southern Germany* (Englewood Cliffs: Prentice-Hall, Inc., 1966).

2. The discussion here follows J. B. Parr and K. G. Denike, "Theoretical problems in central place analysis," *Economic Geography,* **46,** 1970, pp. 568–86.

3. The discussion here follows M. F. Dacey, "The geometry of central place theory," *Geografiska Annaler,* **478,** 1965, pp. 111–24.

4. A. Lösch, *The Economics of Location,* trans. by W. H. Woglom and W. F. Stolper (New Haven: Yale University Press, 1954).

5. *Ibid.,* p. 113.

6. See M. F. Dacey, "An interesting number property in central place theory," *The Professional Geographer,* **17,** 1965, pp. 32–33; J. C. Hudson, "An algebraic relation between the Lösch and Christaller central-place networks," *The Professional Geographer,* **19,** 1967, pp. 133–35.

7. M. J. Beckmann, "City hierarchies and the distribution of city size," *Economic Development and Cultural Change,* **6,** 1958, pp. 243–48.

8. J. B. Parr, "City hierarchies and the distribution of city size: a reconsideration of Beckmann's contribution," *Journal of Regional Science,* **9,** 1969, pp. 239–53.

9. K. G. DENIKE and J. B. PARR, "Production in space, spatial competition, and restricted entry," *Journal of Regional Science,* **10,** 1970, pp. 49–63.

10. H. HOTELLING, "Stability in competition," *Economic Journal,* **39,** 1929, pp. 41–57.

11. See R. G. GOLLEDGE, G. RUSHTON, and W. A. V. CLARK, "Some spatial characteristics of Iowa's dispersed farm population and their implications for the grouping of central place functions," *Economic Geography,* **42,** 1966, pp. 216–72; G. RUSHTON, R. G. GOLLEDGE, and W. A. V. CLARK, "Formulation and test of a normative model for the spatial allocation of grocery expenditures by a dispersed population," *Annals,* Association of American Geographers, **57,** 1967, pp. 389–400; G. RUSHTON, "The scaling of locational preferences," in K. R. COX and R. G. GOLLEDGE, eds., *Behavioral Problems in Geography: A symposium,* Northwestern University Studies in Geography, No. 17, 1969, pp. 197–227.

12. G. RUSHTON, "Postulates of central place theory and properties of central place systems," *Geographical Analysis,* **3,** 1971, pp. 140–56.

13. *Ibid.*

14. L. CURRY, "The random spatial economy: an exploration in settlement theory," *Annals,* Association of American Geographers, **54,** 1964, pp. 138–46; L. CURRY, "Central places in the random spatial economy," *Journal of Regional Science,* **7,** (Supplement), 1967, pp. 217–38.

15. L. CURRY, 1967, *op. cit.,* p. 224.

16. *Ibid.*

17. M. F. DACEY, "A county-seat model for the areal pattern of an urban system," *Geographical Review,* **56,** 1966, pp. 527–42.

18. M. F. DACEY, "A probability model for central place locations," *Annals,* Association of American Geographers, **56,** 1966, pp. 549–68.

C. PATTERNS WITHIN THE CITY

chapter 6

Urban Land Uses

The scale of the analysis now changes and we shall focus closely on the spatial structure of the metropolitan area itself. Now instead of talking about a set of cities, we shall concentrate on the patterns that are revealed within any one large urban area. This does not imply that the approaches to analyzing these patterns are drastically different from those we considered in earlier chapters, for often they are almost the same. But the particular questions that we pose in regard to the patterns are somewhat different and warrant separate consideration.

The distinction between the study of *intercity* relations and *intra-urban* relationships traditionally has been emphasized in urban geography texts. It provides a useful framework on which to organize a review of studies, but it should not be overstressed. We have already noted for example, that the spheres of influences of large urban centers are continually expanding and as a consequence the separation of urban from rural areas is not always clear-cut. Further, as we have hinted at in the opening paragraph above, there are analytical approaches that can be applied equally well at both the intercity and intraurban levels and for these approaches the distinction, therefore, is largely meaningless.

6.1   Generalized Patterns of Land Use

It is convenient to begin with an examination of where different activities are located within a city and what generalizations can be made about these locational patterns and arrangements. Much of the discussion on this question has been influenced by three particular statements concerning the generalized patterns of land use within cities. These statements are qualitative in nature and for the most part are based on an examination of existing patterns and past trends.

Concentric Zone Hypothesis

This hypothesis was developed mainly by a sociologist, E. W. Burgess, of the University of Chicago.[1] He was interested in the social structure of the city and in the manner that the city grew outward from its center. His observations on the changing locations of different occupational, ethnic, and immigrant groups within the city and on the relationships between these distributional patterns and certain social problems led him to suggest that the city's spatial structure could be viewed as a set of concentric zones centered on the city's downtown. Changes occurred as the activities in an inner zone gradually *invaded* the adjacent outer zone and eventually replaced the activities located there. This process has come to be known as one of *invasion and succession*.

In Burgess' city the core was the *Central Business District* (CBD) in which the major commercial, political, and social activities of the city were centered. Here were the central office buildings, the cultural and civic centers, and the large department stores. This core of buildings is still easily identified in any large city and many geographers have devoted much effort to the problems of defining its areal extent, its form in terms of building heights, floor space, and functions, and its dynamics.[2]

The future role of the CBD in the life of any large city is a matter of considerable debate these days. In terms of commercial activity and in particular retailing, it is clear that the relative importance of the CBD in the total city picture has declined as planned regional shopping centers have emerged to cater to the shopping needs of automobile-dependent populations. Also, in many of the cities of the United States the downtown areas have ceased to be attractive places of residence and even employment for a majority of people and they are often characterized by building decay and serious social problems. This has prompted considerable pessimism in regard to the future of these areas in many United States cities. But the downward trend is not everywhere apparent even in the United States and certainly not in cities in other countries. In Canada, for example, the downtown areas of its three largest cities (Montreal, Toronto, and Vancouver) are focal points of development and growth and they function as important centers of social and cultural life.

Burgess described a zone outside the CBD that was *in transition* in the sense that it included old residential districts, many of them slum districts, now being invaded by businesses and manufacturing activities moving out of the CBD. This pattern is still discernible in cities today—the former residence, which in many cases gives the appearance of having been once a large and palatial one, now converted into one or more business offices and destined in the short-term for demolition and replacement by a far less imposing factory or office structure or high-rise apartment building. This pattern of invasion and succession may be understandable in purely economic terms, but to an increasing number of urban citizens it often appears indefensible from the point of view of preserving historical buildings and maintaining the cultural heritage of the city.

In Burgess' view, families sought to escape from this second zone in which he noted marked social disorganization, poverty, crime, and disease to be widespread. Typically, they moved (in the Burgess scheme of things) into the third zone, that of *workingmen's homes*. Here were the ethnic concentrations of immigrant families living for the most part in the rented lower floors of two-storied buildings usually of frame construction. Beyond lay the zones of *better residences* and *commuters* in which single-family homes prevailed and the higher in-income groups were located closer to the downtown.

Burgess has been criticized, very properly, for making such assertions without describing any processes or mechanisms that would do the "sorting and sifting" of individuals and groups over the space of the city as he described. But aside from such criticisms about Burgess' description of the social structure of a city, the concentric zone model has proven to have a fairly broad appeal. First, it is generally consistent with the predictions of a fairly simple model of how the urban land market works, which we shall consider in the next chapter. It is reasonable to expect, within the framework of certain assumptions, that different land uses will be arranged in concentric zones around the CBD, with the most intensive or highest rent-paying uses close to the downtown and the less extensive ones farther out. Also, if one examines the patterns of growth of any large metropolitan area over time, there is usually evidence in support of a concentric zone pattern. In general, as improved transportation methods have emerged, the city has continued to spread outward in broadly concentric zones.

Wedge and Sector Hypothesis

In his writings, Burgess noted that physical features such as rivers, lakes, or railway lines would serve to disrupt the neat concentric zones that he described. But it was left to a later writer, Homer Hoyt, to outline another generalized description of urban land-use patterns that took such features into account.[3]

Hoyt was interested primarily in residential land use, and on the basis of his studies of United States cities he suggested that the residential districts would be arranged like spokes on a wheel outward from the central business district. The residential districts associated with the highest rents would represent one or more sectors and in between these would be the low- and medium-class residential districts.

> High-rent or high-grade residential neighborhoods must almost necessarily move outward toward the periphery of the city. The wealthy seldom reverse their steps and move backward into the obsolete houses which they are giving up. On each side of them is usually an intermediate rental area, so they cannot move sideways. As they represent the highest income group, there are no houses above them abandoned by another group. They must build new houses on vacant land. Usually this vacant land lies available just ahead of the line of march of the area because, anticipating the trends of fashionable growth, land promoters have either restricted it to high-grade use or speculators have placed a value on the land that is too high for the low-rent or intermediate-rental group. Hence the natural trend of the high-rent area is outward, toward the periphery of the city in the very sector in which the high rent started.[4]

This sector model has a certain intuitive appeal as a more general model of urban land use. The historical evidence on urban growth often shows that development usually was channeled along the major transportation routeways and, in the cases of commercial and manufacturing activities that depend on immediate access to transportation facilities, the linear patterns persist today. What has changed in many cases is the orientation. Many of the linear concentrations of industry no longer radiate outward from the downtown. This is the case with the semicircular Route 128 around Boston and the Trans-Canada

Highway 401 that cuts across the northern part of the Toronto Metropolitan Area.

Multiple Nuclei

Contrary to the ideas proposed in the concentric zone and sector theories, the land-use pattern in many cities is arranged around several rather than a single center.[5] In some cities, for example London, these centers may have existed since the beginning of the city; in others, they may have developed with the growth of the city, as in Chicago where heavy industry migrated to the south to serve as a secondary nucleus.

The rise of separate nuclei and differentiated districts in a city may be attributed to a combination of four factors:

1. Certain activities require specialized facilities and locations. For instance, the retail district is attracted to the point of greater intracity accessibility.
2. Certain similar forms of activity often group together. The clothing manufacturing district on lower Manhattan Island in New York provides an example of this tendency. The benefits associated with this concentration are often referred to as *agglomeration economies,* which may stem from the common access to a skilled labor force, from mutual benefits in purchasing and marketing arrangements, from savings in transportation costs, or from the ability to keep abreast of competitive developments. Of course, historical factors also have played a part in the development of many of these concentrations.
3. The opposite of the previous point is that many activities in the city are unattractive to one another and tend to repel one another. This is a force making for separation and dispersion of the different land uses in a city. Such is usually the case, for example, with manufacturing industry and residential districts.
4. Certain activities simply cannot afford high rents and must seek less expensive land on the outskirts of a city. Unfortunately, this is too often the case with recreational land uses.

These factors favor the development within the city's land-use pattern of several *peaks* and around them of dispersed patterns of activities.

What is lacking in all of the above three descriptions of the general land-use pattern of a city is a precise statement of the processes and mechanisms that underlie the observed patterns in the real world. Certain forces are mentioned, but the discussions of these are not tied together in a logical argument that could be used to predict the land-use pattern of any city. Such a framework would, of course, have to allow for the particular physical setting, the peculiar history, and the social and political structure of the city in question. In Chapter 7 we shall see that it is possible to construct such a framework.

Our discussion up to this point has looked at the land-use pattern of the city as a whole. It is now useful to turn to a consideration of some of the major spatial features of each type of land use in turn.

6.2 Commercial Land Use: Hierarchies, Change, and Blight

This particular activity does not occupy a great deal of the land space in the city and it is highly concentrated toward the center of the city. The building of regional shopping centers in the suburbs has tended to weaken this concentration. It is the commercial activity, however, that generates much of the business within the city and helps account for many of the patterns of travel in the city that we shall discuss later.

Commercial Hierarchies

There is clearly a hierarchy of commercial districts within any large city in regard to the types of commercial activities found in the districts and the size of their associated tributary areas. At the top of the hierarchy is the downtown area or the central business district (the CBD). Below this are the regional commercial centers, community shopping centers, the neighborhood centers, and so on, down to the lowest level of the hierarchy, the isolated store or small cluster of stores. The designation and description of these different levels in the hierarchy can be illustrated in the cases of Zurich, Switzerland and Chicago, U.S.A.

Zurich's commercial structure has been described in terms of three major levels of commercial centers.[6] At the top was the Central Business District offering the most goods and the widest selection range, then followed the regional business district, and finally, the neighborhood business district. The comparative sizes of these three districts are shown in Table 6.1. The identification of the number of kinds of champagne and cigars sold and the price ranges existing for wrist watches and jewelry, for example, serve to point up the differences between the three levels of the hierarchy.

In the city of Chicago, the Central Business District remains the largest and dominant retail center in the city.

Table 6.1 Characteristics of the Three Major Levels of Commerical Centers in Zurich, Switzerland. [Based on H. Carol, "Hierarchy of central functions within the city," reproduced by permission from *Annals of the Association of American Geographers*, vol. **50**, 1960, pp. 424–27.]

	Neighborhood Business District (e.g., Seebach)	*Regional Business District (e.g., Oerlikon)*	*Central Business District (Zurich)*
Number of Kinds of Goods Offered			
Champagne	1	3	20
Cigars	112	205	501
Range in Value of Goods Offered			
Wrist Watches	40–200 fr.	60–950 fr.	100–20,000 fr.
Jewelry	30–210 fr.	50–1,050 fr.	100–30,000 fr.
Population Served	5,000–10,000	30,000	500,000
Pedestrian Flow (persons per hour)	200–450	700–1,100	4,480

Retailing in the CBD is little more than a speck in a city map, occupying less than one-half of 1 percent of the city's area, although 5 percent of the total city floor space. On an average weekday 8 percent of all person vehicular trips in the city are made to shop in the Loop, and on these trips 15 percent of the city's retail transactions are completed. Of the CBD's sales, two-thirds are in shoppers goods lines (clothing, furniture, and department stores), and these amount to one-third of the entire city sales of shoppers goods. If simple size be a criterion, the CBD is by far the largest retail center in the city ... But size is not the only criterion for setting apart the CBD.... The CBD provides a greater range of shoppers goods than the outlying centers, and sells them not only to the entire city and metropolitan area, but to the midwestern United States, and for a few things, to the United States as a whole. Eight and one-half percent of the CBD's floor space is accounted for by commercial functions performed for the midwest and nation; another two-thirds serve the entire metropolitan market.[7]

Below the central business district in the commercial hierarchy are four major levels among the larger unplanned outlying business centers. These four levels are described below.

1. *Major unplanned regional centers* typically contain 60 to 70 different kinds of retail and service businesses in one- or two-story buildings. These businesses involve usually as many as 200 or more different firms. As much as three-quarters of the total retail sales in such a center are accounted for by clothing and personal furnishings, department and variety stores, and home furnishings. The total area to which these types of services are provided generally averages about 12 square miles and contains over 300,000 people. In addition, these centers also offer convenience goods and services such as foodstores and drugstores and eating and drinking services, but for these activities the trade area is smaller, averaging only $2\frac{1}{2}$ square miles and serving around 65,000 people.

2. *Smaller unplanned shopping goods centers,* in contrast to the major regional centers, can be further differentiated in terms of the income characteristics of the regions they serve. There are, first of all, the smaller centers offering the same shopping goods as the major regional centers, that is to say, the apparel and personal furnishings, department and variety stores, and home furnishings. Centers like these in the higher-income areas typically perform 50 to 60 different kinds of businesses that might involve as many as 150 different establishments. The trade area of these higher-income centers averages only $4\frac{1}{2}$ square miles and includes around 77,000 persons. The same type of center located in the lower-income areas generally provides fewer types of business, typically 40 or so, with 100 different establishments. However, these lower-income centers generally serve a larger area, around $6\frac{1}{2}$ square miles, and a total population of around 135,000 persons.

3. *Unplanned community centers* provide only convenience goods, that is to say, food, drugs, eating and drinking, whereas the above two classes combine both convenience and shopping goods. Almost all of these community centers are located in the higher-income areas and typically they serve a trade area of 2 square miles with a total population of around 60,000 people. There are fewer different kinds of business, around 36, and there might be 75 to 100 different establishments.

4. *Unplanned neighborhood centers* are found in both the higher- and lower-income areas in the city. In the former they supplement the set of community centers offering convenience goods; in the latter they are the largest centers concerned exclusively with selling the same types of goods. The typical mix of stores includes small food shops, drugstores, restaurants, bars and liquor stores, laundries, barbers and beauty shops, and small

clothing shops. Generally, there are some 25 to 28 different types of businesses involving 40 to 55 stores.

In addition to these different types of unplanned centers, the planned centers generally conform to the same type of hierarchical arrangement. The planned centers usually involve larger individual stores but fewer total establishments and functions.

The above observations relate to the city of Chicago in the early 1960's. Over the past few years the trend certainly has been toward building larger and larger regional shopping centers that offer a wider variety of types of business and involve an increasing number of different establishments. These new planned centers are highly dependent on automobile transportation and they involve large additional areas of space for parking lots.

Although we have been primarily concerned with the hierarchy of unplanned business centers, we should note that there are other levels of commercial establishments within cities such as Chicago. In particular, there are many ribbon-like developments of commercial establishments along the major highways, and in residential areas there are many small isolated clusters of retail establishments.

Specialized Commercial Centers

A second major feature of the commercial structure is that different commercial centers often perform very specialized functions. This is so in Chicago where several different kinds of specialized functional areas exist. By far the most common of these are the so-called *automobile rows* involving strings of new and used car dealers and automobile service shops along major highways. This phenomenon is by no means unique to Chicago and can be found in any major North American city. Other specialized functional areas in Chicago include the medical districts and centers, which are increasingly planned in character, and the clusters of furniture and appliance stores. This tendency for particular commercial establishments to cluster in certain areas finds a very strong expression in the city of New York where such districts as the Wall Street district (finance), Madison Avenue (advertising agencies), and Broadway (entertainment) are renowned the world over. Many similar examples could be cited for other major cities throughout the world. Some of the reasons for this clustering of similar activities in particular zones within the city can be found in the agglomeration economies discussed earlier. The argument, remember, runs as follows. Firms specializing in a certain line of business realize advantages from being located close to their competitors. This enables them to share a common access to a particular market, such as is the case in entertainment districts, and to keep abreast of one another in terms of new marketing strategies and product development, as would be the case in the clothing industry on the west side of Manhattan Island. But the economic argument is easily overdone, and in many cases it seems as though historical accident has been an even more important factor in shaping the character of these particular districts in the city.

Spatial Patterns of Commercial Establishments

In the locational pattern of commercial activity in the city there are a number of distinct components. There are, first of all, the *clusters* of commercial activity noted already in the case of Chicago. These clusters vary in size and range from the central business district that may cover several city blocks down to the small clusters of one or two small stores. In contrast to these clusters of commercial establishments, we noted that in Chicago there are many *linear arrangements* of commercial establishments. In total, these add up to more than 500 miles in the Chicago metropolitan area and contain a total of some 35,000 different commercial establishments. In some cases, they take the form of tentacle-like arrangements of stores extending out from the major commercial centers in the city; in other cases, they occur as isolated ribbons. Many of the establishments in these ribbons (gas stations, motels, and drive-in restaurants) depend wholly on highway traffic; others clearly prefer locations on what have been described as the urban arterials that extend out from the commercial centers. The functions that choose such arterial locations typically include furniture stores, discount stores, lumber yards, nurseries, and so on. "These are the uses for which the householder has an infrequent specialized demand that calls for an occasional special-purpose trip to the store . . . ."[8]

A third way of analyzing the locational pattern of commercial establishments is by way of *point* pattern analysis. Given a set of maps showing the locational patterns of different types of retail establishments in the city as points, we would expect that certain of the maps would show very distinctive patterns. For example, grocery stores should be fairly widely distributed throughout the city, that is, located either within or in relatively close proximity to the major residential districts. Whether or not we define a grocery store to include a supermarket is a question of establishing definitions that would have to be done before the point pattern analysis was begun. In contrast to the situation for grocery stores, more specialized stores, as we have noted, often tend to be clustered in certain areas of the city, perhaps in the downtown area. These suggestions are confirmed in the patterns of retail loca-

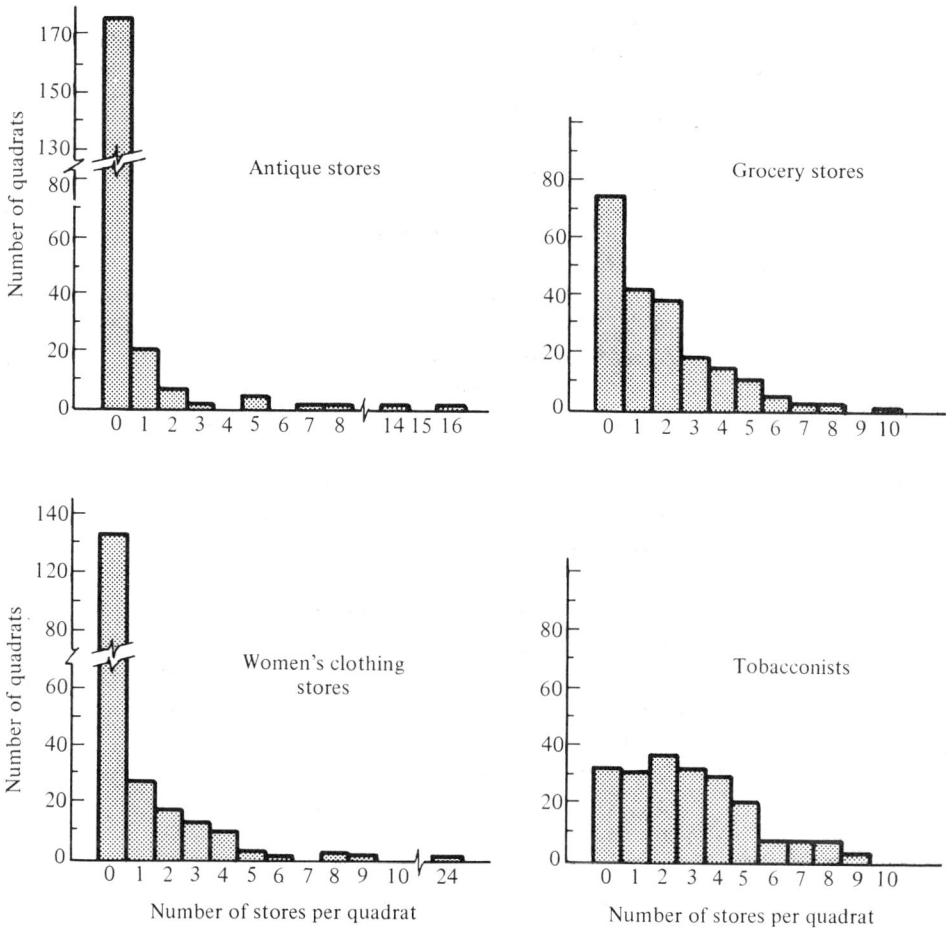

Fig. 6.1 The spatial distributions of selected retail establishments in Stockholm analyzed by the quadrat method discussed in Chapter 5. [Based on R. Artle, *The Structure of the Stockholm Economy* (Ithaca: Cornell University Press, 1965), pp. 136–137. © 1965 by Cornell University Press. Used by permission of Cornell University Press.]

tions in the city of Stockholm, Sweden. There, grocery stores and tobacconists tend to be uniformly dispersed throughout the city whereas antique stores and women's clothing stores are much more clustered (Figure 6.1). Similar results have been reported for other cities.[9]

The same approach has shown that in the city of Lansing, Michigan, as the population and city area have grown over the period 1900–1960, the locational pattern of grocery stores in the city has developed from a clustered one, through a fairly random arrangement, to a more even distribution (Figure 6.2). This trend toward uniformity seems likely to continue.

Dynamics of Commercial Land Use

An important aspect of the structure of commercial activity within the city is that of its *dynamics*. Again, the city of Chicago has proven to be an extremely valuable laboratory for studies of this feature. The changes that took place in the patterns of retail location in that city up until the late 1950's have been summarized as follows:[10]

1. Changes in the economic scale at which retailing could be carried on profitably resulted in larger and larger stores that drew from much wider trade areas and were dependent on automobile transportation. This trend toward increasing scale was balanced by the increasing desire on the part of consumers for greater specialization and by the overall decrease in urban population densities that resulted in higher transportation costs generally.
2. The effect of income and population changes was toward increasing the importance of higher-order goods and, as a consequence, many of the smaller commercial centers that emphasized convenience goods were subjected to increased economic pressure.
3. The planned shopping center dominated the development of new shopping goods stores, a development that was not in line with the expectations of central place theory. In other words, these new planned centers typically were not located in the already developed areas where the population was concentrated, but rather they were often built on the outskirts of the development area. The location of these centers then served to distort the pattern of central places instead of reinforcing it.
4. The planned center was a distinctive level in the commercial hierarchy and was properly regarded as mainly a retailing location. Many of the low-order services were not found in these planned centers.
5. Many of the new planned centers were very specialized in their functions (witness, for example, the medical centers and the discount centers). A consequence was that the centers themselves competed with one another and the whole structure of

Figure 6.2 Spatial distributions of grocery stores in Lansing, Michigan. [A. Getis, "Temporal land-use pattern analysis with the use of nearest-neighbor and quadrat methods"; reproduced, by permission, from *Annals of the Association of American Geographers*, vol. **54**, 1964, pp. 393–94.]

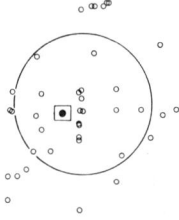

1900

0 _____ 5000
Feet

● STATE CAPITOL

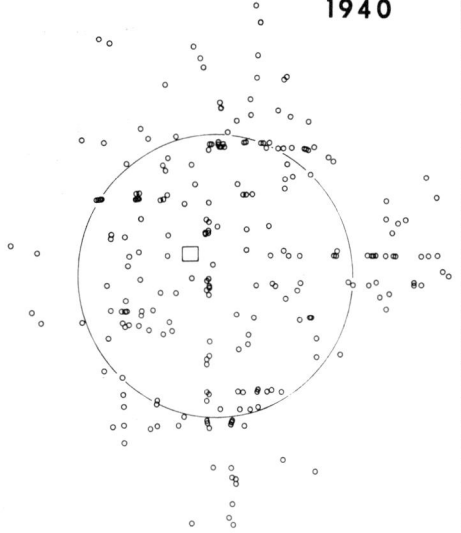

1940

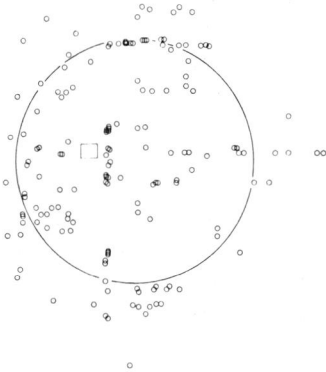

1920

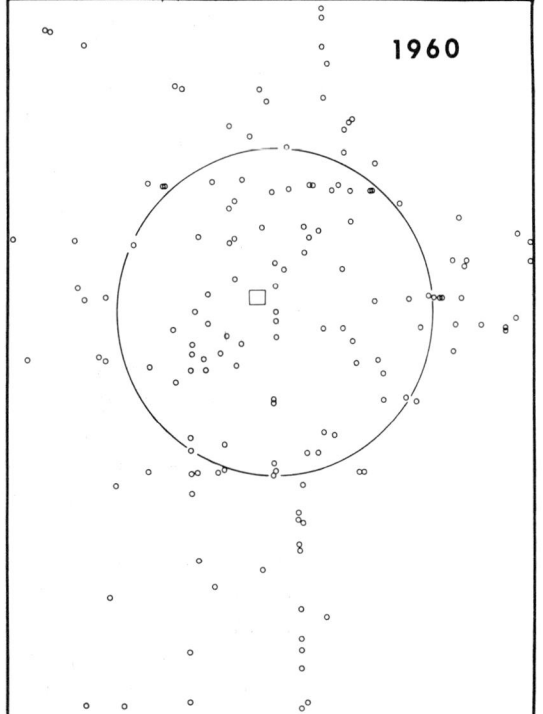

1960

the commercial activity of the city was tending to be organized around the centers instead of around individual establishments or, as was formerly the case, the central business district.

6. The small isolated store continued to disappear in the residential neighborhoods, but this trend was counterbalanced by the expansion of urban arterial shopping areas.

7. The existing unplanned business centers were becoming more tightly defined, retreating at peripheries but increasing in their peak land value at the center. Many functions were abandoning some of the smaller centers so that they could take advantage of larger trade areas, and so on.

8. In the overall pattern of change the importance of population and income changes could not be overstressed. These changes not only accounted for many of the new developments in the commercial pattern of the city but they also helped explain the decline of certain other centers.

9. As the pattern of residential succession moved outward, there were rings of commercial centers that matured and then declined.

An attempt to highlight the forces that prompted change in the retail pattern of Chicago suggested the framework shown in Figure 6.3. The general model postulates that there are certain direct forces such as population and income that affect the assortment of businesses and establishments in the different centers and may be major determinants in the formation of different centers and commercial districts. These factors, in turn, are affected by certain indirect forces such as the level of income, the level of technology, and the growth of the urban system. These affects may be economic or ecological in character or have to do with consumer preference and mobility.

Commercial Blight

One of the consequences of these patterns of change is that considerable downgrading of certain commercial districts may result. Commercial blight may take different forms.[11] *Economic blight* results when changes in consumer demand are reflected in losses of markets. The population of an area served by a particular commercial center may have declined or the relative income levels may have fallen. As a consequence, there are vacant stores and a frequent downgrading of the number and quality of goods and services offered in the center. *Physical blight* generally reflects the age of the buildings and the lack of proper maintenance. *Functional blight*, or technological obsolescence, is a more complex phenomenon and results from changes either in con-

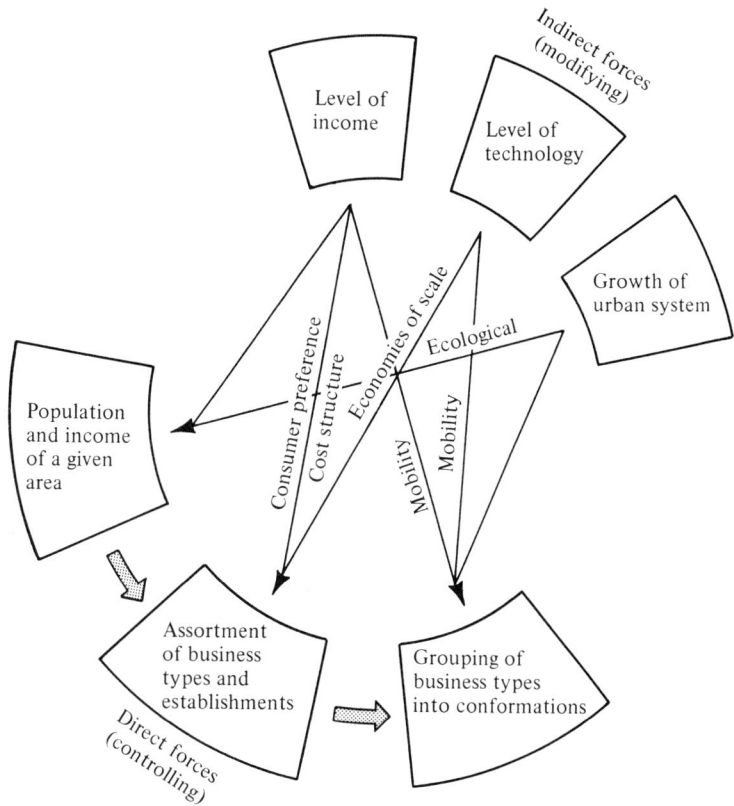

Figure 6.3 Forces leading to change in the retail pattern. [J. W. Simmons, "The changing pattern of retail location," *Research Paper*, Department of Geography, University of Chicago, No. 92, 1964, p. 155. Used with permission of the publisher, The University of Chicago Department of Geography Research Papers.]

sumer demand or the supply side of the commercial activity. As consumers become more mobile and as the technology of retailing changes, many commercial establishments simply become obsolete. This is apparent if one compares the old commercial centers consisting of many stores connected by an outdoor walkway with the modern indoor shopping center. Finally, *frictional* blight resulted from the detrimental affects that a particular business may have upon the surrounding areas or uses, or conversely, when these surroundings have an adverse affect upon the business itself. Examples of frictional blight are the creation of traffic congestion and security and fire hazards as a result of poor planning, and the reduction of land values adjacent to certain commercial activities. All of these different forms of blight may be present in varying combinations in any large commercial center.

6.3   Manufacturing: A Decentralizing Activity

The presence of manufacturing, we have noted, is often basic to the existence of a city and in some cases the city may actually have grown up around a particular industrial concentration. A well-known illustration of this point is the city of Gary, Indiana, which originated in the early 1900's as a planned industrial community dependent on the steel industry.

Within the city area, manufacturing typically is located on or near the major transportation arteries since transportation costs represent an important economic consideration for almost all forms of manufacturing. Hence, the older industrial districts frequently were located near the railway tracks or the rivers and canals, while the more recently established manufacturing areas have preferred locations near the major highways that connect the city with the surrounding region. In the past, the downtown area of the city was often the preferred location for the manufacturing firms; here the transportation routes converged and the resulting accessibility was an advantage not only in assembling raw materials and distributing the manufactured goods but also in obtaining workers. The latter consideration helps account for the fact that clothing factories were, and often still are, typically located near the downtown area, the point of maximum accessibility for the comparatively large number of women workers employed in this industry who make use of public transportation facilities. One consequence of the increased importance of highway locations for manufacturing within the city has been the tendency for new firms to locate in the outer suburbs of the city. We shall say more on this shortly.

Location Patterns

There are any number of specific studies of particular cities that discuss the manufacturing land-use patterns within them. Alan Pred has drawn together some of these different statements into the following classifications:[12]

1. Industries serving essentially the metropolitan market itself, for example, food processing is concentrated near the downtown or Central Business District. These so-called ubiquitous *industries* usually have strong linkages with wholesaling activities and are often located in the same districts as these.
2. Industries, such as job printing, that require close contact with the customer prior to manufacturing also locate downtown. The Manhattan location of the fashion clothing industry pro-

vides an example of a centrally located *communication-economy industry.*

3. Industries serving mainly local markets and using materials produced within the city often randomly locate throughout the city. Examples include the manufacture of ice or concrete blocks and metal-plating and polishing.
4. Industries serving nonlocal markets but producing very high-valued products also locate randomly throughout the city. For these industries, transportation costs are only of secondary importance and specific considerations affect locational choices more heavily. An example in San Francisco, according to Pred, is the manufacture of computers and related machinery.
5. Industries that realize important communications economies from clustering but that do not require a central location within the city. The clustering of electronics and space-age industries along Route 128 around Boston is often cited as an example of this pattern.
6. Industries serving nonlocal markets that seek transportation cost advantages associated with waterfront locations. Petroleum refining, some chemical industries, and sugar refining provide examples of these patterns.
7. Industries with large outside markets and for which transportation costs on finished bulky manufactured goods are significant locate on the sides of the metropolitan area facing the most important market area. The motor vehicle assembly industry in San Francisco, for example, is on the eastern side, almost all of New York's heavy industry is in the west in New Jersey, and Chicago's steel industry is on the south side.

Suburbanization and Decentralization

An issue that has received considerable attention over the years has been the movement of industry out of the central areas of the city into the more suburban locations. We shall now look at some of these movement patterns and the factors that seem to have been associated with the changes in location.

These shifts have generally been summarized by the term *suburbanization* and they have been in response to such factors as the increased cost of manufacturing operation in downtown areas (in turn, a function of the pressure that exists on land values there, the difficulties of access and traffic congestion, the high costs of police protection and other servicing), new planning ordinances that have often legislated against the location of obnoxious industries, especially in the central areas, and technological changes in manufacturing (which have re-

sulted in large single-storied factories in which line assembly is dominant and for which good access to highway transportation routes and
the provision of adequate parking space are essential).

These trends in the suburbanization of manufacturing are illustrated by manufacturing shifts within the Toronto metropolitan area
from 1961 to 1965.[13] There were five main processes, as follows:

1. *Suburbanization* involved the movement of industrial plants from
   the City of Toronto out to its suburbs. Over the period 1961–
   1965 this was the most important component of change and it
   accounted for almost one-fifth of the new job opportunities
   created in the suburbs in that period. Almost all of the plants
   making such a move in Toronto employed around 49 employees, and in the majority of cases, the change in location resulted in an increase in the number of workers. Of the different industries studied, furniture and fixture plants accounted
   for almost all suburbanization moves.
2. *Suburban dispersion* involved the movement of manufacturing
   plants among the suburbs of Toronto. This simply amounted
   to a relocation of plants within the suburbs and such moves
   usually resulted in increased employment in the new locations.
   Metal-fabricating plants tended to dominate in these types of
   moves.
3. *Decentralization* involved the movement of manufacturing plants
   out of the Toronto metropolitan area into other parts of the
   Province of Ontario. This might have been described as an
   extended form of suburbanization, for in the case of Toronto,
   over the period 1961–1965, almost 70% of the decentralizing
   plants moved to new locations within 50 miles of downtown
   Toronto. Again, the shifts generally involved increases in employment and metal-fabricating plants dominated the pattern.
   A map showing the shifts of some of these plants is given in
   Figure 6.4.
4. *Centralization* involved the movement of manufacturing plants
   inward to the metropolitan area, which was the reverse of the
   previous pattern. Almost 80% of the plants studied relocated
   from within a 50-mile radius around Toronto. Almost all of
   the plants taking part in this type of movement were in the
   electrical products and printing industries. For the most part,
   the shifts in location involved small reductions in the number
   of employees.
5. *Dispersion* involved the movement of manufacturing plants from
   one urban center to another. This intercity movement is not

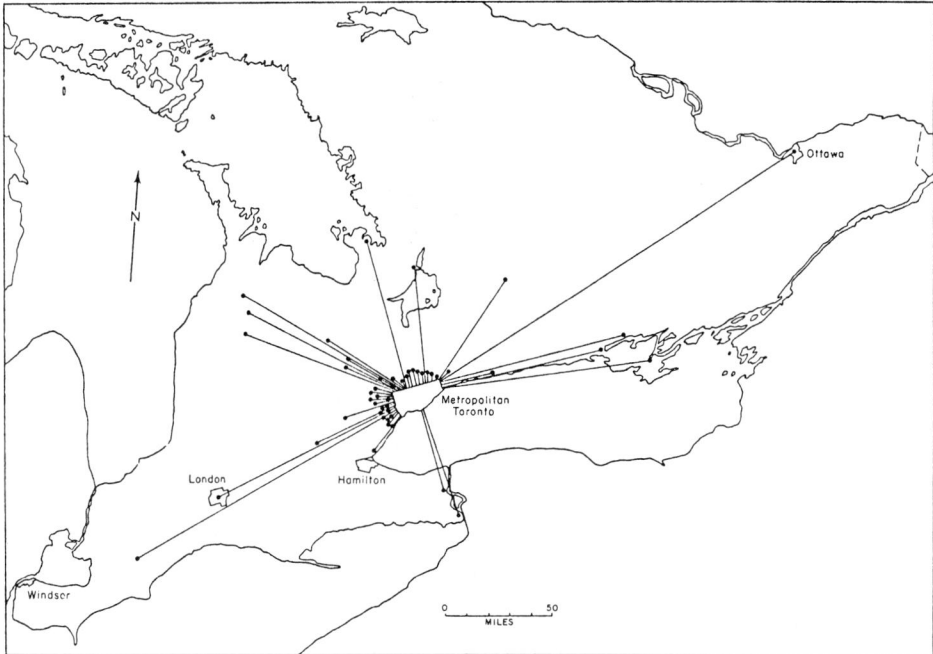

Figure 6.4 Destinations of 51 establishments relocating from metropolitan Toronto, 1961–1965. [L. Collins, *Industrial Migration in Ontario* (Ottawa: Statistics Canada, 1972), p. 97.]

of particular interest when we are dealing with intraurban patterns, but it would be a factor, of course, in accounting for the differential growth of different cities.

The overall effect of these different moves has been described as "the development of an industrial donut around the traditional center of manufacturing activity in the city of Toronto."[14] This trend has been strengthened by the attraction of foreign-owned branch plants that tended to favor locations near the International Airport in the northwest part of the metropolitan area. Also, it is worth noting that Highway 401, the major east–west route through the province, cuts across the northern end of the metropolitan area and has been a major factor in encouraging the decentralization and suburbanization of industry in the metropolitan region.

In different parts of the world, similar patterns of suburbanization of manufacturing have occurred. In the United Kingdom, for example, during the period 1940–1964, the movement of manufacturing firms out of northwest London was much greater than had been expected

Locations of Factories
Established by N.W. London
Firms in Remainder of
United Kingdom, 1940–64

Each individual
factory shown thus   •

100–mile radius ---
from London

20 0   20 40 60 80 100
Mls.

Figure 6.5 The geographical distribution of branch and relocated factories established by N.W. London firms, 1940–1964. [D. Keeble, "Industrial migration from north-west London, 1960–1964," *Urban Studies,* **2**, 1965, pp. 15–32.]

(Figure 6.5). This movement of firms out of London into the zone 15 to 50 miles from the center of the city seems likely to continue and the probable result will be a spreading out of London into a great metropolitan region, another megalopolis.

A similar pattern of manufacturing decentralization has been apparent in Vancouver, Canada. Over the period 1955–1965 there was a large relative shift in the number of manufacturing plants from the core of the city to an intermediate zone some 16 to 35 minutes in travel time from the center of the city and almost all of the gains in this intermediate area were in the metals, machinery, wood, and furniture industries. The largest losses by the core area were in the food and beverages industry and the wood and furniture industry. In the peripheral

Table 6.2 Change in Number of Manufacturing Plants in Selected Industries in Different Zones of Vancouver,
1955–1965. (Based on G. P. F. Steed, "Intrametropolitan manufacturing: spatial distribution and
locational dynamics in Greater Vancouver," *The
Canadian Geographer,* **17,** 1973, pp. 235–258.)

	Food and Beverages	*Wood and Furniture*	*Metals and Manufacturing*	*Transportation Equipment*
Within 15 minutes driving time of downtown	−78	−35	−19	−11
From 16 to 35 minutes driving time from downtown	+21	+45	+65	+21
From 36 to 60 minutes driving time from downtown	−3	+11	+17	+3

zone, defined as lying 36 to 60 minutes in travel time from the center
of the city, there were small relative gains in the wood and furniture
industry and the metals and machinery industry (Table 6.2).

Manufacturing and Urban Economic Change

These trends in the suburbanization of manufacturing have been
viewed as part of a larger pattern of urban change by an economist,
John Kain.[15] After reviewing the trends evident from 1948 to 1963 in
the distribution of population and employment in the 40 largest
metropolitan areas in the United States, Kain suggested that the future
form of the city may be analogous to a donut, with employment opportunities located around the periphery and workers' homes located
in the central city. This form of the city would contrast with that
which is typically observed today in which a cone-shaped form is more
typical and the center of the city still continues to be the most attractive area in terms of employment opportunities.

Others have taken issue with such predictions and have stressed
the following points:[16]

1. The decentralization of population and economic activities in
   United States cities is not a new phenomenon and has been
   underway since the turn of the century.
2. The evidence presented in support of the argument that the
   process has accelerated since 1948 is not consistent. Certainly
   after about 1963 almost all metropolitan areas experienced

either a slowing down or stabilization of the process, and in some cities the trend was even reversed.

3. There is some evidence that the suburbanization trends may be related to regional or national business cycles. For instance, in periods of recession the effects may be more pronounced on central city areas where older, less efficient plants may be the first to be shut down.

4. In almost all large metropolitan areas it is still the central city that contains the largest share of the jobs.

5. The assumptions that suburbanization creates a shortage of jobs in the central city and a mismatching between the low skills of the persons living in the central city and the high-skill characteristics of the few jobs being located there are suspect. Employment opportunities in the central cities are growing, these new jobs are not exclusively high-skill jobs, and there is considerable commuting of suburban blue-collar workers into the central cities to take advantage of these employment opportunities. "Suburban residents hold a substantial number of low- and semi-skilled central city jobs, and it is this—as much as the shortage of such jobs assumed by advocates of the mismatch hypothesis—that helps to explain the high unemployment of unskilled city residents."[17]

6. The argument that the answer to the poverty of the ghettos lies in the suburbanization of the minority group populations at present living there appears weak. The evidence from a number of studies suggests that this ghetto dispersal would do little to significantly improve the overall economic well-being of the minority groups.

6.4   Housing Patterns in a United States City

In any large city the most extensive land use is residential land, which may account for well over one-half of the developed land. Earlier we discussed the sector or wedge hypothesis of how the high-class residential districts in particular developed over time in United States cities. These districts extended out from the center of the city in a wedge-like fashion, often favoring the higher ground or the established lines of travel. The farther away from the center of the city, the greater the availability of land and the larger the lots on which the higher-income groups lived. Alongside of the high-income areas, there were typically intermediate-valued residential areas, while the lower-quality residential areas were found in many different parts of the city, generally toward the downtown area. In Chapter 7 we shall introduce some models that have been proposed to account for the locational preferences of different income groups within the city. At this point, we concentrate on some recent descriptions of the patterns of residential land use and the characteristics of urban housing.

The Baltimore Housing Study

In this detailed and imaginative study, a group of geographers suggested a number of new and informative ways of looking at the patterns of urban housing.[18] Their analysis of the problems of housing deterioration and dilapidation identified five basic components associated with change in housing conditions: (1) the age and structural characteristics of the housing, (2) the tenure arrangements, (3) the density of dwelling units and pressure for conversion to alternative types of housing, (4) the social and economic status of the occupants, and (5) racial change.

Age of Housing

It is estimated that nearly two-thirds of the existing housing stock in Baltimore was built before 1939 and that around 20% of it was probably built before 1900. Nevertheless, the total housing stock in the city is in fact getting proportionately younger. Whereas in 1940 nearly 75% of the houses were more than 40 years old, by 1970 the corresponding proportion had dropped to around 60%. As housing gets older, there is usually a deterioration in the quality of the housing as a result of the physical depreciation of the different building materials and different housing components such as electrical wiring and so on. But in Baltimore the condition of housing is not a straightforward and simple function of age. Much housing deteriorates because no one is interested in renewing it. "It may not be possible to renew, either because there is a prejudice against providing financial support to renovate old housing or because the cost of renovation is so substantial that it is uneconomic to renovate rather than to construct new housing."[19]

The arguments for restoration of old housing rather than demolition in order to make way for new style buildings has become a heated issue in the planning of many modern cities. There are numerous examples of debates that have gone on among developers, city planners, and local citizen groups on this very question.

But the question of adaptability is critical in this context. Some old two- or three-story row houses can indeed be reconstructed into apartment-like dwellings, but other styles of housing, for example, the suburban ranch style house, do not lend themselves to adaptation in this manner. Also, restoration and rehabilitation have to appear as a feasible economic venture in comparison to the cost of providing other types of housing, and the fact that housing codes and regulations are often overly demanding has probably meant that the costs of "planned and publicly supported rehabilitation" are greatly inflated.

A final point on the question of age and housing change is that the nature of the mix of housing types and ages in a neighborhood is critical in influencing patterns of neighborhood change. If all the housing in a particular neighborhood were to age at the same rate, there might result, at some time, serious consequences for the stability of the neighborhood. "Selective redevelopment at different times in the neighborhood, which prevents a massive aging problem at all one point in time, may be more expensive, but it may also avoid some of the incalculable but serious social consequences which stem from the destruction of the social fabric of community."[20]

Ownership Patterns

An examination of the patterns of housing ownership in Baltimore reveals some interesting contrasts. The overall pattern of tenant occupancy shows that the inner city has a heavy concentration of tenants with some sectoral arrangement of other areas out from this core. In Baltimore there has been a considerable increase in the level of tenant occupancy and over the decade 1960–1970 the percent of all housing units that were owner-occupied declined from around 54% to 44.5%. The close relationship between the level of housing deterioration and the patterns of ownership, with high tenancy generally being associated with high levels of deterioration, seems to be explained as follows. The homeowner, in contrast to the tenant, views his property as a form of savings and seeks to build up his equity in the property by maintaining it at a high level of well-being. An alternative view emphasizes that the homeowner has *territorial control* of his property and is free, to a great extent, to do with it as he wishes, but for the tenant, many aspects of housing are beyond his control. The implications of this for the question of housing quality appear to be important.

There is an important contrast in Baltimore in regard to the levels of tenancy and the racial factor. There are very few areas in the city where the level of black owner occupancy is above 40%. By contrast, the levels of white owner occupancy are very high in many parts of the city and sometimes exceed 80%.

The patterns of tenancy and owner occupancy are not static and in the case of Baltimore the conversion from owner occupancy to tenancy is proceeding at a steady rate in certain areas of the city (Figure 6.6). The map shows that around the center of the city there was a general spread of tenancy occupancy and particularly in the northwest section of the city there was a fairly rapid conversion. This process of conversion gives rise to conflict situations in which the dif-

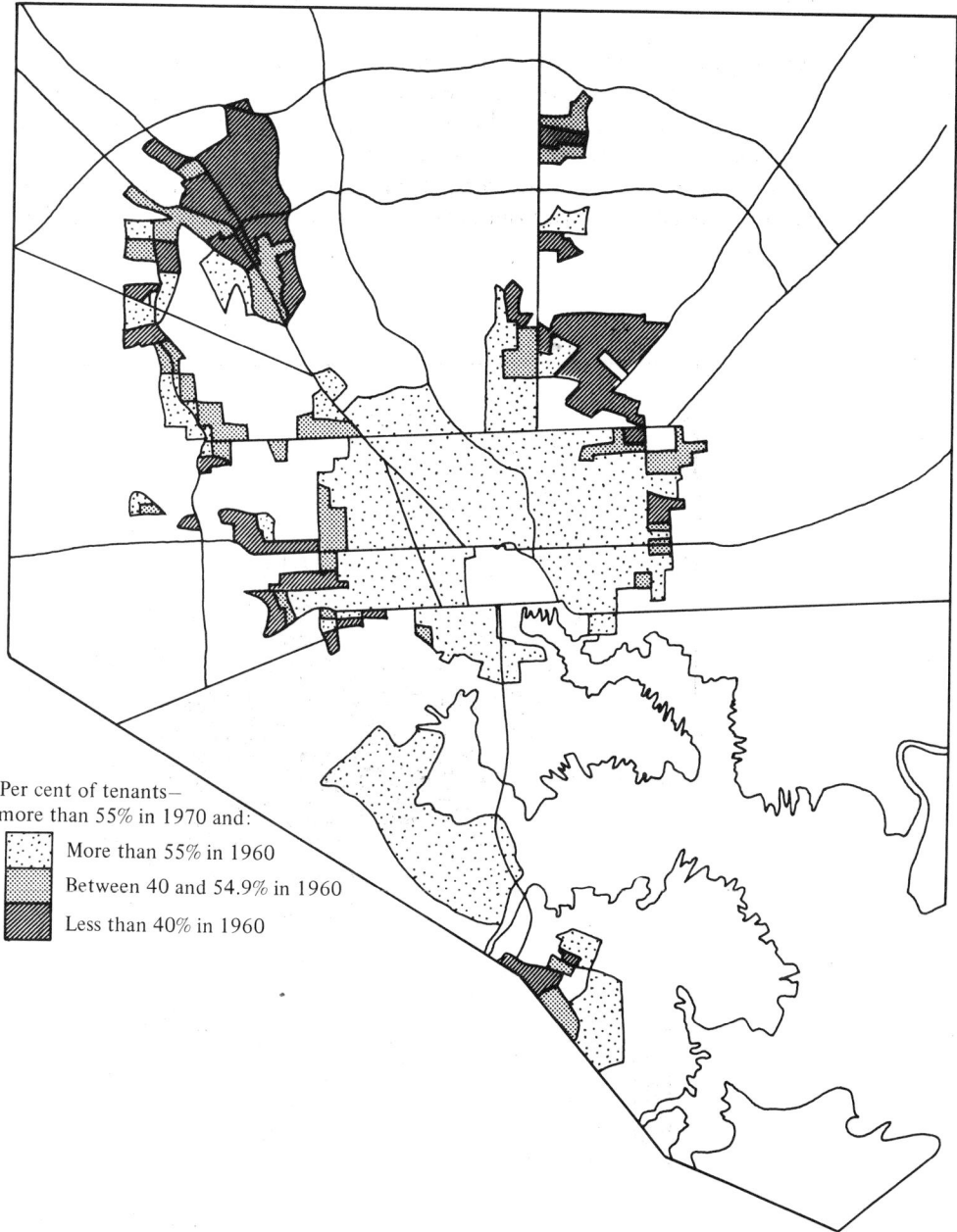

Figure 6.6 Conversion from owner occupancy to tenancy. Increase in tenancy in those Census Block Groups that had more than 55% of housing units under tenant occupancy in 1970, excluding those Census Block Groups in which (1) there was considerable new construction or (2) particularly high median income. [D. Harvey et al., *The Housing Market and Code Enforcement in Baltimore* (Baltimore: The Baltimore Urban Observatory, Inc., 1972), following p. 5.24.]

Per cent of tenants—
more than 55% in 1970 and:

More than 55% in 1960
Between 40 and 54.9% in 1960
Less than 40% in 1960

ferent participants in the housing scene often view the developments in very contrasting ways. For example, what is "normal business practice" for a real estate developer is often seen as speculation and profiteering by homeowners in an area. In any large city in North America today these conflicts are ever present and the pressures they generate create a heavy potential demand for housing inspection and aspects of control.

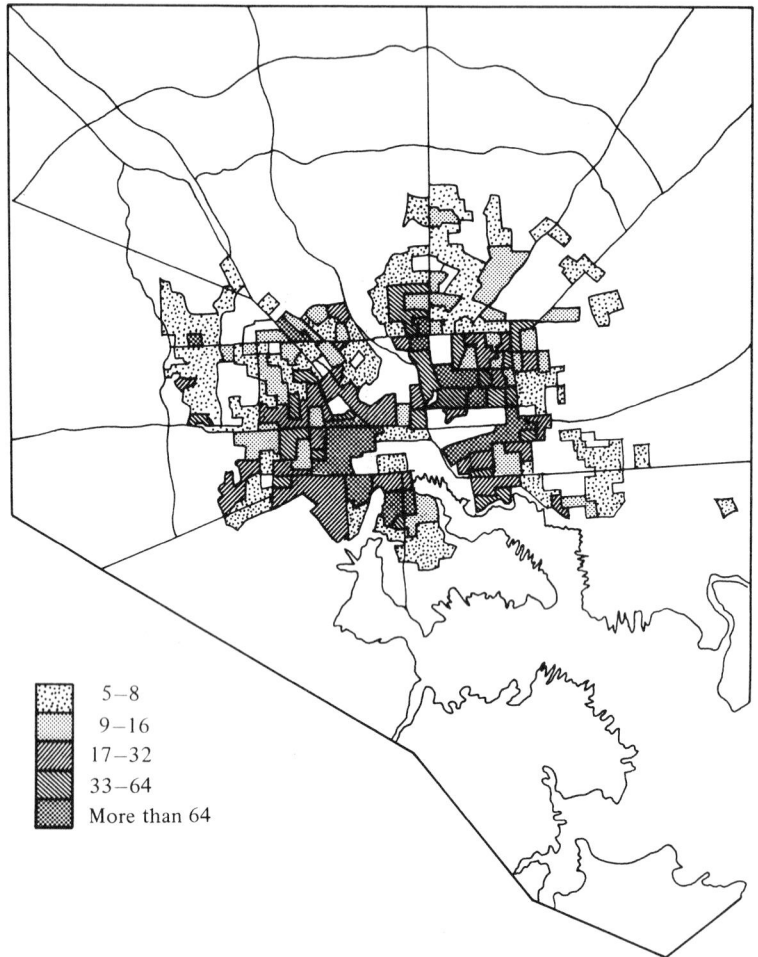

Figure 6.7   Numbers of vacant houses aggregated by Census Block Groups— CRP Survey of 1968 (the CRP Survey Area did not cover the outer city). [D. Harvey et al., *The Housing Market and Code Enforcement in Baltimore* (Baltimore: The Baltimore Urban Observatory, Inc., 1972), following p. 5.30.]

Abandoned Housing

A distinctive feature of the housing situation in many of the larger American cities today is *abandonment*. This is not an easy feature to measure in a city such as Baltimore; often it is only possible to record the number of vacant houses (Figure 6.7). The rate of abandonment seems directly related to mortgage activity and the policies of financial institutions. Some insight into the process that may be at work is provided by a map showing tax delinquency (Figure 6.8). The phenomenon of failure to pay taxes on time shows a marked concentration around the core of the old city, but there are also areas of delinquency in some of the outer zones of the city. A comparison of the two maps, Figures 6.7 and 6.8, shows a strong association between the areas of financial difficulty and the areas in which there are high levels of house vacancy. This prompts the speculation that many of the vacancies involve actual abandonment of the houses.

Housing Zones

A final map from the Baltimore study, Figure 6.9, warrants consideration. This shows the city divided into three general housing market zones. The inner zone is characterized by a general lack of funds and by generally low dollar values per housing unit, low dollar values per capita, and low dollar values per 100 square feet of residential land (Table 6.3). The middle ring of the city, "an intermediate gray area," is a zone in which there is a restricted flow of capital funds and, as can be noted from Table 6.3, very high dollar values per 100 square feet of residential land. Finally, in the outer zone there is adequate financing for individual owner-occupiers of houses and the dollar value per housing unit is very high.

The data in Table 6.3 do not support a generally accepted view of the pattern of land values in a city, namely, that they decrease as one

Table 6.3 Baltimore Housing Zones. [D. Harvey et al., *The Housing Market and Code Enforcement in Baltimore* (Baltimore: The Baltimore Urban Observatory, Inc., 1972), p. 535.]

	Mean Figures		
	Inner City	*Middle Zone*	*Outer Zone*
Dollar value per unit	$3,294	$6,097	$11,478
Dollar value per capita	$910	$1,647	$3,570
Dollar value per 100 sq ft of residential land	$18,973	$34,686	$23,952

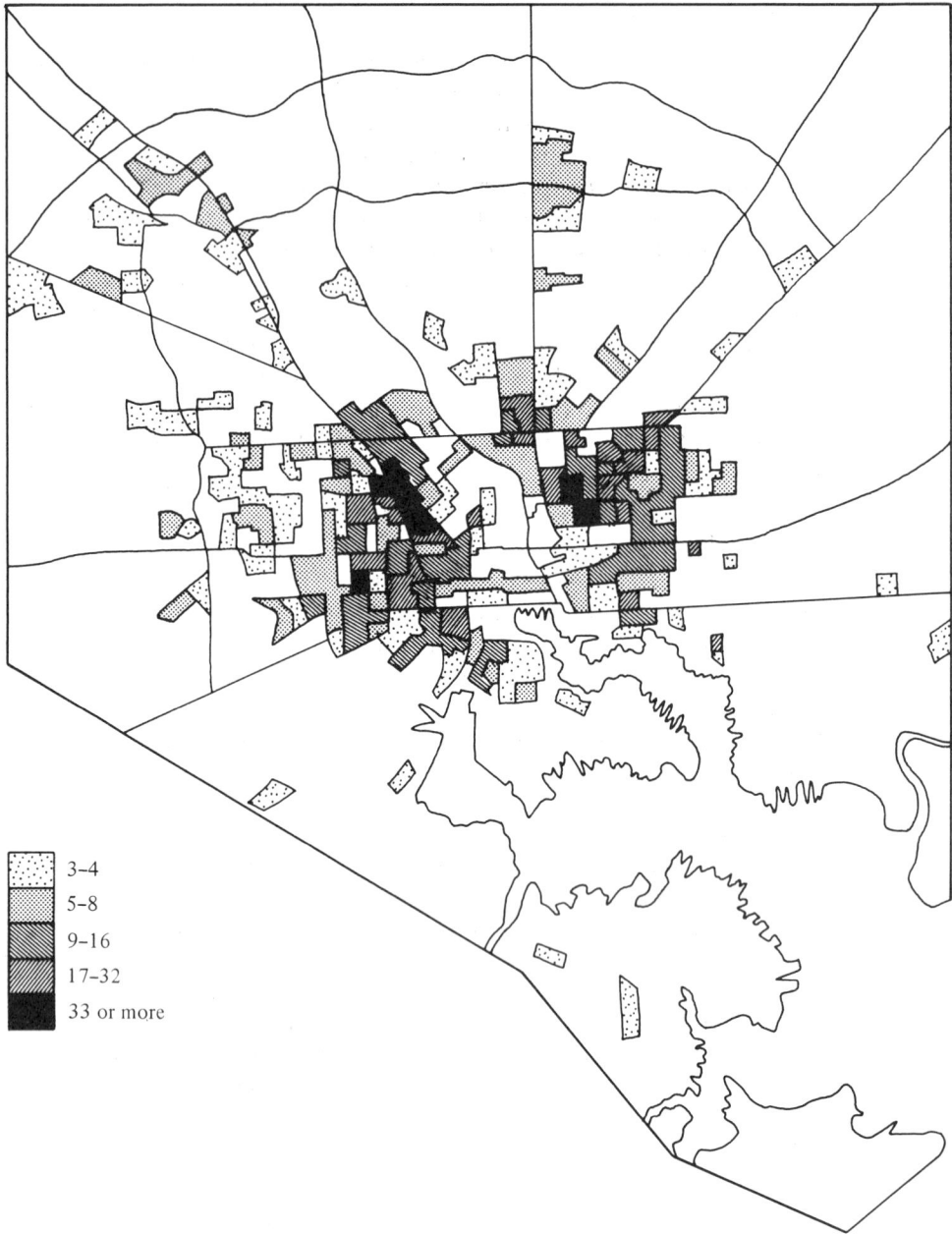

Figure 6.8 Tax delinquency, 1971. Number of properties on which the property tax was not paid on time in 1971, aggregated by Census Block Groups. [D. Harvey et al., *The Housing Market and Code Enforcement in Baltimore* (Baltimore: The Baltimore Urban Observatory, Inc., 1972), following p. 5.30.]

Legend:
- 3–4
- 5–8
- 9–16
- 17–32
- 33 or more

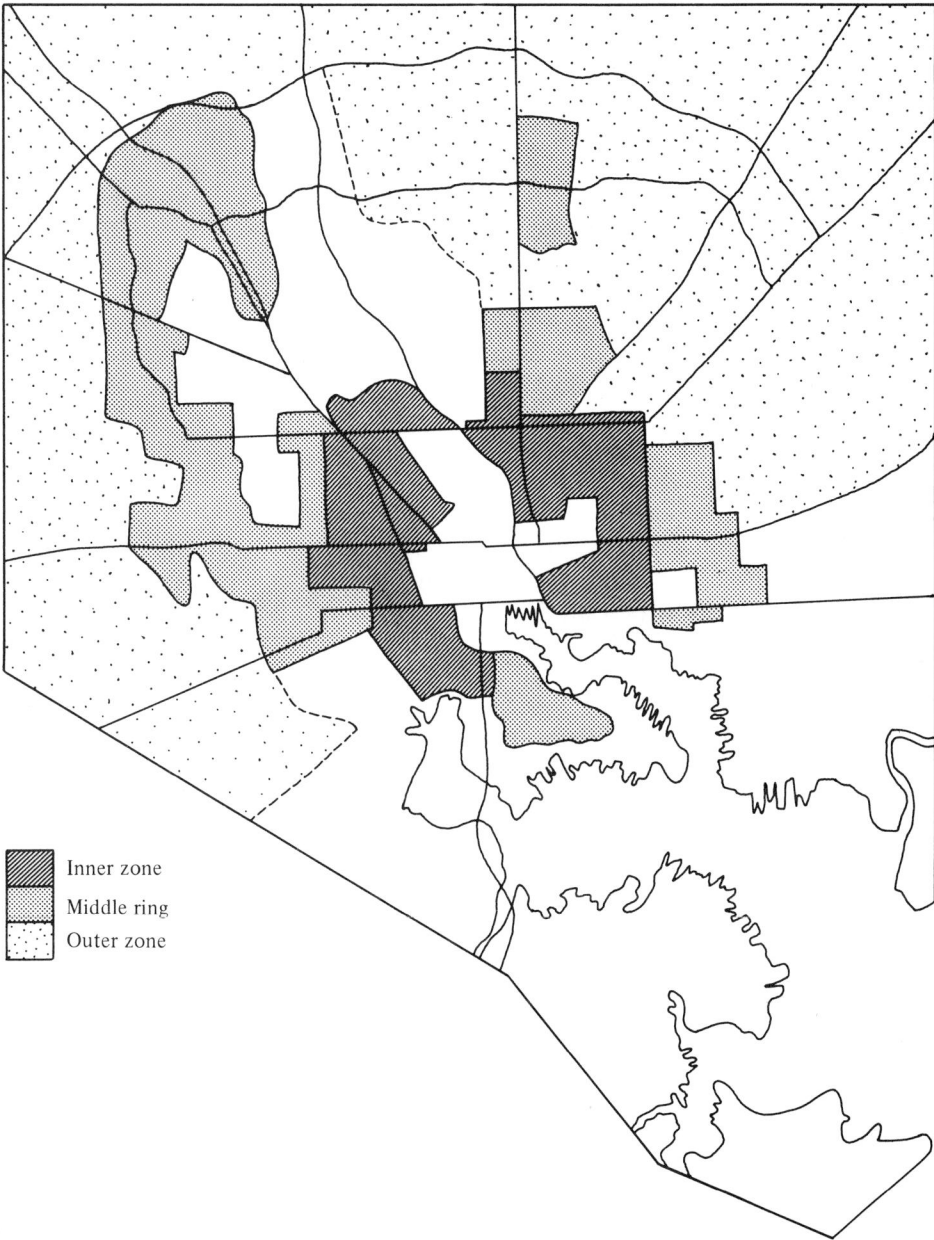

Figure 6.9 Housing market zones. The three distinctive zones within which it is hypothesized that separate housing markets function. The sample block group data were drawn from within these zones. Areas left blank were either areas not under housing or areas that could not unambiguously be assigned to any one particular zone. [D. Harvey et al., *The Housing Market and Code Enforcement in Baltimore* (Baltimore: The Baltimore Urban Observatory, Inc., 1972), following p. 5.34.]

moves away from the center of the city. This inverse relationship between land values and distances from the center of the city has been
discussed in a number of studies. In Chicago, for example, over the
period 1910–1960, the relationship existed at almost all times, although it was stronger in the earlier years.[21] By 1960, however, much
of the land at the periphery of Chicago was in fact becoming relatively
more valuable than land in the middle of the city.

In the case of Baltimore, the relatively lower dollar values per unit
area of residential land in the inner city may be explained largely in
terms of the time lag that is involved in any transition or conversion in
land use. A change in land use is a very expensive business and may
not appear attractive to developers for many years, especially while
there remains good and more easily developable land in the suburbs.
Even allowing for the fact that there is increasing demand for use of the
land in the downtown area because of its more accessible and hence
preferred location, some time may elapse before the land use is actually
changed. The pressure may result initially in increasing densities and
an intensified use of the existing housing which, in turn, may accelerate the deterioration of the housing stock. Only when the value of
the residential property falls very low will the costs of conversion to a
different land use be justified. As Harvey noted, "this is the dilemma
that faces land-use decisions in inner city areas and it helps to explain
the paradox that some of the most valuable land in the city is held under blighted uses without too much action evident to transform it to
higher rent yielding forms."[22]

The Baltimore study gives a detailed account of the spatial characteristics of one metropolitan housing market. The conclusions
drawn, however, are probably applicable to almost all large United
States metropolitan areas. Later in this book, specifically in Chapter
12 when we deal with migration patterns in the city and in Chapter 14
when we discuss planning issues, we shall consider some other topics
relating to urban housing.

6.5 Summary

Our interest in this chapter has been on the patterns of land use within
the city. This is our first close look at the internal form and structure
of a city. We have emphasized the patterns that result from the commercial, industrial, and residential activities within the city, and we
began by considering three generalizations of the overall land-use pattern: the concentric-zone hypothesis, the sector or wedge concept, and
the multiple-nuclei hypothesis. All of these three elements seem to be
present in different degrees in any large metropolitan area.

Commercial activities within the city are arranged in a hierarchy of commercial centers with the Central Business District at the top. In effect, they form a central place system with each center having its own tributary area and particular mix of goods that it offers.

Manufacturing land-use patterns within the city have been changing as the space requirements of new plants have increased, as truck transportation has become dominant, and as environmental considerations have imposed restrictions on many types of industries. The trend toward decentralization of industry in urban areas has been going on for several decades now.

Residential activity is the largest user of space in any urban area. Using Baltimore as an example, we examined some of the interrelationships among age of housing, condition, and occupancy arrangements. The important role of institutions, notably banks and mortgage companies, in shaping the form of the housing market was introduced. Later in the book we shall return to a consideration of urban housing and examine the residential shifts made by people living in an urban area.

With these descriptions of land-use patterns behind us, in Chapter 7 we shall examine some theories of urban spatial structure. This next chapter complements Chapter 5 in its emphasis on theory building. In this case, the subjects of interest are the patterns of population densities and land values that occur within the city. These patterns are expressions of the land uses that we have just discussed.

Notes

1. E. W. Burgess, "The growth of the city," *Proceedings,* American Sociological Society, **18,** 1923, pp. 85–89.

2. M. J. Bowden, "Growth of the central districts in large cities," in L. F. Schnore, ed., *The New Urban History. Quantitative Explorations by American Historians* (Princeton: Princeton University Press, 1975), pp. 75–109.

3. H. Hoyt, *The Structure and Growth of Residential Neighborhoods in American Cities* (Washington, D.C.: Government Printing Office, 1939).

4. *Ibid.,* p. 116.

5. C. D. Harris and E. L. Ullman, "The nature of cities," *Annals,* American Academy of Political and Social Science, **242,** 1945, pp. 7–17.

6. H. Carol, "Hierarchy of central functions within the city," *Annals,* Association of American Geographers, **50,** 1960, pp. 419–38.

7. B. J. L. Berry, "Commercial structure and commercial blight," *Research Paper,* Department of Geography, University of Chicago, No. 85, 1963.

8. *Ibid.,* p. 23.

9. A. ROGERS, *Statistical Analysis of Spatial Dispersion* (London: Pion Ltd, 1974).

10. J. W. SIMMONS, "The changing pattern of retail location," *Research Paper*, Department of Geography, University of Chicago, No. 92, 1964.

11. BERRY, *op cit.*

12. A. R. PRED, "The intrametropolitan location of manufacturing," *Annals,* Association of American Geographers, **54,** 1964, pp. 165–80.

13. L. COLLINS, *Industrial Migration in Ontario* (Ottawa: Statistics Canada, 1972).

14. *Ibid.*

15. J. KAIN, "The distribution and movement of jobs and industry," in J. Q. WILSON, ed., *The Metropolitan Enigma* (Cambridge, Mass.: Harvard University Press, 1968).

16. B. HARRISON, *Urban Economic Development* (Washington, D.C.: The Urban Institute, 1974).

17. *Ibid.,* p. 53.

18. D. HARVEY, L. CHATTERJEE, M. G. WOLMAN, L. KLUGMAN, and J. S. NEWMAN, *The Housing Market and Code Enforcement in Baltimore* (Baltimore: The Baltimore Urban Observatory, Inc., 1972).

19. *Ibid.,* p. 511.

20. *Ibid.,* p. 514.

21. M. H. YEATES, "Some factors affecting the spatial distribution of Chicago land values," *Economic Geography,* **41,** 1965, pp. 55–70.

22. HARVEY ET AL., *op. cit.,* p. 537.

chapter 7

Urban Population Densities
and Land Rents

In the preceding chapter mention was made of the observations about
patterns of land values within large cities and how these patterns
tend to show high values near the center of the city and a general decline as distance away from the center increases. An even more im-
pressive volume of research has focused on the same features in regard
to the patterns of population (and employment) densities within the
city. For the most part, these studies have confirmed a general distance-decay relationship between population (and employment) densities and distance from the center of the city. The typical graph of the
relationship is similar to the two graphs of Figure 7.1. These graphs
for London and Chicago show that over the past century and more the
same form of relationship between density and distance has held; that
is, density has been inversely related to distance, although the slopes of
the two sets of curves have been decreasing over time.

   In this chapter we shall begin with a discussion of the statistical
analyses that have been completed in regard to this density-distance

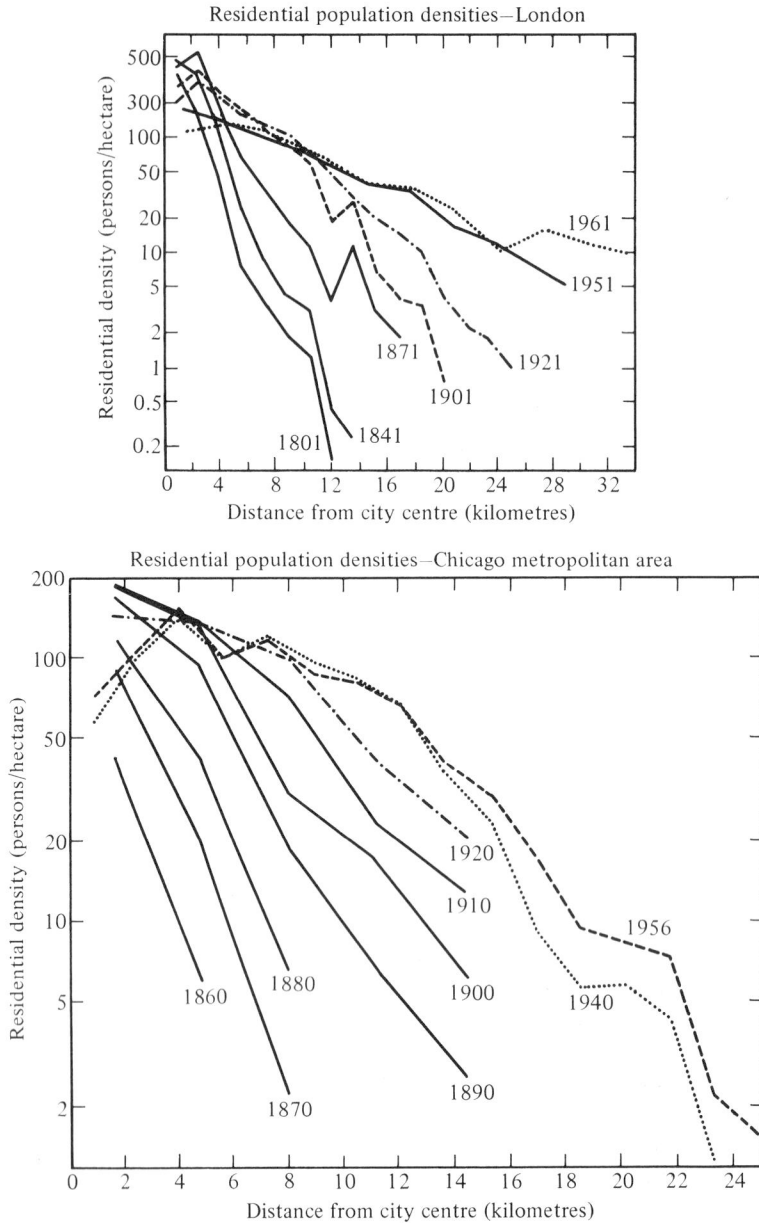

Figure 7.1 Urban population density profiles for London and Chicago. [C. Clark, *Population Growth and Land Use* (New York: St. Martin's Press, Inc., Macmillan & Co., Ltd. 1967), pp. 343–44. By permission of St. Martin's Press, Inc. and Macmillan London and Basingstoke.]

relationship. This provides the introduction to the main part of the chapter, which is concerned with theories of urban spatial structure that seek to provide explanations of these observed patterns of densities and land values.

7.1 Urban Population Densities: Evidence of How They Decline Away from City Centers

Our starting point is the observation that in any large city, regardless of its location in the world, population density tends to decrease as one moves farther away from the center of the city. This rather simple relationship has been observed for some time for different cities throughout the world.

Distance-Decay Model

A particular mathematical model, the negative exponential function, has been used to describe this relationship between density and distance from the center of the city. This model is given by the equation

$$D_s = D_0 e^{-bs}$$

where D_s is the population density at distance s from the center of the city,

D_0 is the density at the city center (distance zero),

s is distance,

b is the rate at which population density declines with increasing distance s,

and

e is a known mathematical constant.

One of the convenient features of this particular model is that if the two variables, population density and distance, are expressed in natural logarithms, the graph of the equation becomes a straight line.

In order to fit the above model, we need for a set of cities measures of the population densities (D_s) at different distances (s) from the centers of the cities. Then, using statistical techniques, we could estimate for each city the appropriate values for the terms D_0 and b in the model. These are called the *parameters* of the model. For most large cities, the negative exponential model seems to describe the real-world observations fairly well as a first approximation.

Density Craters

Population densities do not in fact decline immediately around the city center. They will more likely show an increase away from the center and only beyond some point will the decline in densities become apparent. In other words, there is a *crater effect* in the population density profiles of almost all large cities. This is consistent with the often observed fact that the downtown area is likely to be a zone of office buildings and stores and that it is in the zone of high-rise apartments surrounding the downtown area that population densities peak. Only beyond this zone do the densities start to decline regularly with distance. This crater effect is incorporated into the negative exponential model by adding an additional term in the exponent. The model becomes

$$D_s = D_0 e^{bs - cs^2}$$

where D_s, D_0, s, b, and e are defined as before. The new parameter c has to be estimated along with b. If we assume that parameter b is larger than c, then for short distances the term bs is greater than the term cs^2 and the whole expression on the right is positive; in other words, density increases with distance s. But as distance increases, at some point the term cs^2 becomes greater than the term bs and the expression on the right becomes negative and we have densities decreasing as distance s increases. Again, we could use logarithms and estimate the parameters by using statistical techniques.[1]

Cross-Cultural Comparisons

A number of interesting cross-cultural and temporal comparisons are shown in the diagrams in Figure 7.2. The top diagrams show that in Western cities the central population densities at first increased and then decreased while the gradient (as measured by the parameter b) declined over time, but in the non-Western cities the central densities have continued to increase over time but the density gradient has remained fairly constant. One implication is that in both contexts the areal extent of the cities has been increasing but in the West this spread has been accompanied by a lowering of overall population densities. The same pattern has not held true in the Asian context where the profile of densities has remained remarkably stable.

In the second row of diagrams the parameter b describing the density gradient is plotted against city size. The diagram on the left shows that in the Western cities there is an overall negative relationship between these two values, that is to say, the smaller the city the

WESTERN   NONWESTERN

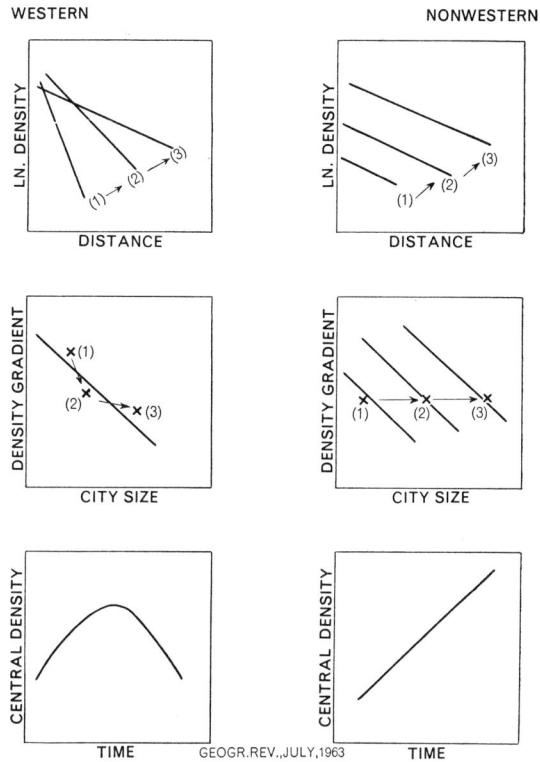

Figure 7.2 Cross-sectional and temporal comparisons of urban density functions in Western and non-Western cities. [B. J. L. Berry, J. W. Simmons, and R. J. Tennant, "Urban population densities: structure and change," *Geographical Review*, **53**, 1963, p. 403.]

steeper the density gradient, but that for any one particular city its gradient has decreased over the three time periods at first rather steeply and then more gradually. By contrast, the right-hand diagram shows that the density gradient for a particular city has stayed stable over the three time periods, as has the general relationship between density gradient and city size.

In the final set of diagrams the central density, the parameter D_0, is plotted against time. The left-hand diagram shows that for Western cities the central densities have increased for a while and then have decreased, but in the non-Western cities they have steadily increased over time. At present, there are too few studies of cities in the non-Western world to be able to place a great deal of faith on such comparisons, but they do point out differences in the spatial structure of cities in the two different realms.

Changes in Density Gradients Over Time

The preceding comments on contrasts in the changing patterns of population densities serve to introduce another topic. An obvious extension of our analysis would be to fashion descriptions of urban population densities as they vary over both distance and time. This requires the construction of dynamic models. These need not be mathematical in character, witness the *wave* model in Figure 7.3. This postulates that there is a zone of high population densities that over time works outward from the center of the city in much the same manner that a ripple or wave moves out over the surface of a lake after a pebble has been dropped into it.

We have already discussed (in reference to Figure 7.2) the observation that both the density gradient parameter b and the central density parameter D_0 in the negative exponential model may change over time. We can develop a mathematical expression of the changing relationship between population density and distance by expressing these parameters as functions of time in the equations given earlier. We begin with the model

$$D_s = D_0 e^{-bs}$$

and first express the two parameters D_0 and b themselves as functions

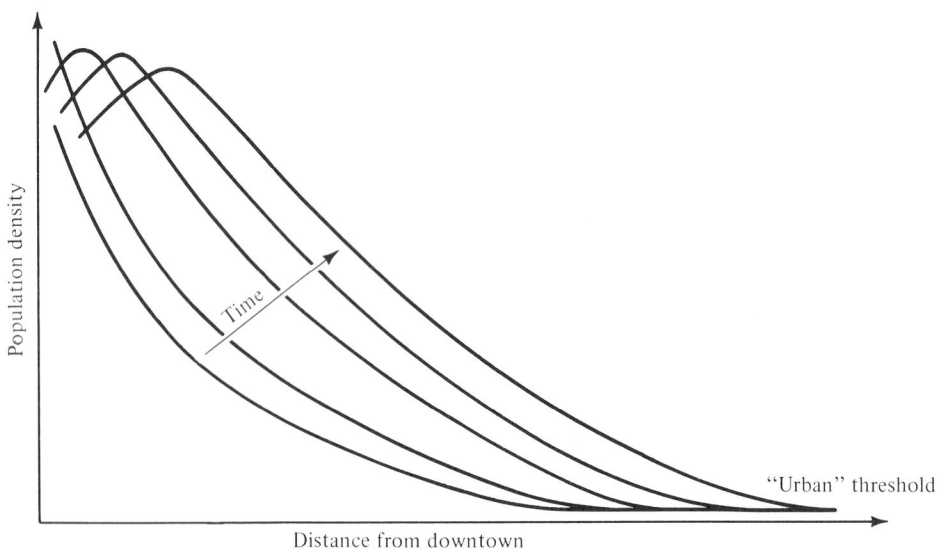

Figure 7.3 Wave-like growth of the urban population surface. [Based on H. M. Mayer, "The spatial expression of urban growth," *Resource Paper No. 7,* 1969, Association of American Geographers, p. 29. Reproduced by permission of the Association of American Geographers.]

218

of time; thus,

$$D_0 = D_0' + D_0''t$$

and

$$b = b_1 + b_2 t$$

These are two equations of straight lines that show both D_0 and b increasing at constant rates as time increases. We then substitute these expressions into our model and obtain

$$D_s = D_0' + D_0''t \ exp \ (-b_1 s - b_2 st)$$

In this equation we use the notation *exp* to represent the exponential term, that is, the constant e and its associated exponent. As before, we could use logarithms to transform this into a linear model and by using data on population densities, at different distances and at different times for sub-areas within a city, we could obtain estimates of the different parameters in the model. It will be noted that instead of the two parameters that we had earlier we now have four parameters to be estimated.

Table 7.1 Population Density Trends over Time and Distance in Montreal and Philadelphia. [Based on E. Casetti, "Testing for spatial-temporal trends: an application to urban population density trends using the expansion methods," *The Canadian Geographer*, **17**, 1973, p. 135.]

	Estimated Coefficients						
	a_0	a_1	b_0	b_1	c_0	c_1	R^2
Montreal (1941–1961)	3.864 (28.42)	—	—	—	−0.079 (10.88)	0.001 (3.69)	0.890
Philadelphia (1900–1950)	4.496 (38.24)	—	−0.213 (3.12)	—	−0.061 (7.15)	0.0008 (11.12)	0.962

NOTE: The equation containing the above coefficients is given in the text. The numbers in parentheses are the "t" values used in establishing the statistical significance of the coefficients shown.

A similar model yielded the results in Table 7.1 for the population density patterns of Montreal and Philadelphia.[2] In this study the author began with a general model of the form,

$$D(s) = exp \ (a + bs + cs^2)$$

where $D(s)$ is the density at distance s, and a, b, and c are the parameters. These three parameters were then written as functions of time and the corresponding expressions were substituted in the above equation, giving

$$D(s, t) = exp\ (a_0 + a_1t + b_0s + b_1st + c_0s^2 + c_1s^2t)$$

The parameters in this model were then estimated statistically. Only those values that were significantly different from zero are shown in Table 7.1. Notice that in the equation for Montreal the term b_0s does not appear but the value of c_0 is -0.07910. The crater effect then is not present. In the case of Philadelphia, both terms b_0s and c_0s^2 appear, but the estimated values are negative. Again, this suggests that no crater effect is present. For both cities, the effect of the last term in the equation is that as time increases, the slope of the population density profile decreases; in other words, the trend is toward a flattening of the initial cone-shaped density surface.

7.2   Why Land Rents Decline Away from a City Center or Market Town

The question that has interested many geographers and other social scientists is why the patterns of population densities and land values discussed above should prevail. In this section we shall consider some attempts to formulate a theory that answers this general question. It is a theory that draws heavily on the economists' theories of how consumers behave in making decisions about the different combinations of goods and services that they can afford to purchase given their income levels and budgets. The patterns of urban population densities and land values are seen as the result of certain decisions made by people acting as consumers. This is not the only way to view the problem and there are theoretical formulations that address the same general question from the viewpoint of persons acting as producers instead of consumers. We shall not discuss this alternative, however.

Consumer behavior theory relies on some basic concepts of economics that we have not yet considered. It is convenient to introduce these concepts by using an example drawn not from the urban scene but from agriculture. This will equip us to discuss a theory of urban population densities and land values.

Land Rents

We shall begin by considering a very simple agricultural situation. Assume that there is a uniform plain extending in all directions and that movement over this plain is not restricted in any way. Assume further that there is one small market town located on this plain and around this center there is a uniform distribution of farms. Now let us consider one of these farms and the decisions that are faced by the farmer. We simplify the problem even further by assuming that he knows how to cultivate only one crop, say wheat, that he does not own his land, that it is realistic to speak of his farm as being located at a certain distance from the market town (the distance might be measured from the center of the town to the gate to his farm), and that the market price for wheat is something that he as an individual farmer can do nothing about.

The first question we consider is how much money can the farmer afford to pay the landowner for the use of the land on his farm? We have noted that the price of a bushel of wheat is fixed as far as the farmer is concerned and also, because of the assumption of a uniform plain the crop yield and production costs are everywhere the same on the plain. The only factor that varies from farm to farm is the distance away from the market town. An equation that describes the money return per unit of land as a function of these other factors can be written as follows:

$$R = Q(p - c) - Qfs$$

where R is money return per unit of land,
             Q is yield in bushels per unit of land,
             p is market price per bushel,
             c is production cost per bushel,
             f is transport rate per bushel per unit of distance,
and
             s is distance from farm to market town.

The assumption that movement is possible in all directions implies that the cost, f, of transporting one bushel of wheat over one unit of distance, say a mile, is the same regardless of where one is located on the plain. It is only distance from the market that varies and this will result in the total transportation charges varying from location to location.

If we graph the above equation, we obtain Figure 7.4. The value of R is highest immediately adjacent to the market town where transportation costs are near zero, and it falls off as distance increases. Eventually, at a certain distance, S_n, the total transportation charges exactly match the money earned by the sale of the wheat in the market (after production costs are taken into account) and R equals zero. Now let us consider our farmer located at S_1. At this location, his growing of wheat will enable him to realize a particular level of monetary

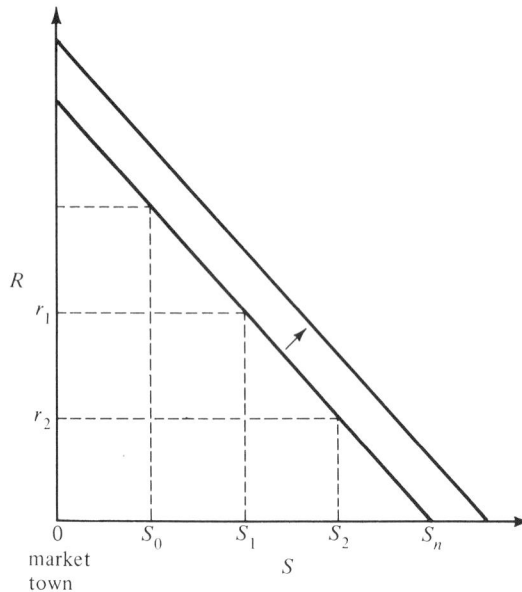

Figure 7.4   Relationship between rent and distance from market.

returns (after he has sold it at the market). On the graph this monetary return is the value r_1. What would happen to this return if he were
to shift to a different location, at say S_2? Then his transportation costs
would be greater and this would be reflected in a lower level of return,
r_2. On the other hand, if he moved to location S_0, his transportation
costs to market would be lower and his return greater. The line in
Figure 7.4 is the graph of the equation given above, and for all locations away from the market it gives the value of the monetary return to
be realized from the growing of wheat in our very simple economy.

Bid-Rent Curves

At this point we wish to give a particular interpretation to this
monetary return. Remember we assumed that the farmer did not own
the land and it was assumed, but not mentioned, that production costs
would include a payment for the farmer's services and skills. The
monetary return, R, is, therefore, a surplus. Economists refer to any
such surplus resulting from the use of a particular factor of production,
in this case land, as a *rent*. As far as our farmer is concerned, this rent
is a surplus that he can afford to pay to the landowner for the use of the
land and, as we have seen, this amount varies from location to location depending only on the distance from the market. The line in
Figure 7.4, therefore, can be thought of as a curve joining all the points

that give the values of the rents the farmer can afford to bid for the use of the land at different locations. It is a *bid-rent* curve. If at a particular location S_1 the farmer is not prepared to bid up to the value r_1, he will lose the use of his land. We are assuming again that there is free entry of farmers into the wheat-growing business and that some other farmer can always come along and offer the landowner the value r_1 and take over the use of the land at that location. Alternatively, no farmer can afford to bid more than r_1 at location S_1, for if he did so, then wheat farming would not be economically feasible there and he would be losing money. Remember that price, production costs, and transportation charges at that location are all fixed and that wheat farming is the only possible activity.

Now what would happen if the market price for wheat went up? If everything else remained the same, then the monetary returns would be increased and higher rents could, and would, have to be paid. A new bid-rent curve would apply (this would be to the right of the old one in Figure 7.4). We can conceive of a whole set (a *family*) of bid-rent curves for the individual farmer. Each curve would be associated with a different market price.

Up to this point we have allowed for only one type of activity, wheat farming, and in this respect our analysis may be described as *partial* in its scope. What happens if we introduce other types of farming into our simple economy?

Competing Land Uses

In our discussion of Figure 7.4 we focused on the individual farmer and his decision making. It is not too big a conceptual step to think now of the rent line in Figure 7.4 as representing the situation for wheat growing in general. In other words, we can assume that the line represents a summing of all the individual situations and describes the rent-yielding ability of wheat growing as an activity. Every type of farming activity will have such a rent curve and in Figure 7.5 three such curves are shown. These curves have different slopes reflecting the different structures of transportation costs for the three activities. The heights of the curves reflect the different market prices for the three products, if we assume for convenience that production costs do not differ among the three activities. Activity A has not only the highest market price but also the highest transportation rate. In a very short distance away from the market the total transportation costs become such that the activity cannot be carried on. By contrast, activity C has the lowest market price and the lowest transportation rate and thus can be carried on over a much wider area.

At a particular location S_1 in Figure 7.5 the three activities yield

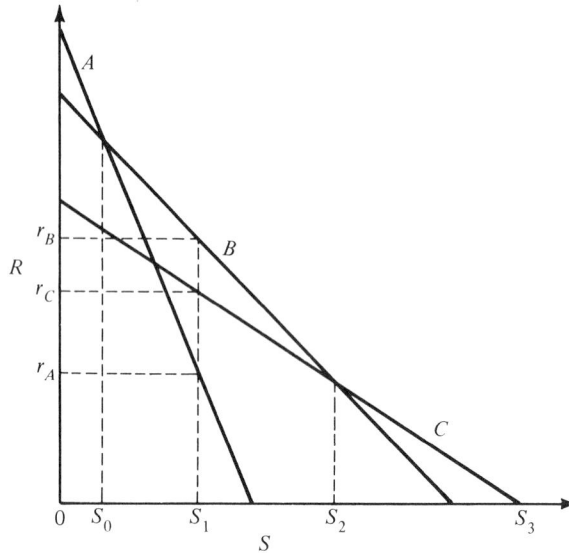

Figure 7.5   Rent curves for different activities.

different returns, and it can be seen that activity B will be carried on there because it allows for the highest rent to be paid for the use of the land. The intersection of the rent curves determines the extent of the areas over which the different activities are carried on. Thus, activity A dominates outward from the market to a distance S_0; at this point activity B takes over and is dominant out to the distance S_2; from S_2 to S_3 activity C prevails. If this pattern exists, then the three farming or land-use activities can be said to be in equilibrium and the patterns will remain unchanged as long as the different prices, production costs, and transportation rates remain unchanged.

7.3   A Theory of Urban Land-Use Patterns and Land Values

The above discussion of a very simple agricultural situation provides a useful introduction to the consideration of urban land uses, population densities, and land values. We can turn now to discuss a theory of land values and land uses in the city proposed by William Alonso.[3]

Alonso focused on the individual household and the business firm, and after discussing the particular characteristics of an equilibrium situation for each of these decision-making units, he considered the general market equilibrium for the land market of a city. Let us review his discussion of these topics and then comment on one or two limitations of his analysis.

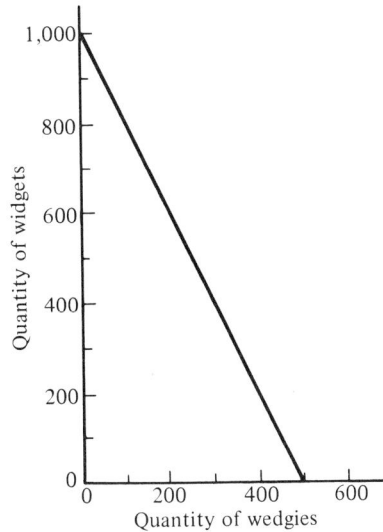

Figure 7.6 Relationship between quantities of two goods purchased with a given income.

Indifference Curves

In order to follow Alonso's discussion of the individual household equilibrium, we must introduce *indifference curves*. Consider an individual who has a budget of $5,000 and intends to spend this on the purchase of two types of goods that we shall call widgets and wedgies. The price of a widget is $5 and the price of a wedgie is $10. The sloping line in Figure 7.6 shows the opportunities that are open to him. If he spends all his money on widgets and none on wedgies, then he can purchase 1,000 widgets. If he spends all his money on wedgies, he can purchase 500 of them. In between these two extreme decisions are a number of other options.

Now let us consider the individual's tastes and preferences. We assume that he will derive some level of satisfaction from the purchase of the two goods and that if there is a small decrease in the purchase of one, then there will be a small increase in the purchase of the other. This level of satisfaction is assumed to be constant over different combinations of the two goods and is associated with the curve drawn in Figure 7.7. This diagram involves no consideration of prices or budget. It simply shows an indifference curve that has a certain level of satisfaction associated with it. The curve has the shape that it does (it is said to be *convex* to the origin) simply because it is assumed that the extra satisfaction derived from an additional unit of one good or the other is not always the same depending on the levels of the goods held. For example, in Figure 7.7 it can be seen that when the quantity of

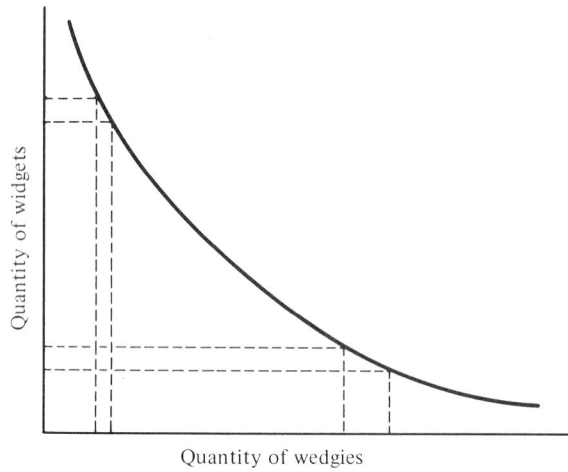

Figure 7.7   Consumer's indifference curve.

widgets is high a certain decrease in that number is compensated for
by a rather small number of wedgies. But when the number of widgets
held is low a corresponding decrease in the number demands a much
larger addition of wedgies.

A number of curves similar in shape to the one shown in Figure
7.7 can be thought of and each one will correspond to a different level
of satisfaction. Now how do we determine the individual's actual
course of action in regard to the purchase of the two goods? In Figure
7.8 four indifference curves are drawn. Each curve represents a different level of satisfaction to the individual. Also included is the line
from Figure 7.6 that shows the different opportunities open to the individual given his budget and the prices. The point at which one of the
indifference curves (and only four of the infinite number possible are
shown) just touches the *opportunity line* defines the equilibrium situation. This point of tangency is shown as Q in Figure 7.8 and it dictates
that the individual will buy q_0 widgets and q'_0 wedgies.

Budget Equation and Utility Function

In Alonso's analysis there are three items of purchase that the individual has to consider—land, transport or commuting, and a composite good that represents all other purchases. The individual has an
income that cannot be exceeded by his purchases. The budget equation, therefore, is

$$y = P_z z + P(s)q + k(s)$$

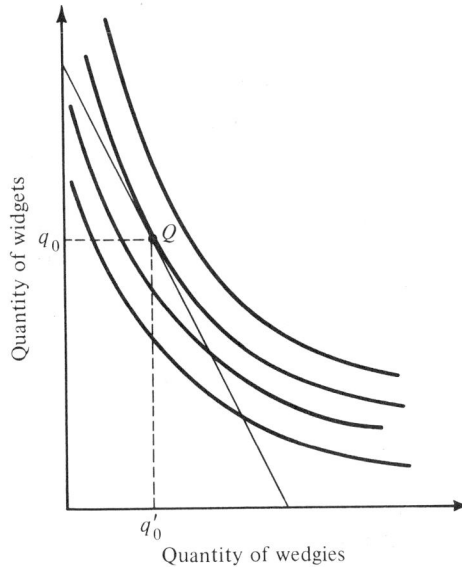

Figure 7.8 Indifference curves and opportunity line for the consumer.

where y is income;
                 P_z is price of the composite good;
                 z is quantity of the composite good;
                 $P(s)$ is price of land at distance s from the center of the city;
                 q is quantity of land;
                 $k(s)$ is commuting costs to the center of the city from distance s.

The equilibrium solution of the household is obtained in the same way as in our example, except that the situation is more complex and mathematics has to be used.

The set of all opportunities is now described by a three-dimensional surface and similarly, instead of indifference curves there are now indifference surfaces. The satisfaction of the individual is now represented by a mathematical function,

$$u = u(z, q, s)$$

which is known as the *utility function*. The aim then is to find values for z, q, and s such that u is as large as possible while making sure that the budget equation is satisfied. This is accomplished by using calculus. The solution at this point in the analysis states that corresponding to the maximum level of utility u_i, the individual will purchase a quantity z_i of the composite good, he will occupy q_i units of land at a distance s_i from the city, he will pay $P(s_i)$ for this land, and he will spend $k(s_i)$ on commuting costs.

Urban Land Values and Land Rents

We now recall the concept of the bid-rent curve, or as Alonso prefers, the *bid-price curve*. How is this derived for the urban resident? For an individual located at a given distance from the center of the city, s_0, the equilibrium combination of quantity of land and quantity of composite good can be determined as before simply by finding the point of tangency between the opportunity line and one of the indifference curves. But now an additional question is asked. What hypothetical price of land would have to exist at any other location in order that the individual would enjoy at that location equal satisfaction to that associated with his present location? Such hypothetical prices for different locations could be regarded as bid prices in the sense that their realization would enable the individual to have the same level of satisfaction regardless of where he was located within the city.

Alonso showed that bid-price curves could be derived for the individual and that these curves had the characteristic that the bid price decreased as distance from the center of the city increased. This was the result of increased commuting costs, and in order to compensate for this, individuals would have to substitute land and the composite good in order to maintain the same level of satisfaction. Land prices, therefore, would have to be lower the farther one was away from the city center.

An individual's equilibrium situation could again be derived by determining the point of tangency between one of his bid-price curves and the curve of actual land prices in the city. In this case, the family of bid price curves is such that the lower the curve, the higher the satisfaction since it involves paying lower prices for land. Hence, in Figure 7.9 bid-price curve u_n is associated with the highest level of satisfaction.

The case of the urban firm was handled by Alonso in a very similar manner. The focus now was on a firm's profits instead of on individual satisfaction. The bid-price curves expressed the relationship between the hypothetical price of land and distance from the center of the city for given levels of profits. Again, in a family of bid-price curves the lower the curve the higher the profit since it involved lower land prices. The equilibrium solution for the firm was determined by the point of tangency between the lowest bid-price curve and the curve of actual land prices in the city. Once the location and land price of this equilibrium were known, the quantity of land used by the firm could

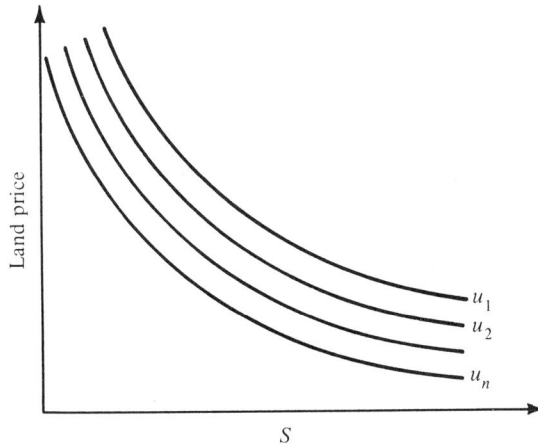

Figure 7.9 Family of bid-price curves.

be determined from equations relating profits to business volume, operating costs, and land costs (the latter two are related to the quantity of land used by the firm).

Alonso's formulation was weakest in its consideration of the market equilibrium. He was able to show that in general individuals or activities with the steeper bid-price curves would be located closer to the center of the city. But he was unable to determine an overall market equilibrium in which the distribution of land prices as a continuous function of distance from the center of the city would be specified. The major difficulty was that the particular locational arrangement of residents within the city was not known. Although it was possible to determine an equilibrium for any individual resident, it was not possible to obtain an ordering of all such individuals in terms of their distance away from the center of the city. Consequently, the distributions of both land values and population densities could not be derived.

7.4   An Alternative Formulation

The derivation of continuous functions relating land prices and population densities to distance from the center of the city (or any central point) is possible when an important change is made in the above framework.

Identical Households

It requires the assumption that all households are identical and that in order to allow for the existence of a spatial equilibrium these households are able to attain a maximum level of satisfaction (or utility) that is the same everywhere throughout the urban area. That is, "all households will attain the same optimal utility level irrespective of their location in the urban area."[4]

This alternative formulation runs as follows. A utility function and a budget equation are defined for the household and are identical to the ones in Alonso's theory. Then for a given distance s, the values $\bar{z}$ and $\bar{q}$ that maximize the utility function while satisfying the budget equation are solved for. Thus,

$$\bar{z} = \bar{z}[s, P_z, P(s), k, y]$$

$$\bar{q} = \bar{q}[s, P_z, P(s), k, y]$$

where the terms are defined as before. It is assumed that $P(s)$ is known. The maximum utility level, $\bar{u}$, is also derived. Recall that the optimal utility level for a household is assumed to be the same throughout the city and, therefore, it is invariant over distance. This spatially constant utility level is denoted by $\bar{\bar{u}}$.

The problem is to find the spatial equilibrium land price function corresponding to $\bar{\bar{u}}$. This involves solving for $\bar{\bar{P}}(s)$. The optimal quantity of land used by a household at distance s, given the existence of the spatial equilibrium, is obtained from the earlier equation as

$$\bar{\bar{q}}(s) = \bar{q}(s, P_z, P(\bar{\bar{s}}), k, y)$$

Then, by dividing this term $\bar{\bar{q}}(s)$ into a unit of land the number of households per unit of land is obtained, and since these households are identical, the equilibrium population density can be derived. This is stated as

$$\bar{\bar{D}}(s) = \frac{m}{\bar{\bar{q}}(s)}$$

where m is a constant giving the number of persons per household. The total population of the circular city of a given radius can then be obtained by using integral calculus.

This formulation does yield the continuous distributions of land prices (or values) and population densities and, depending on the form in which the utility function is stated, these derived distributions will have certain characteristic forms. It is indeed theoretically possible to derive the same mathematical descriptions of population density patterns that we discussed earlier. This is an important result and perhaps a surprising one in view of the strong assumption in this formulation that the households are identical.

7.5 A System of Multiple Centers

The above formulations assume that there is only one central location from which distance is measured. In almost all discussions this central location is taken to be the center of the metropolitan area, the central business district, but from the theoretical viewpoint this particular identification is not essential. All that need be assumed is that there is a central location where the employment and/or other opportunities are concentrated.

An extension of the theory considers several centers and the distances to them.[5] It begins by assuming the existence of an unbounded, homogenous region containing a number of urban places ordered into a central place hierarchy. Households located throughout the region are identical in their desires for space and accessibility, and for any one such household utility is defined as a function of the levels of congestion and accessibility.

Vector of Distances

In the case of several centers, accessibility becomes a function of the distances to them. In other words, the centers at a particular level in the hierarchy are assumed to be the same in terms of the employment opportunities and the goods and services they offer. Therefore, the resident will travel to the closest center of a particular order or hierarchical level, and associated with his location will be a set of distances to the nearest centers of the different orders. This set of distances, designated by the vector $(s_i, i = 1, 2, \ldots n)$, becomes part of the accessibility term and appears, therefore, in the expression for the equilibrium population density, $\bar{\bar{D}}$, as follows:

$$\bar{\bar{D}}(s_i; \quad i = 1, 2, 3, \ldots, n) = exp \ (a - \sum_i b_i s_i)$$

This generalized model might apply at three different levels:

1. At a regional level where the urban places are treated as points and the highest-order point is the metropolis.
2. At an intrametropolitan level where the highest-order point is the Central Business District.
3. At a regional level where the above two possibilities are combined and intraurban centers and separate urban centers are considered together and where the highest-order point becomes the Central Business District of the metropolis.

The equilibrium population density, $\bar{D}$, attains its maximum value (within the system of places being considered) at the highest-order place. This might be thought of as the *global maximum*. At other urban centers local maxima occur. The farther away the centers are from higher-order places, the smaller they are. No peaks or maxima occur other than at urban centers, but it is possible for some centers not to show up as corresponding to local maxima.

Land Prices in a Central Place System

The topic of land prices in a central place system involves a synthesis of the formulations considered above.[6] A central place system is defined as in the multiple-center formulation and for any household there is given the set of distances $(s_i; \quad i = 1, 2, \ldots, n)$ to the different order places. The households located in the region are assumed to be identical in their incomes, tastes, and preferences, a familiar assumption in our discussion thus far.

The household's utility function reflects the different order goods and services and the distances to the centers. Hence,

$$u = u(z_i, q, s_i) \qquad \text{for } i = 1, 2, \ldots, n$$

Now z_i is the composite consumption good of order i in the central place hierarchy of goods and services, and s_i is the distance to the nearest center offering these.

The budget constraint shows the same modifications,

$$y = \sum Pz_i + P(s_i)q + \delta(s_i) \qquad (i = 1, 2, \ldots, n)$$

where Pz is price of composite good of order i;
              $P(s_i)$ is price of land at a location s_i units of distance away
                    from the center of order i;
and
              $\delta(s_i)$ is total transportation costs for that location.

For a household with a given location and, hence, a particular set of distances $(s_1, s_2, \ldots, s_n)$, the values of z_i and q that yield a maximum utility level can be obtained. The assumption is made, as earlier, that the maximum utility level attainable by the households is constant throughout the region. This is a necessary condition for the existence of a spatial equilibrium. It means that no one will seek to relocate within the city because no one can improve his utility level by doing so. Given this assumption then, it is possible to solve for the distribution of land prices $\overline{\overline{P}}(s_i)$ and the quantity of land used by a household at equilibrium $\overline{\overline{q}}$.

A theorem results that states the following:

1. The spatial equilibrium land prices $\overline{\overline{P}}(s_i)$ have a global maximum at the location of the highest-order center.
2. The values of local maxima $\overline{\overline{P}}(s_i)$ corresponding to jth-order centers decrease as the distances between these jth-order places and highest-order places increase.
3. The local maxima correspond only to the locations of centers, given a finite number of centers.
4. Some centers may not correspond to points of local maxima.

Although the emphasis is on a central place system of urban places, the theorem is general in the sense that no sharp distinction need be recognized between urban and rural regions. The system can be thought of as a plain inhabited by identical households and served by any hierarchical arrangement of centers ranging from small clusters to the central business district of the major metropolis.

Future Extensions

It would be inappropriate in this text to attempt to explore further the theoretical issues that still command attention in this research field.[7] We have sketched some of the important contributions to one main theoretical stream and in so doing have highlighted some of the challenges that lie ahead. The assumption of identical households, for example, is a restrictive one and has been relaxed in some other studies by differentiating between households on the basis of income.[8] Similarly, the analyses reviewed above are typically partial in the sense that they deal with residential households and ignore competing forms of land use. But it is afterall the competition between these potential users that helps shape the pattern of land prices in a city.

The market for land in a city also contains many imperfections, and the different institutional factors and the power structures they represent exercise significant influences on the value of urban land. In this regard, it might be noted that a number of geographers take issue with what they regard as the simplistic analyses of urban rent that have been discussed in this chapter. They argue that urban rent is something more than a differential payment resulting from the variations in transportation costs away from the center of the city (or multiple centers). They prefer the Marxian analysis that considers rent as something arising from the monopolistic power of landowners. Landowners are seen as having the power to create an artificial scarcity of land, simply by insisting that they receive a positive return on all land in use, and also to extract excess profits and rents from their monopoly control of land and other resources. David Harvey is a leading proponent of this approach and he has shown how, in the case of the Baltimore housing markets, the different participants (namely, the speculators, landlords, developers, banks, mortgage companies, and government agencies) all interact to create submarkets in which so-called *class-monopoly rents* are realized.[9] These "arise because there exists a class of owners of 'resource units'—the land and the relatively permanent improvements incorporated in it—who are willing to release the units under their command only if they receive a positive return above some arbitrary level."[10]

7.6   A Related Probability Model for Commercial Establishments

We shall now consider a city that is assumed to be of infinite area and with a population density surface described by a particular probability law, the circular normal distribution (Figure 7.10).[11] Around the center of the city, commercial clusters are distributed within the urban area, also in accordance with a circular normal probability law. Each cluster has a size in terms of the number of establishments within it,

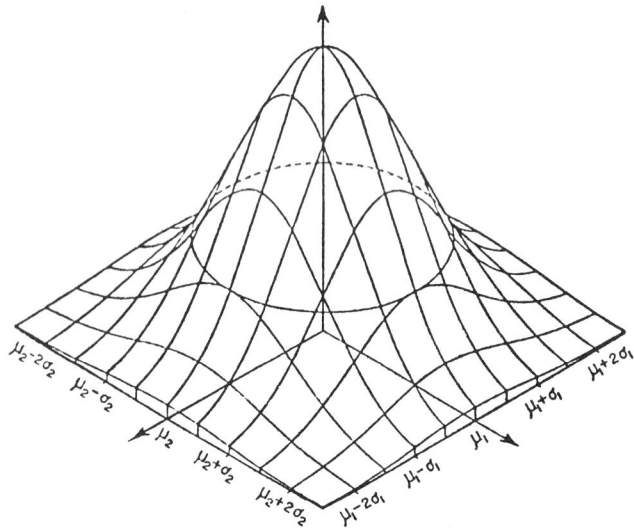

Figure 7.10   A hypothetical circular normal probability distribution.   This function is used to describe the patterns of urban population densities and commercial centers in the city in the model in Section 7.6 of this text.

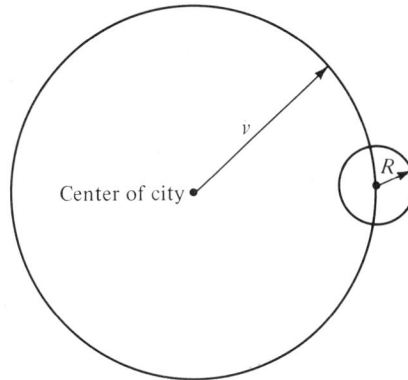

Figure 7.11 Diagrammatic representation of the problem considered in Section 7.6 of this text.

and these cluster sizes are also described by a random variable. All of the establishments within each cluster are assumed to be located at its center, a rather restrictive assumption. Nevertheless, given these assumptions, it is possible to answer the following questions:

1. What is the probability law for the random variable $\mathcal{Z}(R, v)$, which is the count of establishments in circular disks of radius R whose centers are located uniformly and independently on the circumference of another circular disk of radius v and center corresponding to the center of the city (Figure 7.11)?
2. What is the probability law for the random variable $\mathcal{Z}(R)$, which is the count of establishments in disks of radius R that are independently located around the city center according to the circular normal distribution law?

In both cases, the probability laws are shown to be compound Poisson laws.

This model can be generalized to allow for (1) the existence of a central focus, the Central Business District, which is not possible in the above model, and (2) for the dispersion of establishments within a cluster around its center.[12] To date, none of these models has been tested using observations of existing urban patterns.

7.7   Summary

In this chapter we have once again considered theories and models. In Chapter 5 we were interested in theories of the number, size, and location of cities in any large region, but in this chapter we have been concerned with theories of urban population densities and land values.

As we noted in the beginning of the chapter, the theories are based on certain notions of consumer behavior and economics. Essentially, we have proceeded from the general assumption that people living in the city have a desire to live near some central point, which may be the Central Business District or their place of employment, and that they are prepared to face certain costs in seeking such a preferred location. These costs include the rent for the use of a parcel of land, commuting costs, and the trade-offs that have to be made in regard to the quantities of all other "goods" that they are able to afford. We have assumed that the mix of these different choices—the location, the amount of space, the level of other goods—yields a certain level of satisfaction or "utility" to the person. Faced with a fixed budget, the person must then choose that mix that makes his utility as high as possible. We have seen how it is possible to work from these and related assumptions to develop theories that yield predictions about the distribution of population densities and land values within the city.

In a final section on the location of commercial activities in the city we gained a sense of how the theoretical results on population densities and land values might be used as the building blocks for other theories. We could imagine that in the same manner consideration might be given to determining optimal transportation networks, property taxation schemes, and the location of public services and facilities. All of these questions relate in some way to the spatial patterns of populations and land values.

In concluding Chapter 5 we commented on the fact that the theories discussed in that chapter often did not appear very realistic. Although some critics, David Harvey to name but one, would insist that the same is true of the theories of urban spatial structure discussed in this chapter, it does seem plausible that persons act within certain budget constraints in choosing the locations of their residences and that in doing so they strive for some form of maximum satisfaction.

What is disappointing about many of the theories is that the roles of institutions, such as the mortgage companies, banks, and public housing corporations, in further constraining and even shaping people's choices and actions are not considered. Nor do they deal adequately with such factors as racial prejudice and discrimination and investment speculation in land and housing as forces shaping the spatial structure of the housing market.

These points underscore, once again, the obvious. Theories represent one way of looking at urban society and as such they present only a partial view. We must supplement our reading of them with other accounts if we are to fully appreciate the complexity of the city.

Notes

1. For a general discussion, see E. Casetti, "Alternative urban population density models; an analytical comparison of their validity range," in A. J. Scott, ed., *Studies in Regional Science* (London: Pion Ltd, 1969), pp. 105–16.

2. E. Casetti, "Testing for spatial-temporal trends: an application to urban population density trends using the expansion method," *The Canadian Geographer,* **17,** 1973, pp. 127–37.

3. W. Alonso, *Location and Land Use* (Cambridge: Harvard University Press, 1964).

4. E. Casetti, "Equilibrium land values and population densities in an urban setting," *Economic Geography,* **47,** 1971, p. 17.

5. See G. J. Papageorgiou, "A generalization of the population density gradient concept," *Geographical Analysis,* **3,** 1971, pp. 121–27; "The population density and rent distribution model within a multicenter framework," *Environment and Planning,* **3,** 1971, pp. 267–82; "A theoretical evaluation of the existing population density gradient functions," *Economic Geography,* **47,** 1971, pp. 21–26.

6. G. J. Papageorgiou and E. Casetti, "Spatial equilibrium residential land values in a multicenter setting," *Journal of Regional Science,* **11,** 1971, pp. 385–89.

7. G. J. Papageorgiou, ed., *Mathematical Land Use Theory* (Lexington, Mass.: D. C. Heath and Co., 1976).

8. See M. J. Beckmann, "On the distribution of urban rent and residential density," *Journal of Economic Theory,* **1,** 1969, pp. 60–68; E. Casetti, Spatial equilibrium in an ideal urban setting with continuously distributed incomes," *London Papers in Regional Science,* **4,** 1974, pp. 129–40.

9. D. Harvey, "Class-monopoly rent, finance capital and the urban revolution," *Regional Studies,* **8,** 1974, pp. 239–55; D. Harvey and L. Chatterjee, "Absolute rent and the structuring of space by government and financial institutions," *Antipode,* **6,** 1974, pp. 22–36.

10. Harvey, *op. cit.,* p. 241.

11. M. F. Dacey, "An explanation for the observed dispersion of retail establishments in urban areas," *Environment and Planning,* **4,** 1972, pp. 423–38.

12. M. F. Dacey, "A central focus cluster process for urban dispersion," *Journal of Regional Science,* **13,** 1973, pp. 77–89.

chapter 8

The City As a Social Space
and the Related Impressions of People

Cities, we have emphasized, are complex societies that perform many different functions for many different people and organizations. But different cities also have common features that can be summarized at a variety of scales and from a variety of viewpoints. In this chapter, we shall discuss two different approaches to describing cities. The first is a statistical method that seeks to discover spatial patterns in the ecological structure of cities. The second approach concentrates on finding out what people know about cities, and as a result, on determining the spatial structure of cognitive images of cities.

8.1   Social-Area Analysis and Factorial Ecology Studies

The emphasis in this work is on the social structure of the city as it is portrayed by different measures of population characteristics (for example, age structure, sex ratios, ethnic backgrounds, mobility rates, and educational levels), economic characteristics (for example, income levels and occupations), health and welfare levels and housing quality (for example, proportion of houses in need of repair or age of housing), to mention only the major measures that are usually considered. These measures are obtained for different sub-areas of the city, which are usually census tracts in the case of United States cities, and the aim is to identify those key combinations of the different measures that provide an adequate basis upon which to differentiate the different sub-areas from one another.

The first major study of this type was one of the two cities of Los Angeles and San Francisco.[1] It established that three composite indices satisfactorily differentiated between and classified the census tracts in each of these two cities. These indices were *social rank, urbanization,* and *segregation.*

This study predated the widespread use of computers in social science research and it is perhaps not surprising that when these tools became available, other researchers took up the task of extending and refining the methods of this *social-area analysis.* The set of variables could now be expanded to include many other measures that would have been impossible using only hand calculations. New techniques of statistical analysis could also be employed, especially factor analysis, which seeks to represent the covariation among a set of variables, no matter how large, in terms of a much smaller set of underlying factors or dimensions. These factors were the counterpart of the above indices. Scores could then be computed on these factors and the resulting spatial patterns of values mapped for the different sub-areas of the city. This multivariate statistical approach has come to be known as *factorial ecology analysis.*

Urban Factorial Ecology Studies

There are completed factorial ecology studies of numerous North American and non-American cities. Given this wealth of information, it is all the more disappointing to note how few generalizations can be drawn from the results of these studies, an unfortunate consequence of the fact that the choice and definition of variables and the design of the analysis all too often vary from study to study.

Philip Rees has drawn some interesting comparisons between Chicago and Calcutta on the basis of factorial ecology studies.[2] A factor analysis of some 57 variables for the census tracts of the Chicago metropolitan area yielded 2 important differentiating characteristics, namely, the *social-economic status* and the *stage in the life cycle* of the resident population. In turn, the analysis of 37 variables for the 80 wards of Calcutta suggested that 4 underlying factors could reproduce the main patterns of covariation of the variables over the sub-areas of the city. These factors were identified as follows:

1. "A land-use and familism gradient—family status."
2. "Muslim concentrations—ethnic status."
3. "Axiality in literacy—social status."
4. "The substantial residential areas—social status."

It is possible to detect in the vagueness associated with these names one of the major problems associated with factor analysis, namely, the subjectivity involved in identifying the factors. But it must be conceded that this very problem has been persistent in social-area analysis from the outset.

A mapping of the sub-area scores on the factors for the two cities produced the diagrammatic maps shown in Figure 8.1. Rees noted the following with respect to these maps:

> In both instances the high status residential areas front superior amenities (Lake Michigan in Chicago and the Maidan in Calcutta). On the other hand, the geographic pattern of the other three social areas is inverted from one city to the other. In addition, particular areas of social space are picked out and given labels: "Lakeshore and near Lakeshore tracts" and "skid row tracts" or "exclusive residential areas along Maidan" or "city core." The regions of social

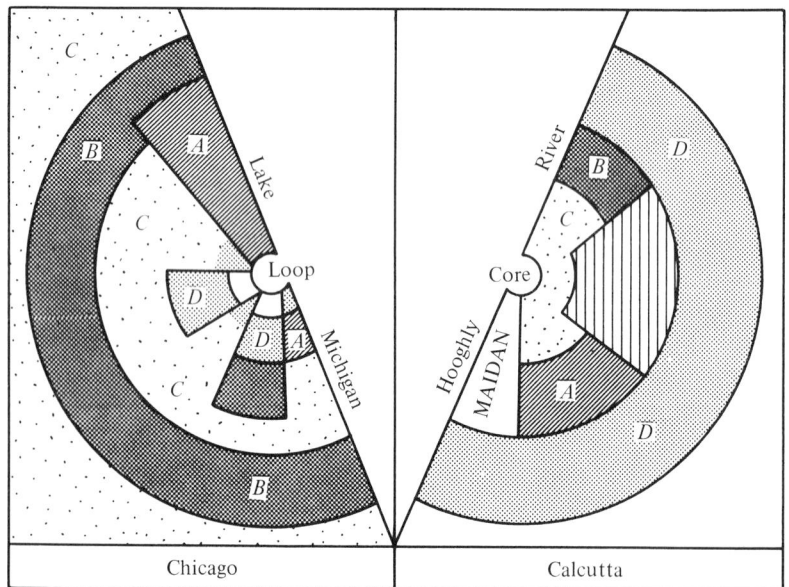

Figure 8.1 The generalized social areas of Chicago and Calcutta mapped. [P. H. Rees, "Problems of classifying subareas within cities," in B. J. L. Berry, ed., *City Classification Handbook* (New York: Wiley Interscience, 1972), p. 300.]

space are classified according to external correlates of race, housing tenure (Chicago), or location and function (Calcutta), all attributes not included in the original factorial ecology. Similar segments of the social space of the two cities are occupied by somewhat analogous areas, though the dimensions making up the social space have a greater significance in describing the social economic patterning of residences in Chicago than in Calcutta.[3]

In summary, what social-area, or factorial ecology, analysis provides is a very generalized description of certain complex patterns of social phenomena over the areal extent of the city. The statements that result are very aggregative ones and there is no real explanation of why any such patterns should exist. Nor does it seem very worthwhile to pursue any quest for such explanation when the descriptions are couched in such general and often vague terms. It is one thing to consider why differences in incomes or educational levels exist within the city, but a very different thing to ask why there are contrasts in social-economic status or family status. The former question can be tackled by using rigorous approaches; the latter question, however, prompts so many secondary-level questions (such as, What is meant by status?) that it seldom produces any satisfactory answers.

Nevertheless, as a form of description of the spatial structure of the city, social-area analysis and the factorial ecology studies provide distinctive results that could prove useful in urban planning activities. For example, neighborhoods that are favored by many planners as the basic unit in their city plans might well be delimited in this way as areas having a measure of internal homogeneity in their cultural, social, and economic characteristics. We shall say more about neighborhoods in Section 8.3.

8.2 People's Mental Images of the City

Factorial ecology depends primarily on objectively measured variables collected at an aggregate level (for example, for census tracts). Some researchers have used more subjectively defined variables to provide insight into the structure of cities. In studies of the urban areas of Boston, Los Angeles, and Newark Kevin Lynch discussed the various elements of city images and the characteristics of urban phenomena that impress themselves on people and influence the formation of their mental maps of those areas.[4] Lynch argued that any city can be decomposed into a number of spatial components—paths, edges, districts, landmarks, and nodes.

Spatial Components of the City Important in Mental Images

Paths are the channels of customary movement or the lines of regular transportation that are used by individuals in their movements around the urban area. For many people, *paths* are the predominant elements in the urban image and, for them, an urban image consists of a series of origin and destination nodes connected by *well-known* paths. It is also argued that almost all environmental elements that an individual retains in his mental map are related to these well-known paths in some way.

Edges are linear elements not considered to be paths but rather breaks in the continuity in the urban structure. Examples such as railroad cuttings, seashores, river banks, and freeways are edges that tend to break up the urban area into recognizable subsets or subdivisions.

Districts are two-dimensional subsets of the city. Both the paths and edges are linear elements and either bisect or define districts. Individuals in the urban area tend to identify with certain districts and in this way place themselves either inside or outside the districts. The sum total of the districts individuals can identify represents the areal extent of their map of the urban area that is retained in the mind.

Landmarks are the physical elements of the city that people use as reference points. In a sense, landmarks emphasize the special and the unique instead of the communal elements of urban areas.

Nodes are the orientation points for the building of mental maps. Nodes represent the origin and destination points that are visited regularly on trips in the urban area; they include the workplace, home, and regular places of shopping, recreation, education, and so on.

An individual's ability to recognize all these elements and link them together determines the degree to which he will be able to produce a recognizable mental map of an urban area. Obviously, the complexity of the *city of the mind* will depend on the amount of information that one has been able to collect about the urban area, particularly its linear, nodal, and district type elements, and also on the individual's ability to link these together into some coherent pattern.

Ciudad Guayana, Venezuela: An Example

The significance of cognitive representations of urban areas has been made particularly clear in the case of new, planned communities such as Ciudad Guayana. Studies of this community have indicated a divergence between the spatial plan of the new city as envisaged by the *designers* and the attributes and components that are significant enough to *residents* to act as anchors for their cognitive images. In such a study, 75 persons were randomly selected from each of 4 different environments in the city: (1) a model middle-income community (Puerto

Orday); (2) a spontaneous rancho settlement (Castillito); (3) a self-help rancho area (El Roble); and (4) an expanded colonial-style village (San Felix). Twenty more persons were interviewed in the elite residential areas of the Country Club and the C.Y.G. Site Engineer's Camp. Information was collected through open-ended questionnaires, map drawings, journey recall, and verbal descriptions of trips through the city. The people were also asked to describe their "ideal" and "worst" cities and to express a level of satisfaction with Ciudad Guayana as compared to other cities.[5]

The overwhelming impression obtained from this study was of the parochial nature of residents' perceptions. Very obviously, their urban knowledge was based on local orientation nodes such as home, workplace, shopping center, or places of previous residence. Their views of the city basically correlated closely with the ways they used it. Other interesting conclusions were that distance-decay effects were directionally biased and that length of residence had the effect of simplifying views of the city instead of making them more complex.

Implicit in the responses were some interesting structural components that varied in character from topological to positional (Figure 8.2). Specific styles for representing urban places cognitively included (1) *linear* elements that were fragmented, chain-like, or branches or exhibited network properties and (2) *areal* elements that were scattered, mosaic, linked, or grouped together into specific patterns.

This variety of styles for structuring cities underscores the differences that exist between individual cognitive representations of urban places and the simplified structural models (such as concentric zones, wedges, and sectors) that are frequently used as a basis for design and for describing the spatial structure of cities. Given that such differences exist, it seems desirable that more attention be paid to the cognitive structure of cities as the basis for actions by planners and designers.

Familiarity Maps of Cedar Rapids, Iowa

It is reasonable to suppose that persons living in a city will have more knowledge about certain areas of the city than about other areas. A study that investigated this idea in relation to Cedar Rapids, Iowa, relied upon responses from persons living in two different residential areas of the city.[6] The two areas were selected so that two contrasting populations from different spatial but internally homogeneous socioeconomic areas were chosen. The first was a low-income area in the central city known as the Oak Hill-Jackson area; the second was an upper middle-income area on the western perimeter of the city known as Cedar Hills. A sample of approximately 200 adults was obtained in

Topological

Sequential   Spatial

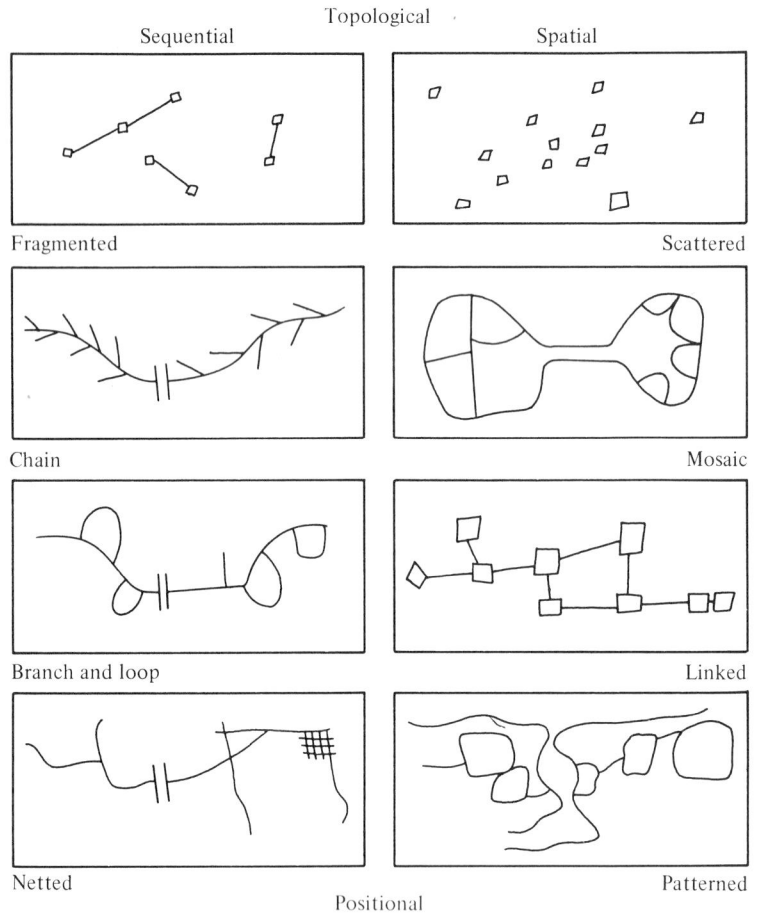

Fragmented   Scattered

Chain   Mosaic

Branch and loop   Linked

Netted   Patterned

Positional

Figure 8.2 Structural styles recognized in subjects' responses on their images of Ciudad Guayana. [Reprinted from *Planning A Pluralist City* by D. Appleyard by permission of The M.I.T. Press, Cambridge, Massachusetts. Copyright © 1976 by The Massachusetts Institute of Technology.]

each area. Sample members were restricted to those who had access to private transportation.

To determine the levels of information that residents had about the whole city, residents were asked to rate some 27 sub-areas on a familiarity scale. From the analysis of the responses, segments of the city were defined that had similar degrees of familiarity to the individuals in each sample. The results were maps of the urban area that showed differences in the levels of familiarity with the city depending on the locations of the respondents (Figure 8.3).

For the low-income Oak Hill-Jackson area, there was a general

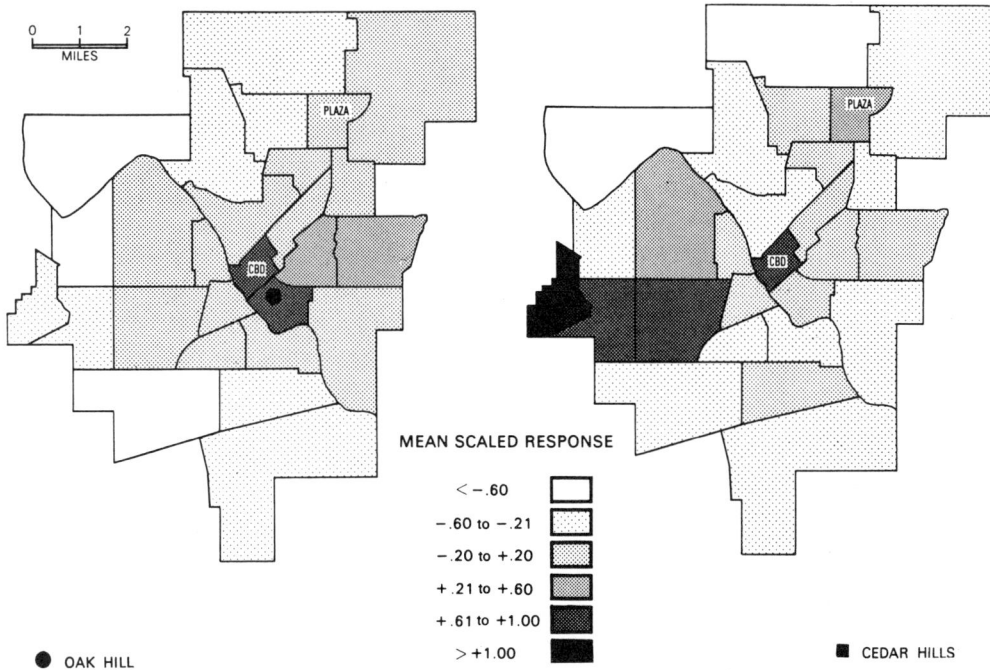

Figure 8.3 Familiarity-mean scaled responses for two communities in Cedar Rapids, Iowa. [F. E. Horton and D. R. Reynolds, "Effects of urban spatial structure on individual behavior," *Economic Geography,* **47,** 1971, p. 44.]

tendency for a pronounced familiarity to exist with the home area and the adjacent central business district. As distance from the home area increased, unfamiliarity also increased. The one exception to this was a relatively higher level of familiarity with areas in the northeast of the city that were joined to the sample area by a major thoroughfare. This northeastern area also had the major regional shopping center located within it.

The mean familiarity responses of the middle-income residential group differed somewhat from those of the low-income group. For sample members in the Cedar Hills area, the familiarity map of the city was highly linear. The highest familiarity was again the home area and the areas along a major road link between the home area and the central business district. An isolated suburban area containing the major shopping plaza also stood out with a high familiarity rating. In this case again, familiarity generally decreased with distance from the home or with distance from the home-central business district link. Apparently, therefore, there is some difference in the way individuals build familiarity maps of urban areas based on their location.

Relations Between Cognitive and Objective Components

This work on the cognitive components of a city has indicated that there are sets of characteristics of the physical structure of urban areas that apparently influence individuals in their attempts to represent the city to themselves in some coherent way. These factors include such things as the dominance of the visible form of physical elements of the city, noticeable hierarchies in structural features of the city, the simplicity of the feature, the frequency of exposure to features, the relative social and cultural values attached to various city elements, and a range of economic, social, and psychological characteristics of people themselves. Constructing a coherent mental map implies that individuals are able to generalize from individual features to surrounding areas. Some of the basic concepts that are part of our everyday vocabulary are specifically generated to describe parts of the city based on, say, the dominance of visible forms of elements of those cities. The terms *slum, high-class residential area, shopping center,* and so on, all describe elements of the city in terms of what are imaged as dominant characteristics or components found in some specific area of the city. For example, in areas where some slum characteristics dominate, the entire area may be designated as slum. In other words, there is in operation a principle of *grouping by proximity* that allows this type of generalization to occur. Frequency of exposure or frequency of sighting are also stressed as major factors in selecting elements for inclusion into mental images of the city. We shall take up this point again in Chapter 12.

8.3   Images of Suburbs and Neighborhoods

In the preceding section we discussed the mental images that people have of a city when it is thought of as a spatially extensive and continuous area. Now we shall ask how the images are formed of the particular suburbs and neighborhoods that are familiar to people.

The Case of Staten Island, New York

We shall discuss a study based on (1) some 1,950 sketch maps drawn by residents of and commuters to Staten Island (see, for example, Figure 8.4) and (2) 138 extended interviews with residents of the island.[7] The aim was to examine the role of formal and informal learning in building cognitive maps of the island. More than one-half of the maps showed an orientation similar to that of commercial maps, but frequently respondents were unclear about the cardinal direction and often included significant distortions in their maps. For example,

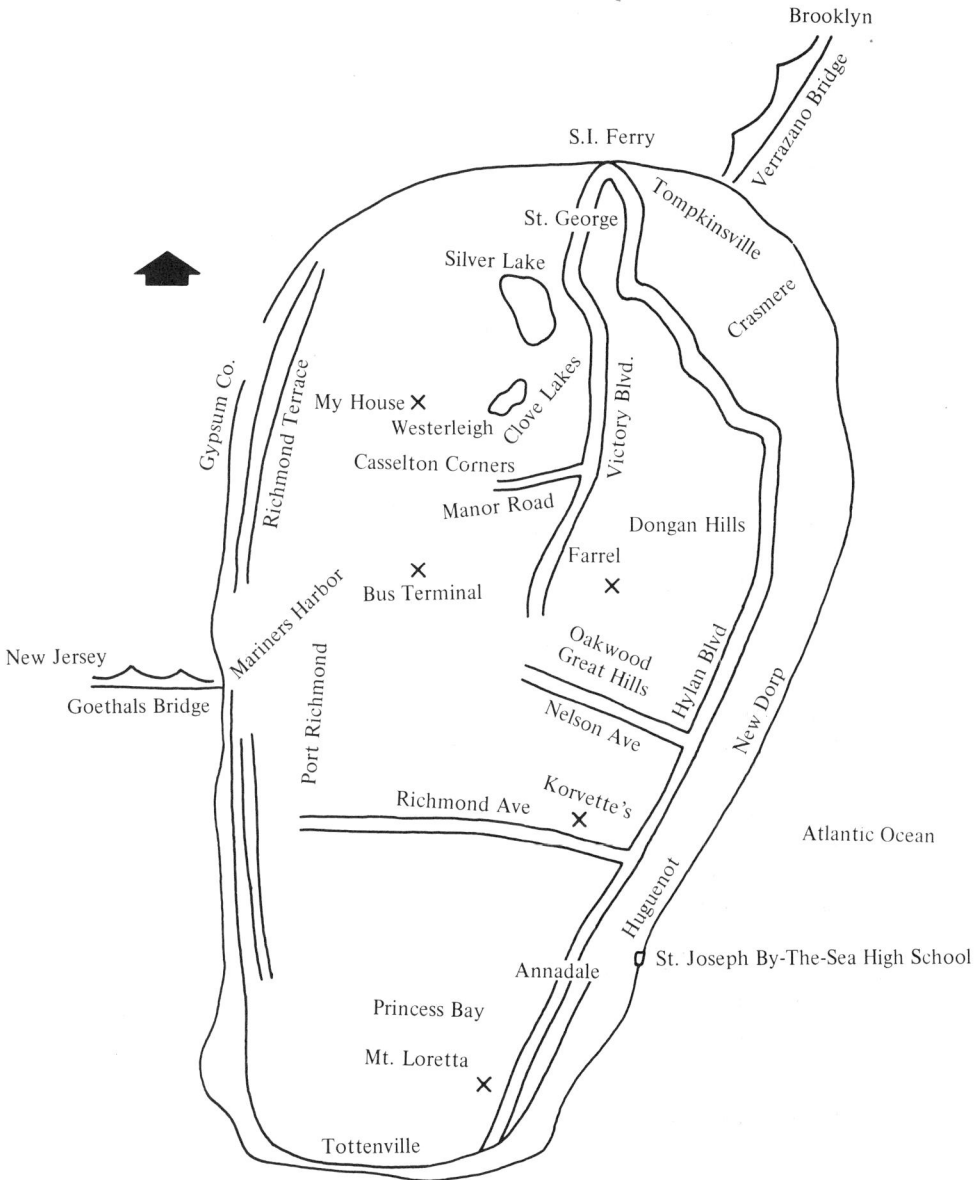

Figure 8.4 Standard orientation with north shore displacement. [R. W. Howell, "A study of informal learning," *Final Report,* Project No. 8-B-125, Grant No. OEG-2-9-420125-1009, U.S. Department of Health, Education and Welfare, 1969, p. 34.]

the western shore facing New Jersey is sparsely populated and tends to disappear from many sketched maps because it is considered to be of little interest or importance. As a result, the north shore of the island is drastically curved toward the south (Figure 8.4).

A close examination of the maps showed that, for the most part, areas of the island that were not considered relevant for individuals were not included on the maps. Commuters tended to show those landmarks and transportation routes that guided them to their destinations on the island. In fact, individuals who used their own transportation, whether by walking or driving, tended to show changes of direction as an important occurrence on their maps. Those who were passively transported (as on the train) more frequently depicted routes as a straight line even if they knew that there were curves and turns in them. For some, the island itself consisted primarily of a series of highly connected routeways. For others, it was a series of communities. For others, the dominant features of the island were the connections with the other parts of the city.

Whenever there was imperfectly understood formal knowledge, such as the correct shape of the island according to commercial maps, there appeared many gross distortions. For example, some residents on the north shore reversed the north–south arrangement of communities while preserving the original north–south orientation of the outline of the island (Figure 8.5). Another common result was to build the map in a mirror image of itself (Figure 8.6). Although many individuals were able to construct in reasonable terms a map of the island and many of its constituent paths, some residents were unable to identify with the island at all, indicating that they had very little local involvement and very little interest in recording information about the island. The most detailed and technically accurate maps were provided by individuals who exhibited a lively interest in the island and who combined the kinds of information available on commercial maps with the kinds of information obtained by direct experience moving around the island.

Neighborhoods

A number of researchers argue that the basic unit of many urban areas is the *neighborhood*. This is an area that has both a physical and a psychological existence. The physical existence consists of an area of space with which an individual identifies. The psychological neighborhood represents the area in which many social or neighboring activities take place. Both the physical and the social–psychological structure of city neighborhoods are apparently so intertwined in the minds of individuals that they can barely be separated. Therefore,

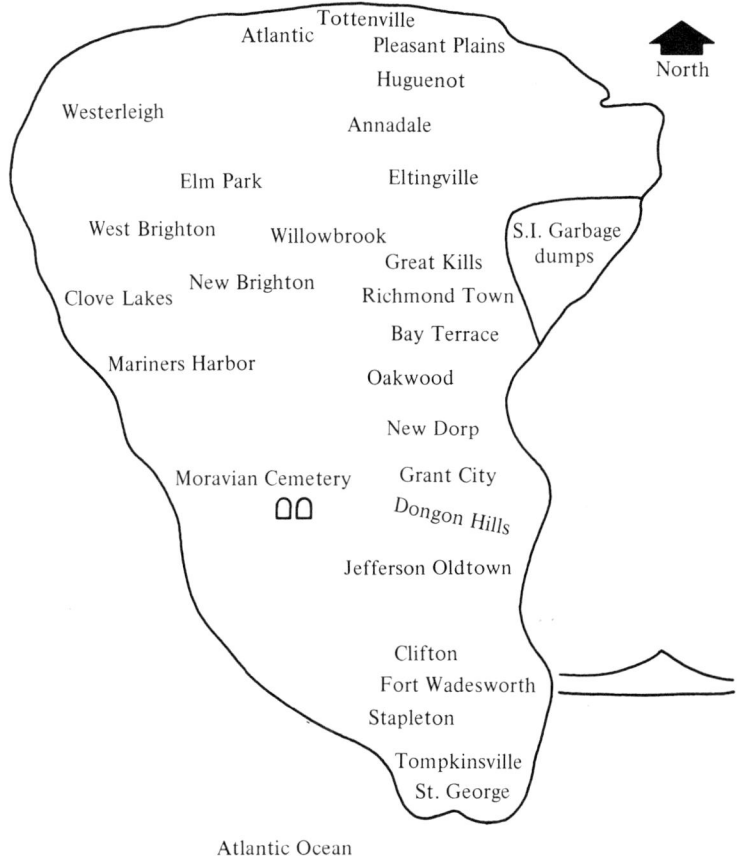

Figure 8.5 North shore orientation with reversals. [R. W. Howell, "A study of informal learning," Final Report, Project No. 8-B-125, Grant No. OEG-2-9-420125-1009, U. S. Department of Health, Education and Welfare, 1969, p. 37.]

some authors argue that any city can be entirely described if one can piece together the number and sizes of all distinct neighborhoods that comprise the urban area.

Recognition of the extent of neighborhoods has taken place at both a gross level and at an individual level. At a gross level, planners have argued that an area encompassing something like 10,000 individuals in a relatively large city can be treated for planning purposes as a neighborhood. This may be an area with reasonably uniform socioeconomic, ethnic, or other functional and structural characteristics. Rarely, however, is it an area determined on the basis of how individuals perceive the neighborhood or on the basis of how they interact.

Attempts have been made in recent years to determine small areas within the city that are relatively uniform from the point of view of the

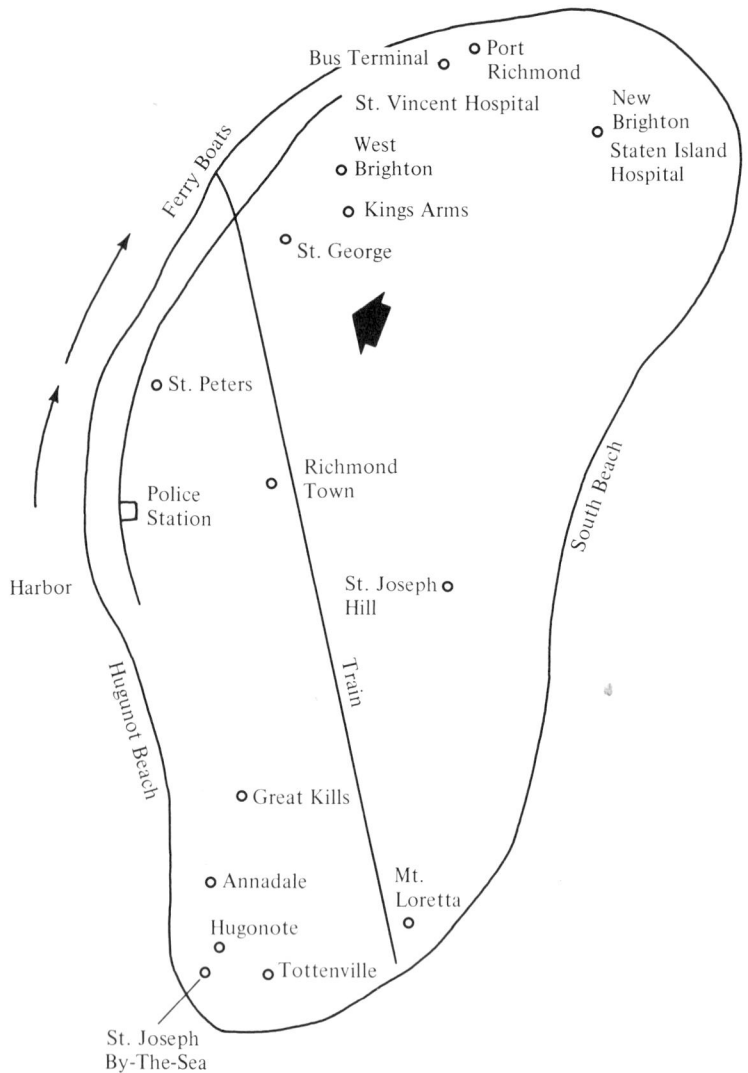

Figure 8.6 Representative "mirror" map. [R. W. Howell, "A study of informal learning," *Final Report*, Project No. 8-B-125, Grant No. OEG-2-9-420125-1009, U. S. Department of Health, Education, and Welfare, 1969, p. 33.]

people who reside in them. This definition has most commonly relied on individual perceptual processes that are seen as forming the basis of our movements through space:

> . . . thus when we learn to find our way about a neighborhood, we develop a system of images and ideals about the relative position and distance in roads, houses, and natural features.

For instance, we know that when we come to such and such
crossroads we must turn right and proceed until we reach a
certain house (which we image), and then branch left, and
so on. Most people can acquire such patterns of images and
ideas; and they also learn to relate them to plans and maps
which symbolize those topological relationships.[8]

This hypothesis has been investigated in a number of studies of which
we shall now give an example.

The Case of Cambridge, England

A study of this community suggested that the concept of the
neighborhood was a prominent one for almost every household interviewed.[9] Almost everyone was able to draw a line around that part of
the urban area that he considered as his neighborhood. This idea of
neighborhood was a very individualistic one, and there was tremendous variation in the neighborhoods constructed by even a sample of
householders in a terrace-row of corporation houses (8 of them within
about 100 yards of each other). Their outlines of the neighborhoods
showed almost no coincidence, despite the fact that the entire area
from which this sample of persons was drawn was labeled as a "neighborhood" by almost everyone interviewed. Admittedly, the city was
only a moderately sized one with no great variations between high-
income and low-income areas, and this may have accounted for the
fact that the average areas of the perceived neighborhoods in both the
outer middle-class suburbs and the higher-density slums were almost
the same. This prompted the conclusion that individuals delineate
neighborhoods not in terms of the population they contain, not in
terms of the number of houses, but only as a space.

Three of the more significant variables that explained the size and
shape of the areas delineated as neighborhoods in Cambridge were the
number of local friends, the number of local clubs and organizations
to which one belonged, and the tendency to use local shops instead of
downtown or major regional centers. Other significant variables appeared to be the social class of the respondent, his length of residence
in the area, the age of the respondent and the location of his workplace.
Summarizing these findings into a *schema*, it seems that there is a continuous input of sensory information from the physical and social objects in the urban environment into each individual. This input arises
from repeated transactions among individuals (such as neighbors,
tradesmen, children, and so on) and the physical elements of the environment (such as buildings, parks, shops, and so on). As the sensory input changes, or as people become more familiar with areas, then
the schema becomes better formed in the mind. It is constantly being

modified by new and relevant experience, but at any particular point in time information as to its content and existence can be extracted.

Although these schema are being constantly changed over time, they are probably rarely, if ever, complete, even for a small segment of space. Consequently, there is no reason to believe that the schema developed in the mind of the individual bears any relationship to the physical reality that lies outside the individual. It can be hypothesized that the degree of coincidence between the schema and the objective reality will increase as the individual is exposed more frequently to the given environment. Individuals who have lived in an area longer than others should have a more complete schema, should be able to remember more elements of the environment, and should be able to locate them more accurately than relative newcomers.

8.4 Are There Relationships Between Physical and Social Structure, Mental Images, and Behavior Patterns?

Despite an increasing amount of research on the social and cognitive structure of cities, there are still many unsolved questions concerning the degree of correspondence between cognized and objective urban environments. There is even less of a concensus on the relationships between cities, their images, and people's behavior. One attempt at answering some of these questions began by conceiving of urban environments as consisting of *stimuli* or cues (such as buildings, parks, shopping centers) and *supports* (such as the paths used by individuals in their movements throughout the city).[10] It was argued that people build their cognitive images from the existing environmental features by selecting and organizing features that are meaningful to them. The study considered a number of hypotheses.

City Structure and Environmental Cues

The first hypothesis was that city structure itself is significant in explaining variations in the average importance assigned to environmental features by the respondents. The bases for this hypothesis were the established relationships between actual and imaged environments (that is, we all recognize that the actual structure of the environment considerably influences the image that we form of it).

The second hypothesis was that land-use features of a city would have a greater average importance in environmental cue selection in concentric zonal types of city structures and that traffic features would be more important in sectoral city forms. In concentrically zoned cities an individual should see several land-use changes along the route as he moves from the periphery to the city center. Hence, it is plausible to expect land-use changes to be dominant in both image formation and environmental cue selection for persons living in such cities. In a sectoral type city, each sector consists of one dominant type of land use that is bounded by major traffic arteries and extends from the center toward the periphery. The individual may see few profound land-use changes on his trip to and from the city center. Therefore, it is suggested that traffic features are likely to be more important in forming images of the urban environment.

Personal Characteristics and Cue Selection

The third hypothesis was that the actual form of the city would be of greater importance in the environmental cue selection process and in cognitive image formation than any of the personal characteristics of individuals. In other words, *what is seen* is *what is remembered*. This is a far more critical factor in image formation than the personal characteristics of the observers.

The final hypothesis was that of all the personal characteristics considered, length of residence in an urban place and type of previous urban experience would be important in determining which cues were critical in forming city images. It was assumed that the longer an individual had lived in an urban area (or the longer his term of urban experience), the more likely he would be to choose critical discriminatory environmental features in finding his way about an urban area. Also, he would be increasingly better able to select from the mass of urban detail certain critical cues to anchor his cognitive representation.

These hypotheses were tested by using a fourfold experimental design and information on three Ohio cities (Marion, Newark, and Columbus). Four different environmental displays were used, each display representing a different level of abstraction. The displays included maps, scale models, slides, and field trips. For example, black-and-white maps were built to portray six dominant land-use types in each city. Locations of traffic lights, railroads, streams, and streets were also added to the land-use information. The *scale models* were built of Styrafoam and included all the features found on the maps, as well as a number of features such as churches, named commercial establishments, and other features unique to each of the cities investigated. At a less abstract level, subjects were presented with a series of *slides* of actual environments in each of the urban places and were asked to suggest where the particular environmental feature shown might be found in the city. The final stage of the experiment involved taking subjects on field trips through each of the urban areas and asking them specifically to name the cues that they used to identify their position in the city on each of the routes that were selected.

The hypotheses were tested by using different forms of statistical analysis. The relative importance of the different cues was shown by deriving measures of their average (or mean) rating over the set of responses. The set of environmental cues identified is shown in Table 8.1.

Table 8.1 Environmental Cues Used in Ohio Study. [G. Zannaras, "An analysis of cognitive and objective characteristics of the city: their influence on movements to the city center" (unpublished Ph.D. dissertation, Department of Geography, The Ohio State University, Columbus, Ohio, 1973), p. 57.]

1. Shopping centers
2. Railroad tracks
3. Direction signs
4. School buildings
5. Banks
6. Churches
7. Movie theaters
8. Restaurants
9. Open space areas such as parks or green space
10. Speed-limit signs
11. City skyline
12. Traffic congestion
13. Traffic lights
14. Street width changes
15. Billboards
16. Bridges
17. Neon lights in business areas
18. Rivers
19. Hills*
20. Freeway system
21. Number and spacing of freeway exits
22. Industrial buildings (factories)
23. Public buildings
24. Residential quality changes
25. Residential density changes (spacing of houses)
26. Smog
27. Buildings become more numerous and closer together
28. Major department stores
29. Slums
30. Construction work

NOTE: This table includes the features that solicited the most responses.

*This feature had a mean of 2.83; all other features had means above 3.0 on a 5-point scale of frequency of use.

Interpreting the Results

As far as the importance of city structure is concerned, it appears that it does influence the process of forming images of urban environments. The selection of both general types of cues and place-specific cues appears to be facilitated more in sectoral zoned cities than in either of the other types. By contrast, the hypothesis on the importance of land-use cues in cities with different structures was not confirmed by the results. The hypothesis on the relative importance of city structure as opposed to personal characteristics in way-finding tasks and in forming cognitive images appeared to be confirmed by the analysis. This finding was somewhat reinforced by the fact that the length of residence in a city did not show up as an important or statistically significant discriminating variable. Instead, a series of variables that related to the activities of individuals instead of to their length of residence proved to be more valuable to the sample observers in discriminating between cues and in selecting routes around the city.

8.4   Summary

This chapter has presented a mix of views on the social and cognized structure of cities. Comments on social areas were confined to the city-wide scale. It was pointed out that results of such analyses have varying degrees of comparability and they frequently suffer from the use of complex concepts such as social status to interpret their dimensions.

Whereas social-area analysis primarily uses aggregative data to impose a structure on cities, cognitive analyses rely more on individual subject responses and attempt to define common elements of those responses. These common elements, such as nodes, paths, edges, and so on, are the principal components of cognitive images of urban environments. There appears to be some overlap between social-area analysis and many cognitive studies, for both break down cities into component parts, recognize the importance of small homogeneous units (such as a neighborhood), and relate the organizational structure they define to spatial behavior. This last point was clearly emphasized in the study of the three cities in Ohio. It is safe to conclude, therefore, that whether the components of cities are analyzed in an aggregated or disaggregated manner, it is important to understand them if one is to be successful in planning for livable and enjoyable city environments.

Notes

1. E. SHEVKY and W. BELL, *Social Area Analysis: Theory, Illustrative Applications and Computational Procedures* (Menlo Park: Stanford University Press, 1955).

2. P. H. Rees, "Problems of classifying subareas within cities," in B. J. L. Berry, ed., *City Classification Handbook* (New York: Wiley Interscience, 1972), pp. 265–330.

3. *Ibid.,* p. 299.

4. K. Lynch, *The Image of the City* (Cambridge: The M.I.T. Press, 1960).

5. D. Appleyard, "Styles and methods of structuring a city," *Environment and Behavior,* **2,** 1970, pp. 100–17.

6. F. E. Horton and D. R. Reynolds, "Effects of urban spatial structure on individual behavior," *Economic Geography,* **47,** 1971, pp. 36–48.

7. R. W. Howell, "A study of informal learning," *Final Report,* Project No. 8-B-125, Grant No. OEG-2-9-420125-1009, U.S. Department of Health, Education and Welfare, 1969.

8. M. D. Vernon, *The Psychology of Perception* (Baltimore: Penguin Books, 1962), p. 135.

9. T. Lee, "Psychology and living space," *Trans. of the Bartlett Society,* **2,** 1964, pp. 11–36.

10. G. Zannaras, "An analysis of cognitive and objective characteristics of the city: their influence on movements to the city center," Unpublished Ph.D. dissertation, Department of Geography, The Ohio State University, Columbus, Ohio, 1973.

D. MIGRATION AND INTERACTION BETWEEN AND WITHIN CITIES

chapter 9

Relations Between Cities and Rural Areas

In preceding chapters the shape and form of different urban environments, ranging in scale from single urban centers to regional and national urban systems, have been discussed in detail. The broad purpose of this discussion has been to show that physical properties of the urban environment can be analyzed so as to extract and order a mass of information about cities and settlements. It should be recalled that when human activities were discussed, they were discussed generally as static patterns and analyzed only at a macro or aggregative level. In other words, emphasis was placed mainly on the distribution of population densities, the spatial arrangement of social and ethnic groups, and the location of different types of economic activities within the city.

At different places in these earlier chapters, however, we referred to the activities of persons as decision makers. This was the case, for example, in the discussion of urban residential choice in Chapter 7, in which people considered as members of households were seen as making choices among alternatives subject to the constraints of their budgets. Then in Chapter 8 we referred to the images that people form and have of the city and how these images might be related to patterns of behavior, including travel within the city. Now in this, and the following three chapters, we shall look specifically at the patterns of human movement and interaction, first as they relate to the relations between rural and urban areas, then to the relations between cities, and finally to the relations among places and locations within any large urban area. The emphasis in this first chapter of the set is on the patterns of migration from rural areas to cities and on the travel patterns associated with rural consumers shopping and trading in urban settlements.

9.1   Migration As a Spatial Process: Some Concepts

It has been suggested that the following 20 important propositions can be stated about migration:[1]

1. The propensity to migrate decreases as the age of the person increases. Those most likely to move are people in the 20–29-year-old group.
2. The tendency to migrate does not differ significantly from males to females, but
3. it does vary directly with level of education. The more educated the persons, the more likely they are to be involved in migrations.
4. Professional and managerial groups are also more migratory than other occupational groups and, generally, the more highly skilled persons will move greater distances than will other workers.
5. Persons who rent their accommodations are more likely to move than are homeowners.
6. Mobility is more highly correlated with career pattern variables than with life-cycle variables.
7. Distance is a barrier to migration and, in general, the level of migration between any two places will be greater the closer they are located to one another.
8. Many forms of migration have definite directional components. For example, moves often are made from smaller urban places to larger ones or from the central city to the suburbs.
9. With the development of any society from a basic rural-agricultural one into a more advanced technological urban-industrial one, the importance of economic factors such as

the income and unemployment differentials between places diminishes as a factor influencing migration.

10. As economic development takes place and urban centers emerge and grow rapidly there will be high levels of rural-urban migration.

11. On the individual level, the decision to migrate in a developed economy such as the United States is mainly influenced by work-related and economic considerations.

12. Related to the previous point, it is factors such as job transfers, moves after retirement, armed forces postings, and college student migration that are important in shaping regional migration patterns in the developed economies, much more so, in fact, than in developing economies.

13. The pull factor of increasing income at a destination is much stronger than the push effect of decreasing income at an origin so far as the level of migration between the two places is concerned.

14. Persons who are unemployed are more likely to migrate than persons who are employed. The push effect of lowering unemployment at the origin outweighs the effect of raising unemployment at the destination as a deterrent.

15. The levels of migration between places tend to persist over time.

16. In general, migration flows cannot be explained in terms of rational individual behavior that seeks to maximize benefits over costs.

17. The ability of any potential migrant to weigh the costs and benefits of a move will be directly related to his level of educational attainment and information about alternative places of residence.

18. If there is disharmony between an individual's present and expected life-style and the life-style norm where he lives at present, then migration often occurs as a response.

19. In terms of their probabilities of migration at any time, persons can be classified into (a) chronic movers who move often and repeatedly, (b) movers who have a low degree of mobility, and (c) stayers who have little or no mobility over time.

20. The longer a person lives in a region, the less likely he is to move away from it.

In the following sections of this chapter and the next two chapters some of these propositions are developed and elaborated upon in specific contexts.

9.2   Rural-Urban Migration in Developing Societies

Rural-urban migration represents a basic transformation of the structure of a society in which people move from generally smaller (mainly agricultural) communities to larger (mainly non-agricultural) communities. Apart from the spatial dimension of the move, there is also a socio-economic dimension involving a permanent transformation of skills, attitudes, motivations, and sometimes behavioral patterns.

As a corollary of economic development, rural-to-urban migration has been going on in the developed countries of Europe and North America for more than a century. By contrast, in many of the developing societies the process is a much newer one and, consequently, it is more easily identified and studied. In these developing societies, prior to Western contacts, the settlement structure typically consisted of isolated and relatively self-sufficient villages and the probability of any rural-urban migration taking place was rather low. This partly reflected the requirements of the communities for full-scale participation of their inhabitants in the subsistence activities and also the lack of cities in such areas that would attract potential migrants. This situation was typical of much of tropical Africa until comparatively recently, but today rural-urban migrations characterize many parts of the continent and have lately been assuming spectacular proportions. The rural areas, in other words, can no longer be regarded as isolated or even self-sufficient.

The Example of Nigeria

A geographer, Akin Mabogunje, has analyzed these demographic trends for his own country, Nigeria.[2] He argued that it is the set of forces set in motion by increasing economic development that has produced change and that although many of the forces of change were initiated by colonial administrations, they have been reinforced in recent years by the activities of the new African governments. These governments have adopted programs aimed at decreasing isolation by improvement of transportation and communication methods, and they have adopted development programs aimed at integrating rural economies into the respective national economies instead of leaving them at their local subsistence levels. Such integration makes rural economies more responsive to changes in wages and prices, consumer preferences, and the overall vagaries of demand and supply changes within a country. Decreasing isolation also means that there is a movement toward greater social and cultural integration of both rural and urban areas. The overall effect of bringing the rural and urban systems into closer harmony has been twofold: either agricultural areas have been stimulated to produce more goods so that they can enter the exchange economy and gain access to the advantages contained therein or persons migrate to urban areas in an attempt to sell labor directly in exchange for wages that are used to buy desired goods and services. This, then, is the environment within which a system of rural-urban migration in a developing economy may be conceived of as operating.

Checks on Migration Movements

Just as there are forces that prompt the migrant to move from the land to the city so there are a number of fundamental checks that serve to inhibit this flow. Mabogunje noted that apart from the ties that a potential migrant has with his family, which must be resolved before a move can take place, the village community itself may act as a control subsystem. Its controlling role often is not as direct as that of the family, but it operates in terms of the types of activities that it sponsors or encourages. For example, the village community that adopts the idea of cooperative farming or marketing may consequently improve its economic conditions and thereby discourage (at least in the short run) permanent migration. It should be remembered, however, that a village that actively undertakes a program to upgrade the social, economic, and productive life of its community may inadvertently stimulate migration to urban areas by making younger generations more enlightened, better educated, and more highly motivated to improve their economic positions.

At the macro level, urban systems themselves act in both stimulating and checking movements. Barriers or checks may exist in the form of poor information about the advantages in the urban system; there may also be a relative lack of job opportunities for in-migrants or a poor public policy on housing potential migrants.

As far as employment opportunities are concerned, the city frequently is regarded as a place for the sale of specialized skills. A migrant who is uneducated and unsophisticated in terms of urban living is frequently seen as belonging to the lowest level of the occupational hierarchy. To some extent, as an individual moves up this urban hierarchy he becomes more and more committed to an urban way of life. Thus, we see that it is a relatively crucial matter for the migrant to determine what type of job he is likely to be able to get before he undertakes a move to a particular place.

Attraction of Large Cities

If we look at the hierarchy of urban places from the migrant's point of view, we can see that size would probably have a fairly important role in the selection of urban destinations. Clearly, smaller urban centers have fewer tiers of specialization and more restricted employment opportunities than larger ones, although in some cases, competition for the positions available may be less intense in the smaller centers.

The dominance of a large primate city as the major point of attraction in the migration streams of a developing economy is illustrated well in the case of Bangkok in Thailand. This country is predominantly agricultural with over 80% of the economically active population employed in agriculture. The patterns of internal migration are dominated by the attraction of the greater Bangkok metropolitan area, which from 1955 to 1960 gained over 66,000 inhabitants by net inter-regional migration. This gain represented 72% of all internal population shifts in the country.

Stepwise Movements

An aspect of the spatial patterning of migration that is illustrated well in rural-urban migration in developing societies is that there are often steps involved in an individual migrant's history. In other words, a person may move up through the different levels of the urban hierarchy by way of a number of migration steps, moving first from, say, the agricultural village to the small town, then to an intermediate-sized town, and finally to the large city (Figure 9.1).

This pattern of migration has been discussed in regard to Sierra Leone.[3] The idealized pattern shown in Figure 9.2 was drawn on the assumption that migration in that country would occur simply as a

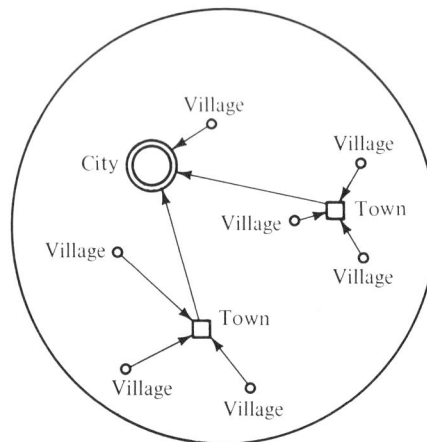

Figure 9.1 A schematic representation of stepwise migration patterns from villages to towns to cities. The arrows show the paths of the migrations.

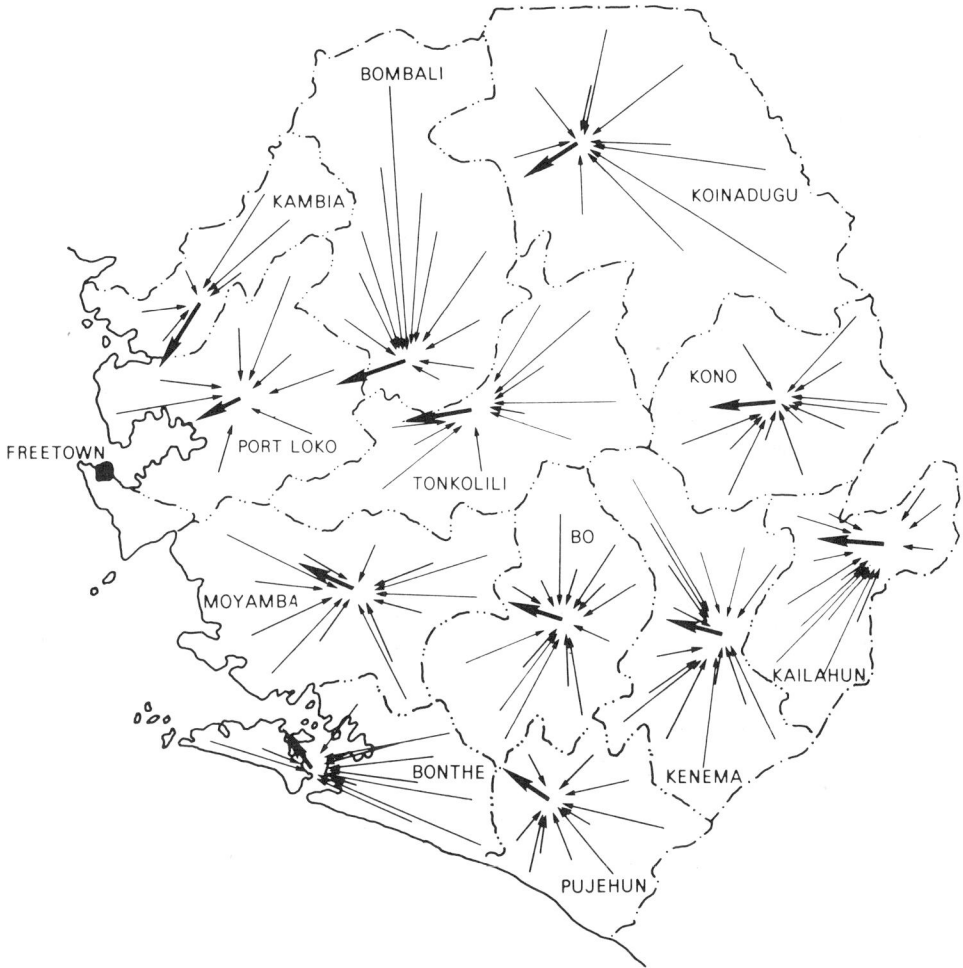

Figure 9.2   Idealized stepwise migration flow pattern. [J. B. Riddell and M. E. Harvey, "The urban system in the migration process: An evaluation of stepwise migration in Sierra Leone," *Economic Geography*, **48**, 1972, p. 277.]

function of the attraction of the nearest larger places in a three-tiered urban system based on Freetown as the highest-order center. In Figure 9.3 the actual pattern of migrations for 1963 is shown. Note that the two patterns agree for only a limited number of regions in the country. This may be attributed to the fact that some centers were too close to Freetown and hence migrants often bypassed the intermediate-sized centers. Second, in some regions the urban system was too poorly developed and the patterns became almost random. Third, the effect of the diamond fields in Kono was to distort some of the flow

Figure 9.3 Actual pattern of dominant inter-chiefdom migration flows. [J. B. Riddell and M. E. Harvey, "The urban system in the migration process: An evaluation of step-wise migration in Sierra Leone," *Economic Geography*, **48**, 1972, p. 278.]

toward that area. Finally, in some regions poor accessibility detracted from the attractiveness of centers in those regions.

In the next chapter we shall return to the topic of migration and examine the movement of people between different urban places and cities. At this point, however, we shall consider some other aspects of rural-urban interaction, specifically the travel patterns associated with the trading and shopping activities of rural residents.

9.3 Periodic Markets: A Dynamic Form of Rural-Urban Interaction

A different form of rural-urban interaction is represented by the shopping trips made by farmers into nearby urban market centers. This form of interaction is present both in developing economies and in those that are economically advanced.

In developing economies, in many cases, the markets are *periodic* in the sense that they are not open for trade every day. Periodicity also occurs in terms of the frequency with which traders attend different markets. For example, in some of the larger places in which markets are located, market activity occurs every day of the week just as in urban places in developed economies. However, in the developing economy even though the market may be open every day, the same mix of traders may not be there. This means that the same mix of functions may not be present in the market on successive days. It is not unusual for a trader in these societies to visit a number of fairs or markets within the same week. Consequently, the degree of seller mobility is much greater.

Characteristics of Periodic Markets

The periodicity in the periodic markets, therefore, appears to be tied to the behavior of both the seller and the buyer. Many sellers, for example, are also the producers of the product. Since they require time for production, they cannot sell in the market on a continuous basis. In addition, some sellers offer trading goods that require a rather substantial threshold population in order to provide an adequate income. If this threshold population is not available within the trading area of a particular market, then the seller may well sell in other markets in order to gain access to this required threshold.

The rural-urban interaction pattern associated with the process of consumption in many developing economies (particularly those that can be described as peasant societies) is a bewilderingly complex system. The potential consumer has to have some idea of the periodicities of the visits of each of the traders from whom he wishes to buy. He then has to match his own potential movement activity with the trader's movement activity. In peasant societies in which many potential consumers are also potential sellers of products, determining periodicities in seller behavior and consequent choice of markets on the basis of these periodicities is an extremely important part of the day-by-day routine.

In the case of periodic markets, the economic aims of viability, profits, lower retail prices, and the forestalling of competition are achieved by splitting overhead costs over a variety of activities and markets. Of course, seller mobility can then only be successful if the time spent in traveling between markets does not diminish sales substantially and if the cost of travel does not offset the cost made by splitting overhead costs. Also, the markets visited would have to be independent entities for seller mobility to achieve an economically satisfactory return.

In peasant societies and in some developing economies the contact between a town or an urban place and its hinterland has to be immediate, tangible, and direct. Given the shortage, for example, of modern food storage and preservation facilities in such economies, a complex and flexible marketing system must develop in order to provide daily foodstuffs for urban populations. These market sites then mesh supply and demand in both a spatial and temporal way and in doing so perform the economic functions of local exchange, internal trade, and service activities.

Types of Periodic Markets

With reference to the spatial structure of periodic markets, it is possible to recognize five classifications of markets (Table 9.1). This classification emphasizes the periodicity schedule, the main function, and the market orientation. Some forms of markets involve horizontal trade that is "synonymous with village and interregional trade" and is

Table 9.1 A Market Classification for Northern Nigeria. (E. P. Scott, "The spatial structure of rural northern Nigeria: Farmers, periodic markets, and villages," *Economic Geography,* **48**, 1972, p. 317.)

Market Types	Periodicity Schedule	Central Function	Exchange Orientation
Village and roadside market	Daily	Retail (emergency items)	Horizontal
Weekly evening market	Once weekly	Retail	Horizontal
Two-day market	Twice weekly	Retail and incipient bulking	Vertical
Weekly day market	Once weekly	Retail and bulking	Vertical
Urban daily*	Daily	Retail (emergency items) and transportation	Vertical

*Urban daily markets are normally located in provincial capitals (Katsina, Sokoto, Kano, etc.) and are synonymous with what are termed here "regional bulking markets."

represented by the movement of goods and food from rural to urban areas in the same region. Others involve vertical trade, which means that the goods and food move from the rural areas to urban centers in distant regions.

Patterns of trader visitation for selected markets in rural Nigeria are shown in Table 9.2. In both cases, it is fairly clear that almost all trader movements are local in nature, the more so in the case of Kaita which is visited mainly by traders from a nearby town, Katsina (Figure 9.4). By contrast, Ajiwa is more nationally integrated than Kaita, attracting traders from a greater range of distances; these traders generally then visit more distant markets than their counterparts who serve Kaita. One conclusion is that "the central importance of rural periodic markets is related more to their orientation to a segment of the

Table 9.2 Data on Visits Made by Traders in 1970 at Two Nigerian Markets, Kaita and Ajiwa. (Based on E. P. Scott, "The spatial structure of rural northern Nigeria: Farmers, periodic markets and villages," *Economic Geography*, **48**, 1972, pp. 326–327.)

(a) Percentage of the traders' trips over particular distances from their homes to markets.

Type of Trader	Number in Sample		Distances (miles)		
			0–9	10–49	50 and over
farmer/trader	Kaita	12	100%		
	Ajiwa	44	73%	27%	
local/contract	Kaita	142	20%	80%	
	Ajiwa	167	25%	75%	
long-distance trader	Kaita	47			100%
	Ajiwa	218			100%

(b) Percentage of the traders' trips over particular distances from Kaita and Ajiwa to their final destination markets.

Type of Trade	Number in Sample		Distance (miles)		
			0–9	10–49	50 and over
farmer/trader	Kaita	12	58%	25%	17%
	Ajiwa	29	52%	38%	10%
local/contract	Kaita	139		75%	25%
	Ajiwa	162		54%	46%
long-distance trader	Kaita	50	28%		72%
	Ajiwa	223			100%

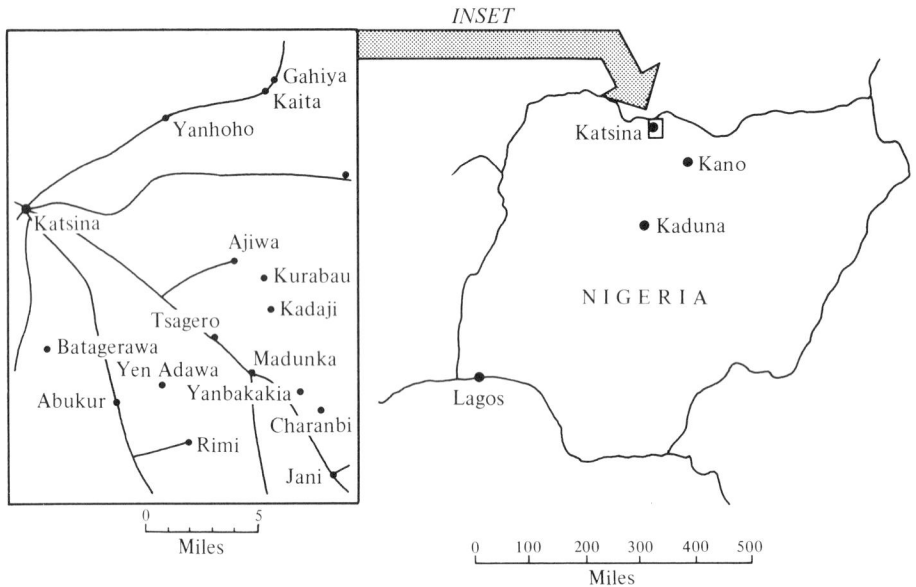

Figure 9.4   Villages in northern Nigeria. [After E. P. Scott, "The spatial structure of rural northern Nigeria: Farmers, periodic markets, and villages," *Economic Geography*, **48**, 1972, p. 328.]

exchange system than to demand-density in the complementary region."[4]

Trader Mobility

One of the dominant characteristics of rural-urban consumer behavior in peasant societies is the mobility of the trader. For example,
in northeastern Ghana traders who travel to several markets in the
Yendi area (Figure 9.5) average approximately 25 to 50 miles per day
and regardless of the distance traveled, almost all traders in the area
return home each night.[5] In Figure 9.6 there are mapped the travel
routes of six itinerant traders who were based in Bimbila and who sold
clothing. It is noteworthy that some traders went to the much smaller
markets of Wulensi and Kpandai which were south of Bimbila even
though on the same days, 1–7, the much larger Yendi market was
meeting in the north. Choice of markets appeared to be based on the
volume of sales, price level, transportation costs, and social factors.
The number of markets visited by traders also varied according to the
number of different goods they offered. This general feature of the
periodicities of movements varying as the type of good offered for sale
varies is common to many periodic marketing patterns.

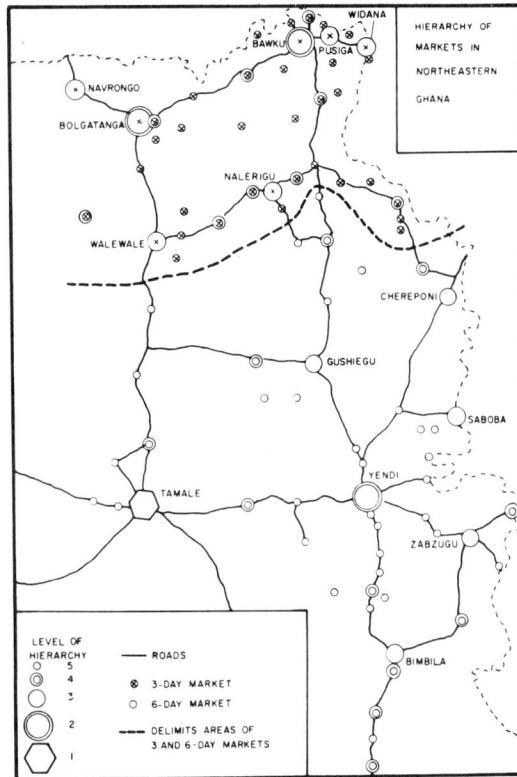

Figure 9.5 Hierarchy of markets in northeastern Ghana. [W. McKim, "The periodic market system in northeastern Ghana," *Economic Geography,* **48,** 1972, p. 337.]

9.4   Shopping Trips in the United States Farming Midwest

The examination of rural-urban consumer behavior in developed economies typically has been set within the frameworks of central place studies.   Recall that the classical central place theory we discussed earlier in Chapter 5 suggests that urban functions that are more widely distributed throughout a farming area would have the lower threshold values and would attract consumers only from the immediately adjacent rural areas. By contrast, functions that were less widely distributed throughout the area would be concentrated in the upper levels of the urban hierarchy, would draw people from longer distances, and would also attract consumers from towns that were lower in the central place hierarchy.   Figures 9.7 and 9.8 illustrate both urban to urban and rural to urban consumer behavior patterns for

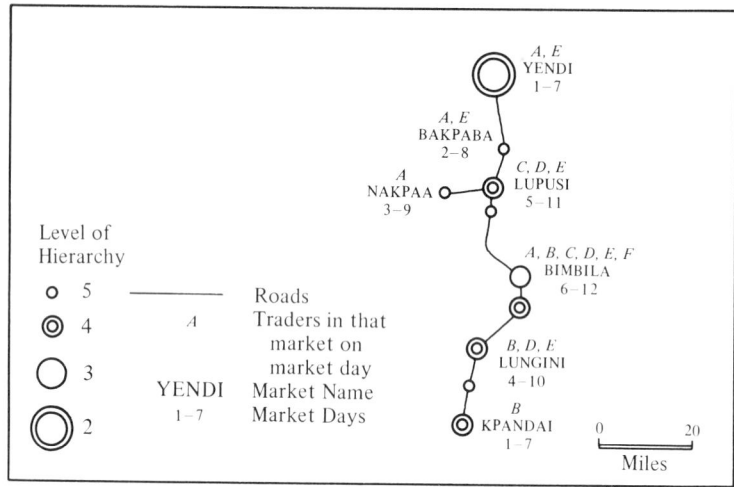

Figure 9.6 Travel routes of six traders in northeastern Ghana. [W. McKim, "The periodic market system in northeastern Ghana," *Economic Geography,* 48, 1972, p. 342.]

two functions—a low order function, "barber service," that attracted people only from its immediate hinterland, and a higher order function, "furniture," attracting consumers from greater distances.

Distances Traveled

Studying the mapping illustrated in Figures 9.7 and 9.8, we might examine more closely the actual distances traveled by rural consumers and consider how closely these agree with distances predicted by central place theory with its emphasis on the attractiveness of urban centers.

A study undertaken in 1959 by the Iowa Bureau of Business and Economic Research asked a sample of farm households located throughout the state to keep logbooks in which they recorded all their household expenditures and where these were made over a twelve-month period. Some of the information obtained from this survey is summarized in Table 9.3. The table shows that some goods and services were distributed throughout the state more widely than others,

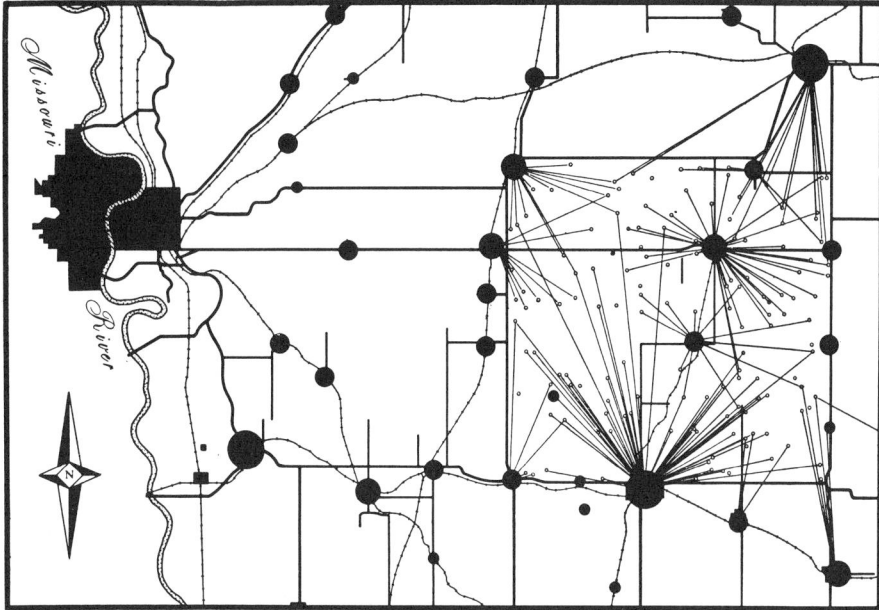

RURAL   1st CHOICE SHOPPING

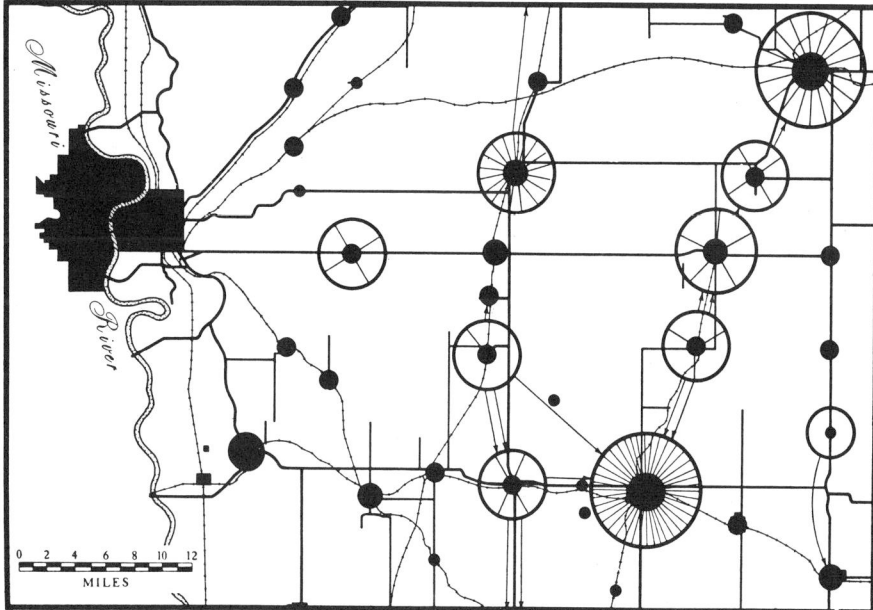

URBAN

0 2 4 6 8 10 12
         MILES

Figure 9.7 Trips made for barber service by both rural and urban residents. The rural residents travel to the nearby towns while the urban residents obtain the services in the towns in which they live. [B. J. L. Berry, H. G. Barnum, and R. J. Tennant, "Retail location and consumer behavior," *Papers*, Regional Science Association, **9**, 1962, p. 85.]

RURAL   1st CHOICE SHOPPING

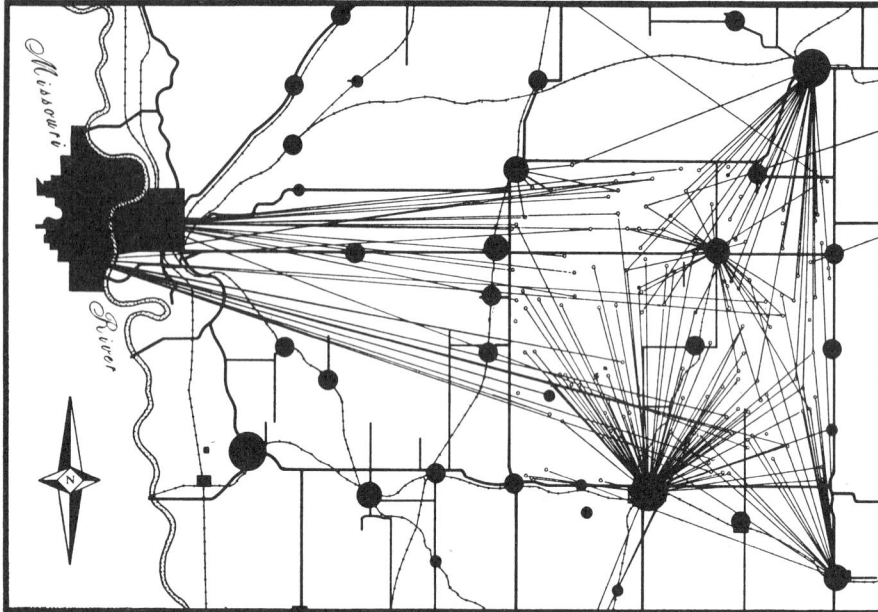

URBAN

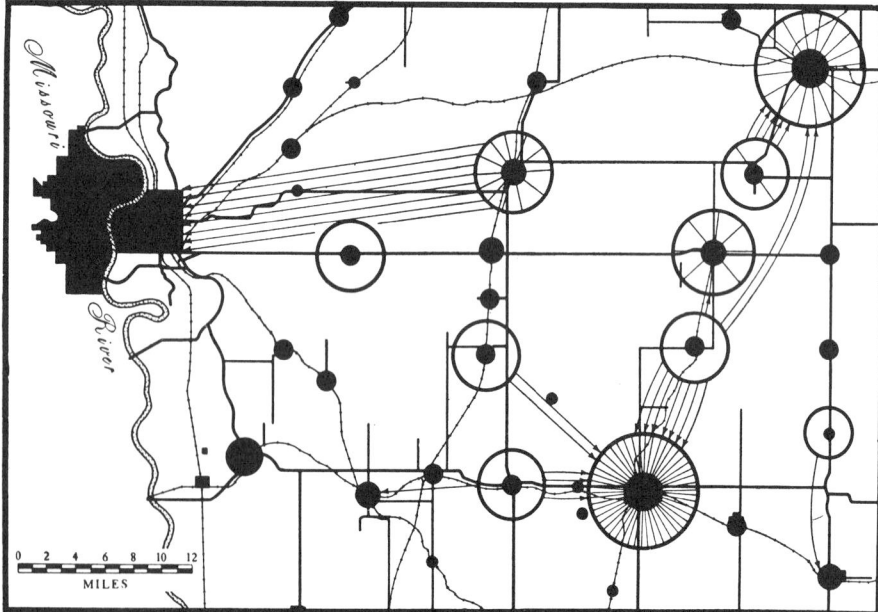

Figure 9.8 Shopping for furniture. In contrast to the patterns in Figure 9.8, the rural residents make longer trips to larger centers and many urban residents also shop outside their hometowns. [B. J. L. Berry, H. G. Barnum, and R. J. Tennant, "Retail location and consumer behavior," *Papers,* Regional Science Association, **9,** 1962, p. 91.]

272

Table 9.3   Distances Traveled by People in Iowa Sample for Various Types of Goods and Services. (Based on R. G. Golledge, G. Rushton and W. A. V. Clark, "Some spatial characteristics of Iowa's dispersed farm population and their implications for the grouping of central place functions," *Economic Geography*, **42**, 1966, p. 263.)

Goods and Services	Number of Observations	Distance to Maximum Purchase Town (Miles)		Distance to Nearest Purchase Town (Miles)		Difference Between Mean Values
		Mean	σ	Mean	σ	
Food and drink away	432	10.7	12.1	6.9	5.8	3.8
Male clothing	459	15.6	17.0	8.2	6.0	7.4
Female clothing	433	30.3	57.7	14.1	33.9	16.2
Major appliances	116	14.5	24.5	13.8	24.3	0.7
Furniture	171	18.7	17.6	17.6	17.1	1.1
Fuel (house)	452	8.0	7.0	6.9	6.3	1.1
Physician	378	13.6	23.5	10.4	11.7	3.2
Dentist	318	11.1	7.6	10.9	7.2	0.2
Medicines (prescribed)	248	11.5	19.3	10.8	18.9	0.7
Medicines (not prescribed)	339	9.2	7.6	8.6	7.4	0.6
Movies	254	16.7	31.5	13.9	23.0	2.8
Sporting goods	231	14.1	19.5	10.2	14.8	3.9
Running cost of car	430	7.2	7.4	5.4	3.4	1.8
Church	400	5.4	4.1	5.2	3.8	0.2
Beauty and barber	432	7.4	9.5	6.1	4.4	1.3
Dry cleaning	424	10.5	9.5	10.3	9.5	0.2
Shoe repair	318	9.5	6.0	9.3	5.6	0.2
Repairs (T.V. and appliances)	333	7.9	5.9	7.6	5.6	0.3
Car purchases	78	19.7	23.9	18.8	23.0	0.9
Food (groceries)	459	7.8	5.3	5.2	3.6	2.6

this being shown by the fact that the average distances that people *actually* needed to travel in order to obtain them were less than ten miles. In the case of some goods and services it is also worth noting that the difference between the average distance actually traveled to those centers in which the major purchases were made and the average distance to the nearest urban place in which the same goods were available was relatively small. This was so for travel to church, travel to obtain dry cleaning and shoe repair services, and travel to dentists. This suggests that at least for these goods and services consumers acted in a spatially and economically rational manner. These sets of goods and services are mainly "convenience" goods which are required on a fairly frequent basis and which give relatively little reward for extensive "shopping around" activities.

For other types of functions, the distances to both the nearest location of the function and the place where the major purchase was made
were substantially larger than those for the above functions. This implies that the functions were less widely distributed than the others,
that they probably required a higher threshold level of support, and
hence, they were likely to be located only in the larger urban centers.

If we examine the entries in the table for functions such as furniture and especially clothing, the impression is that the closest occurrence of these functions was not always the one that was regularly
patronized. In fact, there are frequently substantial differences between the average distance to the maximum purchase town and the
average distance to the nearest occurrence of the function. The standard deviation (σ) associated with the average distance traveled for
these goods also provides a clue as to the way consumers behaved. Almost all of these goods (shopping goods) generated a greater range of
trip distances; that is, they had larger standard deviation values than
did many of the other functions. In other words, the individuals
shopped around before making a purchase and the shopping patterns
for these goods and services may be said to be *spatially flexible,* in contrast to those for most convenience goods which are more *spatially inflexible.*

Opportunity Sets and Revealed Preferences

The above observations suggest that for any particular consumer
or household selected randomly in a study area there is a "feasible
opportunity set" available to him for each particular good or service
that he wishes to obtain.[6] This feasible opportunity set is defined by
the limit of the willingness, or ability, of the household to travel in
order to obtain the function. For example, for consumers in the Iowa
study it was rarely the case that an individual traveled more than 25
miles to make a grocery purchase. Consequently, the range of opportunities available in this case could be defined as that set of grocery
opportunities that lie within a 25-mile radius of any farm location.
Similarly, it is possible to define ranges of locational types that are
available to each consumer for all other functions and these define the
total opportunity set available to him. Figure 9.9 defines this set of
locational types for grocery purchases for consumers in the study area.
In this diagram each cell indicates a type of location available to a
sample farm household in Iowa. For example, type *a* indicates the set
of opportunities at which groceries could be bought at a center that
has a population less than 500 and is located within 5 miles of the

Figure 9.9 Simple two-way classification of locational types.

```
Urban center population
8,000 ┤   u     v     w     x     y
      │
4,000 ┤   p     q     r     s     t
2,000 ┤   k     l     m     n     o
1,000 ┤   f     g     h     i     j
  500 ┤   a     b     c     d     e
      └────5────10────15────20────25
            Distance to urban center (miles)
```

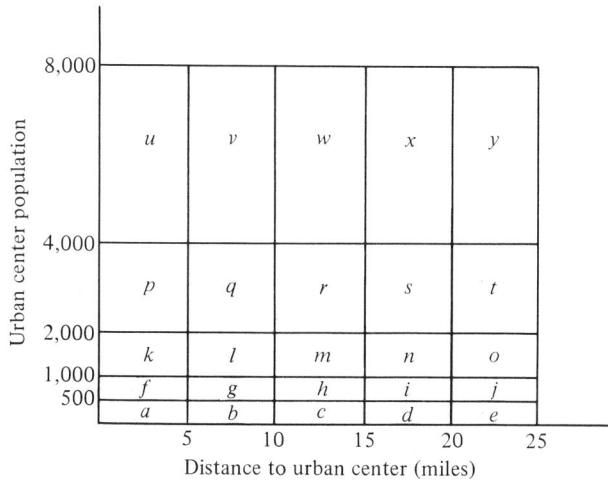

Figure 9.9 Simple two-way classification of locational types. [Based on G. Rushton, "The scaling of locational preferences," in K. R. Cox and R. G. Golledge, eds., *Behavioral Problems in Geography: A Symposium,* Northwestern Studies in Geography, No. 17, 1969, p. 203.]

Table 9.4 The Space Preferences of Selected Respondents in Iowa, 1960. (Based on G. Rushton, "The scaling of locational preferences," in K. R. Cox and R. G. Golledge, eds. *Behavioral Problems in Geography: A Symposium,* Northwestern University Studies in Geography, No. 17, 1969, p. 204.)

Household	a	b	c	d	e	f	g	h	i	j	k	l	m	n	o	p	q	r	s	t	u	v	w	x	y
1		n	n	n	n				n	n			n		n	y									n
2	n	n	n	n	n			n	n	n	y	y	n	n				n							
3		n	n	n	n	n		n										n						y	
4	n	n	n	n	n		n	n										n						y	
5	n	n	n	n	n		y	n	n					n	n										
6	n		n	n	n		y	n	n					n				n							
7	n	n	n	n	n	n	n				n					y									
8	n	n	n	n	n			n		y	n		n												
9		n	n	n	n	n		n	y					n				n							
10	y	n	n	n	n						n		n	n		n		n							

NOTE: *n* identifies the case where the particular locational type was rejected by the respondent. *y* identifies the case where the locational type was chosen and patronized. Blanks indicate that the locational types were not present.

farmstead. Type *l* gives the number of places with populations between 1,000 and 2,000 located between 5 and 10 miles from the consumer. Each urban place lying within 25 miles of any consumer can therefore be allocated to one of the cells of the diagram. For any given consumer the distribution of cells that results is his opportunity set for grocery purchases. By examining actual expenditures it is possible to determine which locational types are preferred to others. In some cases, *indifference* might exist between different town-size and distance combinations.

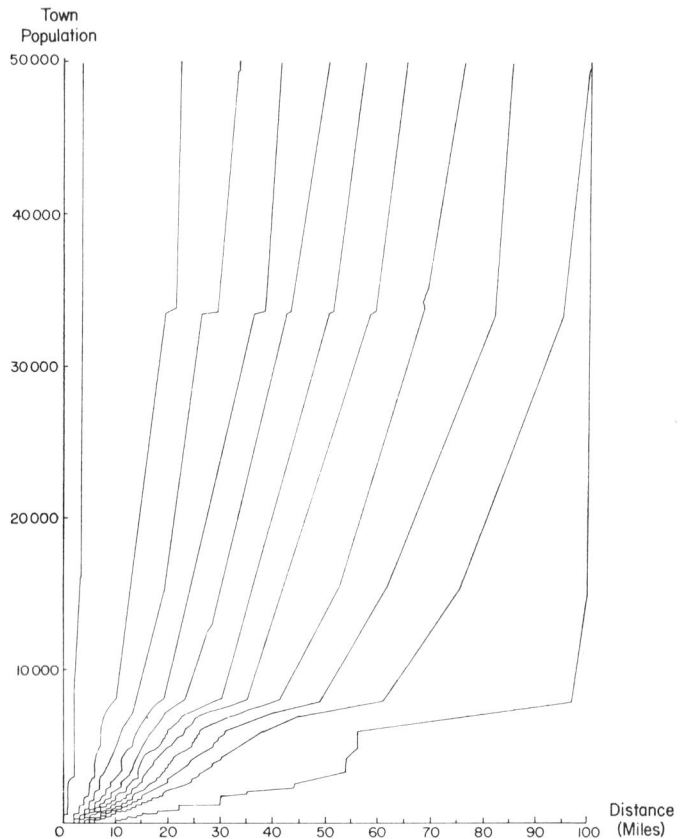

Figure 9.10 Graph of generated distances (redrafted from computer-drawn originals). The curve on the left gives the *closest* distance between respondents and towns of particular sizes. The remaining curves are for percentiles of the population from 10% on the left to 100% on the right. A point on one of the curves gives the percentage of the population located within distance *x* of a town larger than population *y*. [W. A. V. Clark, G. Rushton, and R. G. Golledge, "The spatial structure of the Iowa urban network," *Geographical Analysis*, **2**, 1970, p. 306. Reprinted by permission.]

The actual expenditure patterns of consumers *reveal* their preference for certain locational types over others. Table 9.4 summarizes such information for a sample of consumers in the Iowa area. Here the letters n identify the locational types that were available to each household and the y's indicate the locational types in which major purchases for groceries were made (that is, those locational types that were revealed as being preferred to all others).

If the revealed preference structure for the entire sample of households is plotted on the diagram of locational types, isolines can be drawn to show the general pattern of preference for the different combinations of town-size and distance. On the basis of this type of isoline map (illustrated earlier in Figure 5.18), it is possible to think of sets of generalized indifference curves that present the town size-distance combinations between which households exhibit indifference.

An alternative way of summarizing the above information is to determine, from the town size-distance relations, the maximum distance that consumers would have to travel to reach towns of a certain size.[7] These are portrayed in Figure 9.10. In this case, the rightmost curve shows the maximum distances that individuals would have to travel to any town of a certain size. For example, 100% of the population is within 100 miles of a town of 50,000 population or larger. It can be seen from this graph that the distance that has to be traveled to places increases generally up to a size of about 8,000 population and tends to level out thereafter.

9.5 Summary

In this chapter we have isolated some spatial characteristics of rural-urban movements that are of considerable importance to growth, development, and the day-by-day functioning of urban systems. Understanding migration patterns in developing economies is of the utmost importance in planning and directing rural and urban growth, in seeking an equitable distribution of well-being, and for solving problems of welfare and employment.

Many developed economies such as the United States have become concerned about the continuing viability of small urban places. The study of consumer behavior suggests that there is a continuing need either for a set of widely distributed small urban places or for an ever increasingly complex and efficient transportation system which, by improving travel times to the larger urban centers, can obviate the need for numerous small places. The second alternative tends to eliminate many of the differences between "convenience" and "shopping" goods and may also eliminate many single-purpose shopping trips for lower-order functions.   Regardless of which strategy is adopted, it can readily be seen that urban systems in both developed and developing countries are always in a state of flux and that analysis of movement patterns yields insights into many aspects of these dynamics.

Notes

1. R. P. SHAW, *Migration Theory and Fact. A Review and Bibliography of Current Literature.* Philadelphia: Regional Science Research Institute, Bibliography Series, No. 5, 1975.

2. A. L. MABOGUNJE, "Systems approach to a theory of rural–urban migration," *Geographical Analysis*, **2**, 1970, pp. 1–18.

3. J. B. RIDDELL and M. E. HARVEY, "The urban system in the migration process: an evaluation of step-wise migration in Sierra Leone," *Economic Geography*, **48**, 1972, pp. 270–83.

4. E. P. SCOTT, "The spatial structure of rural northern Nigeria: Farmers, periodic markets and villages," *Economic Geography*, **48**, 1972, p. 331.

5. W. McKIM, "The periodic market system in northeastern Ghana," *Economic Geography*, **48**, 1972, pp. 333–55.

6. G. RUSHTON, "The scaling of locational preferences," in K. R. COX AND R. G. GOLLEDGE, eds., *Behavioral Problems in Geography: A Symposium*, Northwestern University Studies in Geography, No. 17, 1969, pp. 197–227.

7. W. A. V. CLARK, G. RUSHTON, and R. G. GOLLEDGE, "The spatial structure of the Iowa urban network," *Geographical Analysis*, **2**, 1970, pp. 301–13.

chapter 10

City to City Interaction

In this chapter we shall discuss the patterns of human interaction that exist between cities of various sizes. For example, air-passenger traffic flow patterns are examined to show the extent of the dominance of the larger urban centers over the smaller centers in the generation of traffic. Analyses of migrations and the volumes of telephone calls between places of different sizes further illustrate these patterns. As these different forms of interaction between places are examined, a substantial body of empirical information is produced to support the idea that urban places can be differentiated on the basis of their degrees of dominance over other centers. Furthermore, if an examination is made of the diffusion of goods, ideas, and so on, there is a noticeable pattern of movement again dominated by critical centers that diffuse innovations to places within their spheres of influence. The important concepts that arise from all of these different studies and that we wish to stress are the grouping of urban places based on some form of dominance, the distance-decay effect (for example, in the rates of inter-

279

action and diffusion as distance from an originating node increases), and the idea that some centers are tributary to others. These concepts can be formalized in models of interaction such as the social gravity model and various diffusion models.

10.1 Short-Term Travel Patterns: The Example of Airline Traffic

Air passenger traffic flow patterns have been studied extensively by geographers.[1] The studies have shown that there are a number of distinctive features about these patterns.

Patterns of Traffic

First, it is clear that as far as generating flows of air-passenger traffic, the larger urban centers dominate over the smaller ones. This is shown in Table 10.1 which gives data on the number of scheduled departures and the total number of passengers associated with the major airports in the United States. The airports are in the Standard Metropolitan Statistical Areas. The population ranks of the cities in 1970 are listed in the left-hand column of the table. It is obvious that New York, Chicago, and Los Angeles, which are the three largest population centers, also lead in terms of total number of scheduled departures and total number of passengers. A mapping of the major airline connections (direct flights) for 1969 again emphasizes the dominant role of these three urban centers (Figure 10.1).

Table 10.1 shows that those airports which are more important in terms of number of departures and total number of passengers than their population size would suggest, notably Atlanta, Dallas-Fort Worth, and Miami-Fort Lauderdale are all important regional centers either for domestic traffic or international flights.

A second major finding is that in the patterns of air-passenger movement the larger centers typically dominate groups of smaller urban centers. This point is illustrated graphically in Figure 10.2. Related to this observation is the fact that a hierarchy of urban centers considered as traffic generators can be identified (Table 10.2).

Although only fairly gross indicators of intercity interaction are provided by such tables and maps, it is clear that there is abundant evidence to further illustrate some of the concepts mentioned in earlier chapters. The idea of cities dominated by larger ones, the greater strength of attraction between larger centers, the falling off in fre-

Table 10.1   Leading Air Centers and Levels of Service, 1969 (Domestic Operations; over 1,000,000 enplanements). (After R. B. Adams, "Airline connectivity matrix: Growth and disequilibrium," paper presented at Mid-Continental Division Meeting, Regional Science Association, Winnipeg, Manitoba, 1971, p. 5.)

1970 Population Rank	SMSA* (number of airports)	Scheduled Departures	Number of Passengers (miles)	Service Level†
(1)	1. New York (5)	319,172	14.0	21
(3)	2. Chicago (2)	300,746	13.7	44
(2)	3. Los Angeles (3)	179,744	8.0	19
(20)	4. Atlanta	154,770	7.2	112
(7)	5. Washington, D.C. (2)	135,222	5.6	47
(6)	6. San Francisco (2)	112,718	5.4	37
(16)	7. Dallas-Fort Worth (2)	110,811	4.8	48
(25)	8. Miami-Fort Lauderdale (2)	97,803	4.2	70
(5)	9. Detroit-Ann Arbor (2)	94,044	3.5	22
(8)	10. Boston	92,962	4.3	34
(4)	11. Philadelphia-Camden	87,092	3.1	18
(10)	12. St. Louis	84,453	3.1	36
(9)	13. Pittsburgh	82,936	2.8	35
(27)	14. Denver	74,534	3.2	60
(12)	15. Cleveland	68,690	2.5	34
(15)	16. Minneapolis-St. Paul	62,406	2.5	35
(13)	17. Houston	61,556	2.2	31
(26)	18. Kansas City	60,483	2.1	49
(30)	19. New Orleans	51,366	1.9	50
(11)	20. Baltimore	51,249	1.5	25

NOTE: For the year ending June 30, 1969. Compiled from *FAA Statistical Handbook of Aviation* and *FAA Air Traffic Activity,* Department of Administration, Federal Aviation Administration, Washington, D.C. Operations of certificated domestic air carriers.

*The New York Metropolitan Area also includes the SMSA's of Newark, Jersey City, and Paterson-Clifton-Passaic. The Los Angeles Metropolitan Area also includes the SMSA's of Anaheim-Santa Ana-Garden Grove and San Bernardino-Riverside-Ontario.

†Annual plane departures/1,000 persons in the metropolitan area.

quency of interaction as the size disparity increases and distance between places increases, and the existence of hierarchical structures can all be illustrated from the airline passenger flow data and maps. What these analyses do not tell us, of course, are the factors lying behind the observed patterns of interaction. For a discussion of these, we often have to look elsewhere in the literature.

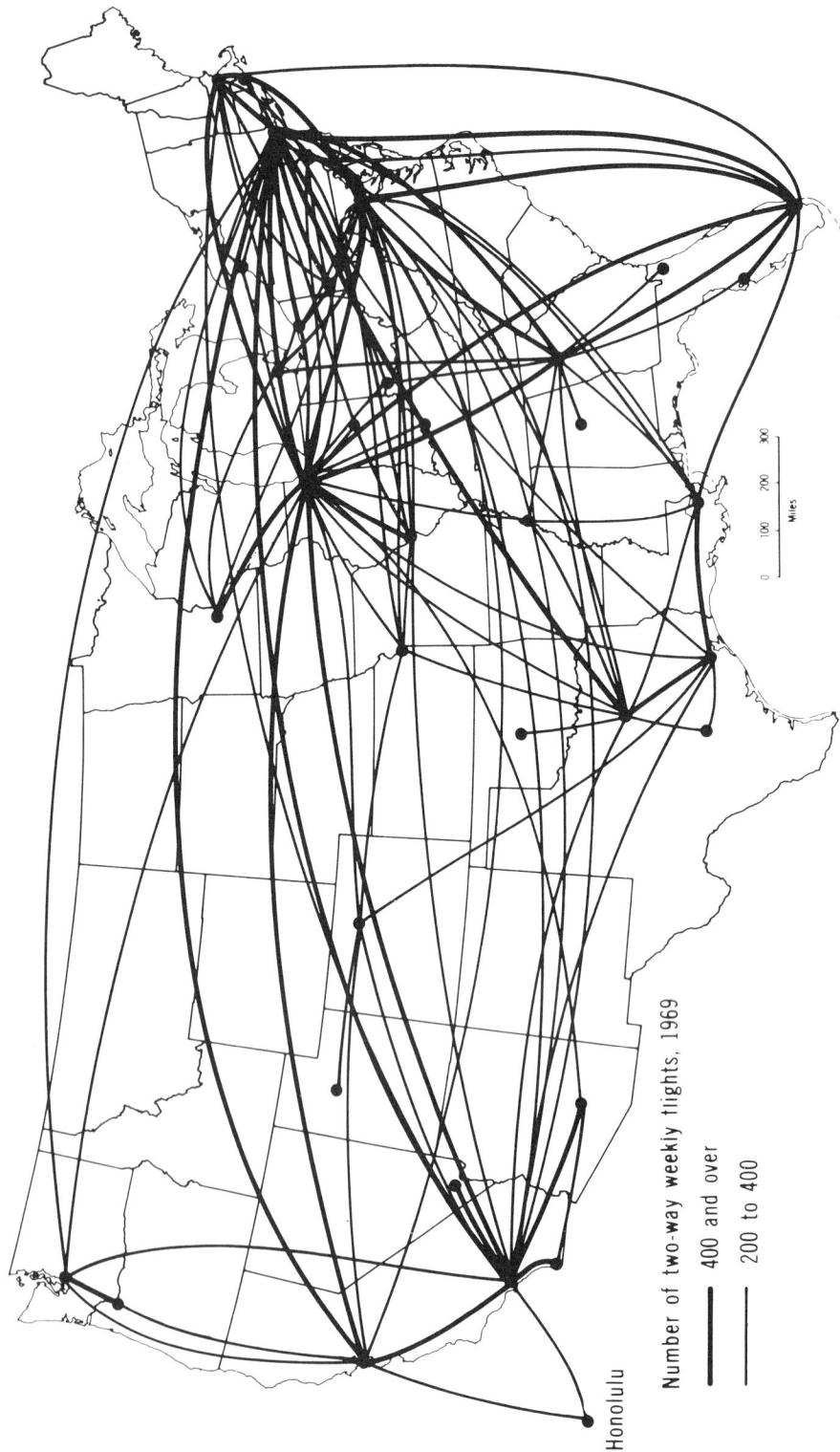

Number of two-way weekly flights, 1969

——— 400 and over

——— 200 to 400

Honolulu

Figure 10.1 Major airline connections (direct flights). [R. B. Adams, "Airline connectivity matrix: Growth and disequilibrium," paper presented at Mid-continental Division Meeting, Regional Science Association, Winnipeg, Manitoba, 1971, p. 5.]

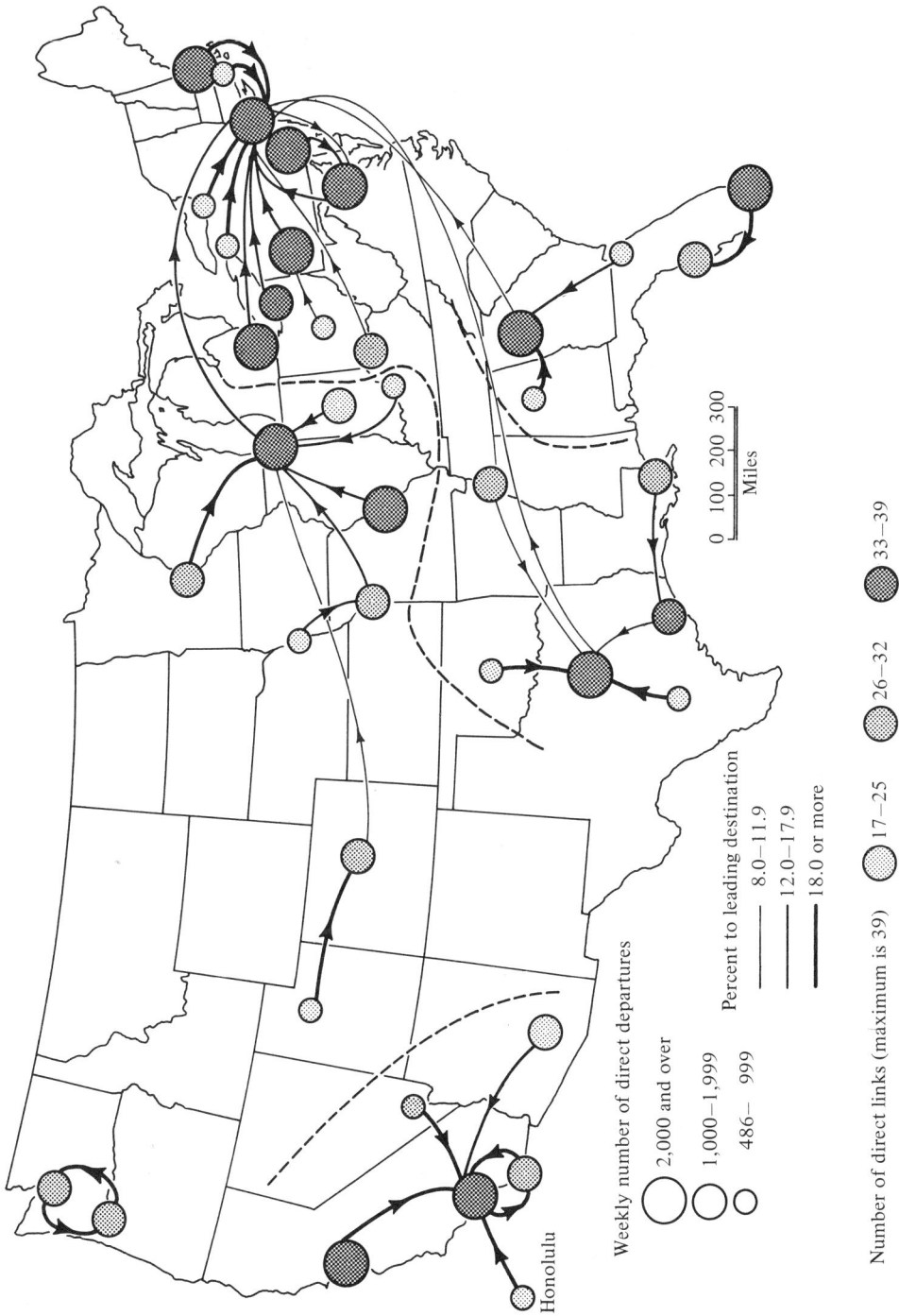

Figure 10.2 Departures, connectivity, and primary flow. [R. B. Adams, "Airline connectivity matrix: Growth and disequilibrium," paper presented at Midcontinental Division Meeting, Regional Science Association, Winnipeg, Manitoba, 1971, p. 8.]

Weekly number of direct departures

2,000 and over

1,000–1,999

486– 999

Percent to leading destination

8.0–11.9

12.0–17.9

18.0 or more

Number of direct links (maximum is 39)   17–25   26–32   33–39

Honolulu

0 100 200 300
Miles

Table 10.2   Hierarchy of United States Air Centers: Domestic
Operations. (R. B. Adams, "Airline connectivity
matrix: Growth and disequilibrium," paper presented at Mid-Continental Division Meeting, Regional Science Association, Winnipeg, Manitoba,
1971, p. 12.)

Rank	Center	Index*
1.	Chicago	10.0
2.	New York	9.4
3.	Washington, D.C.	9.3
4.	Atlanta	9.2
5.	Los Angeles	9.0
6.	Dallas	8.8
7.	San Francisco	8.6
8.	Detroit	8.5
9.	St. Louis	8.4
10.	Pittsburgh	8.4
11.	Philadelphia	8.2
12.	Denver	8.1
13.	Cleveland	8.1
14.	Minneapolis-St. Paul	8.0
15.	Boston	7.7
16.	Kansas City	7.5
17.	Miami	7.2
18.	Houston	7.1
19.	New Orleans	7.0
20.	Seattle	6.5
21.	Memphis	6.4
22.	Cincinnati	6.4
23.	Phoenix	6.0
24.	Buffalo	6.0
25.	Las Vegas	5.8
26.	Tampa	5.7
27.	Portland	5.5

*Based on multiple criteria of weighted-sum of departures,
connections, and flight time (accessibility).

Demand for Air Travel

Air travel from one city to another typically involves the three following major components:

1. Trips made to obtain goods and services offered at the destination city.
2. Trips made for business meetings.
3. Personal trips made to visit friends and relatives.

The demand for these different trips may be considered a function of the features of the origin and destination cities and also of certain alternative cities. In the case of the demand for trips made to purchase goods, the important elements are the prevailing prices of the goods in the destination city and the alternative cities and the transportation cost back to the origin. These factors determine the delivered price of the goods in the origin city, and, consequently, the decisions by businessmen in that city whether to buy the goods from the destination city. The demand for business trips, however, should be more proportional to the population sizes of the origin and destination cities because "the larger the population of the city, the greater the number of firms and, due to agglomeration economies, the larger the firm size. Thus, average cost of making interfirm contacts is lowered and average sale per contact is increased."[2]   Again, travel costs must be considered. Finally, the demand for personal visit trips is a function of the travel costs, and hence distance, and the population sizes that affect the probability of personal relationships existing between individuals in the different cities.

Analysis of intercity air traffic between the 13 largest Standard Metropolitan Statistical Areas in the United States for the years 1960–1963 suggested that the population sizes of the origin and destination cities and the intervening distance did very well to explain the level of air traffic between pairs of cities.[3] The explanation improved when the average distance from the origin city to alternative cities was taken into account; that is to say, the more distant the alternative cities were from the origin, the greater the number of air trips to a given destination. Other economic variables that showed up as being important were as follows: The *level of per capita income* in the origin city proved to be significant in that the larger this income in the origin city, the more air trips there were to a given destination.   The *price of goods* (ignoring transport costs) was significant in the following respect.   The higher the factory price at the origin city relative to the destination, the more air trips there were between the pair of cities.   Surprisingly, it did not appear as though the existence of higher factory prices at alternative cities relative to the destination resulted in an increase in the number of air trips made to the destination.

10.2 Migrations from City to City:
Search for Explanations

The movements of people between different cities as passengers on the airlines generally represent short-duration trips made for various purposes.   Only a small proportion of these trips represents permanent moves on the part of the travelers.   Those that do form part of a larger

pattern of human movement between different regions and cities.
These are known as *migration patterns*. At any one time, we know that
there are many people changing their places of residence or places of
work and that as a result of these changes they move about from one
city to another. Usually, national censuses provide information on
patterns of migration. Geographers and other social scientists have
used these data to pursue three major lines of work. The first has to do
with the description of the spatial patterns of migration, the second
with identifying the factors that affect migration, and the third with
determining the effects of migration on regional levels of income, employment, and unemployment.

Migration Fields

Description of the spatial patterns of migration allows for the
identification of the *migration fields* of the different metropolitan areas.
These are the regions or sets of cities that provide almost all of the migrants who move into the particular metropolitan area in question.
Some examples of these findings are given in Table 10.3 which is taken
from a study of the patterns of migration between the 100 largest
metropolitan areas in the United States over the period 1955–1960.[4]
The results confirm that distance is the overriding consideration and
with but few exceptions, the metropolitan areas draw almost all their
migrants from nearby cities. It should be noted, however, that some
metropolitan areas draw migrants from cities located some distance
away (San Francisco is a good example). The migration field of this
metropolitan area extends as far north as Seattle and as far west as
Denver, and it overlaps with the field of Los Angeles in competing for
migrants from the San Diego area.

Push-Pull Factors

Studies that have attempted to account for the differing levels of
migration between various cities have tended to emphasize either *push*
factors or *pull* factors. Push factors tend to force migrants out of certain cities or regions and may involve economic factors (such as the
level of unemployment or differences in earnings and cost of living)
and/or sociological factors (such as the quality of living, the crime
rate, the density of population), and the quality of services (such as
education). Pull factors may also be defined in economic terms (such
as the availability of better housing or educational facilities), or physical factors (such as climate). These studies usually rely on census data
to establish the correlations between migration levels and the different

Table 10.3   Metropolitan Areas Included in the Migration Fields of the Major SMSA's. (Based on L. A. Brown, J. Odland and R. G. Golledge, "Migration, functional distance and the urban hierarchy," *Economic Geography*, **46**, 1970, pp. 477–78.)

New York
  Jersey City
  Miami
  Newark
  Paterson

Los Angeles-Long Beach
  Bakersfield
  El Paso
  Fresno
  Phoenix
  Salt Lake City
  San Bernadino
  San Diego
  Tucson

Chicago
  Davenport
  Gary
  Indianapolis
  Memphis
  Milwaukee
  Peoria
  St. Louis

Philadelphia
  Allentown
  Baltimore
  Harrisburg
  Lancaster
  Newark
  New York
  Paterson
  Reading
  Wilkes-Barre
  Wilmington

Detroit
  Flint
  Grand Rapids
  Indianapolis
  Lansing
  Toledo

San Francisco-Oakland
  Albuquerque
  Bakersfield
  Denver
  Fresno
  Los Angeles
  Portland
  Sacramento
  Salt Lake City
  San Bernadino
  San Diego
  San Jose
  Seattle

Washington D.C.
  Baltimore
  Norfolk
  Richmond

Boston
  Hartford
  New Haven
  New York
  Providence
  Springfield
  Worcester

Pittsburgh
  Erie
  Johnstown
  Youngstown

St. Louis
  Chicago
  Gary
  Indianapolis
  Kansas City
  Memphis
  Milwaukee
  Peoria

Baltimore
  Norfolk
  Richmond
  Washington
  Wilmington

Cleveland
  Akron
  Canton
  Charlestown
  Cincinnati
  Columbus
  Dayton
  Erie
  Johnstown
  Pittsburgh
  Toledo
  Youngstown

explanatory factors, but in some cases they may be based on questionnaire surveys of "potential" migrants. For example, a survey of some 159 residents of Southern Ontario confirmed that economic considerations, mainly income opportunities, tended to dominate in the formation of the mental images that these people had of places to which they might move.[5] Many of the different findings of these explanatory studies of migration were summarized earlier in Chapter 9 under the 20 propositions about migration.

Consequences of Migration

There have been many discussions of the effects of migration on regional income, employment, and unemployment levels. For United States metropolitan areas, for example, over the past two decades (1950–1970) the relations between levels of in-migration and out-migration, on the one hand, and growth in income, employment, unemployment, and size of labor force, on the other hand, have been summarized as follows:[6]

1. In-migration of members of the labor force induced greater employment growth in urban areas. The affect was a two-way one. Migration responded to growth in economic opportunities and, in turn, migration further induced growth.
2. Out-migration did not encourage income growth such that regional income differences were significantly reduced as a result of migration.
3. The 1950–1960 results did not provide a good basis for predicting the 1960–1970 trends. Much more detailed information on a regional instead of on a national level would be required before such forecasting would be reliable.

In Canada it has been found that out-migration even from regions of high unemployment may have adverse effects on the level of employment in those regions. The point is that even unemployed persons maintain a certain level of living expenditures and when they move these expenditures are lost to the region. In the eastern Maritime provinces of Canada, for example, for every five unemployed persons who left the region, two additional persons in the region became unemployed.[7]

The Canadian migration and metropolitan growth picture reveals some interesting patterns. Over the period 1966–1971 the three largest cities of Montreal, Toronto, and Vancouver absorbed about 60% of total net migration, both internal and foreign. When the composition of the total in-migration to the various cities is examined, several contrasts are apparent (Figure 10.3). These have prompted the suggestion that

> At a first stage, the smaller urban areas with 100,000 to 150,000 inhabitants generally attract their in-migrants from other, non-urban counties in the same province. The second

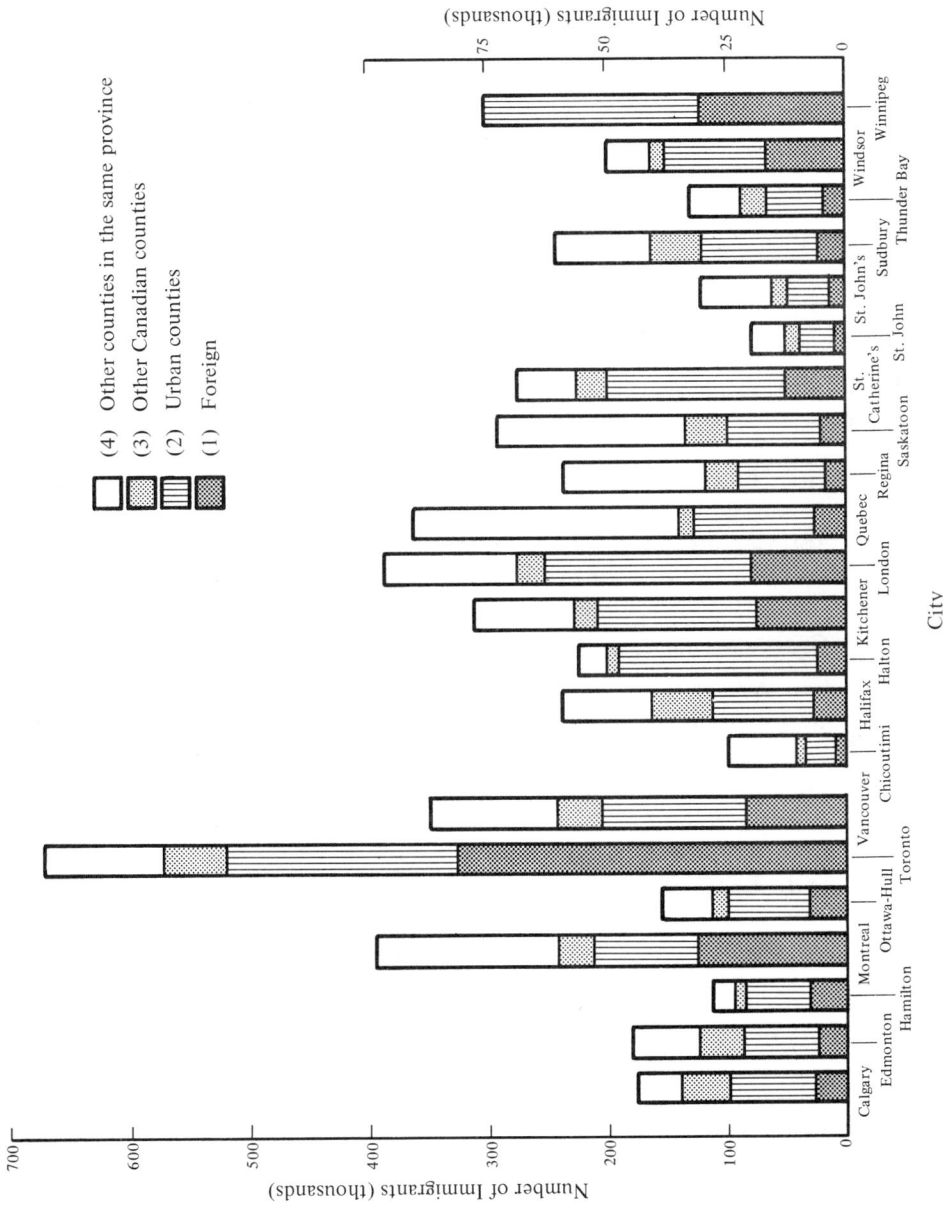

Figure 10.3 Origin of the in-migrants (1966–1971 period). [Canada Manpower and Immigration, *Internal Migration and Immigrant Settlement* (Ottawa: Information Canada, 1975), p. 58. Reproduced by permission of the Minister of Supply and Services Canada.]

stage occurs once they have reached a size of around 300,000; and the urban centers draw their migrants predominantly from other urban areas. When metropolitan areas have surpassed this size, at a third stage they generally begin to attract an appreciable number of foreign immigrants in addition to attracting internal migrants from other urban areas; the three main metropolises exhibit different patterns of in-migration. Toronto's flow is dominated by foreign immigrants, Montreal's by migrants from other non-urban countries in Quebec, and Vancouver's by migrants from other urban areas.[8]

10.3 Predicting Flows and Traffic Levels Between Places

The movement of people, goods, and ideas between cities and within cities has been the subject of a great deal of research by both social scientists and planners. So far in this chapter we have reviewed certain approaches that have been followed in this research and we have summarized some of the empirical findings.

Gravity Model

A frequently used model for predicting the levels of flows of persons or goods between cities and/or between regions is known as the *gravity model*. The analogy is with celestial mechanics and the well-known physical law that the relative attraction of any two bodies is directly related to the product of their masses and inversely related to the square of the distance between them. In the social science context, the model was written typically in the following form:

$$I_{ij} = \frac{(kP_iP_j)}{D_{ij}^b}$$

where I_{ij} is interaction between regions i and j;
P_i, P_j are population size of regions i and j;
D_{ij} is distance between i and j;

and k and b are parameters.

Although this model and variations on it were widely used in studies of migration patterns, commodity flows, air-passage traffic, urban shopping trips, and so on, it has never provided a very satisfactory approach to predicting these different phenomena. It clearly lacks any explicit behavioral basis and those rationales that have been provided, for example, the argument that larger places offer more opportunities and are therefore more attractive, have always appeared shallow and often circular in their logic. Also, from the numerical viewpoint the model can only accommodate changes in the population sizes (or whatever measure of mass is used) by providing inflated estimates of what the effects might be upon interaction.

Modified Gravity Model

Alan Wilson has recently outlined a theory of a modified gravity-model type in which the element of uncertainty is given explicit acknowledgment.[9] The mathematics involved is not simple and we only sketch the main features of the work. A good elementary introduction to the mathematics of Wilson's work is published elsewhere.[10]

Consider a simple table (Table 10.4) which has a set of cities listed as origins down the side and the same set of cities listed as destinations along the top. Now assume that there is a known total, T, of workers in the urban system who are going to be traveling to work in the cities and that we wish to predict the values for the cells in the table that are the T_{ij}'s, that is, the number of workers living in city i and working in city j.

Now consider the first cell and the value T_{11}. This total can be chosen from the total set of workers available, T, assuming for the moment that we disregard where the people live. In other words, assume for illustration purposes that the value of T is only 4 and that T_{11} is thought to be 2. How many different assignments of workers could give rise to T_{11} being 2? If we label our four workers as A, B, C, and D, then clearly the following assignments could be made to T_{11}:

$$AB, AC, AD, BC, BD, CD$$

The number is 6 and we note that this could have been calculated by using the formula $T!/T_{11}!\,(T - T_{11})!$ where the symbol ! denotes the *factorial*. Thus, in the case of T_{11} being 2, we have

Table 10.4 Simple Origin-Destination Table.

		Destinations				
		D_1	D_2	D_3	D_4	D_5
Origins	0_1	T_{11}	T_{12}	T_{13}	T_{14}	T_{15}
	0_2	T_{21}	T_{22}	T_{23}	T_{24}	T_{25}
	0_3	T_{31}	T_{32}	T_{33}	T_{34}	T_{35}
	0_4	T_{41}	T_{42}	T_{43}	T_{44}	T_{45}

$$\frac{T!}{T_{11}!(T - T_{11})!} = \frac{4!}{2!(4 - 2)!} = \frac{4 \cdot 3 \cdot 2 \cdot 1}{2 \cdot 1 \cdot 2 \cdot 1} = 6$$

Compare this value with the one that we would have obtained had we estimated T_{11} to be 4. Then we would have had

$$\frac{4!}{4!(4 - 4)!} = \frac{4 \cdot 3 \cdot 2 \cdot 1}{4 \cdot 3 \cdot 2 \cdot 1 (0!)} = 1$$

In other words, only one assignment of our total T workers would give rise to T_{11} being 4. The corresponding number of assignments for T_{11} being 0, 1, or 3 could be calculated.

Now what about T_{12}? This value can be chosen from $(T - T_{11})$; again, the number of assignments in general will be

$$\frac{(T - T_{11})!}{T_{12}!(T - T_{11} - T_{12})!}$$

Similarly, for T_{13} we have

$$\frac{(T - T_{11} - T_{12})!}{T_{13}!(T - T_{11} - T_{12} - T_{13})!}$$

Combining all these for the complete table involves multiplying the expressions for T_{11}, T_{12}, T_{13}, and so on, and this is written in the form,

$$\frac{T!}{\prod_{ij} T_{ij}!}$$

where the symbol $\prod$ denotes multiplication of the T_{ij}'s for the different values of i and j.

At this point, we recall that our intention was to predict the flows of workers between the places of work and employment. In the case of T_{11}, we showed how, depending on the estimated value of T_{11}, there would be a varying number of assignments that would be possible. If we are uncertain what the values of the T_{ij}'s are, then our best strategy would be to use those estimates that can be generated by the greatest number of assignments. For example, in estimating T_{11} in our sample case we would be taking a chance in estimating it to be 4 since there was only one assignment of the total workers that could give rise to this. By contrast, there were six different assignments that gave rise to T_{11} being 2.

If we denote the total number of assignments or states as

$$W(T_{ij}) = \frac{T!}{\displaystyle\prod_{ij} T_{ij}!}$$

then we are saying that we wish to choose the T_{ij}'s such that $W(T_{ij})$ is as large as possible. These we would feel would be the most probable T_{ij}'s.

There are some constraints on the solution. The workers live in particular cities and the jobs are only available in certain other cities. This implies that

(10-1) $$\sum_j T_{ij} = O_i$$

that is, the number of workers traveling out of city i to the different places of employment j must equal the number of workers living in city i,

(10-2) $$\sum_i T_{ij} = D_j$$

that is, the number of workers arriving in city j from all cities i must equal the number of jobs available there, and

(10-3) $$\sum_i \sum_j T_{ij} c_{ij} = C$$

which imposes a budget constraint. Each trip has an associated cost c_{ij} and the total transportation expenditures must equal some total budget available, C.

Wilson has shown how a solution for the most probable T_{ij}'s can be obtained given the above definitions of $W(T_{ij})$ and the different constraints. The models that he has developed have been used widely in actual planning situations in the United Kingdom.

10.4 Diffusion of Information: A Different Form of Spatial Interaction

The diffusion of innovations (new ideas, fads, technological changes, and so on) within urban systems provides yet another example of the spatial expression of intercity interaction. In this case, a detailed discussion of the reasons for adopting an innovation—be it a household or a business innovation—can be ignored for the moment.

Types of Innovations

Innovations can diffuse through a system of cities in any one of three ways:

1. By a contagious process similar to a wave moving away from an epicenter.
2. Hierarchically, with the innovation appearing first at a higher-order center and then filtering down to the smaller dominated centers.
3. Horizontally among centers of the same magnitude at a given time period and perhaps hierarchically or by contagion thereafter.

Several types of these flows may operate simultaneously in any urban system. For example, there may be an innovation that diffuses among the cities at the same hierarchical level as the innovating center, while at the same time it is also moving upward or downward through the urban hierarchy, depending on the location of the innovating center. Almost all innovations diffuse through space and filter through an urban system until over time a maximum adoption pattern has been reached.

Diffusion probably also proceeds in a number of different ways in concurrent time periods. For example, the extensive interaction exchange between the *elites* in the larger centers of an urban system probably accounts for the transfer of innovation information much more quickly than the transfer of information to much closer and more obviously dominated centers. This point has been made in a study of innovation diffusions in Latin America, where the introduction of innovations often occurred in the large cities, the national capitals, or port cities where there were the highest exchanges of ideas, people, and products with cities in other countries.[11] At the same time that there is this transference among the individuals in the upper order of centers of an urban system, there is not only diffusion downward through the places that they directly dominate, but also lateral diffusion as contacts are made with individuals in places of similar size with which the innovators interact on a regular basis.

A United States Example

A form of intercity diffusion is seen in the pre-electronic age spread of selected innovations in the United States.[12] In the pre-electronic age, public as well as private information could only circulate over long distances as an accompaniment to human spatial interaction. Thus, sources of information such as newspapers, journals, and other printed matter, which were the only forms of public information at that time, could only be moved from place to place if personally carried or shipped in vehicles. The spread of any particular innovation could be related to the existence of specific forms of transportation systems and the degrees to which integrated urban systems were developing concurrently.

As an example of the time differences between the availability of information in selected cities, it has been pointed out that in 1790 the average time lag between the occurrence of an event in London or Paris and publication of the news of that event in New York or Philadelphia was respectively 67.5 and 80 days.[13] Similarly, the Philadelphia reader at that time found on an average that his news from relatively nearby cities such as Baltimore was 6 days old, while that for more distant cities such as Boston (12 days) and Savannah (33.6 days) was much older. This considerable time lag between the obtaining of information, when added to the substantial amount of illiteracy and relatively slow transportation factors, gives a reasonable indication of the factors that slowed or retarded the diffusion of any particular innovation through space.

Examples of diffusion in the pre-electronic age are the introductions of newspapers, interurban and street railways, diseases, and bank panics. For instance, the first daily newspaper appeared in 1784 in Philadelphia, which was the largest city in the country at that time. Six years later (1790) there were three dailies in New York, four in Philadelphia, and one in Charleston (then the nation's fourth ranked city). There also had been unsuccessful efforts to establish one in Baltimore. By 1800 there were six dailies in Philadelphia and five or six in and around Washington, D.C. Almost all of the latter were founded in the same year that the city was made the capital. Between 1790 and 1800 short-lived dailies operated in Boston and Richmond.

As far as local-passenger street railways were concerned, the New York and Harlem Railroad, which began operation in 1832, is usually acknowledged to have been the first in the United States, although in 1831 horsedrawn B&O railroad cars used the streets of Baltimore to provide terminal access. Other pre-1844 adoptions of local-passenger street railways occurred in New Orleans in 1835 when the city ranked fifth in the country and in Cleveland and Buffalo in 1834 where services ceased during the financial panic of 1837.

Whereas our earlier discussions of air-passenger movements and migration patterns emphasized the static interpretation of flows between places, these diffusion studies concentrate more on the time series of the dates of adoption or the dates of exposure to the phenomenon being studied. In other words, the focus is on the behavior of people in urban environments in a time-space framework.

10.5 Diffusion in an Urban Hierarchy: A Model

We are interested here in a model of the diffusion process in a hierarchical urban system. We assume that the communication or influence associated with the process flows down from the largest urban center to the smaller centers.

One such model relates to a Christaller-type central place system with the following properties.[14] The distance between the smallest places in the system, the zero-order places, is equal to one and the distance between nearest-neighboring places of order i is $q^{1/2}$ for $i = 0, 1, \ldots, M - 1$. Every place, therefore, dominates $(q - 1)$ places of every lower order. Each link in the hierarchy is defined as one time lag. It is then possible to derive the number of places of a given order that are so many time lags away from the origin, that is, the top of the hierarchy. This, in turn, allows for the derivation of the proportion of places, $p(t)$, located t-lags away from this origin. This expression is

$$p(t) = \binom{M - 1}{q}\left(\frac{q - 1}{q}\right)^t \left(\frac{1}{q}\right)^{M-1-t} \qquad t = 0, 1, \ldots, M - 1$$

where M is the order of the system. This expression turns out to be a well-known probability law, the *binomial law*.

In the above model any place can influence other places not only at the hierarchical level immediately below it but also at still lower levels. A second model involves the more restrictive assumption that a place can only influence other places at the level immediately below it. This means that diffusion proceeds strictly from the largest to the smallest without any levels being bypassed. In this case,

$$p(t) = \frac{k^t(k - 1)}{(k^M - 1)}$$

where $k =$ number of centers at level $i - 1$ dominated by ith level place and t and M are defined as before.

A third model involves a more relaxed assumption about the hierarchical structuring of influence flows. In contrast to the above two models, no particular assumption is made about how the urban places are arranged hierarchically. Information or influence is assumed to flow randomly among the places. Then $p(t)$, defined now as the proportion of places that are affected by the diffusion process by time t, equals

$$\sum_{i=1}^{\infty} p_i(t)$$

where $p_i(t)$ = proportion of places located i time lags from the origin. In order to obtain an expression for $p_i(t)$ in this case, it is necessary to define a parameter α for the rate of contact with the source and to consider the eventual proportion of cities located i-lags from the source or origin. The result obtained is as follows:

$$\lim_{t \to \infty} p_i(t) = \pi(i) = \frac{\alpha[\log_e(1 + 1/\alpha)]^i}{i!}, \quad i = 1, 2, \ldots$$

This is also a form of a well-known probability law, the *Poisson law*. By taking into account a multiplier that relates population size to the central place system, it is possible to derive the time-lag distribution for the populations as well as for the cities.

10.6 Summary

Many interactions between cities consist of isolated or irregularly repeated events, such as air-passenger flows and individual migrations. Summing these individual events, however, produces a pattern of strong and persistent ties between places—their interaction linkages. These linkages appear directly related to population size, distance apart, economic opportunity, and local and regional growth rates. Examination of these interaction patterns helps to define linkages between places, to determine the major directions of flows, and even to construct highly probable settlement patterns based on interaction intensity.

Knowledge of the frequency and magnitude of intercity interactions, therefore, adds a further dimension to our understanding of urban systems. Not only do we know *where* places are and *why* they are there, but we also know the complex sets of relations that integrate the isolated places into a functioning urban system. Since cities exist to serve people, the human interaction dimension is of considerable importance in obtaining knowledge about how urban systems serve mankind.

In this chapter we have illustrated some of the different forms of human interaction that take place between cities. There are many other patterns that could have been examined and numerous examples that could have been discussed. The ones that we have chosen, however, illustrate the various features that emerge from such studies. Cities are shown to be grouped into hierarchical systems; large cities dominate smaller ones; the levels of interaction between places reflect the relative sizes of the places, the differing levels of opportunity, and the friction of distance; and the search for an explanation of the observed patterns demands that consideration be given to aspects of human decision making.

Notes

1. R. B. Adams, "Airline connectivity matrix: growth and disequilibrium," Paper presented at Mid-continental Division meeting, Regional Science Association, Winnipeg, Manitoba, 1971; E. J. Taaffe, "The urban hierarchy: an air passenger definition," *Economic Geography*, **38**, 1962, pp. 1–14.

2. W. H. Long, "The economics of air travel gravity models," *Journal of Regional Science*, **10**, 1970, p. 355.

3. *Ibid.*

4. L. A. Brown, J. Odland, and R. G. Golledge, "Migration, functional distance and the urban hierarchy," *Economic Geography*, **46**, 1970, pp. 472–85.

5. D. Demko, "Cognition of southern Ontario cities in a potential migration context," *Economic Geography*, **50**, 1974, pp. 20–34.

6. M. J. Greenwood, "A simultaneous-equations model of urban growth and migration," *Journal of American Statistical Association*, **70**, 1975, pp. 797–810.

7. J. Vanderkamp, "The effect of out-migration on regional employment," *Canadian Journal of Economics*, **3**, 1970, pp. 541–49.

8. Canada Manpower and Immigration, *Internal Migration and Immigrant Settlement* (Ottawa: Information Canada, 1975).

9. A. G. Wilson, *Entropy in Urban and Regional Modelling* (London: Pion Ltd., 1970); "A family of spatial interaction models and associated developments," *Environment and Planning*, **3**, 1971, pp. 1–32; *Urban and Regional Models in Geography and Planning* (London: J. Wiley, 1974).

10. P. R. Gould, "Pedagogic review: entropy in urban and regional modelling," *Annals*, Association of American Geographers, **62**, 1972, pp. 689–700.

11. P. O. Pedersen, "Innovation diffusion within and between national urban systems," *Geographical Analysis*, **2**, 1970, pp. 203–54.

12. A. R. Pred, "Large city interdependence and the pre-electronic diffusion of innovations in the U.S.," *Geographical Analysis*, **3**, 1971, pp. 165–81.

13. *Ibid.*

14. J. C. Hudson, *Geographical Diffusion Theory* (Evanston: Department of Geography, Northwestern University, 1972).

chapter 11

Movements and Interactions
Within the City

In this chapter we shall present the city as a web of linked human activities. The scale of analysis is micro-level. As an introduction comments are made on activity patterns generally; this is followed by a discussion of regular periodic spatial acts such as going to work and shopping and by a summary of what people are likely to see and remember as they move about the city. Less frequent events, such as migratory moves, are then examined, and the chapter concludes by illustrating the cognized structure of a city with its various spatial disturbances and directional distortions.

11.1   Activity Patterns in the City

When we alter the scale at which we are examining patterns of human interaction and shift to the intraurban level, it is useful to emphasize the study of activity patterns. An activity approach to urban analysis relies on the very simple assumption that activities, that is, the things that people do in the urban area, provide the greatest insights into the functioning of urban areas and into their spatial structure. In other words, the activity analyst views the metropolis or urban place as a collection of individual activities, actions, reactions, and interactions. Thus, urban places are described in terms of what is going on in them instead of in terms of quantities of land uses of various types. The rationale for this approach is simply that by knowing how people actually use an urban area, how they respond in choice situations, how they sequence their activities and the duration of their activities, and the relation of each of these things to changes in their own circumstances, the analyst will be in a better position to evaluate public policies designed to change the urban environment and in a better position to describe the city as it is used by the people living in it.

Episodes and Routines

In this discussion we refer to *activities* as discrete episodes that occur at uniform intervals in the life of a person (or household). They have some motivations behind them that are derived from a set of prior values and antecedents, and an activity results (produced by a choice mechanism) that has a spatial manifestation.

Activities can be viewed in terms of routines. A *routine* is a recurring set of episodes in a given unit of time. Recurrence may not imply the same length of time for each activity, for different routines require different periods of operation, for example, a daily work trip versus the annual holiday. Schematically, activities can be said to be produced as follows:

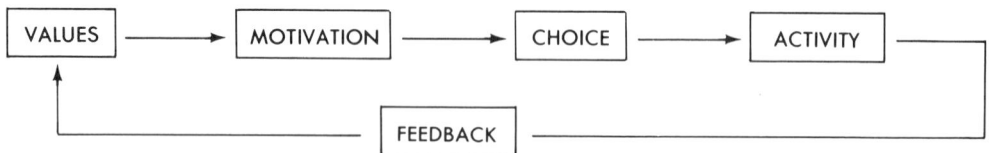

Activities are modified on consecutive trials until feedback no longer substantially alters the activity and a routine (habit) is formed. Almost all frequent routines are daily, weekly, seasonal, and life cycle.

In this section we shall concentrate on daily routines in one particular context, that of household decision making, in an attempt to explain periodicities of activities and variations in behavioral patterns. We shall endeavor to define the main components (episodes) of household activity patterns in terms of how the available time is budgeted and to suggest how they should be aggregated in order to provide meaningful sets of data for, say, planning purposes.

The fundamental activity systems of an urban area are those of its people. These collectively generate the need for, and set in operation, other entities that develop their own activity systems. For example, activities associated with shopping, commuting, and recreation may progress to the stage where business or governmental activities may have to be started in order to cope with them; as a consequence, the environment in which the activities take place changes. Schedules of individuals may have to be adapted to conform with the schedules of institutional entities in such things as working hours, transportation times, and so on.

Obligatory and Discretionary Acts

Activity systems consist of obligatory and discretionary acts. Obligatory acts include sleep, work, and school. Discretionary acts include recreation, some shopping activities, and leisure. Obligatory activities occur more or less in cycles with timed regularity. The identification of these cycles is the first phase in being able to predict and plan for activities in cities.

If we can determine the number of people performing the act (that is, the likelihood of performance) and the number hours devoted to it, we can determine the probability of an act taking place within a given time sequence. For instance, on any given weekday there is a low probability that an individual will perform an out-of-home discretionary activity.

On the typical weekday, approximately 18 hours per day are expended on obligatory activities such as sleep, work, home-making, and shopping (Table 11.1). Of the remaining 6 hours available for discretionary activities, almost all of them (on the average) are spent at home. This stresses the importance of the home and its neighborhood in the life of city dwellers and it has implications also for the allocation of public resources for leisure time facilities. Discretionary acts vary from household to household and produce some variation of behavior within groups. Discretionary acts may be deliberately decided upon by people and reflect the people's initiatives or they may stem from chance happenings.

Factors Influencing Daily Activity Patterns

Three major components of daily activity patterns are the time of activity, the space over which the activity takes place, and the type of activity, all of which are highly interconnected. Time is taken into consideration in two ways:

Table 11.1   Activity Classes and Durations. [After Table 1
from F. Stuart Chapin Jr. and Richard K. Brail,
"Human activity systems in the metropolitan United
States," *Environment and Behavior*, Vol. 1, No. 2
(December, 1969), p. 115; by permission of the
Publisher, Sage Publications, Inc.]

Activity Class	Average Duration (hours)	Percent of Population Performing Activity
In-home:		
Relaxation	1.65	48
Arts, hobbies, sports	2.76	10
Reading	1.34	29
TV and radio	3.08	66
Family	1.65	10
Socializing	1.81	14
Obligatory (housework, meals)	5.67	100
Out-of-home:		
Discretionary	2.71	15
Family	2.33	11
Socializing	2.64	13
Work-related	8.69	47
Shopping and personal services	1.72	35
Obligatory (medical care, errands, etc.)	1.57	49

1. In terms of the duration of each activity.
2. In terms of the time of occurrence of the activity.

The duration of each activity is, of course, a basic ingredient in the
account of a day's activities, but at present relatively little is known
about this. The time of day that activities occur is also important and
it may be critical in determining whether or not an activity *will* take
place together with others that are needed during the daytime. Of
course, one may also suggest that the duration of an activity is directly
related to the time of day in which it occurs.

The distribution of facilities in space for particular activities appears to be of prime importance in determining whether or not a given
activity will be performed, and perhaps more so in determining the
frequency with which an activity will be performed. It is feasible to
hypothesize that activities will have longer duration when access is
easy rather than when it is difficult. We should also note that the distribution of potential places of activity is viewed by the individual from
a certain perspective, that is, from where he is located in the urban
area. This means that the activity approach must necessarily be tied

into the approach designed to find orientation nodes within urban areas. It is a reasonably well-established fact, for example, that an individual's view of opportunities available for interaction changes as he moves about an urban area. The selection of any given activity can be explained in terms of motivations, needs, wants, and capabilities of individual performers. The whole range of socio-economic characteristics of individuals and family units thus comes into play in any attempt to explain the structure of various activity patterns. In addition, one must also consider that activities may be a function of preferences, tastes, information, habits, and financial circumstances.

The above concepts are illustrated in a study of activity patterns in Buffalo, New York in 1962.[1] Information was obtained on the type, location, duration, and time of day of some 92,000 out-of-home activities performed by 55,000 members of 16,000 households on a selected weekday. Each record also contained socio-economic information on the individual and household and on the transportation used. Records of movements were arranged sequentially for the 24-hour period studies. Approximately 80% of all trips recorded in this origin-destination (O-D) study were home based in that either the origin or destination was the home of the trip maker. Consequently, only about 20% of the trips made were from one out-of-home activity to another. Apart from the home-based trips, approximately 41 other out-of-home activities were determined (Table 11.2).

Among the conclusions derived from the Buffalo study were that (a) members of black households generally were less likely to make multiple-activity journeys than members of white households; (b) the likelihood of multiple-activity journeys by all members of a household was inversely related to the age of the head of the household—the older the head, the fewer nonhome-based trips there were; (c) the likelihood of multiple-activity journeys was directly related to household income and car ownership, that is, the higher the household income, the more likely a person was to link activities; (d) if the household owned a car, the person was more likely to link activities than if the household did not own a car; if the household owned two cars, it was even more likely that linked activities would take place; (e) the likelihood of multiple-activity journeys was related to the occupation of the head of the household (ranked from high socio-economic status to lower socio-economic status).

A Disadvantaged Group: The Urban Poor

A number of studies have examined the problems faced by various disadvantaged groups in the city in finding employment and traveling to the workplace. One such study of Indianapolis began by noting two

Table 11.2 Out-of-Home Activities Recognized in the Buffalo
Study. (After G. C. Hemmens, "Analysis and
simulation of urban activity patterns," *Socio-
Economic Planning Sciences,* **4,** 1970, pp. 53–66.)

Work/residential	Eat meal/residential land
Work/retail	Eat meal/restaurant or club
Work/service and offices	Personal business/residential land
Work/wholesale	Personal business/personal services
Work/durable manufacturing	Personal business/medical dental
Work/nondurable manufacturing	Personal business/business service
Work/institutional	Personal business/other services
Work/recreation	Personal business/manufacturing and wholesaling
Work/transportation terminals and facilities	Personal business/hospitals, etc.
Work/other	Personal business/church
Shop/food, drug, liquor	Personal business/other public buildings
Shop/other convenience goods	
Shop/department store	
Shop/other shopping goods	
Shop/automotive	
Shop/miscellaneous other	
School/elementary	
School/secondary	
School/other, including college	
Social-recreation/residential land	
Social-recreation/eating and drinking	
Social-recreation/indoor	
Social-recreation/clubs	
Social-recreation/schools, museums, libraries	
Social-recreation/hospitals, etc.	
Social-recreation/church	
Social-recreation/outdoor	
Social-recreation/local parks	
Social-recreation/spectator sports	
Social-recreation/miscellaneous	

residential processes that are common to American cities, the movement of the middle- and high-income whites to the suburbs and the
movement of poor and mainly black persons into the central areas of
the city.[2] In these central poverty areas, as we have noted, high population densities, housing shortages, and unemployment are pronounced.

A graph showing the relative availability of clerical and manufacturing jobs at different public transit traveling times away from the
center of Indianapolis is shown in Figure 11.1. Clerical jobs are the
most accessible to the centrally located poor, but they are frequently
demanding of levels of skills that the poor have not had the opportunity
to acquire. A large proportion of the manufacturing jobs lies outside
of the range of the public transit system and hence the jobs are in-

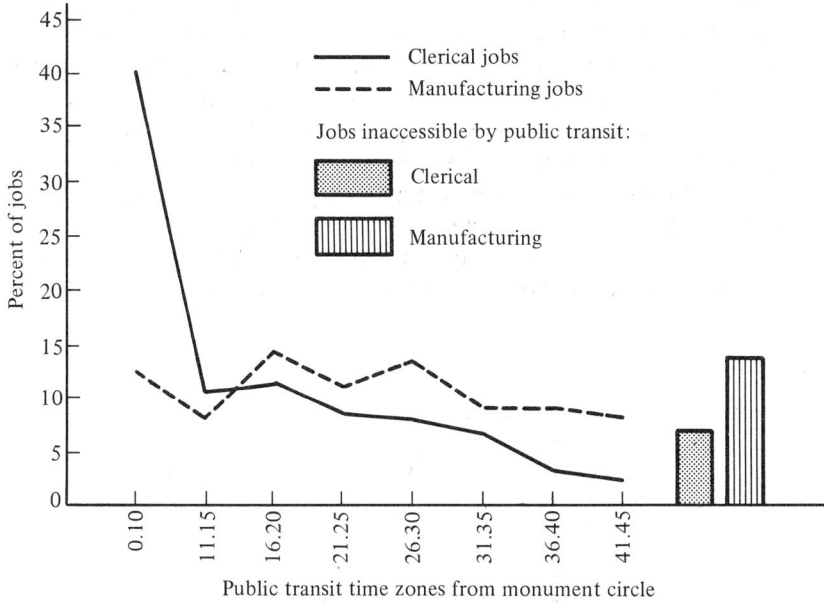

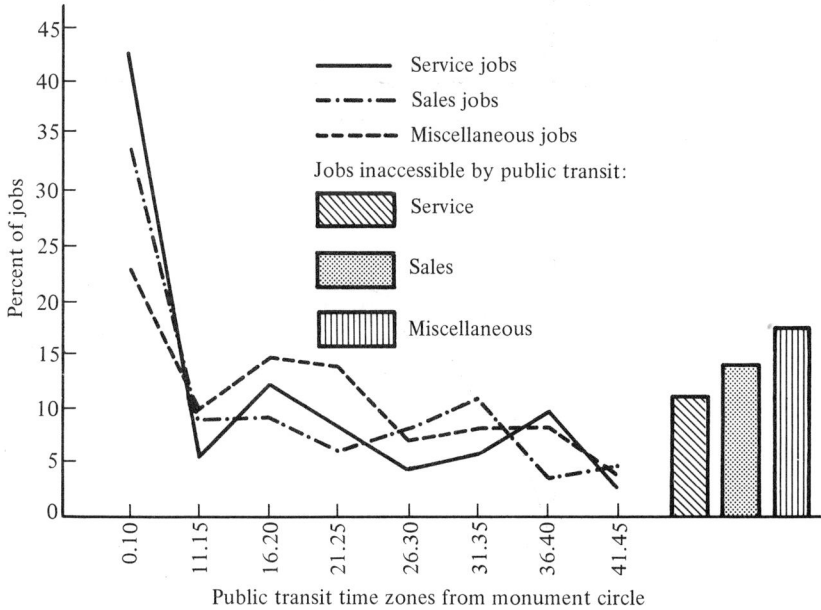

Figure 11.1 The distribution of low-skilled clerical, manufacturing, service, sales, and miscellaneous jobs over public transit time zones in Marion County, 1968. [S. Davies and M. Albaum, "Mobility problems of the poor in Indianapolis," in R. Peet, ed., *Geographical Perspectives on American Poverty* (Worcester, Mass.: Antipode Monographs in Social Geography, 1972), p. 73.]

accessible to the disadvantaged who have low levels of private car ownership. It is significant that the differences in the distances traveled to work either by bus or car are not great between the poor blacks and the poor whites, but as would be expected, the average distance traveled by either group in cars is about one mile longer than the average distance for bus travel (Figure 11.2). These average car distances would be much shorter than the corresponding trip distances for the more affluent suburban residents. A partial solution, it has been suggested, might be to redesign the public transit system, which in this city involves only bus routes, in order to link the poverty pockets with the outlying centers of employment opportunity.[3]

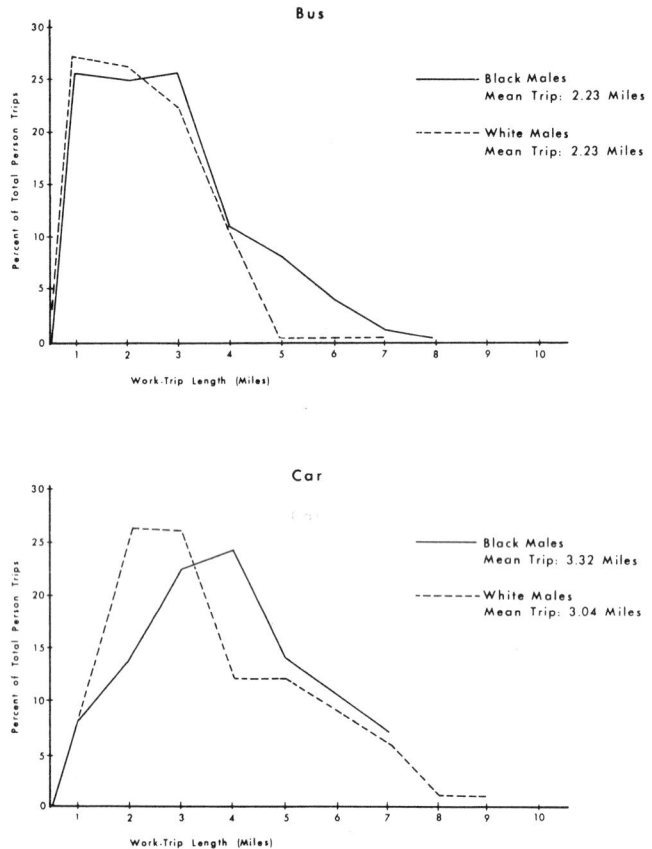

Figure 11.2 Home-based work-trip length distribution of males by race and transit mode. [S. Davies and M. Albaum, "Mobility problems of the poor in Indianapolis," in R. Peet, ed., *Geographical Perspectives on American Poverty* (Worcester, Mass.: Antipode Monographs in Social Geography, 1972), p. 78.]

Shopping Activities

The journey to work is but one of a number of trips that the average urban resident makes in the urban area on any given day. Almost all modeling that has been undertaken with respect to urban movement has concentrated on the journey-to-work behavior simply because this is a relatively invariant and repetitive pattern. But as Table 11.3 illustrates for the city of Cedar Rapids, Iowa, a variety of trips other than for journey-to-work purposes also have a very high repetition ratio. Grocery shopping is an obvious form of such patterned activity whereby the same subset of grocery stores is repeatedly patronized. Column 3 of Table 11.3 also gives some idea of the average distance travelled for certain selected activities in the case of Cedar Rapids residents. As well as grocery shopping, trips to banking facilities, gasoline stations, supermarkets, public offices, and taverns all exhibited a high degree of repetition. In other words, once these par-

Table 11.3   Repetition and Trip Purpose, Cedar Rapids, Iowa, 1949. [D. F. Marble and S. R. Bowlby, "Shopping alternatives and recurrent travel patterns," in F. Horton, ed., *Geographic Studies of Urban Transportation and Network Analysis*, Northwestern University Studies in Geography, No. 16, 1968, p. 69.]

Purpose	Repetition Ratio	Average Number of Stops	Average Distance to Repetitious Stops (miles)	Average Minimum Distance to Stores (miles)	Total Number of Establisments
Grocery	0.92	6.49	0.46	0.18	153
Bank loan and other financial	0.86	1.78	0.89	1.00	59
Gasoline	0.85	1.17	0.93	0.26	97
Supermarket	0.84	3.37	0.72	0.70	10
Public office	0.83	2.84	0.83	0.38	107
Tavern	0.80	1.05	0.63	0.45	63
General store	0.77	4.18	0.92	0.36	34
Restaurant	0.73	3.53	1.68	0.34	98
Theater	0.71	2.49	1.29	0.87	7
Confectionaire	0.70	1.12	0.99	0.50	25
Bottle club	0.69	1.43	1.03	0.91	54
Department store	0.67	2.64	1.61	1.15	5
Variety	0.66	1.97	1.36	0.62	8
Medical	0.64	1.49	1.66	0.76	168
Clothing	0.61	2.09	1.42	1.24	17

Table 11.4 Number of Stores Visited on Sample Trips, Newark, Ohio.   (After J. D. Looman, "Consumer
spatial behavior," unpublished Master's thesis,
Department of Geography, The Ohio State University, 1969.)

| | *Number of Respondents* | | |
Number of Stores Visited	*Sample Location A*	*Sample Location B*	*Total*
1	23	35	58
2	23	21	44
3	11	12	23
4	1	8	9
5	—	1	1
6	—	3	3

ticular travel patterns had been established for any given urban household, they could be predicted with a high degree of success by a relatively simple deterministic model.

As far as shopping is concerned, many of the characteristics exhibited earlier in the rural-urban situation (see Chapter 9) again hold.
For example, the number of shopping centers visited by individuals
within the urban areas for the purpose of purchasing goods such as
groceries typically is more than one and may be as many as three. This
multiple-place shopping (illustrated by the data in Table 11.4), appears to be a characteristic of consumer behavior regardless of the urban environment. There is also considerable multi-purpose shopping
(Table 11.5). Finally, there is often a marked tendency on the part of
shoppers to bypass the nearest commercial center for many functions

Table 11.5 Classification of Trips Made by Respondents, Newark, Ohio. (After J. D. Looman, "Consumer spatial
behavior," unpublished Master's thesis, Department of Geography, The Ohio State University,
1969.)

| | *Number of Stops Made* | | |
Purpose of Trip	*Single-stop*	*Multi-stop*	*Total*
Single-purpose	42%	16%	58%
Multi-purpose		42%	42%
Totals	42%	58%	

Table 11.6 Selected Shopping Patterns for Christchurch, New
Zealand. (Based on W. A. V. Clark, "Consumer
travel patterns and the concept of range;" reproduced, by permission from *Annals* of the Association of American Geographers, volume **58,**
1968, p. 391.)

Goods	*Number of Shoppers in Sample*	*Percent of Sample Purchasing*	*Percent Who Shopped at Center Nearest to Their Homes*
Groceries	495	98.6	57.4
Vegetables	495	67.9	62.8
Meat	495	92.7	46.8

and to shop at more distant ones (Table 11.6). In the case of the households in Christchurch, New Zealand, it seemed that if a shopper did
not frequent the commercial center nearest to his place of residence
then he would be indifferent as to the distances to the alternative centers at which he might shop (Table 11.7). This is suggested by the fact
that there was large variation in the actual distances traveled as measured by the standard deviation values in Table 11.7. Remember that
in Section 9.4 we noted these tendencies in regard to rural consumers
in Iowa.

Table 11.7 Distances Traveled by Consumers in Christchurch,
New Zealand. (Based on W. A. V. Clark, "Con-
sumer travel patterns and the concept of range;"
reproduced with permission from *Annals* of the
Association of American Geographers, volume **58,**
1968, p. 393.)

Goods Purchased	*Average Distance to Nearest Center (miles)*	*Distances to Centers Actually Patronized*	
		Average	*Standard Deviation*
Groceries	.23	.71	1.21
Vegetables	.31	.95	1.12
Meat	.29	.70	.99

11.2 "The City as a Trip": Learning About the City As One Travels Around It

The study of intraurban movements is of such importance in understanding the purpose and functioning of cities that it has led to the
formalization of a hypothesis that "the city is a trip." The argument
is that all one knows about the city and the way one acts within the

city are directly related to the levels and types of information that one gathers as one moves about the city. We examine this hypothesis both from the point of view of active movers, for example, car passengers and drivers as they operate in the city, and also from the point of view of people's ability to recall relative locations. The first view reveals those aspects of a city's structure, that is, environmental cues, that are recognized and used most frequently by urban residents. The second allows us to infer the distance and directional biases that are contained in the cognitive configurations (or cognitive spatial arrangements) of such cues.

In an often quoted study, Carr and Schissler interviewed a number of individuals in the city of Boston in order to identify the types of information the individuals recorded on a given trip within the urban area.[4] The authors adopted a number of unique operational procedures in order to investigate the perceptual processes involved. Their aim was to determine which features of the urban area were noticed and remembered by different individuals. Prior to the day of field testing, the people in this study were asked to state their preconceptions of the trips that they were to make. The people were tested in a laboratory to determine the accuracy and depth of their memory, the angle of their eye movements, and so on. On the actual trip, head-mounted cameras and optical devices fixed on the corneas of the subjects' eyes enabled researchers to identify those points on which eyes were fixed at various places along the route. It was assumed that the psychological principle of grouping by proximity and similarity would be established around those points of fixation, allowing the subjects to describe areas as well as points in the city itself as a result.

Subjects used a variety of verbal, graphic, and descriptive materials in association with trip films to provide a data bank that was then analyzed to find those areas and places in the city that provided the anchors for individual cognitive maps. The frequency with which items were mentioned or observed was recorded; then the total list of items was classified and ranked according to the number of times they appeared in the subjects' responses (Table 11.8).

Differing Responses of Drivers, Passengers, and Commuters

Two of the more interesting results of this study were (1) the difference between the number of items recorded by drivers and passengers and (2) the difference in the number of items recorded by commuters as opposed to first-time travelers. For example, the average driver remembered only 10 objects over a test section of 4 miles of road, but passengers remembered (on an average) 21 separate objects along the route. Commuters who regularly traveled the area remembered an average of 28 objects.

Table 11.8   Individual Items Memory Lists for Passengers, Drivers, and Commuters Going from Best-Remembered Item to Least-Remembered Item. (Table 1 from S. Carr and D. Schissler, "The city as a trip: Perceptual selection and memory on the view from the road" is reprinted from *Environment and Behavior*, vol. **1**, No. 1 (September 1969), p. 21 by permission of the publisher, Sage Publications, Inc.)

Rank	Commuters	Passengers	Drivers
1.	Mystic River Bridge	Mystic River Bridge	Mystic River Bridge
2.	Overpass (early)	Toll booth	Toll booth
3.	Prudential Building	Prudential Building	Overpass (late)
4.	Bunker Hill Monument	Three-Deckers: Chelsea	Sign for Haymarket
5.	State Street Bank	Overpass (early)	Overpass (early)
6.	Three-Deckers: Chelsea	Bunker Hill Monument	Second bridge
7.	Government Center	Overpass (late)	Three-Deckers: Chelsea
8.	Custom House Tower	Government Center	Billboard: John Hancock
9.	Soldier's Home	John Hancock Building	Sign for Downtown Boston
10.	Toll booth	Charlestown residences	Sign for Charlestown
11.	U.S.S. Constitution	Custom House Tower	
12.	Naval Hospital	Charles River Park Apts.	
13.	Sign for Storrow Drive	State Street Bank	
14.	William's School	Sign: Chelsea	
15.	American Optical Co.	North End residences	
16.	John Hancock	U.S.S. Constitution	
17.	Charles River Park Apts.	Colored oil drums	
18.	Colored oil drums	Billboard: John Hancock	
19.	Sign: Fitzgerald Expressway	Twin Tower Church	
20.	Bradlee's Shopping Center	Billboard: Seagrams	
21.	North Station	Residences on Soldier's Home hill	
22.	Sign for High Street		
23.	Sign for Dock Square		
24.	Sign for Chelsea		
25.	Grain Elevators		
26.	Wallpaper Factory		
27.	Barrel Factory		
28.	Cemetery		

The information from all the various perceptual recordings was tabulated and a list of the structural elements of the city was obtained and ranked in order of their probability of being retained by individuals in their mental maps. One important conclusion was that individuals performing different functions tended to remember similar things in the same order of importance after traveling over a selected route. Familiarity of the route changed the range of things that were recorded, but it did not in essence change the fundamental data set. This is indeed a critical feature because it suggests that even newcomers to an area will select approximately the same dominant features when structuring their mental maps as do individuals who are very familiar with an area. This suggests, in turn, that there are some structural properties of the city or urban areas that impress themselves more than others on the memory of either casual or regular observers and that these fixation points become the orientation nodes or focal points in the structuring of mental maps of an urban area. Some areas in the city will be familiar to a given set of individuals while other areas are likely to be poorly represented or poorly remembered in corresponding mental maps. Note also that the difference between the commuters' and noncommuters' lists of environmental cues further indicates that the mental map of the city changes continuously. In other words, the individual has learned a model of the city that he constantly modifies as he travels in the urban area and accumulates further information. Initially, an individual will perhaps build a skeleton-like map of the urban area with the principle elements being origin-destination nodes such as home, work, and shopping places and the paths or edges connecting those particular nodes. As learning proceeds, additional information about places in the vicinity of the nodes and paths is collected and added as fine detail to the perceptual template of an urban area.

Perceptual Structure and Behavior

It is but a short step from recognizing that individuals have mental maps of urban areas to suggesting that it is the mental image and its structure and geometry that influence movements about the urban area rather than the objective physical structure itself. When the perceptual structure is highly distorted, decisions may be made and movements may occur that may not be very easily explained in terms of the location of alternatives, or origins and destinations, in the objective city. On the other hand, when the perceptual city and the objective city approximate each other (that is, when the general learned model of the city conforms to the objective physical reality of the city), one might expect that decision making and movement in the urban area could be much more readily explained in terms of locations, frequencies of occurrence of cues, and distances—the variables that geographers use most frequently in explaining location and movement within urban areas. As represented in memory, therefore, the city as a trip is a highly meaningful thing to almost all individuals. The general structure, sequencing, and dominant elements of trips clarify the social, economic, and technical organization of any city as more information is collected about them. Alternatively, in new urban environments where the structure, sequencing, and dominant elements of the city are not obvious, confusion and obscurity may dominate the mental map. Thus, in order to relate to the urban environment, one must be able to read it or to see what it represents. This is apparently what individuals do in their everyday activities within cities. They attempt to build coherent structures that allow them to operate on a day-to-day basis with a minimum amount of confusion and a minimum amount of effort spent in continuing decision processes.

11.3   Residential Moves Within the City

Residential mobility is a fundamental element of the growth of urban areas. For example, as cities grow, and in the process of growing, age, deteriorate in parts, and alter the locational patterns of their land uses, people also move in response to these changes. For example, when commuting problems become excessive, a change in the location of residence is often substituted for commuting. Also, because of changes in their life cycles, in their economic statuses, and in their tastes and preferences for dwellings and space, people frequently move.

Types of Moves

In the broadest sense there are two types of residential moves within urban areas: voluntary moves and forced moves. Voluntary moves are undertaken in response to changes in city structure and operation and in response to changes in individual (or family) well-being. Forced moves are the result of dislocations produced by programs such as urban renewal, transportation route requirements, and invasion by other economic activities or by public authority.

Conservative estimates of intraurban mobility indicate that between 15% and 20% of urban populations in developed countries change their residences each year.[5] Apparently, this high volume of movement is concentrated among certain segments of almost all urban populations, but even across these segments movement represents an aim of establishing some coincidence between each householder's needs, dissatisfactions, and aspirations.

Involved in each migration are two dominant phases: the decision process undertaken prior to movement and the actual physical movement process. The first of these phases, the residential site selection process, includes both overt and covert stages. The covert stages generally involve (1) reconciling aspiration levels with existing physical, economic, and social conditions, (2) information searching among alternatives in order to reduce the size of the choice population to a set of feasible alternatives, and (3) explicitly formulating housing goals consequent to search activity. The overt stage includes actual spatial movements undertaken in order to examine suspected feasible alternatives and an attempt to define reduced choice sets.

The second stage, that of movement itself, is the actual shift between an origin and destination. This transfer has characteristics of length, duration, and direction. Summed over populations, they can also be interpreted in terms of volumes of flows. Frequently, the elements of the first phase are inferred *a posteriori* by looking at patterns of flow and seeking associations between the flow patterns and sets of spatial, social, economic, and other variables. Since the actual movement is a relatively uncomplicated procedure, it has been examined in great detail in order to help build models of migrations and to assist in predicting future movements.

Who Moves?

There has been considerable agreement between both sociological and geographical investigations on this question.[6] Apparently, the major participants in intraurban migration are younger married couples with small children. Location in the urban area also throws light on the question of who moves: people located in central city areas are generally more mobile than suburbanites. This fact, however, must be tempered by considering the size and growth rate of the city itself, for rapid growth not only promotes new housing investment and encourages suburban migration, but it also increases migration opportunities in older areas.

Almost all studies indicate that intraurban residential change results from *push* factors (such as discontent with one's present neighborhood) instead of *pull* factors (such as job changes). A study of moves made in Seattle, for example, showed that the average length of an intracity move was only 3 miles and that 16% of all changes were less than half a mile, hardly enough to warrant inferences about the attraction of workplace on residential site selection![7] In black housing areas in the same city, the average length of move was 1.2 miles. Usually, upward housing mobility was the basic motive for residential movements. Even in the ghetto areas studies, 42% of the movers listed "dissatisfaction with house and/or old neighborhood" as the primary reason for moving, while increases in family size, income, and changes in the locations of friends were the most important supplementary factors. Another factor apparently influencing change was proximity to arterial roads—changes-of-occupancy rates for housing along arterials in black low-value housing areas was as high as 35%, as compared to 30% for non-arterial housing in the same area. The same differential held true for nonblack low-value areas (16% and 12%).

The majority of movers in urban areas appear to be renters instead of owners. Again, using Seattle as an example, renters had from seven to ten times the turnover rate of owner-occupiers. It also appeared that owner-occupied housing near rental property turned over at a high rate because of contiguity effects. For example, in the black study areas, half of the housing in rental status turned over each year in comparison to only 7% of the owner-occupied residents in the area. In middle- and high-value housing areas, 45% of renter houses changed occupancy in comparison to a 4%-change in the owner-occupied housing.

The Seattle study also argued that people in low-value housing areas moved more than those in high-value areas, that is, those who could least afford to do the moving (in a strict financial sense) moved the most. The 2,254 households studied during a 5-year period produced 2,965 moves. It was estimated that an average of 26% of all housing changed occupancy each year.

Why Do People Move?

This complex question takes us into the areas of economics, sociology, psychology, and politics, as well as geography. On the surface one may argue that the motivations for changing residence vary with each mover. One could hardly expect a teenage entrant into the workforce to change residence for the same reason that an aged person would.

Consider first some economic factors. It seems that a worker moves when his wage is likely to be higher at a destination other than at his present place of work. Although this by itself is an adequate reason for changing jobs, it does not provide an adequate reason for changing the location of residence unless increased commuting costs outweigh the expected benefits. Movements because of economic opportunities seem to be a characteristic of the young more than older age groups; the latter are more subject to sentimental ties and habits and the prospective benefit periods associated with a move may be much shorter for them. In general terms, this explanation revolves around the *pull* of other economic opportunities.

Income attraction or occupational changes are not the only economic forces that produce migrations in the city. As a city grows and as an individual's earning capacity changes, the stock of housing available to him also changes. Thus, as changes take place in the value of property, as the quantity of space available for a given dollar amount changes, and as aging and obsolescence of existing housing stocks occur, movements may take place. In a recent study of residential moves in Milwaukee over the period 1950–1963, it was noted that "the most cogent explanation for about one-quarter of the moves was that they had relatively high incomes and could move fully within the city."[8]

Housing Opportunities

Although we can seek explanations of residential mobility in terms of the personal economics of potential movers, we must also realize that migration is made possible under conditions of weak motivation by various producers of housing in the city. For example, a developer interested in realizing on a speculative subdivision may offer sufficient attractions (in terms of low costs, discounts, or environmental quality) to prompt a move even when personal economic status might remain unchanged. This represents an economic trade-off that brings rewards in terms of longer occupancy life or improved aesthetic values. At the same time there is started a *filtering down* process of housing quality by which vacancies are created that can be filled by individuals newly entering given economic classes. Alternatively, subdivision of the residence into several properties slightly changes the existing housing stock for lower-income groups and may induce locational changes at that level.[9] The possible role of filtering in affecting the supply of housing has been the subject of many studies. One of the few detailed studies of its effects on the housing market of a particular city, in this case Toronto, analyzed the price changes that had taken place in regard to specific properties, all of which had been sold twice during the period 1953–1971.[10] The filtering effect was measured in terms of price changes by calculating for each property at each date it was sold the difference between its sales value and the average sales price of all dwellings being sold at that time. A map showing the pattern of changes in which individual property values have been averaged over census tracts is provided in Figure 11.3. The positive values are taken to reflect upward filtering. This was most pronounced around the central business district (tracts 71–76) and in some outlying areas served by rapid transit. Downward filtering was most noticeable in the eastern end of the city.

One of the conclusions of the Toronto study is worth noting here. The central areas of the city showed upward filtering in response to increased land values as investment in redevelopment took place at a fairly high level. At the same time, the demand for older housing for

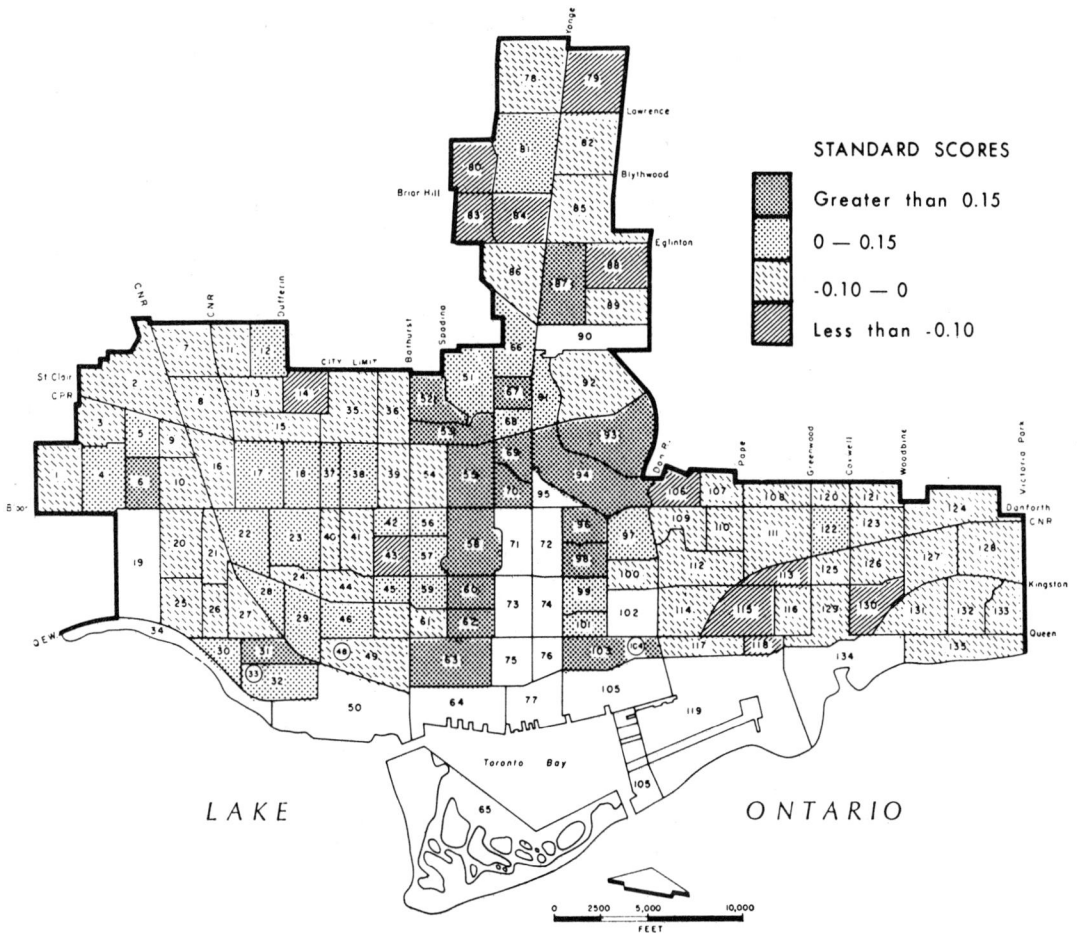

Figure 11.3 Aggregate filtering pattern, 1953–1971 (numbers refer to 1966 census tracts). [C. A. Maher, "Spatial patterns in urban housing markets: Filtering in Toronto, 1953–1971," *The Canadian Geographer,* **18,** 1974, p. 116.]

conversion meant that it was not allowed to depreciate and thereby filter downward, suggesting that "the traditional function of the inner city residential districts as primarily low-income neighborhoods is changing." The conclusion was that filtering is irrelevant as a mechanism for supplying low-income housing.

Social-Psychological Factors

Changing the relationship between a householder and his environment may involve not only economic pressures, but also social and cultural pressures. The householder may change his life-style in the course of growing older, change his family structure, his friendship (or acquaintanceship) fields, his political leanings, or his views on topics such as open housing. Concurrently or independently, his environment may change in terms of accessibility, value, racial mix, noise incidence (pollution), or some other critical variable. The result may be to produce a change in the individual's social psychology that prompts a change of location as a means of adjusting to this change.

Of the various social-psychological factors that produce movements, life-cycle change appears to be the most powerful. It has been argued that this factor can account for more than half of the expected number of moves people make during their lives.[11] Typically, moves take place at the ages of childhood (passive movements as part of a migrating family), maturity (an active move to set up an independent life), and at marriage (an active move frequently involving changes of dwelling space requirements). Thus, as elements of a household form, grow, age, and disperse, there may be accompanying migratory movements.

Of the moves that take place, almost one-third can be classed as involuntary moves. Such migrations occur after major events such as eviction from a residence, marriage, death, or loss of income. Eviction includes displacements produced by natural disasters, renewal projects, and the like. Although a considerable volume of publicity is generally given to displacement (particularly that associated with renewal projects), the volume of total moves resulting from displacement is small. Of the voluntary moves, the most common impetus is the need for more space as single people marry and/or as family needs exceed the space available in the present residence.

Residential Shifts and Segregation

A major social factor generating many of the intraurban residential shifts in North American cities is that of the racial composition of neighborhoods. The phenomenon of what has come to be called the *ghetto* has been the subject of much research and many policy proposals, both good and bad. We are not concerned with the policy issues here but rather with the role that the ghetto plays in the process of residential change and movements within the city.

We begin with the observation that residential segregation in United States cities is very pronounced and shows no signs of disappearing. In Chicago, for example, there has been "a tightening rather than a loosening of the white suburban noose around the black inner city."[12] There, the tendency of the black population to be confined to the center of the metropolitan area increased from 1960 to 1970, while even in the suburbs where only 3 percent of the total black

Table 11.9 Segregation Indices. (F. B. Glantz and N. J. De-
laney, "Changes in non-white residential patterns in
large metropolitan areas, 1960 and 1970," *New
England Economic Review*, March/April, 1973,
p. 6.)

*Metropolitan Area**	*Blacks*			*All Nonwhites*		
	1960	*1970*	*Percent Change*	*1960*	*1970*	*Percent Change*
New York	0.30	0.29	−3	0.30	0.28	−7
Los Angeles-Long Beach	0.37	0.31	−16	0.35	0.27	−23
Chicago	0.37	0.45	22	0.36	0.44	22
Philadelphia	0.39	0.44	13	0.38	0.44	16
Detroit	0.47	0.58	23	0.47	0.56	19
San Francisco-Oakland	0.46	0.52	13	0.36	0.40	11
Pittsburgh	0.54	0.59	9	0.54	0.58	7
St. Louis	0.50	0.57	14	0.49	0.56	14
Baltimore	0.35	0.44	26	0.34	0.43	26
Dallas	0.15	0.29	93	0.15	0.28	87
Atlanta	0.38	0.51	34	0.38	0.51	34
Birmingham	0.20	0.30	50	0.20	0.30	50
Greensboro-Winston-Salem-High Point	0.37	0.40	8	0.37	0.40	8
Boston	0.62	0.66	6	0.59	0.61	3
Average, 14 large SMSA's	0.39	0.45	15	0.38	0.43	13
Boston	0.62	0.66	6	0.59	0.61	3
Providence-Pawtucket-Warwick	0.60	0.65	8	0.57	0.60	5
Hartford	0.60	0.68	13	0.59	0.66	12
Springfield-Chicopee-Holyoke	0.56	0.59	5	0.54	0.56	4
Worcester	0.32	0.48	28	0.29	0.35	21
Average, 5 New England SMSA's	0.54	0.60	11	0.52	0.56	8

NOTE: The higher the value of the segregation index, the greater is the degree of residential concentration.

*Because of data limitations, the indices for the San Francisco-Oakland, Atlanta, Birmingham, Greensboro-Winston-Salem-High Point, and Dallas SMSA's were calculated from Census county subdivision, rather than municipal, data. Census county subdivisions are generally larger than individual municipalities, and this probably results in a downward bias in the values of these indices.

population lived there was a concentration of blacks in only 16 of the metropolitan area's 267 smaller municipalities. The same pattern generally holds true for the other major metropolitan areas. In Table 11.9 segregation indices are given for some 19 different metropolitan areas for 1960 and 1970. The index is so constructed that the closer the value is to 1, the higher the concentration of blacks and nonwhites

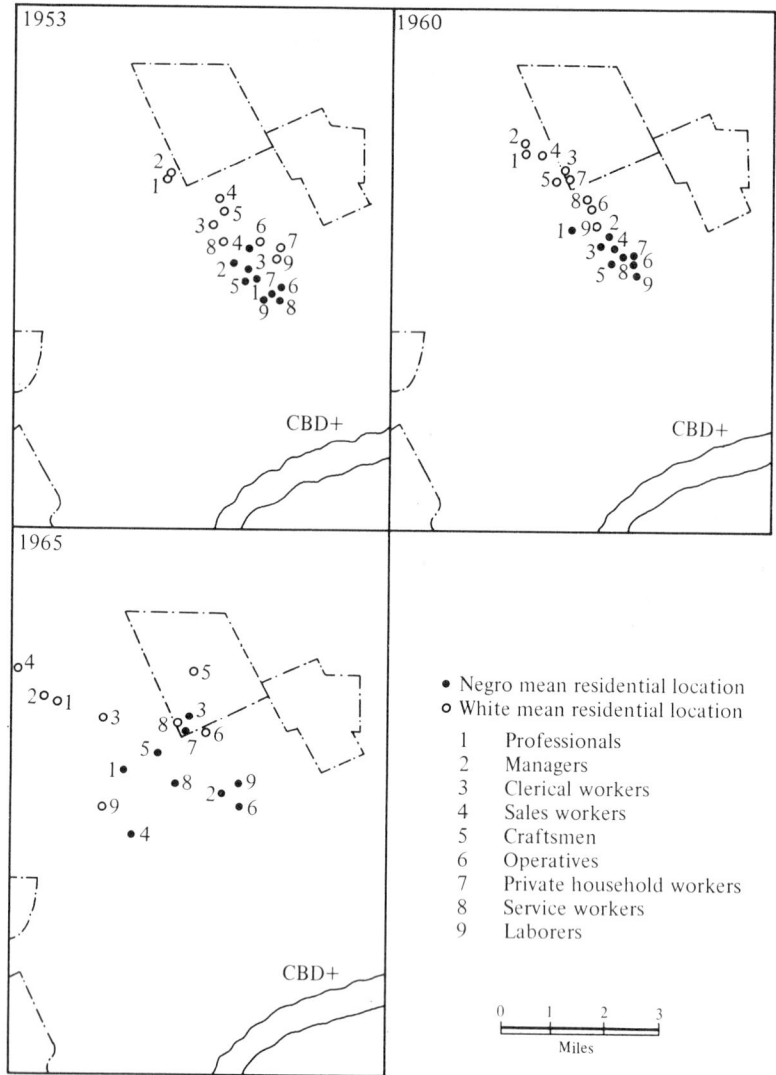

Figure 11.4 Internal structure of Negro and white communities (Detroit 1953–1965). [D. R. Deskins, Jr., *Residential Mobility of Negroes in Detroit, 1837–1965.* (Ann Arbor: Department of Geography, University of Michigan, 19), p. 116.]

in a few residential areas of the city. The values suggest that in almost all cities the spatial concentration of blacks and nonwhites has increased over the decade. The contributory factors of prejudice, discrimination by the real estate industry and financial institutions, legal barriers, power structures, and misguided policies are proving extremely difficult to overcome.

Associated with the ghetto are three major patterns of movement. First, within the ghetto itself there is considerable residential mobility. A very detailed study of the Detroit ghetto, for example, suggested that the internal structure of the ghetto is a *microcosm* of the whole city itself.[13] Within this ghetto there is a concentration of the more affluent black families in the northwestern part away from the central district where the lower-income blacks live. The maps in Figure 11.4 show how the centers of gravity for the locational distributions of the different white and black occupational groups changed from 1953 to 1965. The other movement patterns associated with the ghetto are the movements of black families into the expanding frontier of the ghetto and of white families in response to this expansion or spread.

On the basis of what happened in Seattle (Figures 11.5 and 11.6), Richard Morrill has described the process of ghetto expansion as a contagious diffusion process in which principles of proximity and contiguity dominate.[14] Growth was pictured as a block by block transition process along the edge of the ghetto. There was the initial location of a black family in a white city block adjacent to the ghetto, which may have been the result of a regular property transaction between the

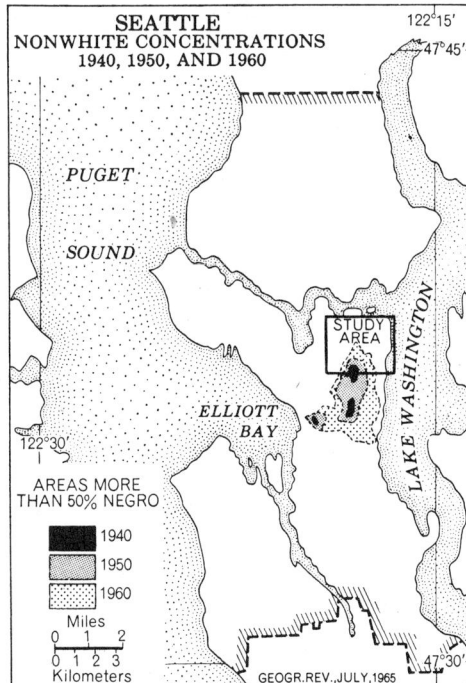

Figure 11.5 The ghetto areas of Seattle. [Redrawn, with permission, from R. M. Morrill, "The Negro ghetto: Problems and alternatives," *Geographical Review,* vol. **55,** 1965, p. 354.]

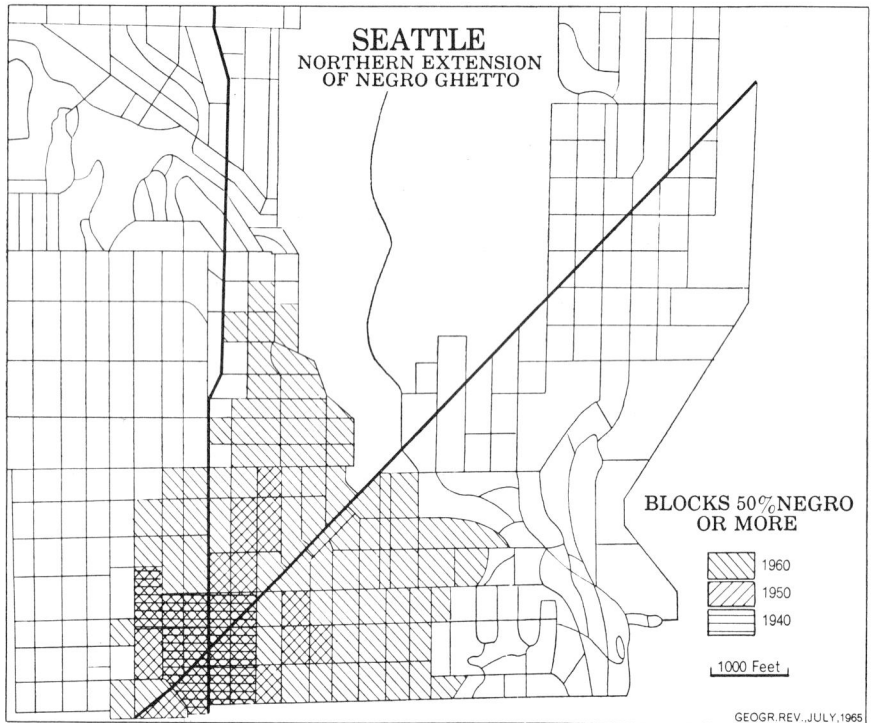

Figure 11.6 Blocks predominantly black in the northern part of Seattle's ghetto. [Redrawn, with permission, from R. M. Morrill, "The Negro ghetto: Problems and alternatives," *Geographical Review*, vol. **55**, 1965, p. 354.]

black family and the white owner but more frequently than not was aided by real estate agents. In the tactic of *block-busting* the real estate agent purchased properties in a white block and then sold to one or two black families. With these established, the pressure on the remaining white families to sell at something less than true market price increased as the real estate agents played upon their fears and false perceptions of drastically falling future property values, deteriorating services, and increasing social problems. Such properties, once acquired by the real estate agent, were then sold at inflated prices to other black families and eventually the block in question switched from white to black in its racial composition. These tactics are now illegal and segregation as such is prohibited by law.

Perceived Environments and Place Utility

Factors influencing intraurban migration are largely individual psychological responses to detailed questions concerning the reasons for movement. Frequently they represent individual perceptions of the environment, both social and physical. A person's perception of his social roles, of the quality of housing and his neighborhood, of the quantity of available dwelling space, his attitudes toward neighbors, and the reconciliation of his expected and perceived levels of aspiration all combine to help influence locational change.

In considering the various factors involved in the migration process, Julian Wolpert defined the term *place utility* as a composite measure of the attractiveness or unattractiveness of an alternative location as perceived by a decision maker.[15] This place utility is a function of levels of information, learning, and search activity, and it enters into the migration decision in two ways:

1. It is a factor in the household's decision to seek a new residence site.
2. It provides a basis for comparing alternative sites.

The measurement of place utility involves the consideration of both household aspiration levels (in terms of the residential environment) and aspects of the existing environment. The relevant variables can be grouped into categories relating to accessibility, the physical characteristics of the neighborhood, the nature of services and facilities, the social environment, and the features of the individual site and dwelling. The maximization of place utility may be viewed operationally as the outcome of matching household aspiration profiles with dwelling unit profiles on each variable.

Movement Destinations and Directions

The final question we ask in regard to intraurban migration is simply, to where do people move? A cursory examination of the individual migration flows for any city shows a complex pattern of crossing lines generally with little clear directional or volume components.

On the city-wide level, certain current trends in the movement of households are illustrated by a study of metropolitan Toronto.[16] In regard to the net flows between areas of the city, outward movements dominate the flow patterns with the inner city and middle suburban areas showing up as the areas losing population (Figure 11.7). When all residential moves are considered, short-distance movements dominate (Figure 11.8); this point has been emphasized in numerous other studies of intraurban movements. Not only are almost all moves short-distance ones, but the frequencies of movements are also reduced as the length of move increases. The findings on Seattle that support this same point were noted earlier in this section. In other words, there

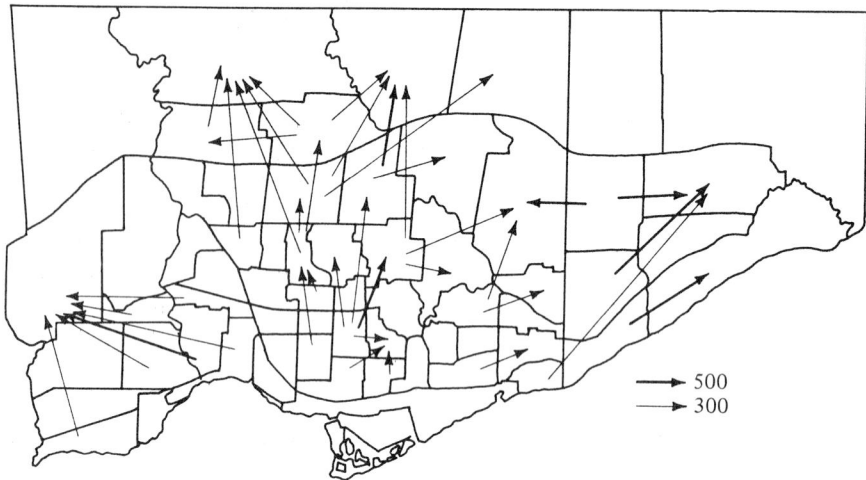

Figure 11.7 Net intraurban migration flows, Toronto, 1958–1964. [J. W. Simmons and A. M. Baker, "Household movement patterns," *Research Report 54*, Center for Urban and Community Studies, University of Toronto, 1972, p. 19.]

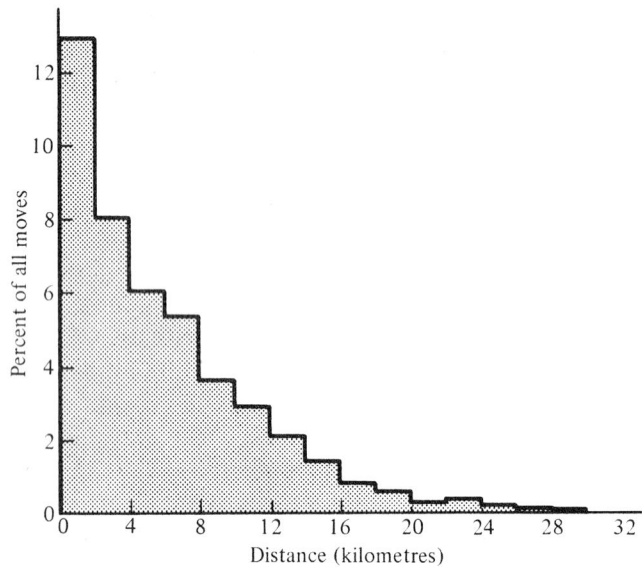

Figure 11.8 Intraurban residential moves by distance. [J. W. Simmons and A. M. Baker, "Household movement patterns," *Research Report 54*, Center for Urban and Community Studies, University of Toronto, 1972, p. 22.]

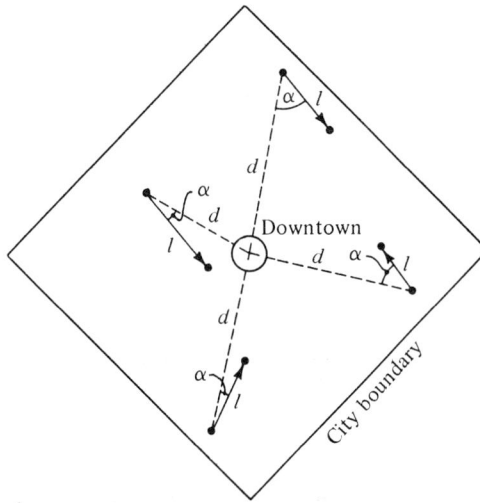

Figure 11.9 Migration moves in a hypothetical urban area. Each directional arrow shows a move from one location to another. The distance of the move is *l*. The direction of the move ($\propto$), is the angle between the line joining the origin and destination locations and a line (*d*) joining the origin location to the center of the city's downtown. [Based on J. S. Adams, "Directional bias in intra-urban migration," *Economic Geography,* **45,** 1969, p. 313.]

is overwhelming evidence that the location of the existing place of residence is a critical factor in determining where people move.

A question related to the one of asking where do people move to within the city is that of asking in what directions are the majority of moves made? The recent research by geographers on this question was stimulated by a study of intraurban migration patterns in the city of Minneapolis.[17] The idea underlying this study was that people in a city have very sharp mental pictures of certain areas of the city and that the best-known areas are likely to form a wedge-shaped sector extending outward to the suburbs and inward toward the downtown area from the place of residence. If we accept this idea, we could expect that when people change their places of residence they would prefer familiar locations within the known sector.

If the direction of a move was measured by the angle between the line connecting the origin and destination and the line joining the origin to the downtown center, then a movement within the same sector should involve an angle close to either 0° or 180° (Figure 11.9). These ideas were tested by using directory data on where samples of people lived in Minneapolis in the 1890's, 1920's, and the late 1940's. When the measurements of the movement angles were related to other measures of the length of the move and the distance of the origin from the downtown area, some interesting patterns emerged. In early

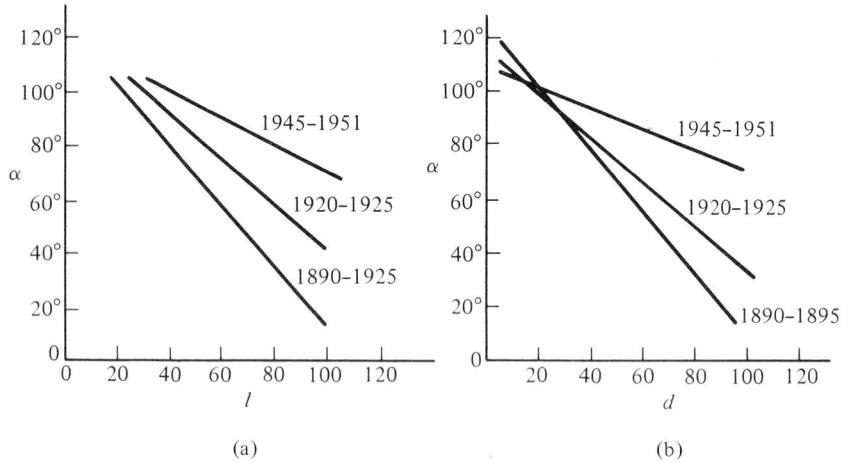

Figure 11.10 Relationships over time between the features illustrated in Figure 11.9. The vertical axis in each graph gives the direction of the migration moves (α), and the horizontal axes involve the distance of the move (l) and the distance from the origin to downtown (d). [Based on J. S. Adams, "Directional bias in intra-urban migration," *Economic Geography,* **45,** 1969, p. 321.]

times, long moves tended to be associated with small angles (inward toward the center of the city) while moves outward (larger angles) tended to be short [Figure 11.10(a)]. The other two lines in this figure suggest that over time this relationship tended to weaken. The relationship between move angles and origin distance [Figure 11.10(b)] suggests that in the 1890's people living in the outer suburbs of the city (large d's) were likely to move inward toward the center of the city (small angles), but that over time this tendency also weakened considerably.

In the few other studies completed so far, the evidence is inconclusive that strong directional biases are characteristic of all intraurban migration patterns. For example, a study of some 5,000 household moves in Christchurch, New Zealand, a city of approximately 250,000 persons, revealed no strong evidence of directional bias in more than two-thirds of the movements that occurred.[18]

11.4   Cognitions of Places and Interpoint Distances

We have already indicated that individuals moving through an urban area accumulate similar bits of information about the area by remembering things in the environment. Now we return to a further discussion of four related questions raised in Chapter 8.

1. Which features of the environment are utilized by individuals in the development of their mental images of cities?
2. Are the features that are selected *structure specific* (that is, are they the same for different city structures or do they differ between city structures)?
3. For certain types of city structures is it easier to develop comprehensive mental images?
4. What influence do variations in physical structure have upon certain types of travel behavior?

Learning About the City

The results of the different studies discussed in this chapter indicate that it is reasonable to assume that in any particular urban environment a selection of critical features or cues will be used by a significant proportion of the population in structuring their *mental maps* of the environment. These cues would also serve as critical places about which to organize information about the city. A list of the more frequently mentioned cues was given in Table 11.8. Let us now consider how we might reconstruct the basic form of an individual's cognitive image of an urban environment by discovering where he thinks places are and how far apart he thinks they are.

It takes time for a person to build a cognitive representation of an environment as complex as a city. How much time we do not know. Let us assume that in order to cope with the demands of everyday living, each individual first develops a skeletal node-path framework that serves as his basic frame of reference for his day-by-day activities in the city [Figure 11.11(a)]. Over time, modifications are made to this cognitive node-path set as information about the external environment is received and classified [Figure 11.11(b)]. We can also assume that initially the preliminary node-path set is tied to the activities of living, working, and recreation and that there are major places in each city that will form part of the skeletal cognitive image for a majority of individuals living there. Learning about an environment then involves the process of continuously adding bits of information to this skeletal node-path set. New locations and new spatial relations among cognitively stored bits of information are added continuously and modifications are made to the image until the relations that exist in objective reality are preserved in the individual's transformed cognitive image [Figure 11.11(c)]. We can also assume that each individual will continue modifying his map until some satisfactory cognitive transformation of objective reality is obtained such that he can operate efficiently on a day-by-day basis in the urban area. At this time, we make no judgments about the nature of the mental transformation used—some

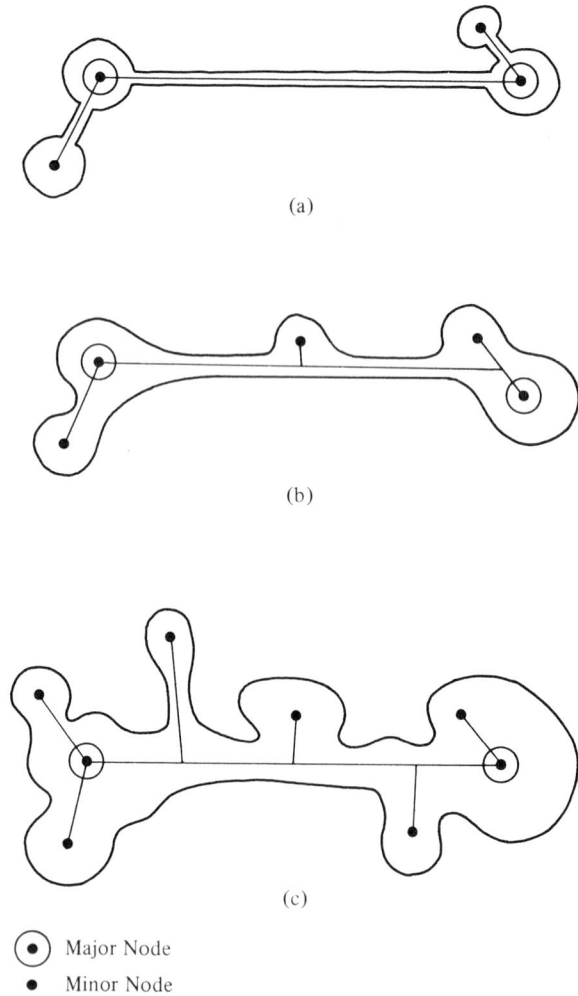

(a)

(b)

(c)

⊙ Major Node
● Minor Node

Figure 11.11 Diagrammatic representation of the development of an individual's cognitive image of a city. (a) Skeletal node-path framework based on home-work relations. (b) Increased awareness of places in vicinity of major nodes. (c) Addition of other minor nodes and increased awareness around major nodes.

urban subgroups and individuals may adopt time transformations of objective reality (that is, distances are expressed in terms of traveling times), some may adopt cost transformations, and others may adopt simple distance transformations. If we accept these assumptions, however, we can reasonably assume that long-time residents of an area and/or populations who are acutely aware of the city will eventually get to know very well (within the limits of their own mental transformation) the relative position of a number of places or environmental cues.

Mental Maps of the City

An extensive study of both student and local population subgroups in the city of Columbus, Ohio, has shown that a number of clearly identifiable distortions of objective reality can be discovered by finding where people think places are and then using this information to produce distorted maps of objective reality.[19] In other words, the approach first establishes the locations of places in the city according to where people think they are and then it derives a series of interpoint distances from these locations and reconstructs a map of the city based on the latent spatial structure represented by these distances. The figures for different individuals, S, in Figure 11.12 show the results of such experiments. The maps are drawn as *contour* maps simply to show

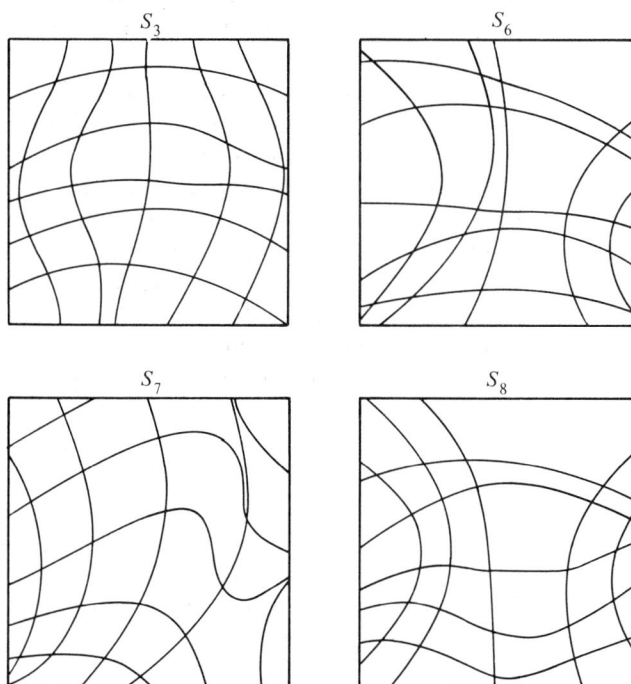

Figure 11.12 Types of cognitive distortions. [After R. G. Golledge, V. L. Rivizzigno, and A. Spector, "Learning about a city: Analysis by multidimensional scaling," in R. G. Golledge and G. Rushton, eds., *Spatial Choice and Spatial Behavior: Geographic Essays on the Analysis of Preferences and Perceptions*, pp. 110–11. Copyright © 1976 by the Ohio State University Press. All rights reserved.]

how the distortion of distances varies away from any point in the city. The distortions are based on the location of the two critical nodes for an individual—the home and the workplace. Three major classes of distortions are shown. First and most obvious is the one in which local (neighborhood) distances are greatly exaggerated producing a transformed map of the city similar to one that might be produced by photographing the city through a fish-eye lens (S_3). A second class of distortions involves a reverse effect (S_6). Here distances in the immediate environment of home and workplace are underestimated while distances to places on the periphery appear overestimated such that interpoint distances on the periphery are exaggerated. A third type of distortion involves either a *northward* pull of downtown locations (S_7) or a *southward* push of these same locations (S_8). Also, in S_6, S_7, and S_8 there is a compression of western locations toward the center of the city. These distortions are significant as far as an individual's use of the city is concerned. *Cognitive distance,* for example, seems to have a much greater discriminatory power in deciding which stores are used for grocery shopping than conventional economic or spatial transforms of distance variables.[20]

An examination of the degree of distortion of various cognitive representations also provides insight into the use of the city by different urban subjects.[21] For example, low-income inner-city residents' maps of the location of well-known places in the city are usually significantly distorted in every direction. Only places in their immediate neighborhood are known with any certainty and incorrect locations of other significant features in the city are very common. By contrast, upper-income suburban residents usually have a greater awareness of the space and range of activities within the urban area, and they are able to locate more correctly the relative positions of places in the city and their approximate distances apart.

In summary, then, the level of information that an individual has about the environment significantly influences his cognitions of distances, proximities, and locations of places within the urban area. This, in turn, influences his behavior within the urban environment in regard to the selection of the routes that he takes to work, his shopping habits, his choice of homesite, and the selection of destinations for many of his day-by-day activities.

11.5 Summary

In this chapter we have examined various patterns of movement within urban areas and have sought explanations of these movements in terms of place utilities, environmental cues, search activity, and individual choice behavior. The lifeblood of a city is the constant movement of people, goods, and ideas. We examined questions related to who moves, why they move, and to where they move. We also detailed some time budgets for activity patterns and suggested that our greatest understanding of the day-by-day functioning of cities derives from knowing why people have to move and what influences their route selections and destinations. To achieve this knowledge, the city was depicted as a trip—a collection of places and paths that sum to form the cognitive images or mental maps that help condition interaction patterns. In doing this, it became obvious that despite everyone's unique information set about any given urban environment, there appears to be a well-defined set of areas, paths, and places that are common to the images of *many* people. These are the city elements that are commonly recognized, commonly used for orientation purposes, and constitute the primary form (or cognitive spatial structure) of the city. Knowing these cues appears to be a critical feature not only for understanding how people use cities today, but also for adequate planning for human use of urban environments in the future.

Notes

1. G. C. HEMMENS, "Analysis and simulation of urban activity patterns," *Socio-Economic Planning Sciences*, **4**, 1970, pp. 53–66.

2. S. DAVIES and M. ALBAUM, "Mobility problems of the poor in Indianapolis," in R. PEET, ed., *Geographical Perspectives on American Poverty* (Worcester, Mass.: Antipode Monographs in Social Geography, 1972), pp. 67–86.

3. *Ibid.*

4. S. CARR and D. SCHISSLER, "The city as a trip: perceptual selection and memory on the view from the road," *Environment and Behavior*, **1**, 1969, pp. 1–35.

5. R. J. JOHNSTON, *Urban Residential Patterns. An Introductory Review* (New York: Praeger Publishers, 1972).

6. See, for example, P. ROSSI, *Why Families Move* (New York: The Free Press, 1955); J. W. SIMMONS, "Changing residence in the city: a review of intraurban mobility," *Geographical Review*, **58**, 1968, pp. 622–51; J. WOLPERT, "Behavioral aspects of the decision to migrate," *Papers*, Regional Science Association, **15**, 1965, pp. 159–69.

7. R. R. BOYCE, "Residential mobility and its implications for urban spatial change," *Proceedings*, Association of American Geographers, **1**, 1969, pp. 22–26.

8. W. A. V. CLARK, "Migration in Milwaukee," *Economic Geography*, **52**, 1976, pp. 48–60.

9. E. CRAVEN, "Private residential expansion in Kent 1956–1964: a study of pattern and process in urban growth," *Urban Studies*, **6**, 1969, pp. 1–16.

10. C. A. MAHER, "Spatial patterns in urban housing markets: filtering in Toronto, 1953–1971," *The Canadian Geographer,* **18,** 1974, pp. 108–24.

11. ROSSI, *op. cit.*

12. P. DE VISE, "Chicago, 1971; ready for another fire?" in R. PEET, ed., *Geographical Perspectives on American Poverty* (Worcester, Mass: Antipode Monographs in Social Geography, 1972), p. 48.

13. D. R. DESKINS, JR., *Residential Mobility of Negroes in Detroit, 1837–1965* (Ann Arbor: Department of Geography, University of Michigan, 1972).

14. R. M. MORRILL, "The Negro Ghetto: problems and alternatives," *Geographical Review,* **55,** 1965, pp. 339–61.

15. WOLPERT, *op. cit.*

16. J. W. SIMMONS and A. M. BAKER, "Household movement patterns," *Research Report 54,* Center for Urban and Community Studies, University of Toronto, 1972.

17. J. S. ADAMS, "Directional bias in intra-urban migration," *Economic Geography,* **45,** 1969, pp. 302–23.

18. W. A. V. CLARK, "A test of directional bias in residential mobility," *Perspectives in Geography 1, Models of Spatial Variation,* 1971, pp. 2–27.

19. R. G. GOLLEDGE, V. L. RIVIZZIGNO, and A. SPECTOR, "Learning about a city: analysis by multidimensional scaling," in R. G. GOLLEDGE and G. RUSHTON, eds., *Spatial Choice and Spatial Behavior* (Columbus, Ohio: The Ohio State University Press, 1976), pp. 95–116.

20. M. T. CADWALLADER, "A methodological examination of cognitive distance," in W. F. E. PREISER, ed., *Environmental Design Research, Vol. II* (Stroudsburg, Penn.: Dowden, Hutchison and Ross, 1973), pp. 193–99.

21. P. ORLEANS, "Differential cognition of urban residents: effects of social scale on mapping," in R. M. DOWNS and D. STEA, eds., *Image and Environment* (Chicago: Aldine Publishing Company, 1973), pp. 115–30.

part 3

Changing the Spatial Organization of Urban Society: Some Possibilities

chapter 12

Cities in Their Regional Settings

In a number of places in this book we have noted the growing size and dominance of the large metropolitan centers in almost all countries of the world. Associated with the growth of these centers have come certain advantages, for example, the achievement of size economies that have allowed activities such as large centers for the performing arts to be supported and for technological developments such as rapid-transit systems to be introduced. It is also in these large urban complexes that civilization finds its highest expression in the whole range of human activities. But there have also come as many, if not more, disadvantages in the form of increased congestion, financial problems, administrative inefficiencies, deterioration of social conditions, environmental pollution, and much degradation of the human condition. Not surprisingly, in the face of such developments there has arisen considerable discussion of the need for national urban growth strategies and development plans that in some way will allow for the curbing of metropolitan growth, the encouragement of urban development at other locations in a country, the removal of regional inequities, and the over-all promotion of an improved quality of life. In this section we shall discuss four particular issues that relate to the city and its regional context and that have been the subject of much attention, namely, the optimal size of cities, the building of new towns, the designation of se-lected urban places as *growth poles,* and the planning of hierarchical urban systems.

12.1   Is There an Optimal Size of a City?

What is the desirable size of a city? This question has generated a great deal of discussion, but, as many critics have pointed out, very little is known about the hard facts of the case.[1]

Minimum Average Cost Approach

A number of studies have approached the question from the point of view of looking at the costs of different urban services and activities as a function of population size. The emphasis is on the shape of the average cost curve and the population size at which this curve has its minimum. The typical analysis is illustrated in Figure 12.1; in this case, city size P_0 would be favored as the optimal size in the sense of minimizing costs. In many studies of North American data this popu-lation size turns out to be around 250,000. But there are at least three weaknesses in this approach, which are as follows:[2]

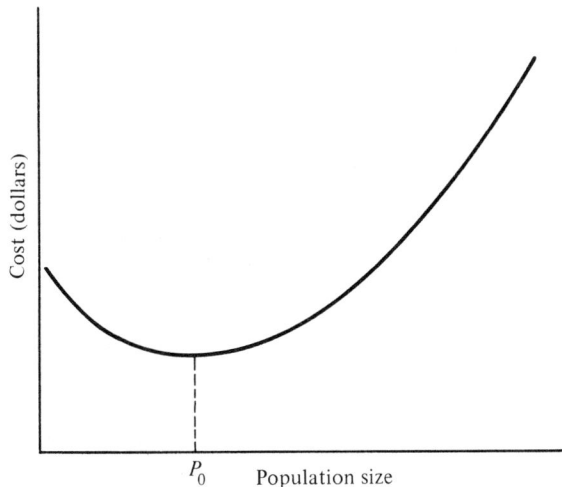

Figure 12.1   Hypothetical average cost curve for urban activities.

1. The studies look at the costs of inputs only and ignore the outputs. If the demand for these outputs is at all responsive to income changes, then in cities with higher incomes much more money may be spent on urban activities and the increased expenditures may not correctly represent any increased expensiveness.

2. The definitions of private goods and public goods in a city are difficult to establish. The costs may either be inflated or deflated in relation to the true costs of city size. For example, how does one put a cost on urban transportation? Is it the cost of public transit or does it also include a cost for private automobile transportation?

3. In a cost-benefit framework it is not always clear which costs should be included. An example would be the teacher cost of education. If in one city high incomes reflect a well-organized teachers' union there, then the cost of education may not be related at all to city size.

An Alternative Model

An economic model of city size in which not only average and marginal costs are assumed but in which there are also given functions for the average and marginal output or benefits is illustrated in Fig-

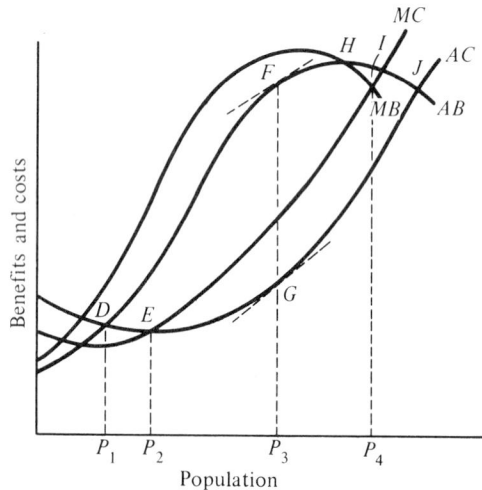

Figure 12.2 Diagram showing urban cost and benefit curves. [After Harry W. Richardson, *The Economics of Urban Size*, p. 11 Saxon House Studies, D.C. Heath Ltd, 1973. Reprinted by Saxon House Studies, Teakfield Ltd, 1977.]

ure 12.2.³ The model assumes that average costs fall and then rise as do marginal costs. Average and marginal benefits are shown as increasing at a faster rate than city size initially, but they then turn downward.

The intersection of the average benefits and average cost curves, P_1, establishes a minimum size for the city since at populations below this the city has higher average costs than benefits. The point of minimum average costs is at P_2, but this is not of interest because it disregards the benefits. There are two other possible city sizes that are of much greater interest. The first is at P_4 where the marginal cost and marginal benefit curves intersect. At this size, then, the cost of adding an additional population unit exactly equals the additional benefits derived, and any national government interested in maximizing total product output, given that surplus labor exists, would aim for this population level. This is, of course, no guarantee that this point exists within a realistic range of population sizes, that is, the curves may not intersect until much farther to the right.

The size P_3 involves a more subtle notion. At this point the slopes of the average cost and average benefit curves are equal and the difference between the two represents a dollar amount that can be thought of as a disposable income per person within the city. At the local city level the interest would be in making this as great as possible and keeping the city size in check. This local interest may well conflict with the national interest referred to above in discussing city size, P_4.

Although it may be possible to hypothesize about the existence of an optimal city size for a city existing in isolation and not as part of an urban system, in reality, cities exist as part of complex urban systems at some particular point in time, and these aspects of city life cannot be ignored when considering the question of the optimal size or probable size of cities of the future. In other words, does the introduction of space negate the value of searching for an optimally sized city? Are urban densities more important than the pure size of population? Another question concerns the influence of location on the optimal size of any given city. For example, if a city is close to a larger city, does this by itself influence the potential optimal size?

What is also important about the general problem of city size is that what may constitute an optimum varies tremendously, depending on the perspective of those making judgments. For example, the optimal size for a manufacturing firm may not represent the optimal size to a city planner. What may constitute an optimal size for a local politician may not constitute an optimal size for the national policy maker. What may constitute an optimal size for an incoming migrant may not constitute an optimal size for a long-time resident.

Pricing of Urban Size Diseconomies

One popular argument in regard to city size maintains that if there were a proper pricing of many of the urban diseconomies such as pollution or traffic congestion, then city size would decrease. But this view has been challenged.[4] For it is possible to show that in a city that produces an export good and a nontraded good, a tax on the effects of pollution associated with the export industry will result under certain conditions in increases not only in the output of all goods in the city, but also in personal utility levels, in immigration into the city, and in the city's overall size. In other words, the popular notion can be refuted.

Two conclusions can be drawn. First, it seems clear that discussions that seek either to establish a unique optimum size for any city in general or for any one city in particular are rather pointless. Second, policies that are aimed at restricting the growth of cities up to certain specified ceilings may be very narrowly conceived and doomed to failure. This seems to have been the case in even the most rigidly planned societies. It has been argued that instead of concentrating on ways of controlling the size of United States cities, much more emphasis should have been placed earlier on the ways of improving their internal organization.[5] In the same vein, it might be argued that it is the role and place of a city in the national urban hierarchy that is the more important question, not simply its size.

12.2   New Towns: A Partial Solution Only

In a number of countries an approach to the decentralization of metropolitan growth has involved the building of new towns. This approach has commanded the most attention in the United Kingdom where, as we shall note below, the passing of the New Towns Act in 1946 was the signal for the creation of some 15 new towns in the period 1946–1951 and this policy has continued. In other countries the approach has won favor only more recently. In the United States, for example, the Demonstration Cities and Metropolitan Development Act of 1966 contained a provision for mortgage insurance for new communities; then in 1968 and 1970 legislation was passed dealing specifically with new communities. Elsewhere, the term *new town* has been applied to new communities created around existing large metropolitan centers, as in the case of those around Paris, or new communities created in association with new industrial complexes, as has often been the case in Eastern Europe and the Soviet Union. In the specific case of the Soviet Union, up until the early 1960's approximately 800 new towns and some 2,000 urban-type settlements had been established

338

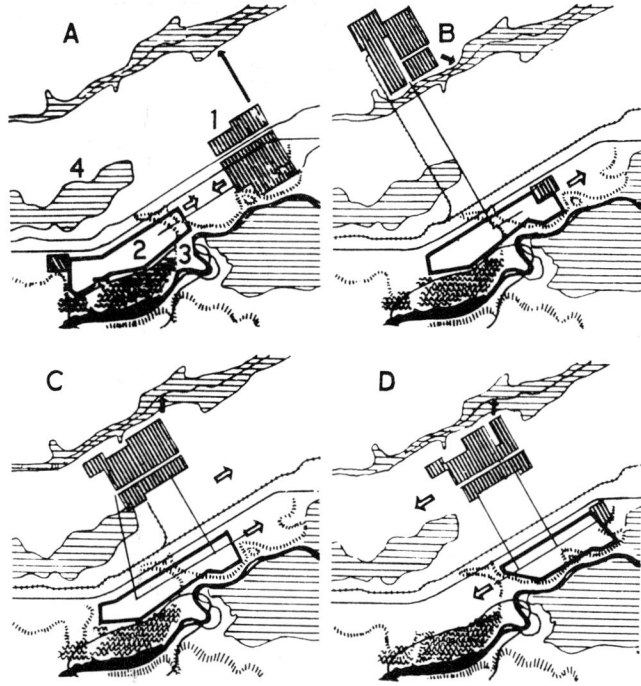

Figure 12.3 New town in the Union of Soviet Socialist Republics. Alternatives considered. The basic alternatives of a new town form centered largely upon the location of oil and chemical industries (1), with certain variations in the location of the residential areas (2), and a common location for recreation (3). Areas unsuitable for development (4) are indicated, as well as areas of possible expansion (arrows). [N.U. Baranov, "Building new towns," in *Planning of Metropolitan Areas and New Towns* (New York: United Nations, 1967), p. 21.]

during Soviet rule.[6] The development of new towns as part of Soviet regional development policies began as early as the 1930's, and cities such as Karaganda, Novokuznetsk, and Magnitogorsk, which were all associated with the development of major heavy industrial complexes east of the Ural Mountains (see Figure 3.7), have now grown into major metropolitan centers. An example of the planning that goes into such new town development in the Soviet Union is shown in Figure 12.3.

New town development associated with industrial development has not been confined to Eastern Europe and the Soviet Union. The development of Gary, Indiana, around the major steel manufacturing complex that was located there early in this century is a well-known example in the United States.

More recently, in Venezuela the creation of the major city of Ciudad Guayana (Figure 12.4), also involving a major steel-making

Figure 12.4 Location of Ciudad Guayana, Venezuela. [Reprinted from *Planning Urban Growth and Regional Development* by L. Rodwin and associates (1969) by permission of the MIT Press Cambridge, Massachusetts.]

complex, has attracted a great deal of attention, perhaps because a team of planners from the United States and elsewhere were involved in the planning of the city from the beginning.[7] The city was built in a region that has rich iron-ore and other mineral deposits and vast hydroelectricity resources. It also lies within 60 miles of large fields of petroleum and natural gas. The planned land-use development of the city is shown in Figure 12.5. The creation of this city was a government enterprise and the plan called for the government to invest $2 billion over the period 1965–1975. During this time it was planned that the city would grow to a size of approximately a quarter of a million people and that it would provide about one-fifth of the country's manufacturing and export products.

One other form of new town development that should be noted is that of the building of capital cities. Washington, D.C. was one such example, but even more recent ones have been built, such as Canberra in Australia, Islamabad in Pakistan, and Brasilia in Brazil. The location and overall plan for Brasilia are shown in Figure 12.6.

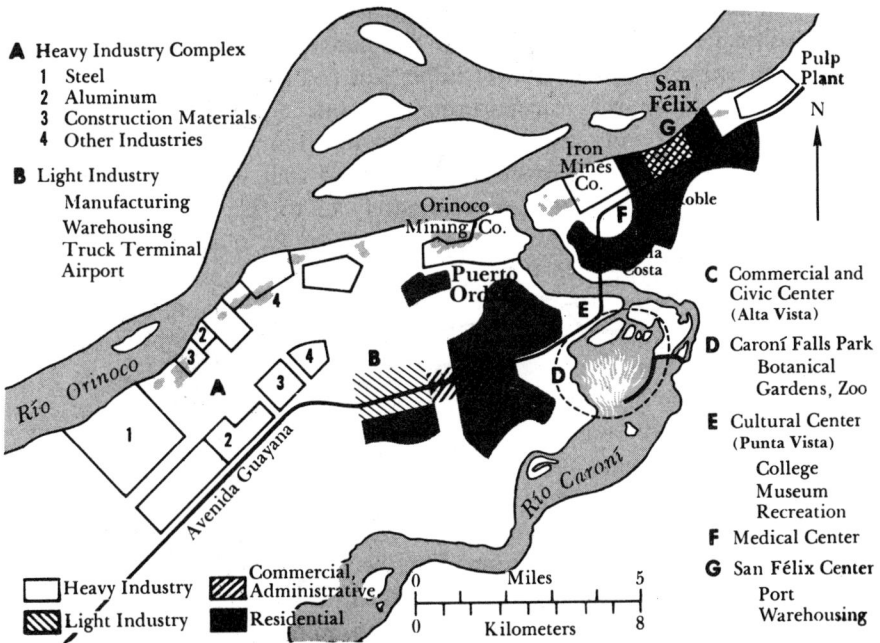

Figure 12.5 Planned land use of Ciudad Guayana. [Reprinted from *Planning Urban Growth and Regional Development* by L. Rodwin and associates (1969) by permission of the MIT Press Cambridge, Massachusetts.]

New Towns in the United Kingdom

The new towns policy in the United Kingdom was formally launched in 1946 with the passage of the New Towns Act, although the idea of building new towns in that country had been under discussion for many decades. In the Britain of the mid-1940's the problems of metropolitan growth and sprawl already were very pressing ones, especially in the London and Glasgow areas. There were already in these large urban agglomerations considerable slum housing and overcrowding, housing shortages and high rent, pollution of the environment, and increasing encroachment upon the existing open spaces.

Each new town was established as a deliberate government act. A Development Corporation was set up to finance and oversee the town construction. By 1950 as many as 14 new towns had been established of which 3, located between 20 to 30 miles from London, were designed to accommodate overspill from that metropolitan region or conurbation (Table 12.1). Two others were overspill towns for Glasgow while 3 of the remaining towns performed a different role in that they were designed to help promote development in specially designated problem

BOA VISTA 1 545
MACAPA 1 105
BELEM 985
SAO LUIZ 950
MANAUS
TERESINA 820
FORTALEZA 1 060
NATAL 1 145
JOAO PESSOA 1 110
POCTO VELHO 1 175
RECIFE 1 065
MACEIO 930
RIO BRANCO 1 395
ARACAJU 800
SALVADOR 665
CUIABA 545
BRASILIA
GOIAMA 110
VITORIA 590
SÃO PAULO 545
BELO HORIZONTE 390
RIO DE JANEIRO 575
CURITIBA 670
FLORIANOPOLIS 815
PORTO ALEGRE 1 005

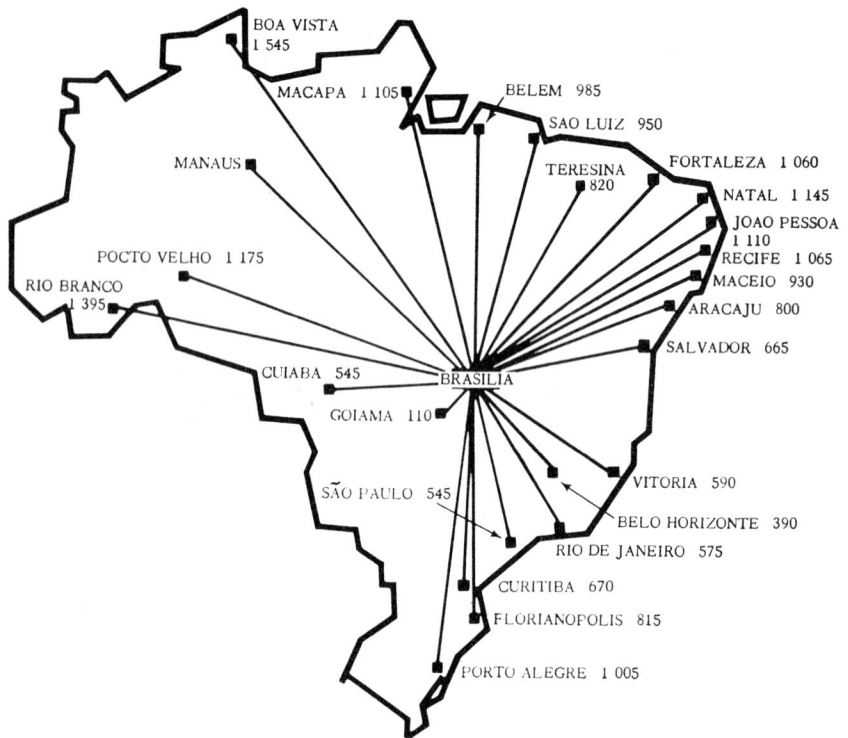

areas. Newton Aycliffe and Peterlee were located in the depressed industrial region of the northeast and Cwmbran was located in South Wales. Corby, the fourteenth center, was built to serve the needs of a major steelwork.

The new towns were intended to be self-contained economically and well-balanced in terms of the demographic, social, and occupational mixes of their inhabitants. The availability of public housing, which comprised at least half of the housing stock in each new town, was offered as an inducement to industries willing to locate in the towns. Almost all of the towns were planned with target populations somewhere in the range 25,000 to 80,000, although many of these have later been revised upward (Table 12.1).

Apart from the development of Cumbernauld in the Glasgow region in 1955, there was no further establishment of new towns during the decade of the 1950's. In 1952, however, there was a significant shift in urban policy marked by the passing of the Town Development Act. Whereas under the provisions of the New Towns Act the government had to take the initiative in setting up a Development Corporation to plan the new town, now a cooperative undertaking was called

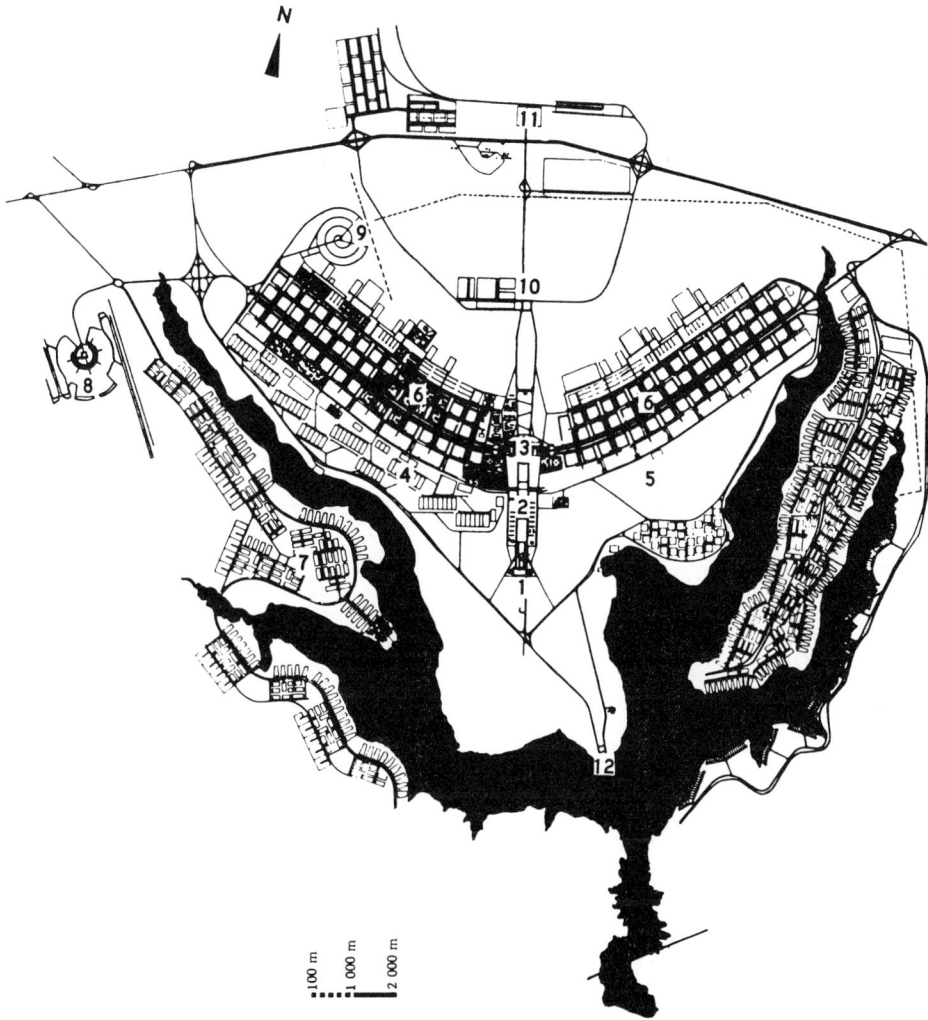

Brasilia

Figure 12.6 Location (see p. 342) and plan (above) for Brasilia, Brazil. *Key:* (1) Plaza of Three Powers, (2) ministries, (3) bus station, (4) embassies, (5) university, (6) residential zone (housing unities), (7) residential zone (individual houses), (8) airport, (9) cemetery, (10) municipal square, (11) railway station, (12) presidential residence. [J. E. Hardoy, "The planning of new capital cities," in *Planning of Metropolitan Areas and New Towns* (New York: United Nations, 1967), pp. 240–41.]

Table 12.1 New Towns in Britain, January, 1971. [M. Clawson and P. Hall, *Planning and Urban Growth: An Anglo-American Comparison* (Baltimore: The Johns Hopkins University Press, 1973), p. 205.]

	Date of Designation	Original Population	Target Population		Distance from Conurbation or City Center (miles)
			Original	Revised	
		(all populations in 1,000s)			
CONURBATION OVERSPILL TOWNS					
Greater London					
Stevenage	1946	7	60	105	32
Crawley	1947	9	50	80	31
Hemel Hempstead	1947	21	80	—	25
Harlow	1947	4	60	90	25
Hatfield	1948	8	29	—	21
Welwyn Garden City	1948	18	36	50	23
Basildon	1949	25	50	133	29
Bracknell	1949	5	25	61	30
Milton Keynes	1967	40	250	—	49
Peterborough	1967	84	190	—	81
Northampton	1968	131	300	—	66
Birmingham (West Midlands)					
Telford (Dawley)	1963	70	90	220	34
Redditch	1964	32	90	—	14
Liverpool (Merseyside)					
Skelmersdale†	1961	8	80	—	12
Runcorn*	1964	28	100	—	14
Manchester (South East Lancashire/North East Cheshire)					
Warrington	1968	122	200	—	18
Central Lancashire	1970	240	430	—	30
Newcastle Upon Tyne (Tyneside)					
Washington*	1964	20	80	—	8
Glasgow (Central Clydeside)					
East Kilbride*	1947	2	45	100	9
Glenrothes*·†	1948	1	32	95	58
Cumbernauld*	1955	3	70	—	14
Livingston*	1962	2	100	—	26
Irvine*	1966	36	116	—	26
DEVELOPMENT AREA TOWNS					
Newton Aycliffe	1947	0	10	45	—
Peterlee	1948	200	30	—	—
Cwmbran	1949	12	55	—	—
Newtown	1967	6	11	—	—
OTHER TOWNS					
Corby	1950	16	40	80	—
TOTAL (28)		1,210	2,709	3,270‡	

*Also served development area purposes and receives development area aid.

†Not originally designated for Glasgow overspill purposes but received this function after failure of original purpose (development of new coal mine in Fife coalfield).

‡Including original targets for towns where these were not revised.

for between the large congested cities seeking relief in the form of houses and jobs for their inhabitants and those smaller communities that were anxious to have the stimulus of planned growth. London has such arrangements with more than 30 smaller surrounding cities.

The policy of building new towns was suspended by the Conservative government in the 1950's, but it was revived in 1961 with the development of Skelmersdale as an overspill community for Liverpool. This second phase of new town development in the 1960's differed from the earlier phase in at least two respects.[8] First, the towns were planned to be larger communities with target populations more than double the size of the earlier new towns. Milton Keynes, for example, was planned to be a city of 250,000 persons, while the Central Lancashire city will be formed by an expansion of an existing urban center of 240,000 into a city of over 400,000 (Table 12.1). Second, many of these newer overspill communities are planned to be at greater distances from the "exporting" metropolitan region than was typically the case with the original new towns. Peterborough, which is to cater to London's overspill is over 80 miles away; Milton Keynes is 49 miles from London (Figure 12.7).

The optimistic planner might interpret these contrasts between the two phases of new town development simply as expressions of the better understanding of how urban size and the distance to larger cities influence a city's economic viability and its cultural and social life. The pessimist, however, might well see the same contrasts as providing further evidence of the continual upward adjustment of target levels and plans that are inevitably forced upon society by the uninterrupted growth of urban populations and the ever-widening spheres of influence of the large metropolitan centers. Besides, the British new towns policy achieved its objectives for only a small minority of people. In other words,

> "a total of 750,000 new residents in public housing in planned communities is a small proportion of the people who have been housed in the $6\frac{1}{2}$ million new dwellings built in England and Wales during this quarter century—a total of people which must amount to close to 20 million if not more."[9]

New Towns in the United States

The United States has not developed new towns in the way that the United Kingdom developed them. Given the tremendous urban growth that has occurred in the United States over the past several decades, it is not surprising that there have been numerous new towns created, ranging in character from company towns (Gary, Indiana, for

Figure 12.7 Location of new towns in United Kingdom. [M. Clawson and P. Hall, *Planning and Urban Growth: An Anglo-American Comparison* (Baltimore: The Johns Hopkins University Press, 1973), p. 203.]

example) to suburban communities (such as Park Forest, Illinois), and even including utopian communities such as New Harmony, Indiana. All of these different communities, however, had one thing in common: They were developed by private enterprise. More recently, the creation of Reston and Columbia both outside but adjacent to the Washington D.C. metropolitan area, reflected this same reliance upon private development and capital. Reston, begun in 1962 and eventually taken over as a development by the Gulf Oil Corporation, is today a community of approximately 25,000 persons. Columbia, which was also launched in the early 1960's, is planned to have a population of around 110,000 by the mid-1980's. This too is a large-scale development financed by private capital.

In evaluating the prospects for a new towns program for the United States, it is probably true that the replication of the conditions on which the British program was based, namely, mass programs of subsidized public housing and public ownership of land, a semi-autonomous public corporation with direct financing from central government, and the means to attract industry to the new towns, would be difficult to achieve in total. Even if the conditions could be established, the contribution of such a program to the handling of the total national population increase could only be very small.

Nevertheless, since 1965 in the United States there has been a growing involvement of the federal government in the encouragement of new town development. This encouragement takes the form of mortgage insurance and different financial guarantees for private developers involved in building the new communities. The main legislative contributions to this federal program are summarized in Table 12.2.

Under the 1970 Act, four main types of development projects were declared eligible for federal assistance. These have been described as follows:[10]

1. "Satellite or suburban new communities ... located within or directly adjacent to metropolitan areas ... as alternatives to urban sprawl."
2. "New-towns-in town ... adjacent to or within existing cities. They may be planned for vacant land or land requiring redevelopment. They serve to revitalize existing urban centers, stabilize surrounding neighborhoods, and provide a full range of housing within easy access of center city populations."
3. "Small town growth centers ... in rural areas with potential growth."
4. "Free-standing new communities ... some distance away from existing urban areas where economic feasibility can be demonstrated."

Table 12.2   U.S. Legislation Related to New Town Development. [H. Mields, Jr., *Federally Assisted New Communities: New Dimensions in Urban Development* (Washington, D.C.: The Urban Land Institute, 1973), p. 22.]

Federal New Communities Programs

Program Title	Legislative Source	Primary Purpose
Mortgage Insurance for Land Development and New Communities* (Title X)	Housing and Urban Development Act of 1965 (Public Law 89-117.79 Stat. 451, 461)	To insure mortgages for land acquisition and site improvement by private developers.
New Communities Program: Loan Guarantees and Supplementary Grants (Title IV)	Housing and Urban Development Act of 1968 (Public Law 90-448, 82 Stat. 476, 513; 42 U.S.C. 390 *et seq.*)	To guarantee bonds, debentures, and notes of private new community developers and to assist in the development of new community facilities through supplementary grants.
New Communities Assistance Program (Title VII)	Housing and Urban Development Act of 1970 (Public Law 91-609, 84 Stat. 1770)	To guarantee bonds, debentures, etc., of private and public new community developers and to provide other development assistance through interest loans and grants, public service grants, planning assistance, etc.

*"New Communities" were made eligible for Title X assistance by Section 401(a) of the Demonstration Cities and Metropolitan Development Act of 1966. Public Law 89-754 approved November 3, 1966, 80 Stat. 1255, 1271.

By the end of 1972 as many as 15 new communities had received guarantees from the federal government under this expanded program. As Table 12.3 shows, the majority of these were satellite-type communities. Another 20 or so plans for new communities also were at various stages of consideration by the federal government at this date.

Possible criticism to the effect that almost all of these new towns in the United States cater mainly to persons in the middle- and upper-income brackets is partially offset by the case of Soul City, North Carolina. This development, the brainchild of Floyd McKissick, a former Director of the Congress for Racial Equality (CORE), is planned as a community principally for those who are at present disadvantaged and poor. Although not designed simply as a community for black inhabitants, it is a project that has been conceived and fought for predominantly by black individuals.[11]

12.3 Cities as Growth Poles: An Unproven Strategy?

In the above discussion of the 1970 Title VII legislation in the United States we referred to the notion of a *growth center*. This idea of a potential growth center, or a *growth pole* as it is commonly called, has commanded a great deal of attention in recent years in regard to regional development policies.

As originally proposed by a French economist, Francis Perroux,[12] the idea of a *pole* was identified with a fast-growing sector of the economy that exerted a propulsive effect on other sectors of the economy. The economic mechanisms by which this effect was transmitted through the economy can be thought of in terms of the input-output framework that we introduced earlier. In other words, industries have linkages with other industries, either as producers or consumers. By using an input-output table we can trace the effects of growth in the sector identified as a pole.

Spatial Growth Poles

The concept of a growth pole was later modified by regional planners to refer to a region or a city whose growth would also generate growth in the surrounding areas.[13] In this sense, a city or region could be thought of as a growth pole, and presumably if investment could be channeled into such centers, there would be beneficial spillover effects into the surrounding regions. But there are difficulties in reconciling these spatial views with those proposed by Perroux. For example, there may indeed exist a clustering or agglomeration of activities in economic space (in Perroux's sense), but there may be no corresponding clustering of these activities in geographical space.[14] Conversely, there may be a geographic concentration of growth industries that may be only weakly related or clustered, if at all, in the sense of economic dependencies and input-output relations.

These difficulties, however, have done little to detract from the growing popularity of the growth pole hypothesis in discussions of regional planning policies in the United States,[15] Europe, Africa, and Latin America.[16]

Appalachian Growth Areas

Within the United States the activities of the Appalachian Regional Development Act in 1965 provide a good illustration of the application of the growth pole concept in an actual planning situation. The Appalachian Development Act stipulated that "the public investments made in the region ... shall be concentrated in areas where

349

Table 12.3 New Town Developments in the U.S. [H. Mields, Jr., *Federally Assisted New Communities: New Dimensions in Urban Development* (Washington, D.C.: The Urban Land Institute, 1973), p. 27.]

Summary of New Communities Guaranteed by HUD*
(Dollars in Thousands)

Community	Type	Guarantee Commitment Amount / Date	Guarantee Issues Amount / Date	Interest Rate	Population (Projected)	Dwelling Units (Projected)	Location
Jonathan, Minnesota	Satellite/ growth center	$21,000 2/70	$ 8,000 10/72† $13,000 6/72	8.50% 7.20%	50,000 in 20 years	16,500 in 20 years	20 mi. S.W. of Minneapolis
St. Charles Communities, Maryland	Satellite	$24,000 6/70	$18,000 12/70	7.75%	75,000 in 20 years	25,000 in 20 years	25 mi. S.W. of Wash., D.C.
Park Forest South, Illinois	Satellite	$30,000 6/70	$30,000 3/71	7.00%	110,000 in 15 years	35,000 in 15 years	30 mi. S. of Chicago
Flower Mound, Texas	Satellite	$18,000 12/70	$14,000 10/71	7.60%	64,000 in 20 years	18,000 in 20 years	20 mi. S.W. of Dallas
Maumelle, Arkansas	Satellite	$ 7,500 12/70	$ 4,500 6/72	7.62%	45,000 in 20 years	14,000 in 20 years	12 mi. N.W. of Little Rock
Cedar-Riverside, Minnesota	New-Town-In-Town	$24,000 6/71	$24,000 12/71	7.20%	30,000 in 20 years	12,500 in 20 years	Downtown Minneapolis

Name	Type			Interest	Projected population	Current target population	Location
Riverton, New York	Satellite	$12,000	$12,000 5/72	7.125%	25,600 in 16 years	8,000 in 16 years	10 mi. S. of Rochester
San Antonio Ranch, Texas‡	Satellite	$18,000 2/72	—	—	88,000 in 30 years	28,000 in 30 years	20 mi. N.W. of San Antonio
The Woodlands, Texas	Satellite	$50,000 4/72	$50,000 9/72	7.10%	150,000 in 20 years	49,160 in 20 years	30 mi. N.W. of Houston
Gananda, New York	Satellite	$22,000 4/72	$22,000 12/72	7.15%	50,000 in 20 years	17,200 in 20 years	12 mi. E. of Rochester
Soul City, North Carolina	Free-Standing	$14,000 6/72	—	—	44,000 in 30 years	12,906 in 30 years	45 mi. N. of Raleigh–Durham
Harbison, South Carolina	Satellite	$13,000 10/72	—	—	23,000 in 20 years	6,750 in 20 years	8 mi. N.W. of Columbia
Lysander, New York	Satellite	§	‖	‖	18,300 in 8 years	5,000 in 8 years	12 mi. N.W. of Syracuse
Welfare Island, New York	New-Town-In-Town	§ 12/72	—	—	18,000 in 7 years	5,000 in 7 years	In New York City
Shenandoah, Georgia	Satellite/growth center	$40,000 2/73	—	—	70,000 in 20 years	23,000 in 20 years	35 mi. S.W. of Atlanta

*Source: Department of Housing and Urban Development, as of February 1973.
†Guaranteed under Title IV; all other guarantees under Title VII.
‡Contingent on water protection studies.
§Eligible for 20% grant from HUD supplementing basic federal grant programs.
‖ First to receive a determination of eligibility for grant assistance rather than federal guarantee of its debt; receives federal assistance under Title VII, Housing and Urban Development Act of 1970.

there is the greatest potential for future growth, and where the expected return on public dollars will be the greatest." With this goal in mind, the Appalachian Regional Commission, in consultation with the states involved, set about designating potential growth areas and channeling investment into the growth centers associated with these areas. From 1965–1969 almost all of the investment was concentrated in the centers listed in Table 12.4. As can be seen, the total level of

Table 12.4 Investment in Appalachian Growth Centers, 1965–1969. [N. M. Hansen, *Growth Centers in Regional Economic Development* (New York: The Free Press, 1972), pp. 271–72. Copyright © 1972 by The Free Press.]

Northern Appalachia	
Greater Pittsburgh (Pa.)	$9,883,216
Cumberland (Md.)	4,993,114
Wilkes-Barre–Scranton (Pa.)	4,441,903
Altoona-Johnstown (Pa.)	3,898,746
Binghamton (N.Y.)	3,537,020
Sharon–New Castle (Pa.)	3,498,638
New Philadelphia–Cambridge (O.)	3,368,493
Hornell (N.Y.)	2,717,173
Parkersburg-Marietta (W. Va./O.)	2,483,329
Williamsport (Pa.)	2,432,975
Huntington-Ashland-Ironton (O./W. Va./Ky.)	N.A.
Hagerstown-Martinsburg (Md./W. Va.)	1,731,948
Elmira (N.Y.)	1,773,357
Erie (Pa.)	1,650,000
Charleston (W. Va.)	1,392,211
Southern Appalachia	
Florence-Decatur-Huntsville (Ala.)	$10,454,584
Gadsden-Anniston (Ala.)	7,168,953
Greenville-Spartanburg (S.C.)	4,914,596
Birmingham (Ala.)	3,491,231
Tri-Cities (Tenn./Va.)	2,997,983
Knoxville (Tenn.)	2,344,287
Asheville (N.C.)	2,133,906
Chattanooga (Tenn.)	1,860,901
Carrollton (Ga.)	1,869,889
Tuscaloosa (Ala.)	1,771,742
Pontotoc-Tupelo (Miss.)	1,479,529
Central Appalachia	
Cookeville-Crosville (Tenn.)	$3,083,841
Paintsville-Prestonburg-Pikeville (Ky.)	2,859,256
London-Corbin-Middlesboro (Ky.)	2,403,480
Appalachian Highlands	
State College (Pa.)	$1,465,523

investment in these centers over that period was less than $100 million, a very modest total indeed when one is talking about creating employment opportunities and providing improved urban services and facilities in a region with an estimated 1966 population of around 18 million of whom probably one-third or more were existing at or below the poverty level.[17]

The Example of Ontario

Provincial planning in Ontario, Canada, provides another illustration of the incorporation of growth center concepts. Under the Design for Development that was fashioned in the 1960's a conscious attempt was made to identify potential growth centers, or *growth points*, in the province (see Figure 12.8). The intent was expressed as follows:

> By stimulating these outlying centres so that they can attract many more residents and commuters, we can reduce the in-

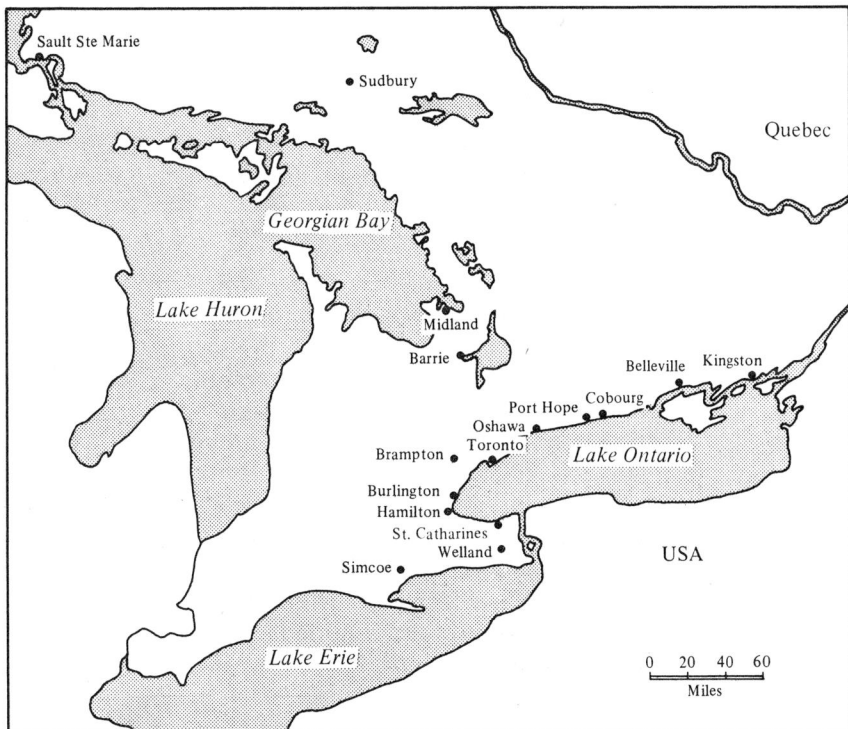

Figure 12.8 Growth centers in Ontario, Canada. [L. J. King, "Conceptual limitations and data problems in the fashioning of growth pole strategies: The case of Ontario, Canada," *Geoforum,* **17,** 1974, p. 62.]

creasing congestion within, and now extending mainly westward from, Metropolitan Toronto. At the same time, we
shall be laying the basic framework for a carefully planned
decentralized urban region of the future.[18]

The analyses completed in connection with this plan identified centers
such as Barrie and Midland in northern Ontario, Port Hope and
Cobourg in the east, and Burlington, Hamilton, St. Catharines, and
Simcoe in the south as having the greater potential for development.[19]

To date, however, there has only been a very restricted program
of economic incentives aimed at encouraging investment and growth in
centers such as these. There still does not exist a clearly defined urban
and regional development program for Ontario.

Growth center policies have been outlined for many other
countries throughout the world. These statements make clear the
tremendous diversity that exists from country to country in the goals
and objectives that are sought and in the growth center policies that
are practiced. The common theme running throughout all of them,
however, is that regional development is seen as a benefit to be gained
from emphasizing growth and investment at a few selected locations
instead of at all of the centers throughout the country. The key, in
other words, is unbalanced growth.

12.4 Hierarchical Urban Systems: A Key to Balanced Development?

Our earlier discussions of central place functions and central place
theory emphasized the existence of hierarchical urban systems, with
cities and towns at different levels performing different roles and offering particular mixes of goods and services. These hierarchical arrangements have been found to be characteristic of urban systems in contrasting cultural realms and also at different periods in history.

Underlying the discussions of these hierarchical systems, and at
times stated explicitly, is the premise that such an ordering of urban
centers is both *efficient* and *equitable* from the points of view of producers
and consumers alike. Whether or not these same conclusions are warranted in the case of actual urban systems that differ markedly from
the *ideal* systems so often assumed in the discussions is a question that
has received little attention. Nevertheless, it is hardly surprising that
many proposals relating to regional development strategies and national urban policies take the position that the establishment of a well-
developed hierarchical urban system is an appropriate means of at-
taining the goals of balanced regional development and more equitable
spatial patterns of economic and social well-being.[20]

Qualitative Application of Central Place Concepts

In the actual practice of regional planning the concept of a hierarchical urban system has provided the basis for many proposals. We can recognize two main streams of work in this regard. There are first of all the many plans and proposals that resulted from essentially qualitative analyses of different planning problems using central place theory as a model. One can point, for example, to the work of the Saskatchewan Royal Commission on Agriculture and Rural Life that recommended that "public policy encourage the reorganization of rural services on the bases of the service center principles demonstrated in (its) report." These were the principles of Christaller's central place theory.[21] Figure 12.9 illustrates the type of analysis that was characteristic of the Commission's report. A similar example is provided in a planning study of Ghana's urban system that proposed the addition of several new urban centers in order that "the increasing quantity of services should be distributed between centres to ensure the maximum benefit from the resources available."[22] In a different context but using similar arguments derived from Christaller's central

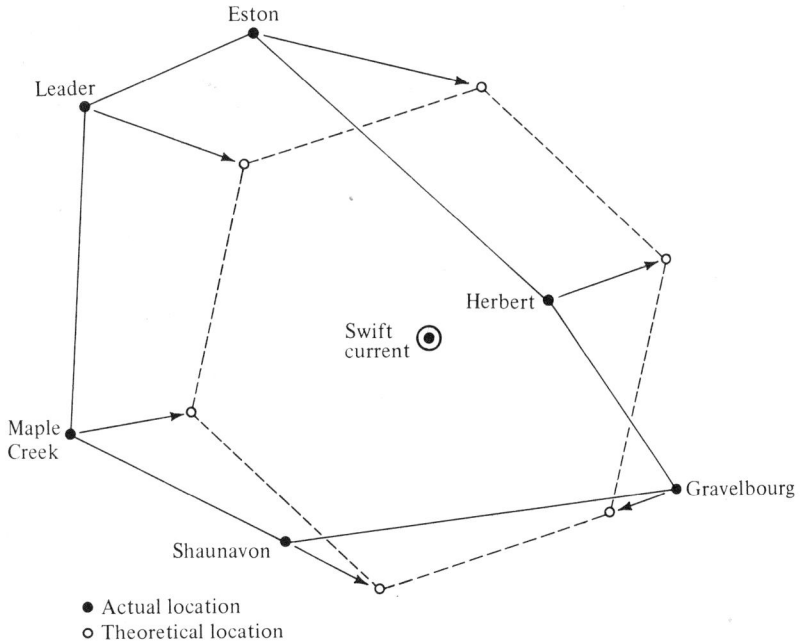

Figure 12.9 Actual and theoretical locations of six towns in Swift Current System, Saskatchewan. [Based on Saskatchewan Royal Commission on Agriculture and Rural Life, "Service centers," *Report No. 12*, Regina, Saskatchewan, 1957, p. 80.]

Figure 12.10 Zuiderzee reclamations. [J. P. Thijsse, "A rural pattern for the future in The Netherlands," *Papers*, Regional Science Association, **10**, 1962, p. 138.]

Legend on figure:

• Existing and planned towns and villages

○ Villages according to Pattern

Scale: 0   10   20   30 km

place theory, Thijsse has criticized the urban patterns developed on The Netherlands' Zuiderzee reclamation areas (Figure 12.10).[23]

Perhaps some of the most fruitful planning work, using central place concepts as its basis, was that completed in Sweden. In the 1950's and 1960's, using central place principles, Swedish geographers profoundly influenced and helped shape national planning policies regarding the location of educational institutions, regional hospitals, and community centers. New administrative regions, the *municipality blocks*, were also devised as part of the reorganization of the country's administrative structure. It has been suggested that "this redrawing of the map of Sweden unquestionably represents the most significant contribution of central place research to that country's planning."[24]

Mathematical Solutions

The second stream of work on hierarchical urban systems is a more recent development and involves mathematical programming solutions to particular planning problems. Banerji and Fisher have illustrated this approach.[25] They were concerned with the question of where to locate certain public facilities (schools, hospitals, and so on) in community development blocks in rural India. Each of these blocks contained on an average 125 urban settlements and had a total population of 125,000. They reviewed two possible solutions. First, one could determine the minimum number of locations needed to serve every settlement in the study area such that no settlement would be more than a given distance away from a facility. This so-called *set-covering* approach generates the output shown in Figure 12.11. But this solution may in fact be a very expensive one. As an alternative, one could determine the best location pattern for a given set of say p facilities, such that the total travel involved in having all the settlements served by these p facilities is minimized. This is the so-called *p-median* problem. Banerji and Fisher combined elements of the two approaches in their plan. They assumed that for some settlements it would be acceptable to exceed the maximum travel distance constraint involved in the set-covering approach. Then, having established a prescribed travel distance standard, they determined how many locations (p) would be needed and sought to locate these p facilities in order to minimize total user (travel) cost. Adjustments could then be made to take into account existing infrastructure. A final solution for one block is illustrated in Figures 12.12 and 12.13.

Another application of the p-median approach began with the existing urban hierarchy in Sierra Leone (Figure 12.14) and the existing pattern of population distribution. It then assigned the different

Location codes of centers chosen after
adjusting results of P-median algorithm

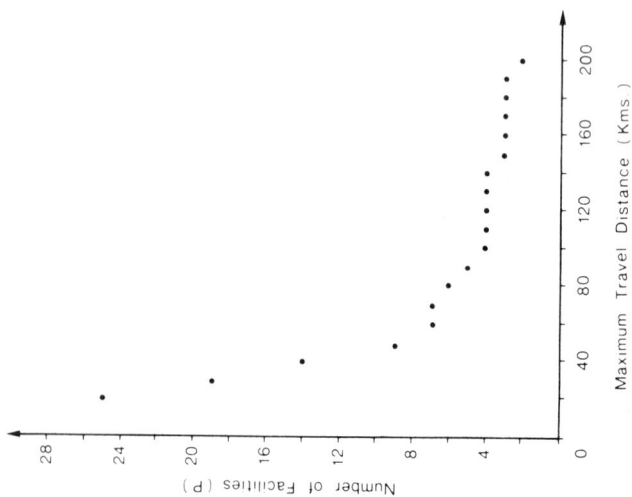

Maximum travel distance, standards,
and values of P determined by
set-covering algorithm

Examples of facilities
planned for each level

$D_{max} = 20$ km
$P = 2$

Hospitals, colleges,
regulated markets, etc.

$D_{max} = 15$ km
$P = 3$

Technical schools
market sub-yards, etc.

$D_{max} = 10$ km
$P = 4$

High schools, primary
health centers, etc.

$D_{max} = 8$ km
$P = 7$

Middle schools,
post offices, etc.

$D_{max} = 3$ km
$P = 19$

Primary schools, market
cooperatives, etc.

20   24

20   26   24

20   26   17   24

19   14   10   17

19   14   10   20   26   17   24

28 29 1   2   3   4   7 11 15 16 18 22

Figure 12.12 Nested hierarchical pattern of the Phirangipuram block. The numbers for the location codes correspond to the numbers in Figure 12.14. [S. Banerji and H. B. Fisher, "Hierarchical location analysis for integrated area planning in rural India," *Papers, Regional Science Association*, **33**, 1974, p. 187.]

Figure 12.11 Minimum number of facility locations to cover all settlements in the Phirangipuram block of Andhra Pradesh. [S. Banerji and H. B. Fisher, "Hierarchical location analysis for integrated area planning in rural India," *Papers, Regional Science Association*, **33**, 1974, pp. 177–94.]

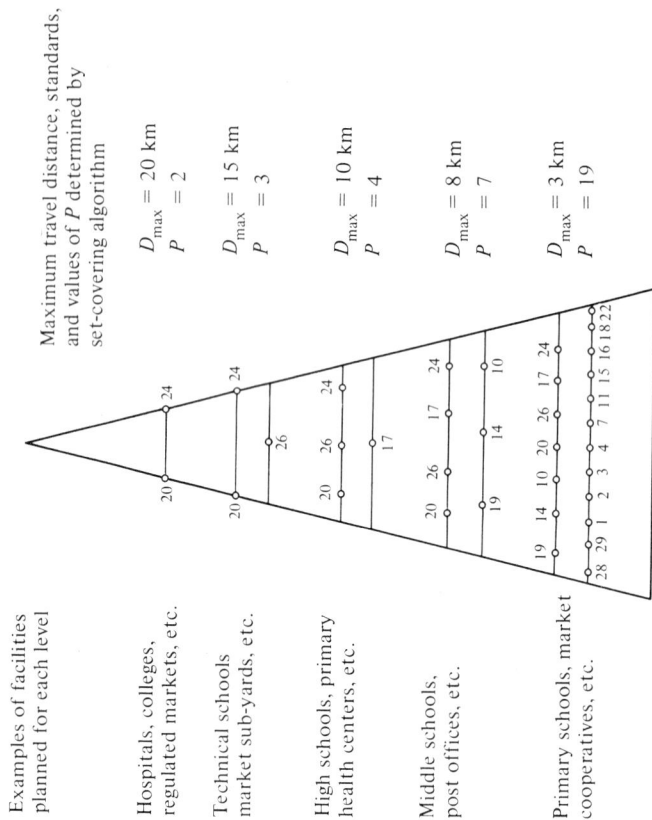

Number of Facilities (P)

28   24   20   16   12   8   4

Maximum Travel Distance (Kms)

0   40   80   120   160   200

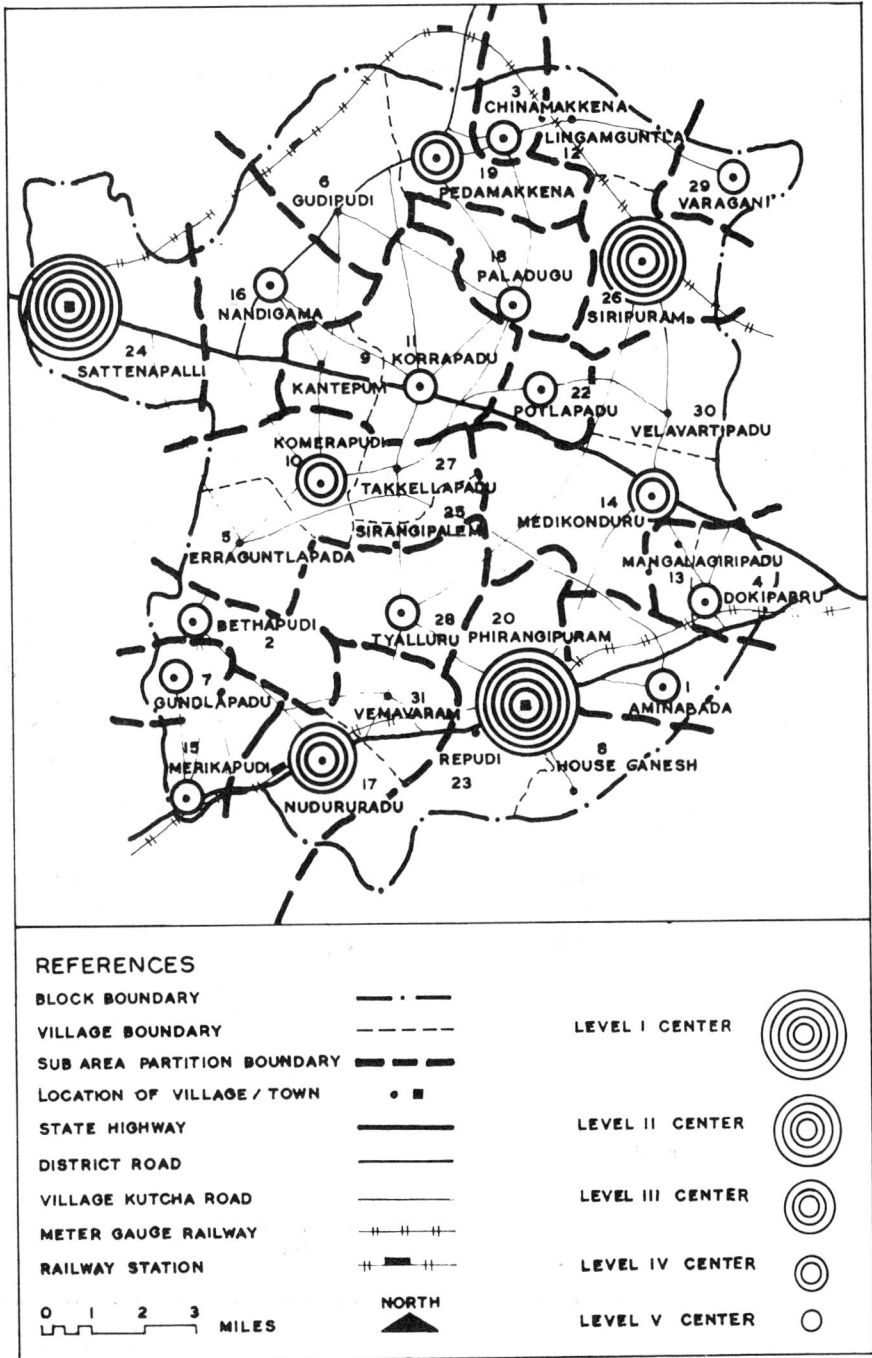

Figure 12.13 Level V of the general settlement plan for the Phirangipuram block of Andhra Pradesh. [S. Banerji and H. B. Fisher, "Hierarchical location analysis for integrated area planning in rural India," *Papers*, Regional Science Association, **33**, 1974, p. 191.]

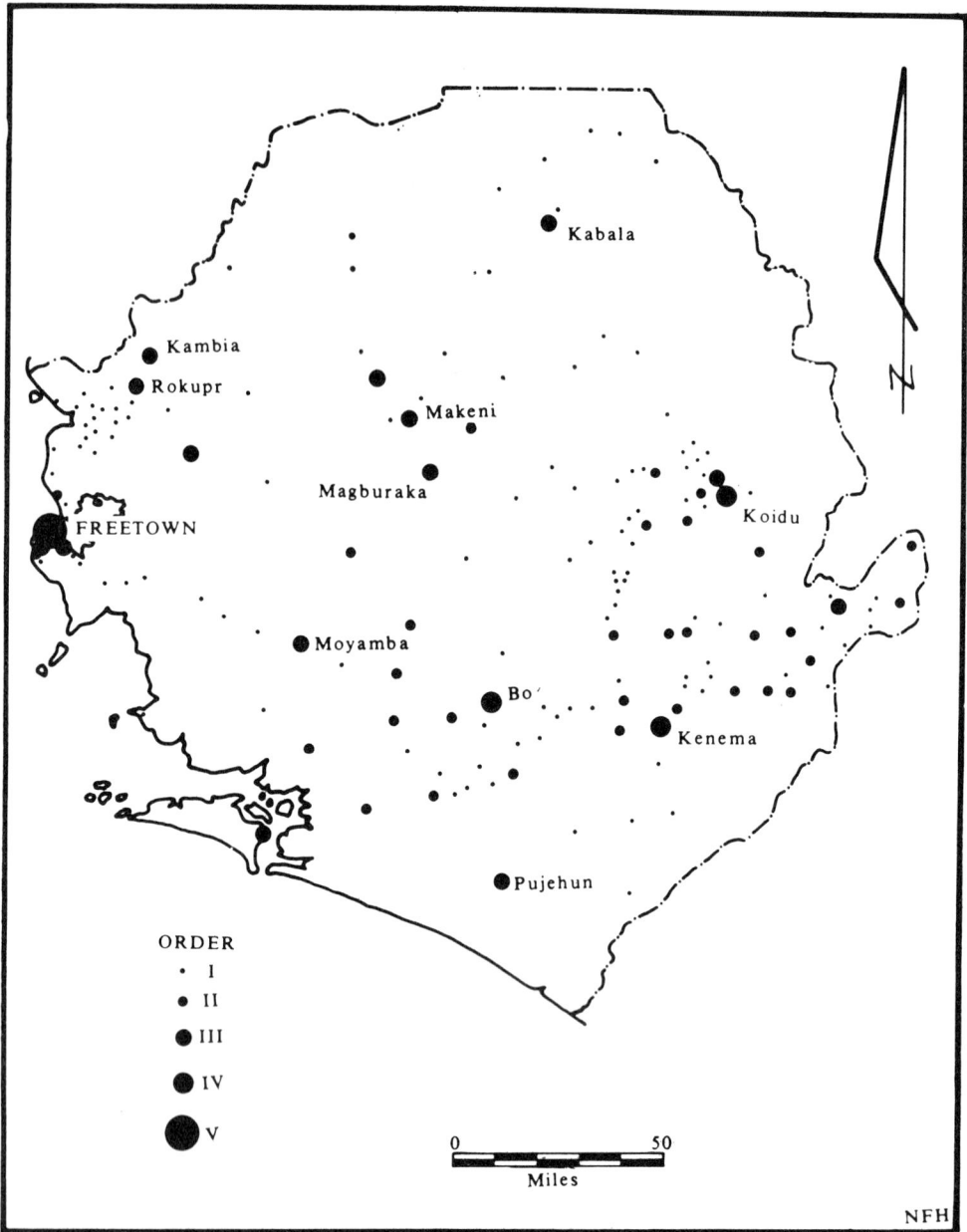

Figure 12.14 Sierra Leone, existing hierarchy of central places. [M. E. Harvey, M. Hung, and J. R. Brown, "The application of a *p*-median algorithm to the identification of nodal hierarchies and growth centers," *Economic Geography*, **50**, 1074, p. 188.]

orders of service centers using the *p*-median approach. The result was the adjusted urban hierarchy and the set of associated service areas shown in Figure 12.15.[26]

These mathematical programming techniques have proven most popular in location planning decisions at the intraurban level. The planning of fire-station locations or new school locations is well-suited to this approach. The techniques are much more difficult to apply on the broader regional level if only because the information on travel

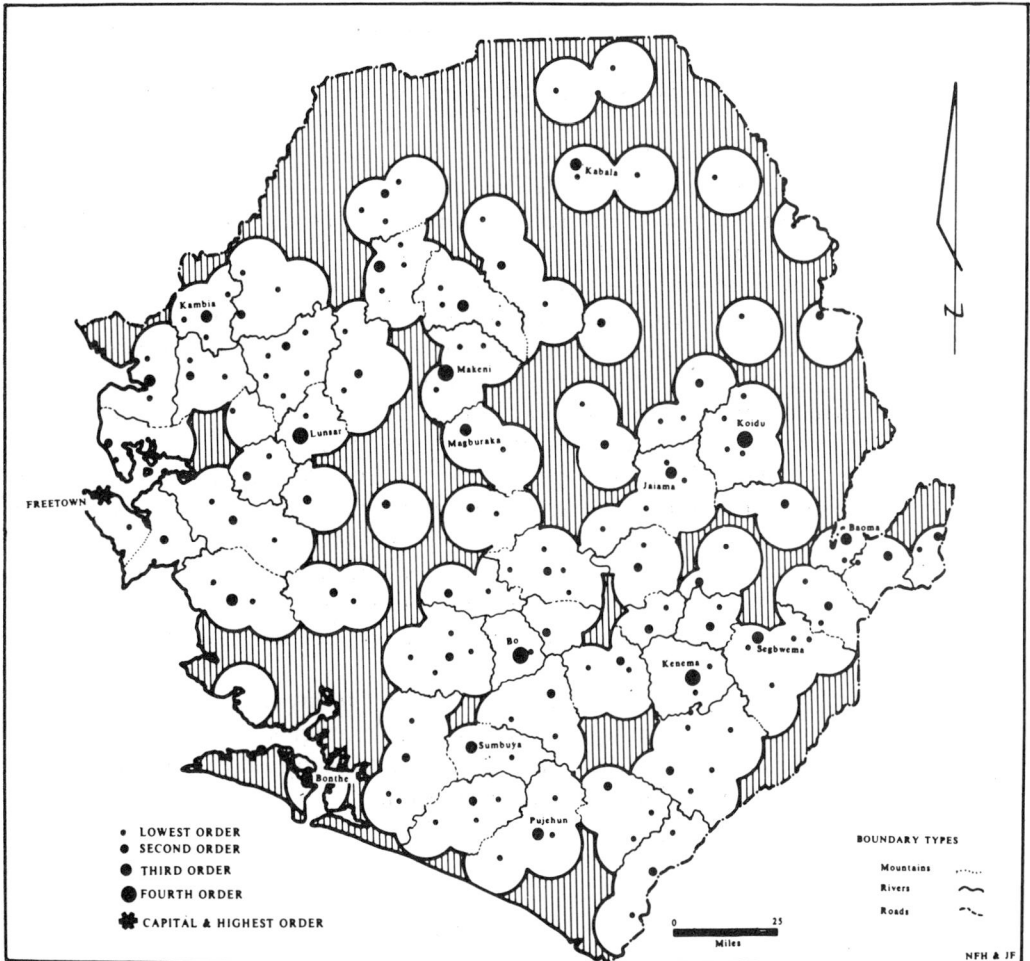

Figure 12.15 Sierra Leone, generated urban system with reconciled catchment areas. [M. E. Harvey, M. Hung, and J. R. Brown, "The application of *p*-median algorithm to the identification of nodal hierarchies and growth centers," *Economic Geography,* **50,** 1974, p. 198.]

behavior that is needed for the solution is usually only approximate information.

12.5   Summary

In this chapter we have examined four specific topics in the planning of regional urban systems. We considered first the question of whether or not there is an optimal size for a city and we concluded that there probably is not. There are certainly costs and diseconomies associated with increasing size, but these seem to be far outweighed by the benefits of size, and as far as the latter are concerned, there seems to be no discernible upper bound.

We then discussed the topic of new towns and noted how this program has had a long history in the United Kingdom and is becoming more popular of late in the United States. Our conclusion here was that the impact of new town construction in absorbing any reasonable share of the projected urban population increase in the United States will be modest at best.

A different strategy of regional and urban development focuses on the role of growth poles, and we noted how this idea has been implemented in a number of countries. Unfortunately, the strategy seems as yet unproven, for it has yet to be convincingly demonstrated that investment in such selected centers has the effect of promoting development in the regions surrounding the centers.

We finally discussed the notion of hierarchical urban systems and the possible effect that such structures have upon the overall pattern of development in a region or country. Again, the hypothesis that a well-integrated hierarchical urban system is a necessary condition for balanced regional development still remains untested, notwithstanding its intuitive appeal to a number of writers on the strategies of national urban development.

All of these topics are popular ones today as people grapple with the question of how national urban strategies might be fashioned. They illustrate well how the spatial dimension enters so forcibly into questions of regional and urban planning.

Notes

1. For example, W. ALONSO, "The economics of urban size," *Papers*, Regional Science Association, **26**, 1971, pp. 67–83; H. W. RICHARDSON, *The Economics of Urban Size* (Lexington: D. C. Heath and Co., 1973).

2. ALONSO, *op. cit.*

3. ALONSO, *op. cit.;* RICHARDSON, *op. cit.*

4. J. V. HENDERSON, "Optimum city size: the external diseconomy question," *Discussion Paper,* Institute for Economic Research, Queen's University, Kingston, Ontario, No. 91, 1972.

5. W. R. THOMPSON, "The national system of cities as an object of public policy," in G. C. CAMERON and L. WINGO, eds., *Cities, Regions and Public Policy* (Edinburgh: Oliver and Boyd, 1973), pp. 99–116.

6. N. V. BARANOV, "Building new towns," in *Planning of Metropolitan Areas and New Towns* (New York: United Nations, 1967), pp. 209–15.

7. L. RODWIN, *Nations and Cities. A Comparison of Strategies for Urban Growth* (Boston: Houghton Mifflin Co., 1970).

8. M. CLAWSON and P. HALL, *Planning and Urban Growth: An Anglo–American Comparison* (Baltimore: The Johns Hopkins University Press, 1973).

9. *Ibid.,* p. 215.

10. H. MIELDS, JR., *Federally Assisted New Communities. New Dimensions in Urban Development* (Washington, D.C.: The Urban Land Institute, 1973).

11. H. MIRON, JR., and F. H. PARKER, "Soul City: the initial stages," *Research Report,* PHS Research EC 00308-02, Center for Urban and Regional Studies, University of North Carolina at Chapel Hill, 1971.

12. F. PERROUX, "Note sur la notion de pôle de croissance," *Economie Appliquée,* **1–2,** 1955, pp. 307–20.

13. For example, J-R. BOUDEVILLE, *Problems of Regional Economic Planning* (Edinburgh: Edinburgh University Press, 1966); J. FRIEDMANN, "A general theory of polarized development," in N. M. HANSEN, ed., *Growth Centers in Regional Economic Development* (New York: The Free Press, 1972), pp. 82–107.

14. J. B. PARR, "Growth poles, regional development, and central place theory," *Papers,* Regional Science Association, **31,** 1973, pp. 173–212.

15. See N. M. HANSEN, "Development pole theory in a regional context," *Kyklos,* **20,** 1967, pp. 709–26; *Growth Centers in Regional Economic Development* (New York: The Free Press, 1972); B. J. L. BERRY, *Growth Centers and Their Potential in the Upper Great Lakes Region* (Washington, D.C.: Upper Great Lakes Regional Commission, 1969); "Hierarchical diffusion: the basis of developmental filtering and spread in a system of growth centers," in N. M. HANSEN, ed., *Growth Centers in Regional Economic Development* (New York: The Free Press, 1972), pp. 108–38; *Growth Centers in the American Urban System,* Vols. I, II. (Cambridge, Mass.: Ballinger Publishing Co., 1973).

16. See A. KUKLINSKI and R. PETRELLA, eds., *Growth Poles and Regional Policies* (The Hague: Mouton, 1972); A. KUKLINSKI, ed., *Regional Development and Planning: International Perspectives* (Leyden: A. W. Sijthoff International Publishing Co., 1975).

17. HANSEN, *Growth Centers in Regional Economic Development,* pp. 266–67.

18. C. MacNaughton, "Presentation of Design for Development: Toronto Centred Region," mimeographed (Toronto: Ontario Department of Treasury and Economics, Regional Development Branch, 1970).

19. L. J. King, "Conceptual limitations and data problems in the fashioning of growth pole strategies: the case of Ontario, Canada," *Geoforum*, **17**, 1974, pp. 61–67.

20. See H. W. Richardson, "Optimality in city size," in G. C. Cameron and L. Wingo, eds., *Cities, Regions and Public Policy* (Edinburgh: Oliver and Boyd, 1973), pp. 29–48; J. W. Simmons, "Canada: choices in a national urban strategy," *Research Paper 70*, Center for Urban and Community Studies, University of Toronto, 1975.

21. Saskatchewan Royal Commission on Agriculture and Rural Life, "Service centers," *Report No. 12*, Regina, Saskatchewan, 1957.

22. D. Grove and L. Huszar, *The Towns of Ghana* (Accra: Ghana University Press, 1964).

23. J. P. Thijsse, "A rural pattern for the future in the Netherlands," *Papers*, Regional Science Association, **10**, 1962, pp. 133–41; "Second thoughts about a rural pattern for the future in the Netherlands," *Papers*, Regional Science Association, **20**, 1967, pp. 69–75.

24. A. R. Pred, "Urbanization, domestic planning problems and Swedish geographic research," *Progress in Geography*, **5**, 1973, pp. 1–76.

25. S. Banerji and H. B. Fisher, "Hierarchical location analysis for integrated area planning in rural India," *Papers*, Regional Science Association, **33**, 1974, pp. 177–94.

26. M. E. Harvey, M. Hung, and J. R. Brown, "The application of a p-median algorithm to the identification of nodal hierarchies and growth centers," *Economic Geography*, **50**, 1974, pp. 187–202.

chapter 13

Problems in Planning
the Internal Structure of Cities

The problems associated with life in our cities today are highlighted in the daily newspapers as well as in the research literature. In general, our attempts to cope with and to solve these problems are piecemeal, and more often than not the proposed solutions create new problems. For example, in the 1950's and 1960's superhighways were built through and around cities in order to relieve the problems of traffic congestion. But it is now apparent that the building of these highways not only often destroyed the cohesion of neighborhoods and the established patterns of interhousehold interaction, but at the same time they also encouraged the spread of urban development into the suburbs and thereby contributed to many of today's urban financial problems.

Many social critics argue that the form of the North American city is in fact both a response to and a means of enforcing the established power structures of society. They view the building of the freeways as an expression of the power of the automobile corporations in shaping the future of the city and the lives of its inhabitants in order to serve the automobile corporations' own interests. Similarly, the large financial institutions can control the level and direction of development in a city simply by exercising their control over the capital available for development. These views of the city and its problems and its future are provocative and should not be dismissed lightly. Unfortunately, at present it is difficult to deduce from the writings of social scholars what forms the alternatives might take. Presumably, a city in which all land is publicly owned by the state might develop very different internal patterns from those in which competition for land and locations finds expression in land values and market mechanisms. But even in countries such as the Soviet Union and China where state ownership of land is the case, the cities still strongly reflect their historical heritages. Truly distinctive urban forms have yet to emerge.

13.1   Some Contemporary Urban Challenges

We shall consider here some of the important issues confronting those who must plan and govern our cities today. Our discussion is by no means complete, but it does at least reference some of the major problem areas.

Urban Poverty and the Ghetto

Poverty is widespread among the urban dwellers of North America, and in the United States the issue seems inextricably mixed up with the issue of racial segregation and the existence of ghetto areas in the cities. This is not to say that poverty is confined to the ghettos; indeed, studies by geographers and others have shown that in almost all United States cities the poverty areas are far more extensive than the area of the nonwhite ghetto (Figure 13.1).[1] But since it is often in the ghetto that the problems of poverty are particularly acute, it is perhaps not surprising that much has been said about the ghetto and the question of how it might fare in the future of the city. Traditionally, the argument has been that the concentration of the nonwhite population in the ghetto areas located in the older central cities has been accompanied by an increasing suburbanization of the employment opportunities and that the poor nonwhites have consequently been increasingly separated by distance from jobs. This has prompted such policies as subsidized transportation systems to improve the accessibility of the less privileged groups to the suburbs. Also, for this and other reasons, arguments favoring the dispersal of the nonwhite population have been put forward, the idea being that if the nonwhites are encouraged to seek suburban residences, then their employment opportunities will be enhanced.

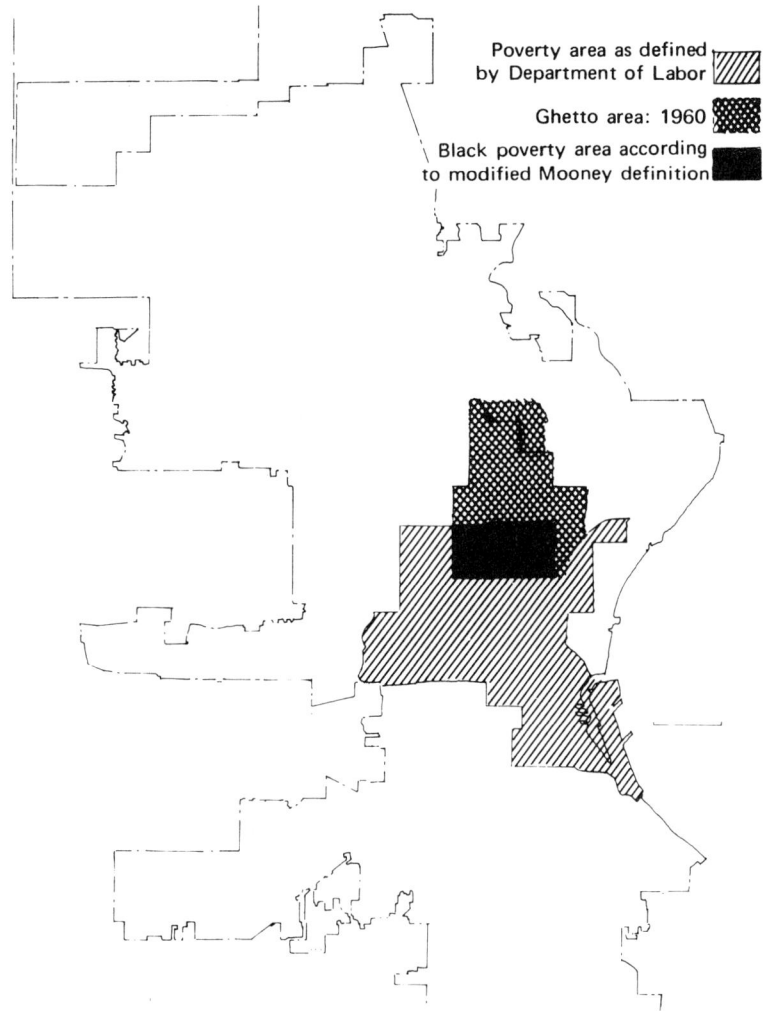

Figure 13.1   Poverty and ghetto areas in Milwaukee, 1960. [From H. M. Rose, *The Black Ghetto. A Spatial-Behavioral Perspective*, p. 54. Copyright © 1971 by McGraw-Hill Inc. Used with permission of McGraw-Hill Book Company.]

We noted in Section 6.3 how this hypothesis has been effectively challenged by other scholars. Recall their argument that the available evidence suggests that nonwhites living outside the ghetto are no better off in economic terms than their counterparts in the ghettos. In other words, the dispersal hypothesis does not seem to hold up. Related prospects are that the outward expansion of the older cities appears to be almost over and that future development will have to occur increasingly as a deepening of activity involving higher densities, new technologies, and new administrative forms. In this process, the economic development of the ghetto appears both feasible and desirable.

Social Well-Being

Considerable concern is expressed today over the levels of crime in cities and over the deteriorating quality of services in the fields of health, education, and other public activities. For example, crime has reached an all-time high in many cities of the world and, unfortunately, it continues to grow both as a reality and a state of mind. Fear of crime and a desire for protection of property and person seem to be escalating and producing a fortress mentality that alters the way people see themselves and the way they live their lives. The fear of crime, in many ways, helps create the conditions that permit crime to increase. Deserted streets, atmospheres of suspicion, and loss of confidence in protection agencies all contribute to a growing environment in which crime expands.

Just as there is a general perception of who commits the crimes, so are there general perceptions of where crimes are committed in cities. A recent study of criminal activity in the city of Akron has shown that people invariably equate the downtown and inner suburban areas with high crime rates.[2] People's ratings of areas in that city on the basis of their perceived safety showed that typically the downtown areas were labeled "unsafe" and "high potential crime" areas. But in actual fact, many crimes occur in the suburban areas and crimes against property are particularly noticeable in the higher economic districts of the city.

Urban crime rates in the United States do seem to increase with city size, but the controlling influences seem to be related more to changes in the ethnic and demographic composition of the populations that occur as cities grow larger than to size itself. Table 13.1 presents index numbers for urban crime rates.[3] The "raw crime rates" (see the top part of the table) generally increase as size increases. But there are a number of intervening variables and the following relationships are important:

1. Increased unemployment is associated with increased property crimes.
2. Higher summer temperatures from city to city are associated with increases in crimes of violence.
3. Increases in the proportions of both the young and the old from city to city are associated with decreases in crime rates.
4. Japanese and children of foreign-born persons are associated with lower crime rates than average, while the percents of non-whites and foreign-born are related to higher than average rates.

Table 13.1   Index Numbers of 1970 Crime Rates, Observed vs. Estimates, as Functions of City Size and Density Only. (I. Hoch, "City size effects, trends, and policies," *Science,* **193**, 1976, p. 860. Copyright 1976 by the American Association for the Advancement of Science. Originally published in *Journal of Urban Economics,* Vol. **1**, 1974.)

SMSA Population ($\times 10^3$)	*Homicide*	*Rape*	*Robbery**	*Assault**	*Burglary*	*Larceny*	*Auto Theft*
Raw crime rates (observed indexes, sample average = 100)							
0 to < 250	85	74	62	85	80	89	61
250 to < 500	94	89	67	95	94	91	75
500 to < 1,000	100	96	91	96	102	104	120
1,000 to < 2,500	118	134	152	112	116	115	128
2,500 to < 9,000	133	154	251	134	126	115	171
9,000 or more	138	106	470	178	156	157	200
Indexes as functions of size and density only							
0 to < 250	96	92	94	104	94	103	73
250 to < 500	96	96	96	97	97	98	86
500 to < 1,000	99	98	104	99	105	108	117
1,000 to < 2,500	110	121	102	101	102	98	119
2,500 to < 9,000	107	66	117	102	103	80	119
9,000 or more	98	65	137	126	136	118	108

*In body of table, percent black-size interactions are not included in indexes as functions of size and density only. When the interactions are included, the indexes are: assault—101, 96, 99, 104, 107, 134; robbery—80, 80, 97, 134, 168, 299. The indexes run from smallest to largest size classes.

5. Increased population density is associated with a decrease in crime, which contradicts many of the qualitative predictions that are made.

When the effects of these variables are taken into account and the crime rates are expressed simply as functions of population size and density, the numbers in the lower half of Table 13.1 result. The size effect is then not so clear and direct.

An approach to measuring the overall quality of life involves the computing of social indicators. Figure 13.2 illustrates the results that can be achieved. In this example, different variables are scored for each census tract within the city and a composite score is obtained for each major indicator that is a weighted combination of the variables listed. The point of this approach is that if the values of the social indicators can be monitored continuously, then the appropriate planning

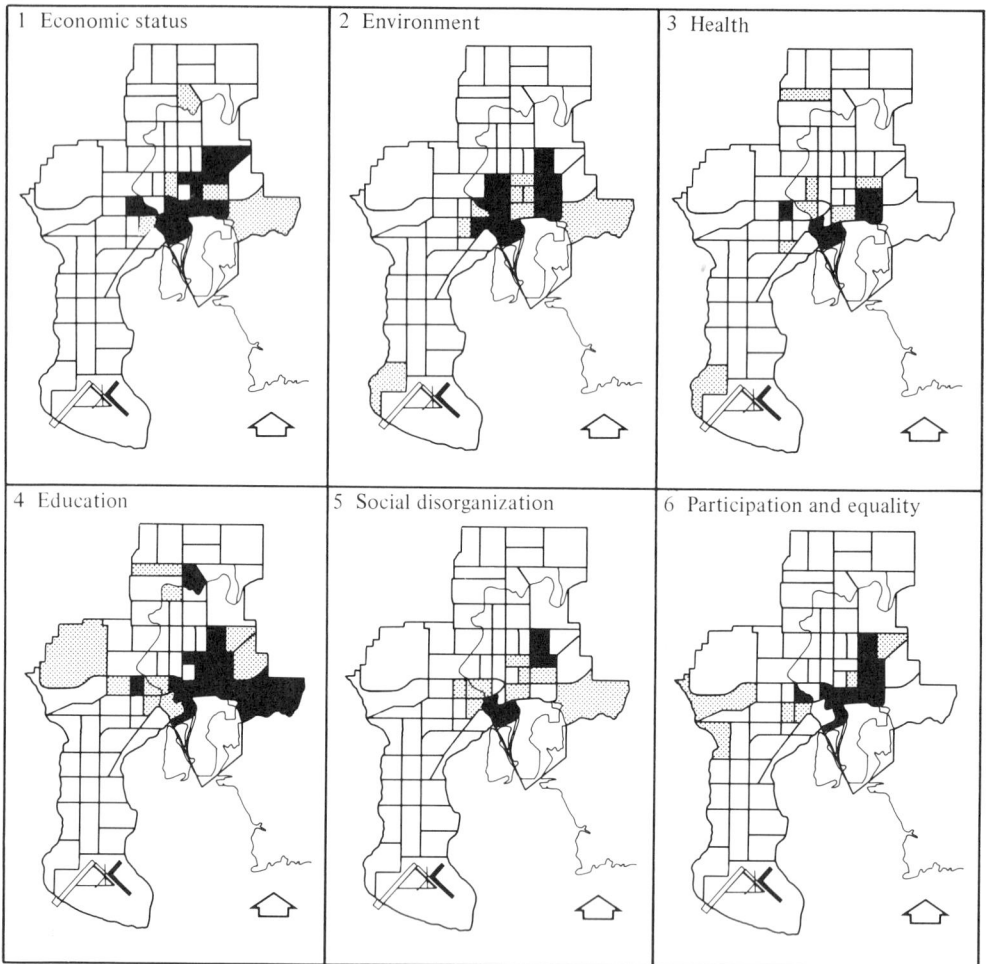

Figure 13.2   The problem areas of Tampa, defined by census tracts with indicator scores of one standard deviation (heavy shading) and one half of a standard deviation (light shading) below the mean. [From D. M. Smith, *The Geography of Social Well-Being in the United States*, p. 125. Copyright © 1973 by McGraw-Hill Inc. Used with permission of McGraw-Hill Book Co.]

policies can be devised and continuously updated to take account of changing conditions in different parts of the city.

Environmental Problems

Whether cities of the future grow outward or concentrate their growth inward and upward, their continued growth will most likely accelerate the process of environmental deterioration that is so evident in many cities today. Until recently, the problem of environmental quality was a much neglected area of urban analysis. In the decade of the 1960's, however, the development of heavy smog in several of the world's large cities prompted concern for general environmental deterioration and exploitation, and this generated a series of acts by governments to begin the process of controlling environmental deterioration. In the United States these included a national environmental policy act of 1969 (signed into law January 1, 1970) and the following year the setting up of the Environmental Protection Agency. This consolidated into one agency major federal programs dealing with problems such as air pollution, water pollution, solid waste disposal, radiation emanating from nuclear power plants, pesticides regulation, and so on.

When one thinks of the general problem of urban pollution, *air pollution* comes quickly to mind. The major sources of air pollution in large urban areas are:

1. Fuel oil burned to heat apartments.
2. Municipal incineration of rubbish and waste.
3. Local on-site incineration.
4. Emissions from cars and other mobile sources.
5. Emissions from industry and power plants.

It is known that air pollution not only contributes to the health problems of urban dwellers, but it also adds considerably to the cost of living and operating in a city. Pollutants produce economic losses through soiling and corrosion, and the higher costs of cleaning contribute significantly to the problem of urban air pollution. It has been estimated that the economic loss in large urban areas averages about $65 per person per year.[4] In the city of New York it has been estimated that the implementation of current air pollution control laws would cost approximately $500,000,000 within the first 3 years. If the per person loss estimate given above is a reasonable one, then the $500,-000,000 would appear to be very well spent because there would be a dramatic per person reduction in the estimated dollar losses.

The question arises then as to how cities of the future might control air pollution. It seems reasonable to assume that considerable attention will be paid to achieving clean air by replacing the relatively inefficient individual apartment heaters with heat supplied from large well-controlled central generating sources. It has proven comparatively easy to control emission from large generating plants either by using pollution-free fossil fuels or by relying on nuclear power, and if such large central generating stations *could* be developed in the vicinity of major urban agglomerations, an extensive network of piped heat could spread throughout the city.

The problem of *waste disposal* is of equal magnitude to that of providing heat. The usual procedures of burying and burning waste appear to have reached their limit in terms of their usefulness to urban dwellers. Places to bury waste are becoming scarce, and we have already noted that the continued burning of waste contributes significantly to air pollution problems in an urban area. The efficient incineration of waste, however, can offer possible solutions both to the waste disposal problem and to the heat generation problem. It has been estimated that incineration of waste reduces its bulk by about 75%. If effective controls can be placed on the emission of pollutants into the atmosphere from such incineration, then a good deal of the bulk of the waste disposal problem might be reduced. For example, it has been estimated that New York City produces over 20,000 tons of refuse per day. Reducing this to about 4,000 tons per day would modify the waste disposal problem for some time, but it would not solve it. In economic terms, burning large quantities of waste could produce significant power or steam generation and, in turn, an economic return of about $2 per ton of refuse burned, or about $12,000,-000 per year. Other solutions to the waste disposal problem include expanding the practice of recycling and encouraging research into new types of packaging other than glass, paper, and metal.

Waste disposal problems also include those associated with *urban sewerage systems*. As concerns for environmental quality have mounted, there has been increasing attention given to the outdated sewerage systems found in almost all large cities. In the past, many cities relied on natural water bodies such as lakes and rivers to carry away partially treated sewerage, but in most cases, critical levels of water pollution have forced a review of these practices. The harmful effects of the large metropolitan complexes located around the western half of Lake Erie on the quality of that body of water have been well publicized. The technology of tertiary treatment systems that would allow for the recycling of treated water has been developed, but cities are faced with tremendous capital costs in installing such systems, and not infrequently other demands are given priority.

Noise pollution may well be a major problem for cities of the future. At present, the main sources of noise include construction machinery, automotive equipment, aircraft, and noises associated with warning systems such as sirens and horns. During the warmer months external air-conditioning units also contribute significantly to the total noise problem. The noise problem is extenuated in many urban areas by the close packing of houses and buildings that tends to reflect and reverberate noise instead of dissipate it. Some attempts have been made to reduce noise pollution by setting noise standards for automobiles, decentralizing airports to locations well beyond the major built-up areas of cities, and protecting highway systems by elevating them or building over them.

At present, industries in many cities consume extremely *large quantities of water* daily. Each individual also consumes a reasonably large quantity (estimated at about 150 gallons per day per person in the United States). Of this, a significant amount (about 15%) is used in disposing of human waste. Obviously, with continued urban population increases, the problem of obtaining sufficient water supplies to meet the needs of all urban dwellers will grow in significance.

Central City–Suburban Fiscal Disparities

We refer here to the growing imbalance between the costs of needed city services and the tax resources that are available to pay for these services. One can conceive of a service needs/tax capacity ratio that would tend to be particularly high in many central cities but much lower in the suburbs. For the most part, the demand for government-provided services and utilities tends to be much greater in central cities than in suburban areas. Unemployment rates are generally higher in central cities, housing stocks are generally of poorer quality or at greater levels of deterioration, transportation systems are often outmoded, utility bases are frequently inadequate, and educational services are frequently rather poor. This means that central cities must provide not only services for their own residents, but also a variety of services for those who live outside their boundaries but use central city facilities frequently. When we add to this problem the tendency over the last decade and a half for industry and commerce to desert central city areas for suburban industrial parks and commercial and financial centers, we find that what remains are aging central cities with declining tax bases. A United States National Academy of Sciences Panel recently noted that "on the average, the central city tax burden (taxes as a percentage of personal income) runs 30% to 50% higher than that of the suburbs. According to the latest data, local taxes on the average constitute 6.9% of personal income in the central cities, while they are only 5.0% in the suburbs."[5]

13.2   Urban Transportation Problems: Who Should Pay for What?

The problems of urban transportation today are visibly evident in the congestion that exists in and around major urban centers. The private automobile contributes far more to congestion than any other form of transportation. In effect, the technology that improved the mobility of the population has created a great deal of immobility in metropolitan areas. At the two major times of the day when the traffic system should best accommodate its users, in almost every city it works at its worst. Attempts to expand the system by constructing new highways to improve the flow of traffic have played havoc with the life-style of inner city residents while doing comparatively little to alleviate the congestion problem. This disregard for the inhabitants of the central cities was a feature of urban transportation development during an extended period of freeway building of the late 1950's and the early 1960's. The systems that were developed were designed and oriented to bring residents of the suburbs into the core of the city for work and recreational and shopping purposes, but it did not follow that they consequently allowed the inner city resident to move outside the urban area to find or reach a job. The massive thruways and freeways that enabled faster auto transportation from the suburbs proved to be comparatively useless to the inner city resident who did not own a car.

Highways and automobiles are not the only contributors to problems of urban transportation. Rapid transit and subway systems have also had serious problems. Fires in subways or commuter trains, power failures, mid-tunnel stalls, or mechanical breakdowns leave passengers trapped in cars (frequently underground) for extended periods of time. In 1970 the bus systems in eight major United States cities collapsed. Cities such as Baltimore, Minneapolis, and Salt Lake City were left temporarily without a viable bus system. Other moderate- to large-sized cities have rapid transit systems that are either losing money or are so close to being marginal that there is a constant threat of closure. For intercity transportation, rail transportation companies such as the Penn Central Company (the largest railroad company in the nation) have suffered severe hardships and sometimes bankruptcy. Many railways in North America have virtually eliminated passenger traffic, but this is certainly not true in other countries of the world.

United States Urban Transportation Policies

By 1975 a number of steps had been taken to help reduce the severity of urban transportation problems in the United States. The areas in which the greatest effort has been expended and the greatest success achieved included the building of more freeways, expressways, and free-flowing arterial roads; the extensive redesign of street systems within urban areas to stimulate one-way traffic flows and to ensure free-flowing traffic through traffic light phasing; and the upgrading of suburban streets.

To help finance necessary changes in the urban transportation systems of many cities, in 1964 Congress passed a bill to provide such assistance, but appropriations have been small by transportation industry standards (only some $600,000,000 were appropriated between 1964 and 1970). Almost all appropriations have gone for re-equipping existing transit systems and for buying new buses or rail and transit cars. A fraction of the funds was earmarked for research and development, and this has produced a variety of innovative and potentially useful operational modes of transportation for cities of the future.

More recently, the Transportation Act of 1970 enacted by Congress has tentatively pledged to put $10,000,000,000 into urban mass transportation between from 1970 and 1982. However, there is and has been little agreement on how the money should be spent. Although the problem of financing rapid transportation in urban areas is still a considerable one, expenditure for the construction of arterial highways in urban communities is still in the magnitude of $4,000,000 per year and urban dwellers are still spending $25,000,000 on new automobiles. Suggestions for using the money allocated to the mass transit program have been numerous, but the implementation of these suggestions is frequently dependent on additional funding by state and local agencies. Some of the improvements suggested so far and, to some extent, implemented, include the development of express bus lanes on freeway systems, a discontinuation of massive freeway building in large cities, a more concentrated effort to redevelop mass transit systems, granting of considerable subsidies to rail and bus companies to pay for modernizing equipment, research and development in construction technology and operating technology, and research into the possible effects of restrictions and regulations on individual auto movements (such as penalizing cars by the number of empty seats, by car size, or by compulsory auto testing every 1,000 miles). In addition to these steps, considerable attention is being paid to the possible success of recent innovations in mass transit such as the San Francisco Bay Area Transportation system and new systems in Montreal, Canada, and Washington, D.C.

People of urban areas may be badly served by urban transportation systems because of system deficiency, poor physical planning, or low income. The first problem can be helped by improving the transportation system itself; the second requires comprehensive urban planning and a design that tries to integrate transportation systems with land-use planning systems; the third is either a matter for income redistribution policy or for the development of a pricing system associated with transportation that makes the system accessible to people of all income ranges.

Transportation system improvements can be facilitated in a number of different ways. Many of these ways are designed to overcome a single overwhelming problem that exists in almost all moderate- to large-size cities—the problem of congestion. Congestion can be said to exist in a traffic artery or network when the number of vehicles trying to move at the same time is so large that the vehicle miles traveled in a given period are substantially fewer than if the traffic flowed freely. Alternatively, one can suggest that congestion exists when the value of time lost because of traffic delay as a result of having too many vehicles in the traffic system exceeds the marginal value of travel for persons traveling at that particular time. Depending on which definition of congestion is acceptable, policies for improving transportation systems might vary. For example, a traffic control policy based on the quantity of movement definition would aim at promoting maximum use of highway and street networks. In other words, one would try to maximize *people-thruput*, or the number of people moving through the system or any part thereof during a given period of time. Alternatively, a policy based on the marginal value of time would seek to maximize the value to users of the network by facilitating the movement of those whose time is worth more while discouraging those whose time is worth less. The second approach might involve a more systematic use of busing systems than does the thruput idea.

One way of implementing the maximum thruput policy is to improve the attraction of mass transit as opposed to individual movement. For example, bus travel time could be improved by giving preference to buses at entrances to arterials and at traffic lights or by reserving lanes for them on major freeways or arterial roads. The speed on road networks can also be improved by familiar engineering devices such as barring on-street parking and designating one-way traffic on some streets. Another successful innovation is to install traffic signaling devices where traffic signals give proportionately more green light time to the dominant flow segment of the road. Other engineering devices monitor the entrance of vehicles to road systems by holding vehicles at entrances until they can be accommodated without causing more congestion.

Pricing of Transportation

In many countries of the world the market price system has been a highly effective mechanism in determining how much should be produced and consumed. As far as transportation use is concerned, however, the pricing system has run into considerable problems when it comes to imposing special charges for the use of road space in congestion-prone areas at congestion-prone times. There is a tendency to resent the imposition of new charges for public services, especially if they were originally provided free of charge. Thus, attempts to establish toll payments on road systems that had been built in the past have frequently not been at all successful because of considerable public and private opposition.

A number of potential advantages to anti-congestion pricing systems are becoming more important as other solutions to the urban movement problem become less effective. For example, pricing systems on roadways may promote the following adjustments in travel habits and could conceivably reduce congestion in the following manner:

1. If a price differential between peak and off-peak traffic were introduced, some traffic would shift to off-peak and the total number of trips would probably be decreased overall.
2. An increase in the amount charged for travel per mile might encourage people to live closer to their jobs or to make adjustments to shorten the average length of trips; it may also influence people to search for relatively less expensive forms of transportation.
3. The higher the price of individual transportation, the greater the use that should be made of less expensive modes such as mass transit facilities.
4. If price differentials were introduced on high-cost and congestion-prone routes, there should be a tendency for some traffic to shift to lower cost routes and thus to even out the intensity of flow in different route segments in urban areas.

13.3   Urban Renewal: Demolition or Restoration

Urban renewal is a program tnat has been suggested to help *save* cities. Antagonists of renewal programs argue that all the problems found prior to renewal will be moved to other parts of the city where urban blight is not yet a problem. Protagonists argue that urban renewal *cleans up* a city physically, economically, and psychologically, and renewal programs should be initiated in blighted areas that appear to be the hard-core centers of deterioration.

The basic questions to be answered by potential renewers are: What constitutes the *life* of a building? When does it become a matter of health, safety, or economy to replace a building with another (or alternate land use)? A mild form of renewal activity constantly goes on in the form of *facelifting, expansion,* and other work on the facade of buildings. Except for this minor work, however, potential renewers are faced with deciding whether or not the costs of demolition, acquisition, and rebuilding are warranted in terms of monetary or other returns.

Renewal Benefits

The major advantages of renewal activity can be summarized as follows: (1) There is a change of aesthetic value which, it is hoped, will be accompanied by changes in health, safety, and morality as a result of the upgrading of facilities; (2) frequently there is no immediate need to provide new utilities (such as power lines, gas and sewerage mains, roads and pavements, street lighting, etc.) and facilities such as schools; and (3) in almost every case, renewal pays its way by producing increased tax revenues from property owners.

However, unless renewal activity is on a reasonably large scale, its chance of realizing on these advantages is reduced. Isolated renewal projects in deteriorating residential areas are often subject to stress, invasion, and deterioration if their influence is not spread into surrounding areas.

A problem often mentioned by renewal agencies is that emphasis on renewal of inner city areas—especially if it is subsidized by government spending—may produce a *housing surplus* at the periphery of cities. Many, of course, would argue that this would be a good thing because it may stop the outward growth of larger cities and depress inflated land values and property values in these areas. This process eventually would recreate a demand at the periphery and the temporarily checked growth process would continue. Of course, with current demands for increased personal space and cleaner environments it hardly seems likely that large-scale renewal would halt peripheral expansion.

Renewal programs frequently need substantial incentives to get under way. These might be in the form of economic, racial, or moral pressures. Economic proposals might include giving tax credits for capital improvements on residential rental buildings, allowing the cost of demolition to be added to the depreciable cost of new development, and on the preventive side of the coin, stopping property owners from benefiting from downward valuation of property as deterioration sets in. This last step discourages parasitic forms of rent capitalism and encourages investment in the maintenance of properties.

Urban Homesteading

In recent years a particularly productive form of urban renewal, called *urban homesteading*, has been undertaken in many large United States cities. This occurs after the city has acquired deteriorating buildings in areas of the city that have potential for regrowth. A list of available housing is published and bids may be called for or a lottery may be established. In the latter case, while there may be no income constraints on entering the lottery, there is a requirement that a person successful in the lottery must *live* in the home he draws for a minimum time period (which may be from 6 months to 2 years) and that considerable improvements be made to the property. The *live in* requirement minimizes short-run speculative activity. The result of this procedure has been to inject new life into some formerly decaying and abandoned neighborhoods and has proven one of the most constructive and successful forms of urban renewal because it combines concern for the physical environment with concerns for human values and the well-being of people.

13.4   Administrative Reorganization: Metropolitan Government

Over the past two decades the population increase of suburban areas has vastly exceeded the population increase of central cities throughout the entire United States. As cities have expanded beyond their original boundaries, a host of administrative and governmental problems has emerged in the wake of this expansion. For example, the more than 200 SMSA's in the United States probably include more than 20,000 local government units. Today, almost all large urban areas spill over into several jurisdictions. This has produced some considerable problems even for the moderately sized cities of today. What will governmental and administrative problems be like in the city of the future?

Interdependent and Overlapping Jurisdictions

The fundamental interdependence of jurisdictional areas in many metropolises has necessitated various innovative methods of administration. Administrative responses to metropolitan problems have ranged from intermunicipal negotiation and cooperation (such as in Nashville) to the creation of supermetropolitan governments (such as in Toronto). Let us recall for a moment the way that people use today's urban places. Many urban residents live in one neighborhood for administrative jurisdiction, work in another, use shopping and entertainment facilities in yet others, and spend additional leisure time in still others. The action spaces of both individuals and economic enterprises, therefore, continually cross and crisscross local government boundaries within a given metropolis. Sometimes, the expanding metropolis has enclosed semi-independent or completely independent communities that developed in earlier eras. The problem of coordinat-

ing the provisions of utilities, services, and transportation and movement systems has become one of the more critical problems facing the
submerged independent communities.

Given that cities expand around independent communities and
overlap a number of jurisdictional areas, one expects that considerable
problems might arise when governmental services have to be provided
for the city as a whole. For some services little action is taken until
crisis points are reached or when conflict develops to such a stage that
stalemates occur and no progressive action whatsoever is taken with
respect to the provision of services. For example, many urban transportation lines carry people from one end of complex urban places to
the other. In the United States those cities that have extensive mass
transit systems have had to generate independent metropolitan scale
agencies in order to manage them. Other city-wide problems, such as
structural unemployment, are left almost completely untouched by
city-wide agencies.

The idea of the establishment of a federated general government
for the metropolis has attracted a reasonable amount of interest as a
panacea for the problems of the future cities. This would require the
creation of an entirely new level of government, however. Theoretically,
such a new level of government would still have to be subordinate to a
state government. But what of the major metropolises and/or mega-
lopolises, that transcend state boundaries? How are necessary functions performed when a jurisdiction is supported to encompass a whole
metropolitan area that has to rely on the largess of a number of states
for the finances needed to provide services? While there may be some
problems in developing some type of federated metropolitan government in the United States cities because of the state boundary problem,
some form of fully fledged general government for the metropolis has
already been manifested in other cities of the world such as London,
Tokyo, Toronto, and Stockholm. The Toronto experience in particular has been reasonably successful and may provide a model for
many governmental units in larger American cities for the next several
decades.

Toronto Metropolitan Government

The Metropolitan Toronto government was first organized in
1953 as a union of 13 local area municipalities, including the City of
Toronto. The structure, however, proved unwieldy and in 1966 the
government was reorganized with 6 municipalities as the members:
the City of Toronto and the boroughs of North York, Scarborough,
York, East York, and Etobicoke, which are shown in Figure 13.3. The

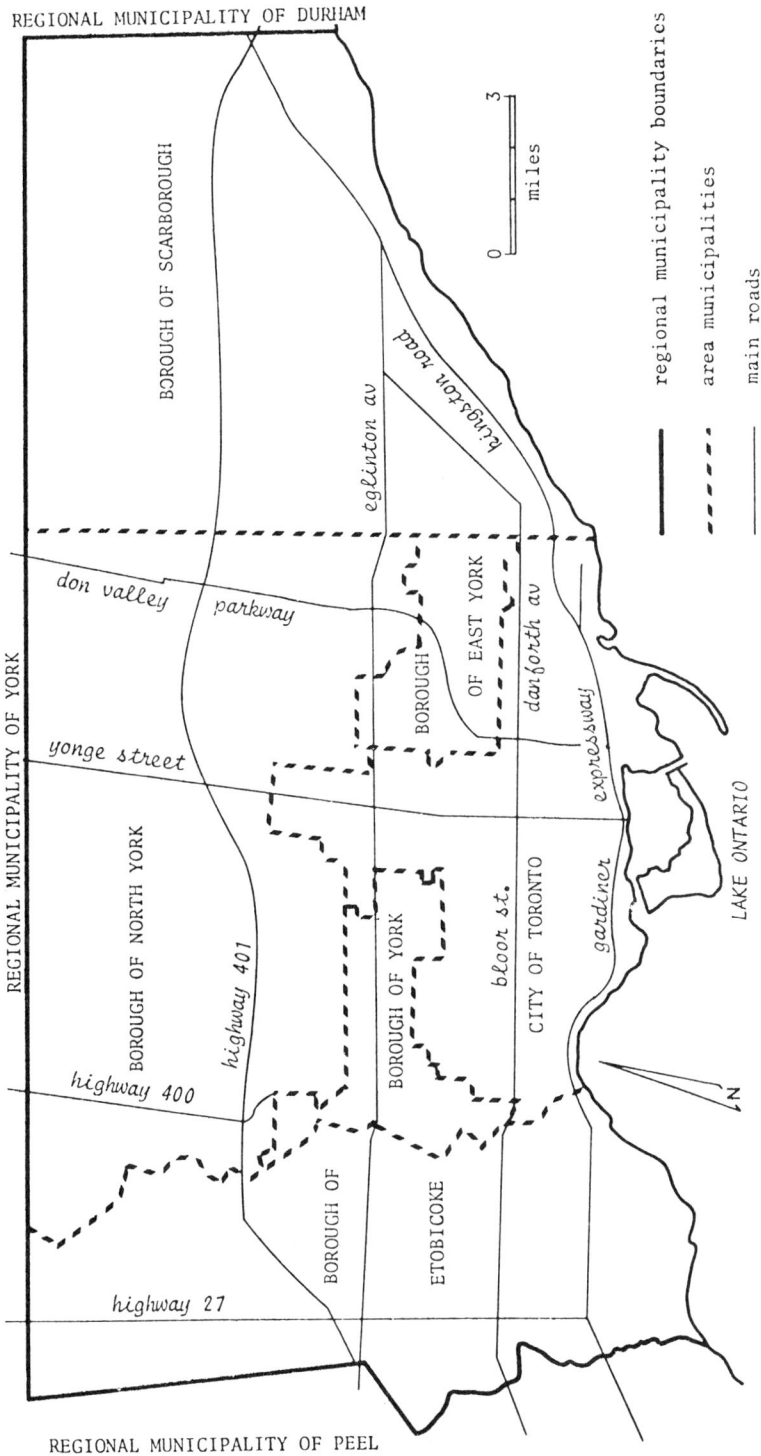

Figure 13.3 Metropolitan Toronto. [A. Bernard, J. Léveillé, and G. Lord, *Profile Toronto* (Ottawa: Ministry of State for Urban Affairs, 1975), p. 5. Reproduced by permission of the Minister of Supply and Services Canada.]

region of Metropolitan Toronto covers an area of about 242 square miles and in 1973 had a population of just over 2.1 million.[6]

The political system is a two-tier one in which locally elected representatives sit on the Metropolitan Toronto Council. As a result of a 1974 amendment to the Metropolitan Toronto Act, there are now 38 members on the Council. These include the 6 mayors of the municipalities, 11 representatives from the City of Toronto, 8 from North York, 5 from Scarborough, 4 from Etobicoke, 2 from York, 1 from East York, and the chairman who is elected by the Council but not necessarily from among its members.

This Council shares responsibilities with the municipalities in the administration of the urban region. Exclusive powers held at the metropolitan level include those of control of the courts, the police, education, water supply, sewage, pollution control, and planning. In order to exercise this authority, the Metro Council makes appointments to a number of intermediary structures such as boards and associations whose officials are both elected and appointed. The more important of these are the Board of Commissioners of Police, the Licensing Commission, the Library Board, the Hospital Planning Council, the Transit Commission, the Planning Board, and the Conservation Authority.

Over the past two decades the Metropolitan government has achieved success in providing reasonably efficient and spatially extensive urban services in one of the faster growing metropolitan areas in North America (in the period 1966–1971 alone the population of Metropolitan Toronto grew by almost 11%). Many of the problems that have plagued United States' cities (for example, the decay of downtown areas, the breakdown of urban services, and the central city-suburban fiscal disparities) have been avoided, at least in any serious form.

But Metropolitan government has brought with it a different set of problems. The emphasis on centralization has been pervasive, and more and more services have become the responsibility of the upper tier, the Metropolitan Council. Local government units often seem threatened with impotency, and citizen involvement in political decision making becomes more and more difficult to ensure and protect.

13.5 · City Forms of the Future: The Role of Architectural Speculations

Throughout this book we have speculated from time to time on the future form of urban society. Our speculations have been those of the social scientist, in particular those of the urban geographer concerned with spatial dimensions. Our inclination always has been to

Figure 13.4 An artist's sketch of a floating city suggested for location off the coast of Oahu, Hawaii. [J. Lear, "Cities on the sea?" *Saturday Review*, September 4, 1971, pp. 84–85.]

view the future largely in terms of what has happened in the past and what seems likely to continue in the future. We have commented on the growth and spread of large urban centers and how these trends, if unchecked, are likely to result in the emergence in the United States of the huge megalopolitan complexes of Boswash, Sansan, and Chipitts. We have reviewed a number of different strategies both at the inter-city and intraurban levels that are aimed at shaping and directing these urban trends in order to ensure that the urban centers in the future are both livable and operable.

There are others who also speculate on the future spatial form of cities. Among these are architects whose speculations are free of any reliance on past trends or patterns; indeed, they often seem almost visionary. In their sketches the city of the future appears in many forms. There are cell-like agglomerations, clipped-on forms of units around large central frames, long-bridged structures, soaring towers, geodesic domes, huge roofed pavilions, and even cities floating on water.[7] An example is shown in Figure 13.4.

At present such suggestions appear to be novel, architecturally intriguing, and grossly expensive propositions. Undoubtedly, in the revitalization of many parts of existing cities and in the design of the new cities that will be built, innovative and contemporary structures should be incorporated. These architectural forms are an expression of contemporary culture and human creativity, and as such they may serve both functionally and inspirationally.

But cities are communities of people, and as many critics point out, too much emphasis on architectural form may involve the sacrifice of human values at the altar of technology. The behavior and wishes of the people should shape the form of the city; the form should not dictate human behavior.

13.6   Summary

We have brought this book to a close with this chapter on some of the issues confronting those who must plan the internal form of the city. This seems appropriate for it is these very same problems that almost all of us must face everyday. They may not touch us directly, but to some extent they involve all of us.

It is easy to talk of solutions to many of these problems simply in terms of reallocating land uses, changing the tax structures, imposing charges on highway users and polluters, restructuring the transportation networks, and so on. But few of these solutions seem to offer much hope as long-range solutions because few of us are willing to change our patterns of behavior and levels of expectations. The *rights* of owning a lot of land and a house on it, of driving a large car by oneself into work each day, of expecting regular postal deliveries and garbage collections, and of enjoying leisure time are things that a majority of city dwellers in North America take for granted. Perhaps the time is fast approaching when we shall have to give up some of these rights, perhaps because they are priced prohibitively high, and adapt to new patterns of urban living. Perhaps the spatial dimension will find a different expression in those new patterns. Communications both between and within cities may be very technologically sophisticated, but in regard to actual movement between cities, distance may once again be a deterrent. Our sense of identification and affiliation with local spatial units may indeed become stronger for many of us than it is today.

Notes

1. H. M. Rose, *The Black Ghetto. A Spatial-Behavioral Perspective* (New York: McGraw-Hill Book Co., 1971).

2. G. F. Pyle, ed., "The spatial dynamics of crime," *Research Paper*, Department of Geography, University of Chicago, No. 159, 1974.

3. I. Hoch, "City size effects, trends and policies," *Science,* **193,** 1976, pp. 856–63.

4. B. J. L. Berry and F. E. Horton, *Urban Environmental Management: Planning for Pollution Control* (Englewood Cliffs, N.J.: Prentice-Hall, Inc., 1974), p. 371.

5. National Academy of Sciences, *Toward an Understanding of Metropolitan America* (San Francisco: Canfield Press, 1974), p. 35.

6. A. Bernard, J. Léveillé, and G. Lord, *Profile Toronto* (Ottawa: Ministry of State for Urban Affairs, 1975).

7. See J. Dahinden, *Urban Structures for the Future* (New York: Praeger Publishers, 1972).

Index